Gustave Masson, Auguste Brachet, Philip Honoré Ernest Brette

The Public School Elementary French Grammar

Adapted for the Use of English Schools and Persons Engaged in Elementary Teaching

Gustave Masson, Auguste Brachet, Philip Honoré Ernest Brette

The Public School Elementary French Grammar
Adapted for the Use of English Schools and Persons Engaged in Elementary Teaching

ISBN/EAN: 9783337167530

Printed in Europe, USA, Canada, Australia, Japan

Cover: Foto ©Paul-Georg Meister /pixelio.de

More available books at **www.hansebooks.com**

THE PUBLIC SCHOOL ELEMENTARY FRENCH GRAMMAR

PART I.—ACCIDENCE

By AUGUSTE BRACHET

Adapted for the use of English Schools and Persons engaged in Elementary Teaching

BY

THE REV. P. H. E. BRETTE, B.D.
HEAD-MASTER OF THE FRENCH SCHOOL, CHRIST'S HOSPITAL,

AND

GUSTAVE MASSON, B.A.
ASSISTANT MASTER AND LIBRARIAN, HARROW SCHOOL,
EXAMINERS IN THE UNIVERSITY OF LONDON

FIFTH EDITION.

Toronto:
JAMES CAMPBELL & SON.
1878.

[*All rights reserved.*]

PREFACE TO THE FIRST EDITION.

THE adapted translation of M. Brachet's "Nouvelle Grammaire Française," published by us at the beginning of the year, and which has been received with such signal success, was intended to meet the wants of pupils belonging to our ordinary Grammar Schools. On the present occasion, we address ourselves to those with whom philological details, and discussions of etymological or scientific problems would be completely out of place.

M. Brachet's "Petite Grammaire" simply gives the various rules both of accidence and of syntax, without attempting to enter into explanations which beginners nine or ten years old could not possibly understand. We have adopted the same method, but introduced into the work all modifications necessary for making our "ELEMENTARY FRENCH GRAMMAR" a practical and useful book for English class-rooms. Each section is followed by a set of questions and by exercises which should be written out and committed to memory after they have been corrected.

In many instances the Accidence alone is required for examination purposes; accordingly we have thought it best to print the Grammar in two distinct parts, containing, respectively, the Accidence and the Syntax, each part being followed by a complete English-French and French-English Vocabulary. As the translation of the "Nouvelle Grammaire Française" is now adopted in most of our English Grammar and Preparatory Schools, so the "Petite Grammaire," by its cheapness and completeness, will commend itself to School Boards and Persons engaged in elementary teaching.

It gives us much pleasure to acknowledge the valuable assistance which Mr. E. JANAU, French Master at Blackheath Proprietary School, has given us in preparing the present volume.

PREFACE TO THE SECOND EDITION.

THE sale of several thousand copies of this little work in less than six months is a sufficient proof that it has met a want felt by the persons for whom it was chiefly designed. The present edition, thoroughly revised and corrected, is accompanied by a very complete French-English and English-French Vocabulary, arranged by Mr. A. DUPUIS, B.A., First French Master at King's College School, to whom we have to tender our thanks for his kind assistance; beginners will thus be spared the necessity of referring to separate dictionaries.

We take the opportunity of reminding our friends that a supplementary set of Exercises on the Accidence and the Syntax will be ready very shortly.

P. H. ERNEST BRETTE,
GUSTAVE MASSON.

TABLE OF CONTENTS.

INTRODUCTION.

PAGE.

Preliminary Remarks on the History and Geography of the French Language 1
Object and Definition of Grammar 5

BOOK I.—STUDY OF LETTERS.

CHAPTER I.

Of the French Alphabet 7
Section I.—Of the Vowels 9
Section II.—Of the Consonants 11

CHAPTER II.

Of Syllables.—Orthographic Signs 14

BOOK II.—STUDY OF WORDS.

CHAPTER I.

Of the Noun or Substantive 18
Section I.—Of Gender in Nouns 19
Section II.—Of Number in Nouns 20
Section III.—Formation of Substantives 23

CHAPTER II.

Of the Article 32

CHAPTER III.

Of the Adjective 34
Section I.—Formation of the Feminine of Adjectives ... 35
Section II.—Formation of the Plural of Adjectives ... 39

SECTION III.—Of the Degrees of Signification in Adjectives ... 40
SECTION IV.—Formation of Adjectives 42
SECTION V.—Agreement of the Adjective with the Substantive 45
SECTION VI.—Determinative Adjectives 45
 I. Numeral Adjectives 45
  Comparative Table of the Numeral Adjectives... 47
 II. Demonstrative Adjectives 49
 III. Possessive Adjectives 50
SECTION VII.—Indefinite Adjectives 52

CHAPTER IV.

Of the Pronoun 53
SECTION I.—Personal Pronouns 54
SECTION II.—Demonstrative Pronouns 58
SECTION III.—Possessive Pronouns 59
SECTION IV.—Relative Pronouns 61
SECTION V.—Indefinite Pronouns 63

CHAPTER V.

Of the Verb 66
 1. Stem.—2. Termination 67
 3. Numbers 67
 4. Persons 67
 5. Moods 67
 6. Tenses 68
Auxiliary Verbs 69
Conjugation 70
SECTION I.—Auxiliary Verbs 71
 I. Conjugation of the Auxiliary Verb **avoir** (=*to have*) 71
 II. Conjugation of the Auxiliary Verb **être** (=*to be*) 75
SECTION II.—Active Verbs 79
 I. First Conjugation.—Verb **aimer** (=*to love*) ... 79
 II. Second Conjugation.—Verb **finir** (=*to finish*) ... 83
 III. Third Conjugation.—Verb **recevoir** (=*to receive*) 86
 IV. Fourth Conjugation.—Verb **rompre** (=*to break*) 89
SECTION III.—Conjugation of Verbs.—1. Interrogatively; 2. Negatively; 3. Interrogatively with a negative ... 92
SECTION IV.—Remarks on the Formation of the Tenses ... 96
SECTION V.—Passive Verbs 98
 Conjugation of the Passive Verb **être aimé** (=*to be loved*) 99

TABLE OF CONTENTS.

Section VI.—Neuter Verbs	101
Conjugation of the Verb **tomber** (=*to fall*)	102
Section VII.—Reflexive Verbs	104
Conjugation of the Reflexive Verb **se reposer** (=*to rest*)	105
Section VIII.—Impersonal Verbs	109
Conjugation of the Impersonal Verb **neiger** (=*to snow*)	109
Section IX.—Irregular and Defective Verbs	110
1. First Conjugation: er	111
2. Second Conjugation in **ir** with Imperfect in **issais**	112
3. Second (direct) Conjugation in **ir**	113
4. Third Conjugation: **oir**	119
5. Fourth Conjugation: **re**	124
Section X.—Formation of the Verbs	139
Section XI.—Rules for the Agreement of the Verb with its Subject	141

CHAPTER VI.

Of the Participle	142

CHAPTER VII.

Of the Adverb	143

CHAPTER VIII.

Of the Preposition	148
Section I.—Formation of the Simple Prepositions	149
Section II.—Formation of Prepositive Locutions	150
Section III.—Government of Prepositions	150

CHAPTER IX.

Of the Conjunction	152

CHAPTER X.

Of the Interjection	154

Conjugation of the auxiliary verb **avoir** (=*to have*) negatively, interrogatively, and interrogatively with a negation	156

Conjugation of the auxiliary verb **être** (= *to be*) negatively,
    interrogatively, and interrogatively with a negation . 160
Models of reflexive verbs conjugated negatively, interroga-
    tively, and interrogatively with a negation 164
Index 169
French-English Vocabulary 173
English-French Vocabulary 193

INTRODUCTION

PRELIMINARY REMARKS
ON THE HISTORY AND GEOGRAPHY OF THE FRENCH LANGUAGE.

Geography.—The French language extends over the whole of France, with the exception of one single province, Brittany, where, out of a population of 1,800,000, one million of individuals speak a language known by the name of **Bas-Breton**, and which is Celtic in its origin. To this important exception three small groups can be further added: the department of the North, where 200,000 inhabitants out of 1,200,000 speak the **Flemish language**, an offshoot from the German; the department of Lower-Pyrenees, where 120,000 persons speak the **Basque**, a very ancient idiom, the origin of which is unknown; finally, the department of Eastern Pyrenees (formerly the province of Roussillon), where 130,000 inhabitants speak the **Catalonian** language, derived from the Latin.

If the domains of the French language do not correspond exactly with the present territory of France, they include, on the other hand, several important districts outside the limits of that country, which represent an aggregate of a little more than 3,600,000 inhabitants, distributed as follows:—Belgium, 1,600,000; Germany, 1,000,000; French Switzerland, 400,000; finally, the Channel Islands, 60,000.

To these numbers we must add, out of Europe, the English colonies of Canada and Mauritius, which have retained the use of the French language, to say nothing of the French settlements (Algeria, Guiana, Senegal, etc.); we find thus 1,500,000 inhabitants more to be placed to the account of the French linguistic wealth.

With reference to the language, France is divided into two regions, **North** and **South**, the limits of which can be marked by tracing on the map a line extending from La Rochelle to Grenoble.

North of this line all cultivated people speak French; the peasants understand French, but make use of *patois* closely connected with it. These *patois* are four in number: 1. The **Norman**, spoken in the western district; 2. The **Picard**, in the northwestern; 3. The **Lorrain**, in the eastern; 4. The **Burgundian**, in the central and south-eastern. The analogy which these *patois* present with the French language has caused them to be collectively designated as *French patois*.

South of the line, linguistic circumstances are entirely different. Cultivated people, indeed, understand and write French; but in the relations they hold with each other they have recourse by preference (even in the large towns) to their own *patois*, which is an idiom as different from French as is Italian or Spanish. The inhabitants of the rural districts, notwithstanding the efforts made by the teachers of elementary schools, seldom speak anything but these *patois*, which are likewise four in number: —1. The **Gascon**, 2. The **Limousin**; 3. The **Languedocian**; and 4. The **Provençal**; the names sufficiently point out the provinces where these idioms are respectively used; they are called collectively *Provençal patois*, in opposition to the *French patois* spoken north of the line mentioned above.

History.—Everyone knows that the earliest inhabitants of Gaul, so far as we are aware, at least, were the *Galli*, who spoke a language belonging to the *Celtic* family, that is to say, akin to the idioms used in France by the natives of Lower Brittany, and, in the British Isles, by the Scotch Highlanders, the Irish, and the Welsh.

In the course of the first century, B.C., the legions led by Cæsar conquered Gaul, and reduced it to the position of a Roman province. Far superior to the *Galli*, in point both of science and of civilisation, the Romans forced upon them the Latin language together with the yoke, in the same way as the French have forced their language upon the Arabs of Algeria.

At Rome, however, just as in the France of the nineteenth century, there were two languages co-existing: that of the people and of the peasants, the **popular Latin**, in a word; and that of the learned and the *literati*, which is known as **classical** or **literary Latin**—the former was less fettered, the latter was more refined; but both often employed different words to express the same idea. Thus, whilst the classical *Latin* had the substantive *equus* as an equivalent for *horse*, the colloquial Latin said *caballus*; whence the French *cheval*.

It is the **colloquial Latin,** naturally, which the Roman soldiers introduced amongst the peasants of Gaul; these, in their turn, transformed it into French, by dint of altering the pronunciation. If we notice how the English, who speak the French language, all modify the pronunciation of the French in the same manner, we shall easily understand how Latin uttered by the *Galli* was altered according to one uniform system; it is precisely this altered Latin which is called *French*. The colloquial Latin thus changed through the Celtic pronunciation, began to make its appearance about the fifth century, at the downfall of the Roman empire, as a distinct language, which the *savants* of the day contemptuously called *lingua Romana rustica* (the Latin of the peasants); hence the designation **Romance language**. The invasion of the barbarians was then destroying the empire; in the storm, everything bearing the Roman stamp disappeared—administration, schools, justice, aristocracy, literature; the *literary* Latin shared the same fate—that idiom which had been both the organ and the result of intellectual activity.

As colloquial Latin produced **French** in Gaul, so it became **Italian** in Italy, and **Spanish** in Spain. In France the *Romance language* was subdivided into two great varieties corresponding with the rival races of the north and south. North of the Loire we find the *Langue d'oïl*, or French, properly so called; south of the Loire, we have the *Langue d'oc*, or Provençal; these curious names result from the custom, frequently resorted to during the Middle Ages, of designating languages by the sign of affirmation *oui* (yes); *oui* was *oïl* in the north, and *oc* in the south.

The northern language, the *Langue d'oïl*, was in its turn divided, during the eleventh century, into four principal dialects: the **Norman**, the **Picard**, the **Burgundian**, and, finally, the **French** dialect, which was originally the one spoken in the province called *Ile-de-France*. (In the Middle Ages the name *Français* was given specially to the inhabitants of Ile-de-France.) These four dialects were equal in power and in influence, because there did not exist then, as there does to-day, one single centre, one capital of the kingdom, capable of setting to the whole country the model of elegant speaking. The Dukes, whether of Normandy or of Burgundy, the equals of the Dukes of France (we mean, of Ile-de-France), employed respectively in their official acts the language of their province, Norman or Burgundian.

How is it that these four languages were subsequently reduced to one? Why is it that the dialect of Ile-de-France was adopted subsequently as the common language, rather than the Burgundian or the Norman? As long as the Capetian monarchs, humble lords of Ile-de-France and of Orléanais, remained destitute of all influence beyond the limits of their royal domain (that is to say, from the tenth to the twelfth century), the French dialect enjoyed no notoriety out of these two provinces. But with the beginning of the twelfth century, the petty Kings of France began to extend their possessions at their neighbours' expense; they annexed successively Berry (1101), Picardy (1200), Touraine (1203), Normandy (1204), Champagne (1361), and carried with them into those newly-acquired provinces the dialect of Ile-de-France, the *French*, which took, in each of them, the place of the native dialect; and being the *language of the king*, it was soon adopted as the type of fashionable parlance. Resisting this invasion, the people alone, in each province, retained their old dialect, and refused to accept the French. As they ceased then to be used in writing, the idioms of Picardy, Burgundy, and Normandy fell immediately from the rank of *dialects* (that is to say, of *literary* languages both written and spoken) to the humble position of *patois* (we mean of idioms not written, but only spoken). This date (the fourteenth century), when the provincial dialects became patois, whilst the dialect of Ile-de-France assumed the place of the common language of the kingdom, marked the death of the *Langue d'oïl* and the historical birth of the *French language*.

The *patois*, which we find at the present day in the rural districts of Picardy, Normandy, and Burgundy, are not therefore, as is commonly believed, the *literary French corrupted on the lips of the peasants;* they are the *débris* of the old provincial dialects reduced by political events from the rank of written languages to that of *patois*.

The *Langue d'oïl* had disappeared to make room for the French, south of the Loire, the *Langue d'oc* likewise vanished away. The terrible rivalry between the inhabitants of the south and those of the north was ended by the Crusade against the Albigenses, and the defeat of the Southerners struck the death-blow at the *Langue d'oc*. In 1272, Languedoc was annexed to France, and the introduction of the French language speedily followed as a matter of course. The *Langue d'oc* ceased to be used as a medium for writing; it fell from the rank of a literary language to that of a patois, and the *Limousin, Gascon, Languedocian,* and *Provençal* patois, which still persist at the present day in the rural districts of southern France, are merely the *débris* of that *Langue d'oc* which shone with so brilliant a lustre in the times of the troubadours.

To sum up: we see that French is by no means formed from the corrupted *débris* of the Celtic language, as some grammarians still persist in saying; and its history may be concisely stated thus: the *popular* Latin, transferred into Gaul by the soldiers of Cæsar, quickly suppressed the native language, the *Celtic*, and, through a series of slow and imperceptible transformations, gave birth to a new idiom, the **Romance language**, to which the barbarians added a certain number of German words (such as *fief*, fief, *sénéchal*, seneschal, *baron*, baron, *échevin*, alderman, sheriff, etc.) relating to the feudal system, to war, and hunting. Towards the eighth century, this *Romance language* was divided into two branches: the *Langue d'oc*, south of the Loire, and the *Langue d'oïl*, north of that river. One of the four dialects of the *Langue d'oïl*, that of Ile-de-France, gradually supplanted all the others, and became, in the fourteenth century, the *French language*.

To the old stock of the language, which may be called **popular French**, two categories of new words have become superadded, from the fourteenth century to the nineteenth.

1st. **Foreign words**, imported as the result of several political circumstances, the principal of which are, in the thirteenth century, the Crusades and the commercial relations with the East; in the sixteenth, the Italian wars, and the influence of the Renaissance; in the seventeenth, the influence exercised by Spain over the court of Louis XIII., and the wars of Germany with France; finally, in the present century, the commercial, industrial, and social relations which the French are carrying on with England, and which are daily increasing.

To the first of these causes is due the introduction of a small quantity of Arabic or Oriental words (*sultan*, sultan, *caravane*, caravan, *derviche*, dervis, *alcool*, alcohol, *sequin*, seqnin, etc.); to the second, the French language is indebted for more than five hundred words of Italian origin (especially terms of war and of the fine arts—*spadassin*, fighter or hired assassin, *brave*, brave, *gabion*, gabion, *parapet*, parapet;—*costume*, dress, *fresque*, fresco, *aquarelle*, water-colour, *galbe*, entasis, *torse*, torso, etc.); the third has contributed a few Spanish words (*mantille*, mantilla, *duègne*, duenna, *matamore*, bully, *hâbler*, to boast, etc.), and a certain number of special German military expressions (*vaguemestre*, baggage-master, *schlague*, military flogging, *bivouac*, bivouac, *blockhaus*, block-house, etc.); finally, the invasion of English words is still going on very steadily (*whist*, *turf*, *spleen*, *tunnel*, *wagon*, *rail*, *coke*, *express*, *fashionable*, *budget*, *jury*, etc.). *

2nd. In addition to the *popular French*, which is the work of the people, and to the *foreign words* imported into France as the result of political circumstances, we must distinguish a third series of expressions created by learned men since the eleventh century, and ever on the increase. This **learned French** con-

---

* For the etymology of all these words, see Brachet's "*Dictionnaire étymologique.*"

sists of words borrowed directly by the *savants*, either from the Greek (*autopsie, aristocratie, microscope, cosmographie*), or from the Latin (as *relation, proportion, préméditation, précession, coordination*, etc.).

As a conclusion to these short historical remarks, let us show by a few numbers in what proportions the three elements—**popular** French, words of **foreign origin**, and **learned** or **artificial** words—have combined to form the French language. We shall take as the basis of our calculation the *Dictionnaire de l'Académie française*, which contains about 27,000 words: out of these we find 600 whose origin is entirely unknown; 1000 are words of foreign extraction, borrowed from the modern languages (English, Italian, Spanish, etc.); whilst 14,000 are of *learned origin*, having been made up by scholars with the help of Greek and Latin. We thus obtain a total of 15,600 words, leaving us rather less than 12,000 constituting what we may designate as *popular French*. Of these 12,000 words, about 8000, such as *pauvr-ette* (= poor creature), *faibl-ir* (= to grow weak), *maigr-ir* (= to get lean, or thin), are immediately created by the French with the help of the simple words *pauvre* (= poor), *faible* (= weak), *maigre* (= lean), etc. The simple words, which constitute the real substratum of the language, are therefore reducible to about 4200, of which 3800 are of Latin origin, whilst the remaining 400 are German words introduced by the Teutonic conquerors at the time of the invasion (fifth century).

OBJECT AND DEFINITION OF GRAMMAR.

We express ourselves by means of **phrases**, which are composed of **words**; words, in their turn, are composed of **letters**.

The French grammar is the series of rules to be observed in the French language for the assemblage of *letters* into words, and the combination of *words* into *sentences*. Hence three divisions in the grammar: the study of **letters**, the study of **words**, and the study of **sentences**.

BOOK I.

STUDY OF LETTERS.

CHAPTER I.

OF THE FRENCH ALPHABET.

1. We express our thoughts by means of *words*, which are composed of one or several *sounds*, represented in writing by signs called *letters*.

2. The collection of all the letters used in a language is called its *Alphabet*.

The French alphabet is composed of twenty-six letters, as follows:—*

A, B, C, D, E, F, G, H, I, J, K, L, M, N, O, P, Q, R, S, T, U, V, W,† X, Y, Z.

These twenty-six letters do not express all the sounds of the French language; there are some other simple sounds which are expressed by joining together two letters of the alphabet, thus forming a new group. *Ch*, for instance, is a simple sound represented by two letters.

Why does the French alphabet follow this curious order in which consonants and vowels are jumbled together indiscriminately? Because it is derived from the Latin, whose alphabet was already arranged in this order. The Latins borrowed their alphabet from the Greeks, and the Greeks took theirs from the Phœnicians.

3. All the sounds of the French language are divided into two classes, viz. **vowels** and **consonants**.

---

* We do not attempt any equivalent pronunciation of the French Alphabet; the pupil must learn from the master how the letters are pronounced.

† W is used in words taken from English and German, and in their French derivatives.

SECTION I.

OF THE VOWELS.

4. The sound produced by a simple emission of the voice (*a, o, u*), is called a *vowel*. There are seven vowels in French—

a, e, i (or **y**), **o, u, eu, ou.**

All the vowels can be pronounced by themselves without the help of any other sound.

5. All the vowels can be either **short** or **long**, according as they are pronounced **quickly** or **slowly**: thus *a* is short in *patte* (=paw, foot), because it is pronounced rapidly; whilst it is long in *pâte* (=dough), because we lay a stress on the *â*. In the same way—

e	is long in	bête (=beast),	and short in	jette (=he or she throws).
i	„	gîte (=lodging),	„	petite (=small).
o	„	côte (=coast),	„	dévote (=devout).
u	„	flûte (=flute),	„	butte (=butt, mound).
eu	„	heure (=hour),	„	jeune (=young).
eu	„	jeûne (=fast),	„	creuser (=to dig).
ou	„	voûte (=vault),	„	toute (=all).

Out of the seven vowels *a, e, i, o, u, eu, ou*, the first five are represented in French by a single letter; the last two are expressed by the junction of two letters, namely *e* and *u*, *o* and *u*. Although appearing to the eye compound vowels, they give to the ear only one sound, *eu, ou*, as simple as that of *a* or *o*.

6. No remarks are needed about *a* and *i*; but *e, o*, and *eu* require some observations to be made—

The letter *e* is used in French to express **three sounds**, which in reality ought to be considered as three distinct vowels :—

1. A very *dull* sound, called **e muet** (mute), as in *homme* (=man), *venir*, (=to come).

2. An *acute* sound, called **e fermé** (close), as in *aimé* (=loved), *bonté* (=goodness). This *e* is generally denoted by the sign ('), called **acute accent** (*accent aigu*).

The *e* is likewise close in words ending by the letter *r* when the *r* is not pronounced. Thus *verger* (=an orchard), *rocher* (=a rock), *aimer* (=to love).

8. A very open sound, which is heard in t*e*rre (= earth, land), m*e*r (= sea), enf*e*r (= hell), succ*è*s (= success), proc*è*s (= lawsuit), and uttered by opening the mouth wide. This **e** is called **ouvert** (open), and is generally marked by the little sign (`), called **grave accent** (*accent grave*). No accent is used when the open *e* is followed by two consonants, as in p*e*ste (= plague), r*e*ste (= remainder), fr*e*sque (= fresco), or when it is followed by a sounded *r* at the end of a word, as in :—

  am*e*r (= bitter)   f*e*r (= iron)
  canc*e*r (= cancer)   hi*e*r (= yesterday)
  ch*e*r (= dear)   hiv*e*r (= winter)
  enf*e*r (= hell)   v*e*r (= worm).

This sound of the open *e* is also rendered either by *ai*, as in :—

  *ai*re (= threshing floor), pronounced *è*re.
  ch*ai*r (= flesh),   ,,   ch*è*re.
  cl*ai*r (= clear),   ,,   cl*è*re.
  écl*ai*r (= lightning),   ,,   écl*è*re.
  p*ai*r (= equal),   ,,   p*è*re.

Or by *ei*, as in :—

  p*ei*ne (= trouble), pronounced p*è*ne.
  S*ei*ne (= Seine),   ,,   sc*è*ne.
  v*ei*ne (= vein),   ,,   v*è*ne.

7. The sound *eu* is represented in French in three different ways, viz. :—

  eu,   as in h*eu*re (= hour),
  œu, ,, b*œu*f (= ox), *œu*f (= egg), s*œu*r (= sister).
 œ and *ue*, ,, *œ*il (= eye), acc*ue*ille (= greet [thou]), c*ue*ille (= pluck [thou]), org*ue*il (= pride),

which are pronounced as if written :—

    acc*œ*uille, c*œ*uille, org*œ*uil.

8. The vowel *y* between two consonants is pronounced *i*, as in anal*y*se (= analysis, parsing), mart*y*r (= martyr), presb*y*tère (= parsonage); but between two vowels it is sounded like two *i*'s, that is to say, that the first *i* is joined to the preceding vowel, as in abo*y*er (= to bark), pronounce *aboi-ier*, and not *aboi-er;* and in p*ay*s (= country), pronounce *pai-is*, and not *pa-is*.

OF THE VOWELS.

9. A **diphthong** is the combination of two simple vowels pronounced by a single emission of the voice, as *ui* in *huileux* (=oily). *Ui*, being a compound of the two vowels *u* and *i*, is a diphthong.

Diphthong comes from the Latin *diphthongus* which, itself, was borrowed from the Greek, and means two sounds.

10. In French, diphthongs are formed with the four vowels *i, o, u, ou*, followed by some other vowel of the alphabet.

Thus *i* forms: **ia**, as in *piano* (=piano)
            ie, ,, *pied* (=foot)
            io, ,, *piocher* (=to dig);
o forms: **oa**, as in *moabite* (=moabite)
            oe, ,, *moelle* (=marrow)
            oi, ,, *roi* (=king);
u forms: **ue**, as in *écuelle* (=bowl)
            ui, ,, *huile* (=oil)
            ,, ,, *suif* (=tallow);
ou forms: **oua**, as in *douanier* (=custom-house officer)
            oue, ,, *fouetter* (=to whip)
            oui, ,, *oui* (=eyes)
            ,, ,, *louis* (=louis)

Exercise 1.

Write out the following words in French and in English.

A. *Underlining with one dash the* **short,** *and with two dashes the* **long vowels** *[see § 5]:—*

pâté	petite	cru	fleur	pôle
thé	chute	crû	malheur	île
âge	fête	du	pécheur	jeûne
sage	épître	dû	pêcheur	jeune
cravate	sucre	mot	mur	tache
fourchette	apôtre	août	mûr	tâche
joûte	châsse	louve	sur	bûche
croûte	chasse	succès	sûr	fou
route				

B. *Underlining the* **e** *mute* (a); *the* **e** *close* (b); *and the open* **e** *or its equivalents* (c) *[see § 6]:—*

(a)	pureté	tenir	somme	élever	sentence
	mener	bijouterie	Rome	batelier	féroce
(b)	aimé	méchanceté	beauté	sobriété	présent
	dîner	légèreté	boucher	boulanger	péril
(c)	excès	élève	hiver	pair	haine
	arrêt	presque	chaise	chair	reine

C. *Underlining the* **eu** *or its equivalents* [see § 7] :—

beurre	fauteuil	deuil	nœud	œuf
cœur	écureuil	cueille	vœu	neuf
chœur	orgueil	écueil	demeure	œuvre

D. *Arranging under two heads those where the* **y** *stands for* **i,** *and those where the* **y** *stands for* **ii** [see § 8] :—

croyant	fondroyant	fuyard	cyprès	presbytère
broyant	rayon	syllabe	style	martyr
paysan	citoyen	symbole	analyse	acolyte

E. *Underlining the* **diphthongs** [see §§ 9 and 10] :—

diable	huile	médiocre	étoile	écuelle
acier	tuile	ennui	poire	queue
cahier	guide	cuir	roue	équestre
péricle	liquide	louage	Louis	quille

SECTION II.

OF THE CONSONANTS.

11. In the French alphabet there are twenty consonants :—

B, C, D, F, G, H, J, K, L, M, N, P, Q, R, S, T, V, W, X, Z,

to which CH should be added.

Several of these consonants express the same sound, thus *s, k, q* have the sound of *c hard, e.g.,* cavalier (=horseman), kakatoès (=cockatoo), qualifier (=to qualify).

S and c are sounded alike in *servir* (=to serve), and cervelle (=brains);

J and *g* in *j*'ai (=I have), and *geai* (=jay), *joli* (=pretty), and geôlier (=jailer);

Z and *s* in zéro (=zero, nought), and déserteur (=deserter), which is pronounced dézerteur.

These letters are called CONSONANTS, from the Latin word *consona* (that which is pronounced with, by the help of), because the old grammarians believed that a consonant could never be pronounced without the help of a vowel.

12. The consonants are produced by three different parts of the vocal mechanism: the *throat*, the *teeth*, and the *lips*. The six consonants, **c, k, q, g, j, ch,** which are produced by the *throat,* are for that reason, called

gutturals (from the Latin *guttur*, throat); two of them, **c** and **g**, have a double sound, viz., *hard* before the vowels *a, o, u*, as in c*a*marade (=comrade), g*a*min (=street Arab), c*o*rridor (=passage), g*o*belet (=goblet); c*u*muler (=to accumulate), g*u*ttural (=guttural); and *soft* before the vowels *e* and *i*, as in c*e*rveau (=brains), g*e*rmer (=to sprout); c*i*rer (=to black, to polish), g*i*bier (=game).

13. **T, d, s, z**, which are produced by the *teeth*, are, for that reason, called **dentals** (from Lat. *dens, dentis,* tooth).

s placed between two vowels is sounded like **z**:—
cloison (=partition) *pronounce* cloizon
poison (=poison) ,, poizon.

14. The consonants produced by the help of the *lips*, and for that reason called **labials** (from the Latin *labia*, lips), are **p, b, f, v.**

15. The two consonants **l** and **r** are called **liquids** (from the Latin *liquidus*, liquid, flowing), because these two letters are easily joined to other consonants, such as *p, b, c*, to form groups of letters quite liquid (*easy to pronounce*), such as *bl* in *bl*anc (=white), *pl* in *pl*aine (=field), *cl* in *cl*ameur (=clamour, outcry), *gl* in *gl*oire (=glory), or *pr* in *pr*emier (=first), *cr* in *cr*oire (=to believe), *br* in *br*uit (=noise), *gr* in *gr*andir (=to grow).

16. The two consonants **m** and **n** are called **nasal** (from the Latin *nasus*, nose), because they give to the vowels a peculiar sound proceeding from the *nose*, as *an* in m*an*ger (=to eat), v*an*ter (=to praise).

The liquid *l* and the nasal *n* become liquid in some cases, that is to say, they are pronounced as if followed by a very weak *i*, audible, for instance, in campag*n*ard (=countryman), and travai*ll*er (=to work).

17. **x** is a double consonant, pronounced sometimes like *cs* (lu*x*ueux=luxurious), sometimes like *gs* (e*x*act=exact).

OF THE CONSONANTS. 13

13. **H** is the weakest of all the consonants, just as *e silent* or *mute* is the weakest vowel. There are two kinds of *h*'s:—

1. *H silent* (or *mute*), which does not represent any sound, and over which leaps the elision of the article *le* or *la*, exactly as if the article was coming into contact with the vowel itself. Examples:—

 L'homme (=the man), *l'habitude* (=the habit);

Exactly as in—

 L'abaissement (=the abasement), *l'obéissance* (=the obedience).

2. *H aspirate*, which in French is not more heard than *h silent*, but which differs from it by preventing the elision :—

 Le héros (=the hero), *la houlette* (=the shepherd's crook).

Care must be taken not to sound *les-zhéros, les-zhou'ettes*.

QUESTIONS FOR EXAMINATION.

1. How are *words* formed?
2. How are *sounds* represented?
3. What is the *alphabet*?
4. How many letters are there in the French alphabet?
5. What is the origin of the French alphabet?
6. What are *vowels*?
7. Give a list of the French vowels.
8. What is a short vowel?—a long vowel?
9. What is the *e* mute?—the *e* close? —the *e* open?
10. What is to be noticed with reference to the letter *y*?
11. What is a *diphthong*?
12. Name the principal diphthongs.
13. How many *consonants* are there in French?
14. Name the *gutturals*—the *dentals*—the *labials*—the *liquids*—the *nasals*.
15. When do the consonants *l* and *n* become liquid?
16. When is *h* a mute letter?—When does it become aspirate?

Exercise 2.

Write out the following words in French and in English.

A. *Underlining the* **guttural consonant** (*see* § 12):—

| cristal | jumeau | kilomètre | question | goût |
| camp | joyeux | requête | chaleur | dégât |

B. *Underlining with one dash the* c *and* g **hard**, *and with two dashes the* c *and* g **soft** :—

| cascade | garçon | courte | céleste | golfe |
| cervelas | géant | gibier | cible | guêtre |

C. *Underlining the* **dentals** (a); *the* **labials** (b); *and the* **liquids** (c) [*see* §§ 13—15]:—

(a) teindre   attentif   dimanche   seigneur   zéro
    tempête   danser   savoir   sucre   zone

(b) poulet   boucle   figure   perte   revers
    peuple   faiblesse verbe   vertu   bible

(c) blé   grand   bruit   plateau   plume
    croisée   blanc   prairie   trouble   prune

D. *Underlining the* **nasal** (a), *and the* **liquid l** *and* **n** (b) [*see* § 16]:—

(a) menton   mensonge   un   fonction   festin
    tenture   leçon   puissance prompt   vilain

(b) mouille   campagne   pille   vermeil   gouvernail
    oreille   règne   aiguille   sommeil   Gascogne

E. *Underlining with one dash the* **x** *employed instead of* **cs**, *and with two dashes the* **x** *employed instead of* **gz**. (*see* § 17):—

luxe   texte   exhaler   exprès   exposé
exemple   exigu   vexer   annexion   exigeant

F. *Underlining with one dash the* **h** **mute**, *and with two dashes the* **h** **aspirate** (*see* § 18):—

habile   hagard   hache   hasard   héritier
baie   habit   habitation herbage   hibou

CHAPTER II.

OF SYLLABLES.—ORTHOGRAPHIC SIGNS.

19. A **syllable** is one or several sounds which are pronounced without interruption, and by a single emission of the voice. Thus *ôté* (=taken away, past participle of *ôter*), is formed of two syllables, the first of which is composed of only one vowel (*ô*), and the second of a consonant (*t*) and a vowel (*é*).

When a syllable ends with an *e silent* (or *mute*), as *me*, in j'aime (=I love), it is called **silent** (or **mute**).

20. The name of **orthographic signs** is given to certain signs used in writing, either to indicate the changes of the same vowel, as *o* and *ó*, *é* and *è*, *ai* and *aï*; or the suppression of a letter, as in *l'épée* for *la épée* (=the sword); or lastly, the joining of two or three words into one, as *arc-en-ciel* (=rainbow), *pied-à-terre* (=temporary lodging, resting-place).

There are five kinds of *orthographic signs*, viz., the *accents*, the *cedilla*, the *diæresis*, the *apostrophe*, and the *hyphen*.

The **accents** are three in number: the *acute* ('), the *grave* (`), and the *circumflex* (^).

The *acute* accent is placed over *close é*: bon*té* (=kindness), san*té* (=health).

The *grave* accent is placed over *open è*: pro*cès* (=lawsuit), suc*cès* (=success). It is also placed over *à* (=to), *là* (=there), *où* (=where), *dès* (=as soon as), to prevent the confusion with *a* (= [he *or* she] has), *la* (=the, *fem. article, or* her, *pers. pronoun*), *ou* (=or), *des* (=of the, *defin. art., or* some, *indefin. art.*).

The *circumflex* accent is placed over long vowels: *cô*te (=coast, shore, rib), *gî*te (=dwelling).

<small>The circumflex accent usually shows that a letter has been suppressed. Thus, the words *tête* (=head), *fête* (=festival), *bête* (=beast), were originally spelt *teste*, *feste*, *beste*, and they preserved that spelling till the middle of the eighteenth century. It was only in 1740 that the *Académie Française* replaced the consonant *s* by a circumflex accent in the above words and similar ones.</small>

21. In order to show, when two vowels following each other are to be pronounced separately, the sign (¨) called **tréma** (diæresis) is placed over the second: thus *uë* in *ciguë* (=hemlock). Without the diæresis this word would be pronounced *cig*, because *ue* would be mute as in fig*ue* (=fig), lig*ue* (=league).

The **apostrophe** (') denotes the suppression of the vowels *a, e, i*, in *le, la, je, me, te, se, de, que, si*, and a few other words before another word beginning with a *vowel* or *h silent*, as in :—

	instead of	
L'épée (=the sword)	instead of	*la-épée*
J'arrive (=I arrive)	,,	*je-arrive*
S'il vient (=if he comes)	,,	*si-il vient*
L'honneur (=the honour)	,,	*le-honneur*

22. The **cedilla** is a sign (¸) placed under the *c* before *a*, *o*, *u*, when it has a soft sound, as in façade (=frontage, façade), façon (=form, shape), rinçure (=rinsings), instead of its regular hard sound before the same vowels, as in camarade (=comrade), colombe (=dove), curieux (=inquisitive).

23. The **hyphen,** called in French **trait d'union,** joins together either the different parts of a cómpound word, as *arc-en-ciel* (=rainbow), *chef-lieu* (=chief or county town), *vis-à-vis* (=opposite);—or the verb with its subject (in the interrogative conjugation), as in *irai-je* (=shall I go)? *viendrez-vous* (=will you come)?—or with its object, as in *croyez-moi* (=believe me), *venez-y-voir* (=come hither and see).

All these signs were introduced into the French language by the grammarians of the sixteenth century. The accents are borrowed from the Greek language, in which, however, they were used for a very different purpose. *Trema* is a Greek word which means "point, dot," or, more properly, "hole." *Apostrophe*, likewise borrowed from the Greek, means "that which wards off," the suppression of the vowel preventing, or *warding off*, the hiatus which would be caused by the discordant meeting of two vowels. The *cedilla* was borrowed from the Italian printers, who called *zediglia* a little crotchet like a *z* placed under *c*, when it was to be pronounced *z* instead of *k*. The Italian word comes from *zeta* (z), and means properly "small z."

24. The three accents just described must not be mistaken for the *tonic accent* (from the L. *tonus*, a tone).

The raising of the voice on a particular syllable in every word is called the **tonic accent,** and the syllable on which falls that accent is called the **accented** or **tonic syllable.**

In French the accented syllable is always the last of the word, as mou**ton** (=sheep), che**val** (=horse), il

aima (=he loved), except when the word ends in
e mute, as table (=table), aimable (=amiable), lisible
(=legible), in which case the tonic accent is carried
back to the penultimate: ta*ble*, aima*ble*, lisi*ble*.

It results from this that, when two mute syllables would otherwise come together at the end of a word, as in the feminine of adjectives, and in verbs (*muet-e* = dumb; *complet-e* = complete; *appeler* = to call, *j'appele* = I call; *acheter* = to buy, *j'achete* = I buy; *mener* = to lead, *je mene* = I lead), the sound of the e in the last syllable but one is increased either by putting a grave accent over it (*complète, je mène, j'achète*), or by doubling the following consonant (*j'appel-le, muet-te*).

QUESTIONS FOR EXAMINATION.

1. What is a *syllable?* — How many syllables are there in *résidence?*
2. What is a *mute* syllable?
3. What is meant by *orthographic signs?*
4. Enumerate the orthographic signs used in French.
5. Where is the *acute* accent placed? — What are the various uses of the *grave* accent? — What does the *circumflex* accent generally show?
6. Where is the *tréma* placed?
7. Explain the use of the *apostrophe*, the *hyphen*, the *cedilla*.
8. State the origin of the various orthographic signs.
9. What do you mean by the *tonic accent?*
10. Which is the *accented syllable* in French words?

Exercise 3.

Write out the following words in French and in English:

A. *Underlining the* **tonic** *syllable (see § 24):*—

| aimant | président | souvent | président (*verbe*) | veille |
| aiment | expédient | trouvent | expédient (*verbe*) | veillent |

B. *Underlining with one dash the* **tonic** *syllable, and with two dashes the* **atonic** *one (see § 24):*—

| édifice | touffe | froment | plancher | soulèvement |
| forêt | avenue | charrue | assiette | fondement |

BOOK II.

STUDY OF WORDS.

25. There are ten classes of words used in the French language, viz. :

1. **Le nom** (noun)
2. **L'article** (article)
3. **L'adjectif** (adjective)
4. **Le pronom** (pronoun)
5. **Le verbe** (verb)
6. **Le participe** (participle)
7. **La préposition** (preposition)
8. **L'adverbe** (adverb)
9. **La conjonction** (conjunction)
10. **L'interjection** (interjection).

These ten kinds of different words, which by their combination form the French language, may be compared to the different parts of the human body, and for that reason have been called by grammarians **parts of speech**—that is to say, *the parts of the language.*

All these parts of speech (with the exception of the article unknown to the Romans) passed from Latin into French.

CHAPTER I.

OF THE NOUN OR SUBSTANTIVE.

26. The **noun** or **substantive** is a word used to name persons, animals, or things.

There are two kinds of nouns: **proper** nouns and **common** nouns.

The **proper** noun applies either to one *person* only, as *Pierre* (=Peter), *Paul* (=Paul), *Louis* (=Louis), or to one *thing* only, as *le Rhône* (=river Rhone), *la Loire* (=river Loire).

REMARK.—Proper nouns begin always with a capital letter.

The **common** noun designates either all the *persons* of the same nature, as *enfant* (=child), *marchand* (=merchant), *soldat* (=soldier); or *things* of the same kind, as *cour* (=court, yard), *jardin* (=garden), *maison* (=house).

27. Collective nouns are those which express a collection of persons or things, as *foule* (=crowd), *troupe* (=troop), *multitude* (=multitude).

Compound nouns are those which, although formed of two or three words, designate one single person or thing, as *chou-fleur* (=cauliflower), *arc-en-ciel* (=rainbow).

28. In nouns two things are to be studied and examined—*gender* and *number*.

SECTION I.

OF GENDER IN NOUNS.

29. Gender is the difference or distinction which is made between male and female beings.

In French there are two genders :—the **masculine**, and the **feminine**.

Men and males of animals, as *le père* (=the father), *le lion* (=the lion), are of the masculine gender. Women and females of animals, as *la mère* (=the mother), *la lionne* (=the lioness), are of the feminine gender.

Moreover, names of things which belong to neither sex have been made, by imitation, masculine or feminine. Thus *le bois* (=the wood), *le château* (=the castle), *le pays* (=the country), are masculine; whilst *la cour* (=the court, yard), *la grille* (=the grate, railing), *la lune* (=the moon) are feminine.

30. Feminine nouns are generally formed by adding an **e mute** to the masculine—

marquis (=marquis)   *marquise* (=marchioness)
ours (=bear)   *ourse* (=she-bear)

When the masculine noun ends with **en** or **on**, the *n* is doubled in the feminine—

    baron (=baron)   baro**nne** (=baroness)
    chrétien (=Christian)   chréti**enne** (=Christian)
    lion (=lion)   lio**nne** (=lioness)

When the masculine ends in **er**, the feminine takes a grave accent (`) over the **e** : *portier* (=door-keeper), *porti**è**re*.

EXCEPTIONS.—About twenty substantives form their feminine by changing e final into **esse**, as—*nègre* (=negro), *négresse* (=negress); *tigre* (=tiger), *tigresse* (=tigress); *prophète* (=prophet), *prophétesse* (=prophetess); *hôte* (=host), *hôtesse* (=hostess), etc. *Chasseur* (=hunter), *pécheur* (=sinner), weaken, besides, the diphthong *eu* into *e* mute, thus making *chasseresse*, *pécheresse* (and not *chasseuresse*, *pécheuresse*).

A few masculine substantives ending in **eur** form their feminine in **ice**, such as *acteur* (=actor), *ambassadeur* (=ambassador), etc., which make *actrice*, *ambassadrice*, etc. *Chanteur* (=singer), *voyageur* (=traveller), etc., have for their corresponding feminine: *chanteuse*, *voyageuse*, etc.

Many nouns, denoting professions generally followed by men, have no feminine: *imprimeur* (=printer), *graveur* (=engraver).

Exercise 4.

Write out the feminine of the following substantives, and give the meaning of each :—

(a) marquis	ouvrier	chien	gardien	Louis
cousin	lion	comédien	mercier	écolier
orphelin	paysan	magicien	portier	ours
châtelain	Européen	jardinier	Anglais	Italien
filleul	Français	Romain	berger	Gascon
(b) pair	chasseur	maître	Suisse	traître
prophète	tigre	défendeur	prince	comte
nègre	chanoine	hôte	pécheur	enchanteur
(c) baigneur	nageur	pêcheur	sauteur	chanteur
voyageur	joueur	travailleur	voleur	faucheur
acheteur	laveur	polisseur	flatteur	danseur
(d) délateur	bienfaiteur	fondateur	conducteur	directeur
acteur	moteur	admirateur	adorateur	instituteur

SECTION II.

OF NUMBER IN NOUNS.

31. The **number** is the difference or distinction which is made between one single thing and several things collected together.

In French, as in English, there are two numbers—the **singular**, to denote one person or one thing, as *le lion* (= the lion), *le livre* (= the book); and the **plural**, to denote several persons or things, as *les lions* (= the lions), *les livres* (= the books).

32. General Rule.—The plural of nouns is formed by adding **s** to the singular: *L'homme* (= man), *les hommes* (= men); *le livre* (= the book), *les livres* (= the books).

The reason why the French forms its plural in *s*, in preference to *m* or *b*, or any other letter, may be briefly stated thus: the French language has borrowed from the Latin accusative both its singular and its plural; and the letter *s* was generally the sign of the accusative plural in Latin.

33. When a noun in the singular already ends in *s*, *x*, or *z*, it does not change in the plural—

le fils (= the son)	*les fils* (= the sons)
la voix (= the voice)	*les voix* (= the voices)
le nez (= the nose)	*les nez* (= the noses).

34. Exceptions.—Nouns whose singular ends in *au* or *eu* take **x** in the plural—

un bateau (= a boat)	*des bateaux* (= some boats)
le château (= the castle)	*les châteaux* (= the castles);

as well as the seven following nouns ending in *ou*:

le bijou (= the jewel)	*les bijoux* (= the jewels)
un caillou (= a pebble)	*des cailloux* (= some pebbles)
un chou (= a cabbage)	*des choux* (= some cabbages)
le genou (= the knee)	*les genoux* (= the knees)
le hibou (= the owl)	*les hiboux* (= the owls)
un joujou (= a toy)	*des joujoux* (= some toys)
un pou (= a louse)	*des poux* (= lice).

N.B.—All the other nouns ending in *ou* follow the general rule, and take *s* in the plural—

un clou (= a nail)	*des clous* (= some nails)
un verrou (= a bolt)	*des verrous* (= some bolts).

This irregularity is one of the remains of the old language. The French *s* in the plural is always silent: *roses, fleurs,* and in the Middle Ages, we find it spelt either *s* or *z*, in *nes* for *nez*, *vois* or *voiz* for *voix*, for instance.

That license has remained in the words *bijou, genou*, etc., which are still written *bijoux, genoux*, whilst the plural of *clou* and *verrou* is spelt *clous, verrous*.

35. Nouns in *al* change *al* into *aux* in the plural—.

le cheval (= the horse)   les chevaux (= the horses)
un mal (= an evil)   des maux (= evils)

EXCEPT:—bal (= ball [to dance at])   chacal (= jackal)
carnaval (= carnival)   régal (= regale, feast, treat)
which take **s** in the plural:—des bals (= balls)

Seven substantives ending in *ail* follow the same rule—

un bail (= a lease)   des baux (= leases)
le corail (= coral)   les coraux (= the corals)
l'émail (= the enamel)   les émaux (= the enamels)
un soupirail (= an air-hole)   des soupiraux (= air-holes)
le travail (= work)   les travaux (= the works)
le vantail (= the leaf of a door)   les vantaux (= the leaves of doors)
un vitrail (= a stained glass window)   des vitraux (= stained glass windows).

N.B.—The word *bestiaux* is used as the plural of *bétail* (= cattle).

But all the other substantives ending in *ail* follow the general rule, as—

un gouvernail (= a helm)   des gouvernails (= helms), etc.

At the birth of the French language—that is, in the time of Hugh Capet—*al* became *als* in the plural: un cheval, des chevals, un mal, des mals; but in the thirteenth century (about the time of St. Louis) *al* was softened, and became *au* before a consonant. Traces of this alteration are found in the expressions: *cheval-léger* (= a light dragoon), and *Vaugirard*, still used instead of *cheval-léger*, *Val Girard* (le vallon de Girard = the vale of Girard): *chevals* then became *chevaus*, and, subsequently, *chevaux*. (See § 34.)

36. The following nouns have two plural forms, one regular, the other irregular. The irregular generally leaves to the noun the same meaning it has in the singular, whilst the regular gives it a peculiar signification:—

IRREGULAR.

l'aïeul* (= the grandfather)   les aïeux (= the ancestors)
le ciel (= sky, heaven)   les cieux (= the heavens)
l'œil (= the eye)   les yeux (= the eyes)
le travail (= the work)   les travaux (= the works).

REGULAR.

les aïeuls (= the grandfathers)
les ciels (= skies in pictures, bed-testers)
les œils, in compound nouns, as œils-de-bœuf (= oval windows)
des travails (= a minister's reports, or brakes for shoeing vicious horses).

* Aïeul keeps its original meaning in the regular plural.

QUESTIONS FOR EXAMINATION.

1. How many kinds of words are there in French?
2. What is the meaning of the expression: *parts of speech*?
3. What is a *common* substantive?—a *proper* one?
4. What is a *collective* noun?—a *compound* one?
5. What are the two points to be studied in connection with nouns?
6. What is meant by the *gender* of a noun?—How many genders are there in French?
7. What is the general rule for the formation of the feminine in French nouns?
8. Give the feminine of the following nouns: *chien—traître—lecteur—chanteur—pêcheur*.
9. What is meant by the *number* of a noun?—How many numbers are there in French?
10. How do you form the *plural* of French nouns?
11. How do you account for *s* being the sign of the plural in French?
12. How do you form the plural of nouns ending, 1. in *s, x, z*; 2. in *au* or *eu*; 3. in *ou*?
13. How do you explain the irregularity in the case of nouns ending in *ou*?
14. How do you form the plural of nouns ending, 1. in *al*; 2. in *ail*? —What are the exceptions?
15. What is the origin of the plural in *aux*?
16. Give the plural of *aïeul, ciel, œil*.

Exercise 5.

Write out the plural of the following substantives, giving the meaning of each:—

(a)
vaisseau	homme	maître	excès	château
richesse	mer	siècle	bambou	hameau
pois	trou	élève	tableau	caillou
vice	ami	navigateur	vertu	acajou
verrou	oiseau	perdrix	noix	

(b)
maréchal	canal	régal	camail	gouvernail
cheval	arsenal	bal	détail	rail
bocal	cristal	carnaval	éventail	vitrail
signal	végétal	chacal	bail	travail
amiral	vassal	soupirail	corail	général
mal	journal	attirail	émail	capital

SECTION III.

FORMATION OF SUBSTANTIVES.

37. New substantives are formed by joining together, either:

1. **two nouns:** un *chat-tigre* (=a tiger-cat),
2. **a noun and an adjective:** une *basse-taille* (=a bass voice),
3. **a noun and a verb:** un *tire-bouchon* (=a cork-screw),
4. **a noun and a preposition:** un *sous-officier* (=a non-commissioned officer),
5. **a verb and an adverb:** un *passe-partout* (=a master-key),
6. **two nouns joined by a preposition:** un *arc-en-ciel* (=a rainbow).

38. From a simple substantive, as *boutique* (=shop), two new words can be derived in French:

(*a*) A **derivative**, with a new termination called **suffix** (from the Latin *suffixus* = *affixed to* or *after*) placed *after* the word, as *ier* in *boutiquier* (=shopkeeper). The part of the simple word which remains unaltered, and to which the suffix is added, is termed *root* or *stem*.

(*b*) A **compound**, with the help of a new word called **prefix** (from the Latin *præfixus* = *affixed before*), which is placed *before* the simple word, as **arrière**-*boutique* (=back-shop).

PREFIXES.

39. The prefixes used in French to form new substantives are—

après,	as in	une *après*-midi (=an afternoon)
avant,	„	un *avant*-coureur (=a forerunner, precursor)
arrière,	„	une *arrière*-boutique (=a back-shop)
contre,	„	un *contre*-ordre (=a counter-order)
entre,	„	une *entre*-côte (=a rib of beef)
non,	„	un *non*-sens (=a nonsense)
sans,	„	un *sans*-façon (an off-handed manner)
sous,	„	un *sous*-officier (=a non-commissioned officer)

The three particles, *bis, mi, vice,* are also used to form compound nouns—

bis (=twice), as *bis*aïeul (=great-grandfather); *bis*cuit (=biscuit, *lit.* twice baked)

mi (=half), as la *mi*-carême (=mid-Lent); la *mi*-juillet (=the middle of July); *mi*nuit (=midnight)

vice (=instead of, in the place of), as *vice-roi* (=viceroy), *vice-amiral* (=vice-admiral).

SUFFIXES.

40. Derivative substantives are formed in French by adding to substantives already existing, to adjectives, or to verbs *eleven* suffixes: **ade, age, ain, ard, at, é, ée, er (ier), ie (erie), esse, iste.**

FORMATION OF SUBSTANTIVES.

1. *Substantives formed from substantives already existing.*

From *colonne* (=a column), we get colonnade, i.e. a collection of columns.
 plume (=a feather)   ,,   plumage, i.e. a collection of feathers (=plumage).
 chapelle (=a chapel)   ,,   chapelain (=a chaplain).
 bille (=a ball)   ,,   billard (=a billiard table).
 marquis (=a marquis)   ,,   marquisat (=a marquisate).
 comte (=a count *or* earl)   ,,   comté (=a county *or* earldom).
 bouche (=a mouth)   ,,   bouchée (=a mouthful).
 horloge (=a clock)   ,,   horloger (=a clockmaker).
 pomme (=an apple)   ,,   pommier, (=an apple-tree).
 boucher (=a butcher)   ,,   boucherie (=a butcher's shop, butchery).
 âne (=an ass)   ,,   ânesse (=a she-ass).
 journal (=a journal *or* newspaper)   ,,   journaliste (=a journalist).

41. There is a particular class of suffixes which indicating *diminution*, are used to form derivatives, whose meaning is less than that of the simple word. For this reason they are called *diminutive suffixes*. Such are, for instance, **illon** in *négr*illon=*petit* nègre (=little negro); *eau* in *chevr*eau=*petite* chèvre (=kid).

Some of these suffixes, whilst lessening the signification of the simple word, give to it, at the same time, a meaning of depreciation and contempt, as *aille* in—

 la ferr-aille (=old iron), from *fer* (=iron)
 la valet-aille (=flunkeys), ,, *valet* (=valet, footman), &c. &c.

42. The diminutive suffixes are six in number—

1. **aille**: valet (=valet), valetaille (=flunkeys);
2. **as**: plâtre (=plaster), plâtras (=rubbish of plaster); (*in the feminine,* **asse**); paille (=straw), paillasse (=straw-mattress).
3. **et**: livre (=book), livret (=small-book); (*in the feminine,* **ette**); chanson (=song), chansonnette (=little song, ditty), hence the compound **elette**: goutte (=drop), goutelette (=small drop).
4. **on**: âne (=ass), ânon (=foal of an ass); hence the compounds **illon** and **eron**: carpe (=carp), carpillon (=small carp); mouche (=fly); moucheron (=gnat).
5. **eau**: prune (=plum), pruneau (=small plum); (*in the feminine,* **elle**), prunelle (=sloe).

The suffix **eau** makes **elle** in the feminine, because the old French language had the masculine termination *el* instead of *eau*; thus, *chapel*, the old form of *chapeau* (=hat), subsists still in *chapel*ier (=hatter).

6. **ot**: île (=island), îlot (=small island).

2. *Substantives derived from Adjectives.*

43. New substantives are formed by adding to adjectives the five following suffixes: **esse, ise, ie, té, ure.** All these nouns, thus derived from adjectives, are feminine—

    la faiblesse (=weakness) from *faible* (=weak)
    la sottise (=foolishness) ,, *sotte, f.* of *sot* (=foolish)
    la maladie (=illness) ,, *malade* (=ill)
    la pauvreté (=poverty) ,, *pauvre* (=poor)
    la courbure (=bending) ,, *courbe* (=curved).

3. *Substantives derived from Verbs.*

44. New substantives are formed from the verbs in three different ways, either—

(1) by using as substantives the **infinitive**, the **present participle**, and the **past participle**, as *le manger* (=eating), which is the infinitive of *manger* (=to eat); *le tranchant* (=the edge), from *tranchant* (=cutting), present participle of *trancher* (=to cut); *le reçu* (=the receipt), past participle of the verb *recevoir* (=to receive);

Or, (2) by striking off the termination *er* from verbs belonging to the first conjugation; thus, from *replier* (=to fold back) we get *repli* (=fold); from *débuter* (=to begin) we get *début* (=outset); from *appeler* (=to call), we get *appel* (=call, appeal);

Or (3) by adding to the root of the verb the suffixes **ade, age, ance, eur (or isseur), is, ment (or ement), oir, on, aison (or ison), ure.**

Thus from—

    promen-er (=to walk) comes *promenade* (=walk)
    lav-er (=to wash) ,, *lavage* (=washing)
    surveill-er (=superintending) ,, *surveillance* (=superintendence)
    chass-er (=to hunt) ,, *chasseur* (=hunter)
    rég-ir (=to rule) ,, *régisseur* (=steward, bailiff)
    hach-er (=to chop, to mince) ,, *hachis* (=hash, minced meat)
    hurl-er (=to howl) ,, *hurlement* (=howling)
    parl-er (=to speak) ,, *parloir* (=parlour)
    jur-er (=to swear) ,, *juron* (=oath)
    li-er (=to connect) ,, *liaison* (=connection)
    guér-ir (=to cure) ,, *guérison* (=curing, healing)
    bless-er (=to wound) ,, *blessure* (=wound).

FORMATION OF SUBSTANTIVES.

QUESTIONS FOR EXAMINATION.

1. How are new substantives formed in French?
2. Define a *prefix*;—a *suffix*.
3. Form a few substantives with the prefixes *contre*, *sous*, *sans*.
4. What is the meaning of *mi*, *bis*, *vice*?
5. Form a few substantives with the suffixes *at*, *on*, *aille*, *as*, *er*, *iste*.
6. What is meant by a *diminutive suffix*?
7. Form substantives with the suffixes *on*, *eau*, *ot*, *us*.
8. How are new substantives formed from adjectives?
9. What parts of the verbs are sometimes used as substantives?
10. What suffixes are used to form fresh substantives from verbs?— Give a list of substantives formed from the verbs *nettoyer*, *abreuver*, *épancher*, *frémir*, *sentir*.

Exercise 6.

Write a list of the following substantives with the PREFIX *indicated, and give the meaning of both the simple and the compound substantives.*

(a) prefix **après :** coup, midi, demain, dîner
(b) ,, **arrière :** garde, saison, boutique, neveu, pensée
(c) ,, **avant :** poste, coureur, garde, goût, propos
(d) ,, **contre :** coup, sens, marque, amiral, mutité
(e) ,, **entre :** côte, mets, sol, pont
(f) ,, **non :** sens, valeur, payement
(g) ,, **sans :** façon, gêne, dent
(h) ,, **sous :** officier, préfet, maître, intendant, sol
(i) ,, **vice :** roi, président, amiral
( ) ,, **mi :** nuit, jambe, juillet, partie
(l) ,, **bis :** aïeul, sac.

Exercise 7.

Write a list of compound substantives, by adding to the following one of the SUFFIXES *given below, and give the meaning of both the simple and the compound words.*

(a) *suffix* **ade** (*fem.*) :

aube	limon	colonne	poivre	arc
peuple	face	galop	recul	bourg
balustre	rodomont	orange	bourre	œil

(b) *suffix* **at** (*masc.*) :

solde	consul	assassin	syndic
externe	interne	Auvergne	forme
tribun	cardinal	marquis	économe

(c) *suffix* **age** (*masc.*) :

herbe	esclave	bande	jardin	feuille
bord	branche	brigand	corde	ermite
langue	magasin	échafaud	vagabond	ligne
pèlerin	grille	mari	moule	plume
jambe	ferme	coquille	homme	ancre

(d) *suffix* **ain** (*fem.* **aine**):

Masc. {	monde	république *	Rome	proche
	public	Afrique *	terre	Amérique *
	Toulouse	Maroc	quatre	diocèse
Fem. {	Dix †	huit	quarante	cinquante
	soixante	cent	trente	vingt
	douze	quinze		

(e) *suffix* **ard** (*fem.* **arde**):

Masc.: campagne montagne bille
Fem.: poule bombe moût

(f) *suffix* **é**:

Masc: comte doigt
Fem.: parent prévôt

(g) *suffix* **ée** (*fem.*):

assiette	soir	rang	matin	niche
écuelle	jatte	table	cuiller	plume
pâte	bouche	train		

(h) *suffix* **ier** [or **er** *after* **ch, g,** or **ill**] (*masc.*):

cerise	amande	gomme	grenade	pomme
poire	châtaigne	groseille	rose	orange
pêche	forme	douane	barbe	botte
plomb	guerre	bourse	vache	cloche
carrosse	tapis	cheval	école	cuisine
serrure	porte	horloge	couteau	salade
colombe	cendre	sucre	(*O. F. coutel*)	oreille
encre	huile	moutarde	sable	houille

(i) *suffix* **erie** [or **ie** *when the substantive already ends in* **er**] (*fem.*):

acier	berger	boulanger	horloger	pirate
boucher	argent	bois	corde	fruit
ébéniste	gendarme	lait	singe	marbre

(j) *suffix* **iste** (*masc.* or *fem.*):

dent	monarchie	copie	art	journal
mode	auberge	capital	chimie	fleur
morale	ébène	latin	paysage	machine

(k) *suffix diminutive* **aille** (*fem.*):

roc pierre fût mur

(l) *suffix diminutive* **as** (*fem.* **asse**):

papier‡ fil terre (these are *fem.*)

* *Que* is changed into *c*. † The *x* is changed into *s*. ‡ See § 24, and § 34 Note on *eur*.

FORMATION OF SUBSTANTIVES.

(m) *suffix* **et** (*fem.* **ette**):

	Masc.				
	croc*	couple	coussin	livre
	cabine	poule	jardin	vers
	sac*	feuille	coffre	boule

	Fem.				
	broche	fourche	chèvre	poule
	bûche	langue	boule	table
	cache	mie	épaule	chaîne

(n) *suffix* **et** (*fem.* **ette**) *preceded by* **el**:
Masc.: bras   cerveau   château   marteau   manteau
Fem.: bande   côte   goutte   tarte

(o) *suffix* **on** (*masc.*):
1.
jambe   dinde   ceinture   jupe   âne
corde   guide   aiguille   aigle   glace
caisse   caraïe   rejet   médaille lard

2. *preceded by* **ill** (*masc.*):
croix   cotte†   nègre   carpe

3. *preceded by* **er** (*masc.*):
aile   vigne   bûche   mouche   chape

(p) *suffix* **eau** (*fem.* **elle**):

	Masc.				
	chèvre	orme	prune	cave
	tombe	barre	écrit	table
	corde	pomme	plat	tonne

	Fem.				
	canne	prune	tour	ombre
	citron	tonne	dent	rue

(q) *suffix* **ot** (*masc.*):
balle   île   bille   maille   Charles

Exercise 8.

Write a list of the substantives formed by adding to the following adjectives the SUFFIXES *indicated, and give the meaning of both the adjective and the compound noun.*

(a) *suffix* **esse** (*fem.*):
rude   sage   molle   hante   petite
hardie   faible   tendre   juste   triste

(b) *suffix* **ise** (*fem.*):
franche   gourmand   marchand   sotte   fainéant

(c) *suffix* **ie** (*fem.*):
félon   perfide   monotone   barbare   jaloux

* These take *h* before *et*.   † The derivative takes only one *t*.

FORMATION OF SUBSTANTIVES.

(d) *suffix* **erie** *(fem.)*:

| coquette | drôle | espiègle | fourbe | infirme |

(e) *suffix* **té** *(fem.)*:

âcre	âpre	varié	immense	trivial
honnête	chrétien	avide *	intime	facile
pauvre	dure	acide	sincère	absurde
ferme	nette	banal	timide	agile
ancienne	sûre	docile	tranquille	crédule

Exercise 9.

Write a list of the substantives formed from the following verbs, giving the meaning of both substantive and verb.

(a) *by taking the infinitive as a substantive:*

souvenir	sourire	souper	savoir	goûter
manger	déjeuner	devoir	avoir	toucher
rire	dîner	pouvoir	boire	dire

(b) *by putting the verb in the present participle:*

pencher	mendier	débiter	assister	commander
protester	combattre	stimuler	commercer	habiter
assiéger	trancher	passer	conquérir	émigrer

(c) *by putting the verb in the past participle:*

Masc.
| pendre | apercevoir | devoir | contenir |
| procéder | réduire | précipiter | élire |

Fem.
enjamber	bouffer	voler	gorger
armer	revoir	ranger	couver
conduire	aller	étendre	entrer
venir	trancher	arriver	échapper
fumer	monter	renommer	pousser

(d) *by taking off the termination* **r** *to form feminine, and* **er** *or* **tre** *to form masculine nouns:*

Masc.
arrêter	oublier	soupirer	plier
galoper	crier	désirer	débuter
siéger †	soucier	souhaiter	débattre
appeler	rebuter	combattre	rabattre

Fem.
| scier | rallonger | râper | vendanger |

(e) *by adding the suffix* **ade** *to the root:*

| griller | rouler | embrasser | parer |
| enfiler | fusiller | glisser | ruer |

* All the following adjectives change the final *e* into *i* before the addition of *'s*.
† *Siège* keeps the *e*.

FORMATION OF SUBSTANTIVES.

(f) *with suffix* **age** (*masc.*):

| laver | ouvrer | raffiner | piller | trier |
| témoigner | tirer | plier | savonner | chômer |

(g) *with suffix* **ance** (*fem.*):

dépendre	confier	délivrer	suffire	médire
tempérer	croire	espérer	obliger	prévoir
venger	ressembler	reconnaître	répugner	remontrer
assister	souffrir	convenir	naître	obéir

(h) *with suffix* **eur** (*masc.*):

pêcher	pécher	relier	tricher	venger
rire	tailler	compter	ramer	diviser
vaincre	flâner	fournir	enchérir	polir
régir	blanchir	acheter	acquérir	nager

(i) *with suffix* **is** (*masc.*):

| hacher | loger | rouler | gâcher | semer |
| tailler | colorer | cliqueter | laver | croquer |

(j) *with suffix* **ment** *or* **ement** (*masc.*):

affaisser	abattre	agencer	amuser	bâiller
abonner	accabler	accomplir	appauvrir	agrandir
applaudir	amollir	établir	éclaircir	rugir

(k) *with suffix* **oir** (*fem.* **oire**):

Masc.:
- cracher, saler, repousser, moucher
- peigner, fermer, réserver, percher
- promener, mirer, abreuver, parler

Fem.: nager, mâcher, manger, balancer

(l) *with suffix* **on** (*masc.*):

| jurer | plonger | | brouiller |
| boucher | grogner | bâiller | couper |

(m) *with suffix* **aison** (*fem.*):

| combiner | conjuguer | terminer |
| comparer | lier | décliner |

(n) *with suffix* **ison** (*fem.*):

| garnir | guérir | trahir |

(o) *with suffix* **ure** (*fem.*):

aller	border	ferrer	parer	blesser
chausser	user	voiler	couper	flétrir
moisir	meurtrir	polir	élargir	bouffir

Exercise 10.

Write all the derivatives of the following words with the meaning of each.

orange	dent	plume	ébène
rang	barbe	table	bouche
limon	médaille	jardin	corde
bûche	balle	poivre	face

CHAPTER II.

OF THE ARTICLE.

45. The **article** is a word generally placed before the substantive, and agreeing with it in gender and in number.

There are two kinds of articles: 1. the **definite** article, placed before substantives the meaning of which is clearly determined, as **le** *cheval* in the following sentence: **le** *cheval de mon père est noir* (= my father's horse is black). The words *de mon père*, which accompany the substantive *cheval*, serve to determine it.

2. The **indefinite** article, placed before substantives the meaning of which is indeterminate, that is to say, vague, not precise, as **un** *cheval* in the following sentence: **un** *cheval s'est abattu* (= a horse has fallen down).

46. The definite article has both genders and numbers:

SINGULAR.

le (for the masc.)   **le** père (= the father)
la (for the fem.)   **la** mère (= the mother).

PLURAL.

les (for both genders) { **les** pères (= the fathers)
                     { **les** mères (= the mothers).

47. There are two remarks to make with reference to the definite article:—

1. When *le* or *la* comes before a substantive beginning with a vowel or *h* mute, the vowel (*e* or *a*) is cut off and replaced by an apostrophe. Thus—

le-amour (= the love)   must be written   *l'*amour
la-envie (= the envy)   ,,   *l'*envie
le-*h*onneur (= the honour)   ,,   *l'*honneur.
de *le*-amour (= of the love)   ,,   de *l'*amour
de *la*-envie (= of the envy)   ,,   de *l'*envie
à *le*-honneur (= to the honour ,,   à *l'*honneur, etc.

This suppression of the vowel is called **elision**.

The word *élision* (= elision) is derived from the Latin acc. *elisionem*, which means "a striking out *or* forcing out."

2. When the masculine definite article, preceded by the prepositions *de* (=of, from), or *à* (=to), is placed before a substantive beginning with a consonant or *h* aspirate, both the article and the preposition are blended into one word. Thus—

 de le becomes **du**: **du** père (=of the father)
        : **du** héros (=of the hero)
 à le   "   **au**: **au** père (=to the father)
        : **au** héros (=to the hero).

Before all plural substantives, *de les* is changed into *des*, and *à les* into *aux*:—

 des pères (=of the fathers), instead of **de les** pères
 des héros (=of the heroes),   " **de les** héros
 des mères (=of the mothers), " **de les** mères
 aux pères (=to the fathers),   " **à les** pères
 aux héros (=to the heroes),   " **à les** héros
 aux mères (=to the mothers),   " **à les** mères.

This blending of the definite article with the two prepositions *de* and *à* is called **contraction**.

48. The **indefinite article** in French is—

 un = a *or* an, before masculine substantives,
 une = a *or* an, before feminine substantives,
 des = some, before substantives of both genders;

as—
 un homme (=a man), **des** hommes (=some men)
 une femme (=a woman), **des** femmes (=some women).

N.B.—1. *Some* or *any*, which is frequently omitted in English, must be expressed in French, and repeated before every substantive: *Il a* **de** *l'argent* (=he has money); *j'ai* **des** *pommes et* **des** *poires* (=I have apples and pears).

2. If an adjective precedes the substantive, or if the sentence is negative, **de** only is used: *J'ai* **de** *bonnes pommes* (=I have good apples), *je n'ai pas* **de** *pommes* (=I have no apples).

3. The possessive case is expressed in two ways in English: My father's horse, and the horse of my father, but in French only one way (the latter) is used: *le cheval* **de** *mon père*.

The same construction must be used for expressions like: a gold watch, *i.e.* a watch made of gold, *une montre* **d'or**.

Exercise 11.

1. Le pain, du pain, de bon pain. 2. Le père a du pain. 3. Les bateaux sont sur l'eau. 4. Les joujoux des enfants. 5. Les fleurs des champs. 6. Les oiseaux ont des ailes. 7. Le marin est sur le rivage. 8. Donnez-moi des noisettes. 9. J'ai de bonne viande. 10. L'arbre a des branches. 11. Les bijoux de la mère. 12. Le maitre de l'enfant. 13. L'encrier de porcelaine.

[1] livre (m.), [2] nous avons, [3] jeu (m.), [4] reine (f.), [5] racine (f.), [6] tronc (m.), [7] feuille (f.), [8] aile (f.), [9] herbe (f.), [10] rivage (m.), [11] discours (m.), [12] général (m.), [13] ville (f.), [14] chat (m.), [15] souris (f.), [16] marin (m.), [17] rame (f.), [18] voiture (f.), [19] princesse (f.), [20] école, (f.), [21] maître d'école (m.), [22] splendeur (f.), [23] roi (m.), [24] verre (m.).

1. The father has a book.[1] 2. We have[2] some horses. 3. The sports[3] of the children. 4. The queen[4] has some jewels. 5. A tree has roots[5]; a trunk[6] has branches and leaves.[7] 6. The wings[8] of the birds. 7. The grass[9] of the fields. 8. From the boats to the shore.[10] 9. The speeches[11] of the generals.[12] 10. From a village (m.) to a town.[13] 11. A cat[14] and a mouse.[15] 12. A collection (f.) of fans. 13. The sailor's[16] oars.[17] 14. To the carriage[18] of a princess.[19] 15. Some bread, some meat, and some nuts. 16. The owls of the castles. 17. To a school[20] and to a schoolmaster.[21] 18. The eyes of the grandfathers. 19. To the splendour[22] of the heavens. 20. The ancestors of the king.[23] 21. A glass[24] inkstand.

QUESTIONS FOR EXAMINATIONS.

1. What is the *article* ?
2. How many kinds of *articles* are there?
3. What is the *definite* article?
4. When is the article *elided* ?
5. Define the word *elision* ?
6. When is the article *contracted* ?
7. What is the *indefinite* article?
8. How do you translate *some* or *any* ?
9. When do you use *des* and when *de* ?
10. How is the possessive case expressed in French ?

CHAPTER III.

OF THE ADJECTIVE.

49. The **adjective** is a word added to the substantive to express the quality of the person or thing—that is to say, to indicate "what is" that person or thing. Thus, when we say, *L'homme est mortel* (= man is mortal), or, *Le cheval est noir* (= the horse is black), *mortel* makes us know that man is *mortal;* and *noir*, that the horse is *black*. *Mortel* and *noir* are adjectives.

The word *adjective* comes from the Latin *adjectivus*, and means "added to."

50. There are three different sorts of adjectives:—
1. *Qualifying.*
2. *Determinative.*
3. *Indefinite.*

(1.) **Qualifying** adjectives express only the quality, as " les *grands* hommes "=the *great* (celebrated) men.

(2.) **Determinative** adjectives show precisely the object designated by the substantive to which they refer, as "*mon* chapeau"=*my* hat; "*ce* cheval"=*this* horse.

(3.) **Indefinite** adjectives mark that the substantive is used in a vague and general manner, as " *Chaque* pays a ses coutumes "=every country has its customs; "*plusieurs* hommes sont venus "=several men have come.

51. Adjectives take the mark of **both genders and numbers.** (*See* §§ 74-77.)

SECTION I.

FORMATION OF THE FEMININE OF ADJECTIVES.

52. GENERAL RULE.—The feminine of adjectives is formed *by adding an* **e mute** *to the masculine:*

méchant (=wicked)   méchant-e
saint (=holy)   saint-e

53. The masculine and feminine of adjectives ending in **e mute** are the same, as—

un chapeau *large* = a broad-brimmed hat
la rivière est *large* = the river is wide
un homme *maigre* = a thin man
une femme *maigre* = a thin woman
un homme *sage* = a wise man
une politique *sage* = a wise policy.

54. To form the feminine of the adjectives ending in **eil, el, en, et,** and **on**—the final *l, n,* or *t must be doubled* before the final **e mute** is added—

MASC.		FEM.
cruel	=cruel	cruelle
pareil	=alike	pareille
ancien	=ancient	ancienne
européen	=European	européenne
bon	=good	bonne
muet	=dumb	muette

55. *A.* Adjectives ending in **ier, er,** and the six adjectives *complet, concret, discret, inquiet, replet, secret,* instead of doubling the final consonant, take a grave accent on the *e* which precedes the *r* or the *t*.

MASC.		FEM.
complet	=complete	complète
concret	=concrete	concrète
discret	=discreet	discrète
inquiet	=uneasy	inquiète
replet	=replete	replète
secret	=secret	secrète
altier	=haughty	altière
étranger	=foreign	étrangère

(See § 24.)

56. *B.*

beau	=beautiful, becomes	**belle**	in the feminine
jumeau	=twin,	,,	jumelle	,,
nouveau	=new,	,,	nouvelle	,,
fou	=foolish, mad,	,,	folle	,,
mou	=soft,	,,	molle	,,
vieux	=old	,,	vieille	,,

Those adjectives were formerly spelt in the masculine *bel, jumel, nouvel, fol, mol, vieil;* hence the feminine in *elle (belle, jumelle,* etc.). The masculine forms *bel, nouvel, fol, mol, vieil* are still used before nouns which begin with a vowel or an *h* mute; thus we say:—

un *bel* homme=a fine man,	instead of un *beau* homme
le *nouvel* an =the new year,	,, le *nouveau* an
le *fol* enfant =the mad, wild boy,	,, le *fou* enfant
le *mol* édredon=the soft eider-down,	,, le *mou* édredon
un *vieil* ami =an old friend,	,, un *vieux* ami.

57. To form the feminine of adjectives ending in **x**, change **x** into **s**, and add *e mute*, as—

MASC.		FEM.
jaloux	=jealous	jalouse
heureux	=happy	heureuse.

Some adjectives even double that **s**, as—

MASC.	FEM.
faux=false	fausse
roux=sandy (of the hair)	rousse.

(*Exception*—
doux=sweet   douce.

Formerly *faux, roux* were spelt *faus, rous,* the feminine form being *fausse, rousse,* just as the feminine of *gras* is *grasse,* and that of *gros* is *grosse.*

58. The masculine adjectives ending in **f** form their feminine by changing the final **f** into **v**, and adding *e* mute:

MASC.		FEM.
bref	=short	brève
craintif	=fearful, timid	craintive
neuf	=new	neuve

59. Blanc (=white), **franc** (=frank), **sec** (=dry), **frais** (=fresh, cool), have for their feminine, respectively, *blanche, franche, sèche, fraîche*.

But some adjectives ending in *c* hard (sounded as *k*), form their feminine by changing **c** into **que**, as—

MASC.		FEM.
caduc	=decayed	caduque
public	=public	publique
turc	=turkish	turque

N.B. The adjective **Grec** (=Greek), keeps the final **c** before the last syllable **que**—*i.e.*=Grecque.

The feminine of **long** is *longue*, and that of **oblong**, *oblongue*. If *e mute* only had been added to *caduc, public, turc*, we should have had the forms *caduce, publice, turce*, in which the *c* would have lost its hard sound. In order to preserve it in the feminine form, it was necessary to replace *c* by its equivalent *qu;* for the same reason *long* (=long) makes *longue*, and not *longe* (which is a substantive feminine—*e.g.*, "longe de veau"=a loin of veal.)

60. Adjectives ending in **eur** generally form their feminine by changing *eur* into *euse; trompeur* (=*deceptive*), *trompeuse*; *menteur* (=lying), *menteuse*.

Except *meilleur* (=better), *majeur* (=major), *mineur* (=minor), and a few others ending in **érieur**, *intérieur* (=interior), *inférieur* (=inferior), which follow the general rule, and form their feminine by adding an *e* mute to the masculine; *meilleure, majeure, mineure*, etc.

Accusateur (=accusing), *débiteur* (=owing), *protecteur* (=protecting), and a few others, make *accusatrice, débitrice, protectrice*, etc.

Pécheur (= sinful), *enchanteur* (= charming), *vengeur* (=avenging), make *pécheresse, enchanteresse, vengeresse*. We have already seen (§ 30), that *eresse* is only the softening of *euresse*.

FORMATION OF THE FEMININE OF ADJECTIVES.

62. The feminine of *bénin* (= good-natured) is bénigne
,, ,, *malin* (= malicious) ,, maligne
,, ,, *favori* (= favourite) ,, favorite
,, ,, *coi* (= quiet, tranquil) ,, coite
,, ,, *dissous* (= dissolved) ,, dissoute
,, ,, *tiers* (= third) ,, tierce
,, ,, *bellot* (= pretty) ,, bellotte
,, ,, *pâlot* (= palish) ,, pâlotte
,, ,, *sot* (= foolish) ,, sotte
,, ,, *vieillot* (= oldish) ,, vieillotte
,, ,, *bas* (= low) ,, basse
,, ,, *gras* (= fat) ,, grasse
,, ,, *las* (= tired) ,, lasse
,, ,, *épais* (= thick) ,, épaisse
,, ,, *exprès* (= express, positive) ,, expresse
,, ,, *gros* (= big, large) ,, grosse
,, ,, *nul* (= nul) ,, nulle
,, ,, *gentil* (= pretty, amiable) ,, gentille
,, ,, *hébreu* (= Hebrew) ,, hébraïque
,, ,, *traître* (= treacherous) ,, traîtresse
(see § 30).

Notice also that a diæresis is placed over the final **e** in the feminine of adjectives when the masculine ends in **gu**, in order to keep the sound of the **u**: *aigu* (= acute), *contigu* (= contiguous), **aiguë, contiguë;** otherwise the **gue** would be pronounced as in *figue* (= fig).

Exercise 12.

1. Ma tante est riche. 2. L'histoire ancienne est intéressante. 3. La nature du tigre est cruelle. 4. La couleur du vin est vermeille. 5. Cette poire est bonne. 6. Vous êtes trop prudente pour ne pas être discrète. 7. Votre fille est jalouse. 8. La température est douce. 9. Sa chevelure est rousse. 10. Craignez la foudre vengeresse. 11. Cette robe est vieille. 12. Cette paysanne est grecque. 13. La viande est trop fraîche. 14. J'ai rencontré votre sœur favorite chez (at the house of) mon oncle. 16. Sa lettre est très-flatteuse.

[1]dame, [2]L'Espagne, [3]dernièrement, [4]bienfaiteur, [5]des pauvres, [6]je n'aime pas, [7]voix (*f.*), [8]main (*f.*), [9]punit, [10]coupable, [11]je la regarde comme, [12]affligé, [13]flotte (*f.*), [14]armée (*f.*), [15]nouvelle (*f.*).

1. My favourite sister. 2. Your letter is too flattering. 3. This lady[1] is discreet and prudent. 4. Spain[2] is rich in fruits. 5. Have you met this countrywoman lately.[3] 6. The queen is the benefactress[4] of the poor.[5] 7. I do not like[6] (a) red (head of) hair. 8. He has a cruel disposition. 9. Her voice[7] is sweet. 10. The avenging hand[8] of (the) justice punished[9] the guilty.[10] 11. Your aunt is very kind; I consider her as[11] the consoler of the afflicted.[12] 12. The Turkish fleet[13] and the Greek army.[14] 13. The news[15] is false. 14. That child's face is ruddy.

SECTION II.

FORMATION OF THE PLURAL OF ADJECTIVES.

62. GENERAL RULE.—The plural of adjectives is formed like that of substantives, *i.e.*, by adding **s** to the singular:

MASC. SING.	MASC. PL.	FEM. PL.
grand=great, tall	grand**s**	grande**s**
saint=holy	saint**s**	sainte**s**

63. When the adjective, in the singular, ends already in **s** or **x** there is no change in the plural masculine.

MASC. SING.	MASC. PL.
gros =big	gros
épais=thick	épais
glorieux=glorious	glorieux

Examples: *des hommes gros* (=big men); *des murs épais* (= thick walls); *des souvenirs glorieux* (=glorious remembrances).

64. EXCEPTIONS.—I. Adjectives ending in **al** change that termination into **aux**, in the masculine plural, as—

MASC. SING.	MASC. PLUR.
égal =equal	égaux
légal=legal	légaux
loyal=faithful	loyaux

The adjectives *fatal* (=fatal), *glacial* (=icy), *final* (=final), *naval* (=naval), and a few others to be learned by use, form their masculine plural by adding **s** to the singular (*fatals, glacials*, etc.).

II. Adjectives ending in **eau** take **x** in the plural masculine.

MASC. SING.	MASC. PL.
beau =beautiful	beaux
nouveau=new	nouveaux

NOTE ON THE POSITION OF ADJECTIVES.—Adjectives are *generally* placed after the substantive to which they relate; past participles used as adjectives *always* follow the substantive. *Beau*=fine, *bon*=good, *grand*=great, tall, *joli*=pretty, *petit*=little, *meilleur*=better, *tout*=all, *mauvais*=bad, *usually* precede the noun.

Exercise 13.

1. Les généraux sont vieux. 2. Les chapeaux sont neufs. 3. Les fils sont bons. 4. Les souliers sont grands. 5. Les hommes sont égaux. 6. Ces accidents sont fatals. 7. Les palais sont beaux. 8. Les sujets sont loyaux. 9. Les livres sont épais.

[1] élève, [2] église, [3] étaient arrivés, [4] école (*f.*) communale, [5] spacieux, [6] salle (*f.*), [7] bail (*m.*), pl. baux, [8] difficulté (*f.*).

1. The hats are old. 2. These pupils[1] are equal. 3. These books are thick. 4. These men are loyal. 5. The churches[2] are old. 6. The royal palaces are beautiful. 7. The fatal days had come.[3] 8. The parish school[4] has very spacious[5] rooms.[6] 9. These leases[7] are new. 10. Legal difficulties.[8] 11. These books are moral.

QUESTIONS FOR EXAMINATION.

1. What is an *adjective*?
2. How many kinds of adjectives are there?
3. Define the adjective *qualifying, determinative, indefinite*.
4. How is the feminine of adjectives generally formed?
5. Give the feminine of *cruel, pareil, bon*, etc.; also of *complet, concret*, etc., explain the peculiar formation of the feminine of *beau, nouveau*, etc.
6. Account for the formation of the feminine of adjectives in *x*.
7. What is the feminine of adjectives ending in *f*?
8. Give the feminine of *blanc, turc, grec, long, trompeur, protecteur, meilleur, vengeur, bénin, favori*.
9. How is the plural of adjectives formed?
10. Give the plural masculine of *beau*.
11. How do you form the plural masculine of adjectives ending in *al*? State some exceptions.
12. Where is the qualifying adjective placed in French?

SECTION III.

OF THE DEGREES OF SIGNIFICATION IN ADJECTIVES.

65. There are three degrees of signification in adjectives: the *positive*, the *comparative*, and the *superlative*. The **positive** is the adjective itself: *mon cheval est* **noir** = my horse is black; (*noir* = black, which expresses simply a quality, is the *positive*).

66. The adjective is in the **comparative** when it expresses the quality with an idea of *comparison*. The **comparative** may either express—

(*a.*) *superiority*, in which case the adverb **plus** (= more), is placed before the adjective, and **que** (= than), after it, as—

mon cheval est **plus** noir **que** *le vôtre* = my horse is blacker than yours.

OF THE DEGREES OF SIGNIFICATION IN ADJECTIVES. 41

or, (*b.*) *inferiority*, in which case the adverb **moins** (=less), is placed before the adjective, and **que** (=than), after it—

mon cheval est **moins** *noir que le vôtre*=my horse is less black than yours (not so black as yours).

or, (*c.*) *equality*, in which case the adverb **aussi** (=as) precedes the adjective, and **que** (=as) follows it—

mon cheval est **aussi** *noir que le vôtre*=my horse is as black as yours.

In a negative sentence **si** is often used instead of **aussi** :—

mon cheval n'est pas si noir que le vôtre=my horse is not so black as yours.

There are, therefore, three comparatives : (*a*) of *superiority;* (*b*) of *inferiority;* (*c*) of *equality*.

67. *Exceptions.*—The three adjectives *petit* (=little or small), *bon* (=good), *mauvais* (=bad), form their comparative irregularly :—

Petit, comparative *moindre;* **bon,** comparative *meilleur;* **mauvais,** comparative *pire*. (*Petit* and *mauvais,* however, have also a regular comparative—*plus petit, plus mauvais*).

Do not mistake them for the adverbs *peu, bien, mal,* which become *moins, mieux, plus mal,* or *pis* in the comparative.

68. The adjective is in the *superlative* when it expresses—

(*A.*) A quality in the highest degree *without any comparison,* as *mon cheval est* **très**-*noir*=my horse is very black, *i.e.,* my horse is *quite* black. This is called the **superlative absolute,** and is expressed by *très, fort, bien, extrêmement,* etc., all meaning *very*.

(*B.*) A quality in the highest degree either—

(*a.*) *superior, but as compared with other persons or objects of the same kind,* as *mon cheval est* **le plus** *noir de tous les chevaux de la ville*=my horse is the blackest of all the horses in the town.

or (*b.*) *inferior*, as *ma sœur est* **la moins** *forte de nous tous* = my sister is the weakest (*lit.* the least strong) of us all.

These are called **superlatives relative**, and are formed by placing the article or a possessive adjective before the comparative.

The superlatives of **bon** are *très-bon* (absolute) = very good, and *le meilleur* (relative) = the best; **petit** makes *très-petit* (absolute) = very small, and *le moindre* (relative) = the least; **mauvais** makes *très-mauvais* (absolute) = very bad, and *le pire* (relative) = the worst.

Remember that in French **plus, moins**, &c., are generally repeated before each adjective; also that *very much* must not in any case be translated by *très-beaucoup*, but by **beaucoup** only.

Exercise 14.

1. La rose est la plus belle des fleurs. 2. Le meilleur livre de ma bibliothèque. 3. Il est moins aimable que son frère. 4. Vous êtes plus âgé que moi. 5. Il n'est pas si avancé que votre ami. 6. Le moindre mal. 7. Il va mieux. 8. Ce qui est pis, c'est que la bataille est perdue. 9. Ce livre est très-intéressant.

[1] Beau, [2] doux, [3] avancé, [4] eux, [5] santé (*f.*), [6] jeune, [7] mort (*f.*), [8] perte (*f.*), bataille (*f.*), [10] ceci, [11] cela.

1. Fine,[1] finer, finest. 2. Gentle,[2] less gentle, the least gentle. 3. Small, smaller, smallest. 4. A good book, a better book. 5. He is as forward[3] as they.[4] 6. His health[5] is better. 7. I am not so young[6] as your sister. 8. The death[7] of the general is less fatal than the loss[8] of the battle.[9] 9. This[10] is well, that[11] is better. 10. My sister is much better.

QUESTIONS FOR EXAMINATION.

1. What are the three degrees of signification in adjectives?
2. How many different comparatives are there? How are they formed?
3. Give the comparatives of *bon, petit, mauvais*.
4. How is the superlative formed?
5. State what are the different kinds of superlative.

SECTION IV.

FORMATION OF ADJECTIVES.

69. French adjectives are formed in the same way as nouns—that is to say, by *composition* and by *derivation*.

Adjectives formed by *composition:*— (*a.*) either two simple adjectives are joined together, such as *aigre*(=sour) and *doux* (=sweet), to form a compound adjective: *aigre-doux*=sourish; or (*b.*) a prefix is placed before simple adjectives (*see* § 38 [*b.*]), for the purpose of giving them a new meaning; as *bien*-heureux (=happy, blessed); *mal*-heureux (=unhappy), *in*-constant (=variable); *sous*-marin (=submarine); *sur*-humain (=superhuman). The prefixes most often used are: **archi, anti, bien, demi, in, mal, sous, sur. ultra.**

70. New adjectives are formed by *derivation* with the help of substantives, adjectives, and verbs *already existing in French:*—

(*a.*) **Substantives** (*pierreux*=stony, from *pierre*=stone);

(*b.*) **Adjectives** (*noirâtre*=blackish, from *noir*=black);

(*c.*) **Verbs** (*trompeur*=deceptive, from *tromper*=to deceive).

71. New adjectives are formed from substantives by adding to the substantives the terminations **eux, ain, in, é, er, u.** Thus: *courage* (=courage), *courageux* (=courageous); *monde* (=world), *mondain* (=worldly): *enfant* (=child), *enfantin* (=childish); *aile* (=wing), *ailé* (=winged); *mensonge* (=lie), *mensonger* (=untrue, lying); *barbe* (=beard), *barbu* (=bearded).

72. New adjectives are formed from existing adjectives with the help of the four terminations—**âtre, et** (and **elet**), **ot** and **aud.** These are called *diminutive suffixes.*

Ex.: *gris* (=grey), *grisâtre* (=greyish); *aigre* (=sour), *aigret* and *aigrelet* (=sourish); *vieux* (=old), *vieillot* (=oldish); *lourd* (=heavy), *lourdaud* (=clumsy).

73. The French language makes new adjectives from verbs, either by taking the **participles** (*present* or *past*) of the verb, or by adding to the stem of the verb the three suffixes **able, ard, if.** Thus *charmer*

(= to charm) gives *charm*ant (charming); *polir* (= to polish), *poli* (= polished); *compar-er* (= to compare), *comparable* (comparable); *pill-er* (= to plunder), *pill*ard (= plundering); *pens-er* (= to think), *pens*if (= pensive).

Exercise 15.

Write a list of compound adjectives by adding to the following one of the **prefixes** *enumerated below; give the feminine of each, and also the meaning of the compound words:—*

(a.) prefix *archi*, ducal, diaconal, épiscopal, fou.
(b.)   ,,   *anti*, social, fébrile, religieux, monarchique.
(c.)   ,,   *bien*, heureux, séant, aimé, faisant.
(d.)   ,,   *demi*, nu, fin, mort, fermé.
(e.)   ,,   *in*, constant, suffisant, différent, variable.
(f.)   ,,   *mal*, formé, sain, habile, heureux, intentionné.
(g.)   ,,   *sous*, marin, jacent, terrain, axillaire.
(h.)   ,,   *ultra*, libéral, mondain, royaliste, zodiacal.

Write in the same manner a list of derived adjectives:—

a.) From substantives with the suffix:
    eux: pierre, rabot, joie, brume, heur.
    ain: monde, Rome, château, proche.
    in: enfant, mal.
    é: aile, bât, sangle, laite.
    er: message, mensonge, passage, potage.
    u: pointe, barbe, branche, bosse.

(b.) From verbs with the suffix:
    able: comparer, séparer, voler, punir.
    ard: piller, baver, vanter, brouiller.
    if: penser, pousser.

(c.) From adjectives with the diminutive suffix:
    âtre: noir, bel, (beau), rouge, doux.
    et(elet): aigre, rond, mou, fou.
    ot: vieil (vieux), pâle.
    aud: noir, sale, rouge, fin.

QUESTIONS FOR EXAMINATION.

1. How do the French form new adjectives from adjectives already existing?
2. What are the parts of the verb which are used in the formation of adjectives?
3. Give a list of adjectives formed with the prefixes *bien*, *sous*; and with the suffixes *âtre*, *if*, *able*, etc.
4. How are adjectives formed from substantives?
5. What suffixes are added to the stem of the verb?

SECTION V.

AGREEMENT OF THE ADJECTIVE WITH THE SUBSTANTIVE.

74. The adjective takes the same gender and number as the substantive which it qualifies. Thus: *Dieu est* **clément** (=God is clement); *ma mère est* **bonne** (=my mother is good); *les hommes sont* **mortels** (=men are mortal).

75. When an adjective qualifies several substantives in the singular, it is put in the plural. Thus: *le riche et le pauvre sont* **égaux** *devant Dieu* (=the rich and the poor are equal in the sight of God).

76. If the substantives are of different genders, the adjective is put in the masculine plural. Thus: *le roi et la reine sont* **prudents** (=the king and the queen are prudent).

SECTION VI.

DETERMINATIVE ADJECTIVES.

77. There are three sorts of determinative adjectives:

Numeral adjectives,
Demonstrative adjectives,
Possessive adjectives.

NUMERAL ADJECTIVES.

78. Numeral adjectives are those which denote *number, order,* or *rank*.

There are two kinds of *numeral* adjectives: the *cardinal*, and the *ordinal*.

79. Numeral adjectives indicating the *number* or *quantity* of objects, as *trois* (=three), *quatre* (=four), *cinq* (=five), are called **cardinal**.

With the exception of *zéro*, which comes from the Arab, all the numeral adjectives are of Latin origin; for the French number as the Romans did, and have admitted their terms of numeration.

Septante, octante, and *nonante,* were formerly used as synonyms of *soixante-dix, quatre-vingts,* and *quatre-vingt-dix,* respectively. During the Middle Ages the *even decades* (60, 80, 120, 140, etc.) stood thus—

   trois-vingts for 60 *six-vingts* for 120
   quatre-vingts for 80 *sept-vingts* for 140;

—that is to say, three times twenty, four times twenty, etc. Traces of this ancient usage remain even in our day (to say nothing of *quatre-vingts* = 80), as in the hospital " des *Quinze-Vingts* " (15×20=300), founded by St. Louis to support 300 crusaders, whose eyes had been put out by the infidels; so also Bossuet and Voltaire have made use of the expression *six-vingts ans* for 120 ans (= 120 years).

Million (= *million*), and *milliard* (= a thousand millions), are derived from *mille* with the suffixes *on* and *ard.*

NOTE.—Care must be taken not to confound *un* (= a or an) indefinite article, with *un* (= one), numeral adjective.

80. Ordinal numeral adjectives point out the *rank* or *place* occupied by the object. They are formed, with the exception of *premier* (= first), and *second* (= second), by adding the termination **-ième** to the cardinal adjectives, as—

  trois = three *trois-ième* = third
  six = six *six-ième* = sixth
  sept = seven *sept-ième* = seventh
  vingt = twenty *vingt-ième* = twentieth, etc.

When the cardinal adjective ends in *e mute,* that *e* is cut off, as—

  quatre = four *quatr-ième* = fourth
  onze = eleven *onz-ième* = eleventh
  douze = twelve *douz-ième* = twelfth.

☞ *Neuf* (= nine), changes *f* into *v* :
  neuf = nine *neu-v-ième* = ninth.

Cinq (= five), adds *u* before the termination *-ième* :
  cinq = five *cinq-u-ième* = fifth.

Formerly *prime, tiers, quint* were used in French as well as *premier, troisième, cinquième.* Traces of these old forms remain in some few locutions, as *de prime-abord* (= at first sight); *de primo saut* (= spontaneously); *le tiers état* (= the third estate, the Commons); *Charles-Quint* (= Charles the Fifth, Emperor of Germany and King of Spain, the great rival of Francis the First, King of France); *Sixte* Quint (= Pope Sixtus Quintus, the fifth).

NUMERAL ADJECTIVES.

N.B.—The cardinal number is used instead of the ordinal in the following cases: (*a.*) after the names of Sovereigns: Henri *quatre* (= Henry IV.); (*b.*) in speaking of the days of the month: le *trois* mars (= the third of March.)

☞ But *Premier* (= first) is an exception to this rule: François *premier* (= Francis I.); le *premier* mars (= the first of March). In compound numbers, *first* is to be translated by *un*: Le pape Jean vingt et *un* (= Pope John XXI.); le vingt et *un* juin (= the twenty-first of June).

81. Nouns of number which indicate a certain quantity (as *une dizaine** = a collection of ten, *une centaine* = a hundred), are connected with the numeral adjectives, as are also the nouns which denote the different parts of a whole (*le quart* = the fourth; *la moitié* = the half), and those which are used for multiplication (*le double* = the double; *le triple* = the treble, threefold; *le centuple* = centuple, a hundredfold).

A Comparative Table of the Numeral Adjectives.

CARDINAL NUMBERS.	ORDINAL NUMBERS.
N.B.—**Un** is the only cardinal which takes the mark of the feminine: **une**.	N.B.—**Premier** and **second** are the only ordinals which are variable: **première, seconde**.
1. un, une	1*st.* premier, première
2. deux	2*nd.* second,—e, or deuxième
3. trois	3*rd.* troisième
4. quatre	4*th.* quatrième
5. cinq	5*th.* cinquième
6. six	6*th.* sixième
7. sept	7*th.* septième
8. huit	8*th.* huitième
9. neuf	9*th.* neuvième
10. dix	10*th.* dixième
11. onze	11*th.* onzième
12. douze	12*th.* douzième
13. treize	13*th.* treizième
14. quatorze	14*th.* quatorzième
15. quinze	15*th.* quinzième
16. seize	16*th.* seizième
17. dix-sept	17*th.* dix-septième
18. dix-huit	18*th.* dix-huitième

* The article *a* which precedes these collectives in English, in sentences like the following, is expressed in French by *la*: *combien* la *douzaine* (= how much a dozen?).

NUMERAL ADJECTIVES.

CARDINAL NUMBERS—*continued.*   ORDINAL NUMBERS—*continued.*

19. dix-neuf	19th. dix-neuvième
20. vingt	20th. vingtième
21. vingt et un	21st. vingt et unième
22. vingt-deux	22nd. vingt-deuxième
23. vingt-trois	23rd. vingt-troisième
24. vingt quatre	24th. vingt-quatrième
25. vingt-cinq	25th. vingt-cinquième
26. vingt-six	26th. vingt-sixième
27. vingt-sept	27th. vingt-septième
28. vingt-huit	28th. vingt-huitième
29. vingt-neuf	29th. vingt-neuvième
30. trente	30th. trentième
31. trente et un, etc.	31st. trente et unième
40. quarante	40th. quarantième
41. quarante et un, etc.	41st. quarante et unième.
50. cinquante	50th. cinquantième
51. cinquante et un, etc.	51st. cinquante et unième
60. soixante	60th. soixantième
61. soixante et un, etc.	61st. soixante et unième, etc.
70. soixante-dix	70th. soixante-dixième
71. soixante et onze	71st. soixante et onzième
72. soixante-douze	72nd. soixante-douzième
73. soixante-treize	73rd. soixante-treizième
74. soixante-quatorze	74th. soixante-quatorzième
75. soixante-quinze	75th. soixante-quinzième
76. soixante-seize	76th. soixante-seizième
77. soixante-dix-sept	77th. soixante-dix-septième
78. soixante-dix-huit	78th. soixante-dix-huitième
79. soixante-dix-neuf	79th. soixante-dix-neuvième
80. quatre-vingts*	80th. quatre-vingtième
81. quatre-vingt-un, etc.	81st. quatre-vingt-unième, etc.
90. quatre-vingt-dix	90th. quatre-vingt-dizième
91. quatre-vingt-onze	91st. quatre-vingt-onzième
92. quatre-vingt-douze	92nd. quatre-vingt-douzième
93. quatre-vingt-treize	93rd. quatre-vingt-treizième
94. quatre-vingt-quatorze	94th. quatre-vingt-quatorzième
95. quatre-vingt-quinze	95th. quatre-vingt-quinzième
96. quatre-vingt-seize	96th. quatre-vingt-seizième
97. quatre-vingt-dix-sept	97th. quatre-vingt-dix-septième
98. quatre-vingt-dix-huit	98th. quatre-vingt-dix huitième
99. quatre-vingt-dix-neuf	99th. quatre-vingt-dix neuvième
100. cent	100th. centième
101. cent un	101st. cent-unième
102. cent deux	102nd. cent-deuxième
103. cent trois	103rd. cent-troisième
200. deux cents*	200th. deux-centième
300. trois cents*, etc.	300th. trois-centième, etc.

* See Syntax, Chapter III. Vingt and cent take s when multiplied by a number and not followed by another, so deux cent un (=201) has no s.

DEMONSTRATIVE ADJECTIVES.

Cardinal Numbers (continued).	Ordinal Numbers (continued).
1000. mille*	1000th. millième
5000. cinq mille	5000th. cinq millième
10,000. dix mille	10,000th. dix millième
1,000,000. million	1,000,000th. millionième

N.B.—The words *one*, *and*, in expressions like *cent-deux* = one *hundred* **and** *two*, are suppressed. *Million* and numbers above are substantives, and must be followed by *de*.

Exercise 16.

1. Soixante-treize; Charles Quint; Louis quatorze. 2. J'ai six mille volumes dans ma bibliothèque. 3. Le premier janvier. 4. L'an mil huit cent soixante. 5. Cette armée se compose de vingt mille hommes. 6. Il a perdu deux cents francs, et sa sœur en a gagné deux cent cinquante. 7. Une douzaine de chemises. 8. Il a mangé le tiers de sa fortune. 9. J'ai dépensé un millier de francs pendant mon voyage. 10. Il est une heure un quart. 11. Il est deux heures moins dix.

¹ Pape Pie, ² furent massacrés à, ³ perdu, ⁴ combien, ⁷ argent, ⁸ gagné, ⁷ coûtent ⁸ Pouvez-vous manger, ⁹ gâteau (m.), ¹⁰ dépensé, ¹¹ un millier (m.), ¹² livre (f.) ¹² dîners.

1. 99; 2,846,578. 2. (The) Pope Pius[1] the Fifth. 3. The Protestants were murdered in[2] Paris in 1572. 4. The twenty-first *of* January. 5. Your brother has lost[8] 375 francs. 6. How much[4] (of) money[5] have you gained[6]? 25,000 francs. 7. These shirts cost[7] 36 shillings a dozen. 8. Four is the third of twelve. 9. Can you eat[8] thirteen cakes[9]? 10. He has spent[10] about a thousand[11] (of) pounds.[12] 11. It was ten minutes to four. 12. We dine[13] at a quarter past seven.

II.—DEMONSTRATIVE ADJECTIVES.

82. Demonstrative adjectives are used to point out the person or thing spoken of:—

  ce *château* = this castle   ce *héros* = this hero.

The demonstrative adjectives are:—

ce	for the masculine singular:	ce *lion*	= this lion
cette	for the feminine singular:	cette *femme*	= this woman
ces {	for the plural of both genders.	ces *garçons* ces *filles*	= these boys = these girls.

* *Mille*, in dates of the Christian era, is spelt *mil*.

cet is placed before masculine substantives beginning with a vowel or *h mute*, instead of **ce**:—

cet h*omme* = this man, not ce h*omme*
cet e*nfant* = this child, ,, ce e*nfant*.

☞ In order to show whether the person or thing we speak of is **near** or **far** from us the adverbs **-ci** (=here) and **-là** (=there) are joined to the substantive by a hyphen, as:—

cet *enfant*-ci *est brun* = *this* child (*i.e.* close to me) is dark
cet *enfant*-là *est blond* = *that* child (*i.e.* far from me) is fair.

-*ci* is the abridgment of *ici*, adverb of place.

Exercise 17.

1. Cette gravure est très-belle. 2. Cet enfant a un vilain caractère. 3. J'aime ce cheval-ci, mais ce cheval-là est trop vieux pour moi. 4. Ces jardins-ci sont la propriété de mon père. 5. Cette dame est très-aimable. 6. Pourquoi battez-vous ces enfants-là? 7. Que dites-vous de ces jeunes personnes? 8. Ces raisins sont excellents. 9. Ce dictionnaire-ci n'est pas complet. 10. Ces souliers-là sont trop étroits.

Soulier (m.), blessent,[2] jeune demoiselle,[3] dites que,[4] déchiré,[5] aimable vieillard,[6] maire (m.),[7] prenez,[8] mûr,[9] vu,[10] large,[11] propriété (*f.*),[12] caractère (m.),[13] battez,[14] habit (m.) *h* m.

1. This child. 2. These generals. 3. I do not like these old horses. 4. This garden belongs to my father. 5. Those shoes hurt[1] that young lady.[2] 6. You say that[3] this engraving is torn.[4] 7. That amiable old man[5] is the mayor[6] of the town. 8. Take[7] these grapes; they are ripe.[8] 9. Have you seen[9] that dictionary? 10. These hats are too wide.[10] 11. This lady has a fine estate.[11] 12. The temper[12] of that child is abominable. 13. Dust[13] this coat.[14]

III.—POSSESSIVE ADJECTIVES.

83. Possessive adjectives are placed before the noun to point out *to whom the object belongs*:—

mon *cheval* = my horse—*i.e.* the horse which belongs to me
ton *chapeau* = thy hat—*i.e.* the hat ,, ,, thee
son *bâton* = his stick—*i.e.* the stick ,, ,, him.

POSSESSIVE ADJECTIVES.

The possessive adjectives are:—

A. When the object belongs to one person only (**mon** *chien* = my dog):—

SINGULAR.

MASC.	FEM.
mon	ma
ton	ta
son	sa

PLURAL.
(FOR BOTH GENDERS.)
mes = my
tes = thy
ses = his, her, its.

B. When the object belongs to several persons at the same time (**notre** *chien* = our dog; **nos** *chevaux* = our horses):—

SINGULAR.
(FOR BOTH GENDERS.)
notre
votre
leur

PLURAL.
(FOR BOTH GENDERS.)
nos = our
vos = your
leurs = their

☞ The masculine forms *mon, ton, son* are placed before feminine nouns beginning with a vowel or *h* mute, instead of the feminine *ma, ta, sa*, in order to prevent the hiatus which the meeting of two vowels would produce; thus we must say:—

mon *âme*	= my soul,	instead of	*ma-âme*
ton *épée*	= thy sword,	,,	*ta-épée*
son *humeur*	= his *or* her temper,	,,	*sa-humeur.*

In Old French *mon* was strictly kept for masculine, and *ma* for feminine nouns. Whenever *ma, ta, sa* came before a word beginning with a vowel, the *a* was elided, as it is now for the feminine definite article *la*, and people then said *m'âme, t'épée, s'amie*, just as we now say *l'âme, l'épée, l'amie*. Towards the fourteenth century the use of the masculine forms *mon, ton, son* superseded this elision, which has, however, survived in the term of endearment *m'amie, ma amie* (= my love), which later on became, by corruption, *ma mie*; hence came the expressions *ta mie, sa mie* = thy, his lady-love, etc.

NOTE that in French, the possessive adjective agrees with the thing possessed, not with the possessor; also, that it must be repeated before each noun: **son** *père*, **son** *frère et* **sa** *sœur* (= his, or her father, brother and sister).

Exercise 18.

1. Où est votre plume, et où sont mes livres? 2. Notre maison est grande. 3. Je parlerai de vous à mon père. 4. Vos craintes

sont ridicules. 5. Ma montre avance. 6. Ton habit est taché. 7. Je vous montrerai ses gravures. 8. Ma mère est à la campagne. 9. Son cheval est boiteux. 10. J'aime beaucoup nos cousins; ils sont très-aimables.

¹ Amitié (*f.*) pour, ² sincère, ³ loi (*f.*), ⁴ suprême, ⁵ livre (*m.*), ⁶ mère (*f.*), ⁷ à la campagne (*f.*), ⁸ vous montrerai-je, ⁹ sur la table, ¹⁰ gant (*m.*), ¹¹ canne (*f.*), ¹² quand, ¹³ maison (*f.*), ¹⁴ brûlé, ¹⁵ parlerai, ¹⁶ rapporté, ¹⁷ chaque pays, ¹⁸ coutume (*f.*).

1. Your engravings are good. 2. My friendship for[1] you is sincere.[2] 3. His laws[3] are supreme.[4] 4. These books[5] belong to my mother.[6] 5. Our cousins (*m.*) are in the country.[7] 6. I have lost my watch. 7. Shall I show you[8] his horses? 8. My pens are on the table.[9] 9. Give me my coat, my gloves,[10] and my walking-stick.[11] 10. When[12] have you seen your cousin? 11. His house[13] is burnt.[14] 12. I shall speak[15] to your officer. 13. Her friend has brought back[16] his book. 14. Each country[17] has its own laws and customs.[18]

SECTION VII.

INDEFINITE ADJECTIVES.

84. Indefinite adjectives denote that the noun is used in a vague and general manner, as: **aucune lettre n'est arrivée** (= no letter has arrived); **quelque malheur nous menace** (= some misfortune threatens us).

These adjectives are twelve in number:

1. **aucun** (*fem.* **aucune**) = any, no, none; 2. **autre** = other, another; 3. **certain** (*fem.* **certaine**) = some, some one, a certain; 4. **chaque** = each; 5. **maint** (*fem.* **mainte**) = many; 6. **même** = same; 7. **nul** (*fem.* **nulle**) = no, none; 8. **plusieurs** = several; 9. **quelconque*** = whatever, whatsoever; 10. **quelque** = some; 11. **tel** (*fem.* **telle**) = such; 12. **tout** (*plur. masc.* **tous**, *fem. sing.* **toute**) = all, every.

N.B.—**Certain** is an indefinite adjective when it means *un, quelque* = one, some, as: *certain homme* (= a man, some man). But when it means *sûr* (= sure), it is a qualificative adjective, as: *j'en suis certain* (= I am sure of it).

* *quelconque* always follows the noun.

Aucun and **nul** are accompanied by *ne*: *Je ne connais aucun de ses frères* (=I don't know any of his brothers).

Exercise 19.

1. Je n'ai aucune envie de punir un autre élève. 2. Certain renard gascon; d'autres disent normand. 3. Chaque jour amène avec lui son travail. 4. Maint écrivassier se croit poète. 5. J'ai rencontré plusieurs soldats dans la rue. 6. Il n'a nulle pitié. 7. Tel maître, telle maison. 8. Tous les matins je lis un livre quelconque. 9. Tel qui rit vendredi, dimanche pleurera. 10. Plusieurs de vos amis sont ici.

[1] élève (m.), [2] ne sortira vendredi, [3] semaine (f.), [4] écrivassier (m.), [5] voiture (f.), [6] ferait plus de, [7] vu, [8] personne (f.), [9] sentiment (m.), [10] vais, [11] rebelle (m.), [12] renard (m.).

1. Have you (of) such pupils?[1] 2. None of these soldiers shall go out on Friday.[2] 3. Every week[3] my father brings with him many a scribbler.[4] 4. Like master, like man. 5. Your friend has several horses. 6. Are you of another opinion (f.)? 7. I have seen several fine carriages.[5] 8. Another poet would do more[6] work every day. 9. Have you seen[7] the same persons?[8] 10. Every child likes (the) cakes. 11. He has no sense[9] of envy. 12. I am going[10] to punish several rebels.[11] 13. I have met no fox[12] in the street.

QUESTIONS FOR EXAMINATIONS.

1. Give a list of the *determinative adjectives*.
2. What are the *numeral adjectives?*
3. Give a list of the cardinal numbers.
4. What is the difference between *un* indefinite article, and *un* numeral?
5. How do you form the French *ordinal* numbers?
6. What are the numerals which serve to *multiply?*
7. Write down the *demonstrative adjectives*.
8. Remark on the demonstrative adjective *ce*.
9. Give a list of the *possessive adjectives*.
10. State the peculiarities which affect the words *mon, ton, son*.
11. What are the *indefinite adjectives?*
12. Remark on the adjective *certain*.

CHAPTER IV.

OF THE PRONOUN.

85. The **pronoun** is a word which takes the place of the noun. In the sentence **Henri** *est espiègle, mais il deviendra raisonnable* (=Henry is frolicsome, but he will grow steady), the word **il**, being put there instead of **Henri**, is a pronoun.

Pronoun is the Latin *pronomen* (*pro*=instead of, *nomen*=noun).

86. The pronoun takes the gender and number of the noun instead of which it is used. *Les hirondelles partent;* **elles** *vont dans les pays chauds* (=the swallows are on the wing; they go to warm countries). **Elles** is feminine plural, because **hirondelles** is feminine plural. *Votre maison est grande;* **la mienne** *est plus petite* (=your house is large; mine is smaller). **La mienne** is feminine singular to agree with **maison.**

87. There are five kinds of pronouns :—

    1. *The* **personal.**
    2. *The* **demonstrative.**
    3. *The* **possessive.**
    4. *The* **relative.**
    5. *The* **indefinite.**

SECTION I.

PERSONAL PRONOUNS.

88. Personal pronouns are those which point out the persons, and indicate the part they play in the speech.

In the sentence **je** *devine que* **tu** *viens de chez* **lui** (=I guess you come from his house), we distinguish at once three different persons, *je, tu, lui*, as being the actors in this little drama. These actors have different parts, which are indicated here by three distinct words: the *first* part (**je**=I) is that of the actor *who speaks;* the *second* (**tu**=thou), that of the actor *spoken to;* and the *third* (**lui**=him), that of the actor *spoken of*.

These three *characters*, or rather *parts*, are called **personnes**=persons (from the Latin [*dramatis*] *persona*), and represented by the **personal pronouns**, which point out beings *by the part they act in* that short piece called a *sentence*.

89. The personal pronouns are divided into *conjunctive, disjunctive,* and *reflective*.

The **conjunctive personal pronouns**, or pronouns immediately connected with the verb, are :—

PERSONAL PRONOUNS. 55

Singular.

Je = I ; **tu** = thou ; **il, elle** = he, she, it.

Nom.	**Je**=I.	**tu**=thou.	**il, elle**=he, she, it.
Gen.			**en**=of him, her, it.
Dat.	**me**=to me.	**te**=to thee.	**lui, y** (of things)=to it, to them.
Acc.	**me**=me.	**te**=thee.	**le, la**=him, her, it.

Plural.

Nous = we ; **vous** = you ; **ils, elles** = they.

Nom.	**Nous**=we.	**vous**=you.	**ils, elles**=they.
Gen.			**en**=of them.
Dat.	**nous**=to us	**vous**=to you.	**leur**=to them.
Acc.	**nous**=us.	**vous**=you.	**les**=them.

90. All conjunctive pronouns, used as subject, are placed *before* the verb, except when the sentence is interrogative: **il** *vient* (=he comes); *vient*-**il?** (=does he come?).

91. When used as object, all the conjunctive pronouns are placed immediately *before* the verb, unless the verb is in the imperative and used affirmatively: *Je* **le** *connais* (=I know him); *ne* **le** *fais pas* (=do not do it); *fais*-**le** (=do it).

92. When a verb governs two conjunctive pronouns, both are placed before the verb, the dative being put first, and the accusative next: *Je* **te le** *donne* (=I give it to you); **te le** *donne-t-il?* (=does he give it to you?).

However, **lui, leur** are to be put after *le, la, les* : *Je* **le lui** *donne* (=I give it to him).

N.B.—1. All these pronouns are used for both genders, with the exception of:—

il, le, ils, eux, which are reserved for the masculine ; and *elle, la, elles*, which are reserved for the feminine.

2. Vous is used for politeness' sake instead of **tu**, and the adjective remains in the singular: *Paul,* **vous** *êtes triste* (=Paul, you are sad).

3. The pronouns **le, la, les** must not be mistaken for the definite article *le, la, les*, the former always accompany a verb, the latter a substantive: *Voici le livre que je vous ai promis, prenez-*lo (=here is *the* book I promised you; take *it*).

4. **Leur** is a personal pronoun when it means *à eux, à elles* (=to them), and accompanies a verb. In that case it never takes the mark of the plural, as: *Je* **leur** *ai donné un livre* (=I have given them a book). It is a possessive adjective when it signifies *d'eux, d'elles* (=of them), and is placed before a substantive. It must then take the mark of the plural, as: *Ces enfants ont perdu* **leurs** *livres* (=these children have lost their books). **Leur**, possessive adjective, never takes the mark of the feminine: **Leur** *fille* (=their daughter), **leurs** *filles* (=their daughters).

5. **En** is a pronoun when it is used instead of *de lui* (=of him); *d'elle* (=of her); *d'eux, d'elles* (=of them): *J'aime cet enfant et j'*en *suis aimé* (=I love this child, and I am loved by him). Otherwise it is either an adverb, *j'*en *viens* (=I come from thence), or a preposition, *je suis* en *France* (=I am in France).

6. **Y** is a pronoun when it means *à cette chose* (=to this thing), *à ces choses* (=to these things), *à cela* (=to that): *L'affaire est importante, j'*y *donnerai tous mes soins* (=the affair is important; I shall bestow all my care upon it). Otherwise it is an adverb: *Tu* **y** *cours* (=thou runnest there.)

23. The **disjunctive personal pronouns**, or pronouns used apart from the verb, are:—

Singular.

Moi = I; **toi** = thou; **lui, elle** = he, she.

Nom. **Moi**=I.	toi=thou.	lui, elle=he, she.
Gen. de moi.	de toi.	de lui, d'elle.
Dat. à moi.	à toi.	à lui, à elle.
Acc. moi.	toi.	lui, elle.

Plural.

Nous = we; **vous** = you; **eux, elles** = they.

Nom. **Nous**=we.	vous=you.	eux, elles=they.
Gen. de nous.	de vous.	d'eux, d'elles.
Dat. à nous.	à vous.	à eux, à elles.
Acc. nous.	vous.	eux, elles.

94. The disjunctive pronouns are always the same, whether used as subject or as object of a verb. They are used as subject only when it is necessary to establish a distinction between two persons or things, or for emphasis: **Lui** *m'a donné de l'argent,* **eux** *m'ont donné à manger* (=*he* gave me money, *they* gave me to eat); **moi,** *je vous le dis* (=*I* tell you so).

95. These pronouns are used in French after the verb **être,** after a preposition or conjunction, and also in answer to questions: *C'est* **moi** (=it is I); *c'était* **lui** (=it was he); *ce livre est à* **moi** (=this book is mine, belongs to me); *il parle contre* **toi** (=he speaks against you); *il est plus grand que* **moi** (=he is taller than I); *qui vient là?* **Moi** (=who comes there? *I*).

In order to give still greater force to the expression, the adjective *même* is joined by a hyphen to these pronouns, as :—

Singular.
moi-même = myself
toi-même = thyself
lui-même = himself
elle-même = herself

Plural.
nous-mêmes = ourselves
vous-mêmes = yourselves
eux-mêmes } themselves.
elles-mêmes }

soi-même = oneself, himself, herself, etc.

96. The **reflective personal pronoun** (conjunctive, *se*; disjunctive, *soi*) is used only for the third person, and for both genders and both numbers. The first and second persons are formed with the pronouns given above.

N.B.—In modern French, *soi* is only used when the subject of the verb is *on, tout le monde, chacun,* etc., or after an impersonal verb.

Exercise 20.

1. Il travaille avec soin. 2. C'est moi qui irai le voir. 3. Je crois que c'est à toi qu'il parle. 4. Adressez-vous à lui. 5. Elle lui parlera de votre affaire. 6. Je le vois d'ici. 7. Elle est si bonne que je veux la récompenser. 8. Ces fleurs me plaisent

beaucoup. 9. Croyez-mci, consentez-y. 10. J'ai lu votre livre, et j'en parlerai dans la revue.

[1] marche, [2] vois, [3] voyons, [4] pensez, [5] jouent, [6] dansent, [7] donnerai, [8] qui plaisent, [9] croyez, [10] récompenser, [11] consens, [12] parle, [13] venons, [14] en, [15] montrerai, [16] c'était, [17] parlez, [18] souvenez-vous de, [19] loin, [20] allez, [21] allons, [22] font tout, [23] on ne doit jamais parler, [24] flattent, [25] sais.

Conjunctive pronouns : 1. I walk;[1] thou seest[2] these flowers; he has read your book; your sisters are very good. 2. She works with much (of) care; we see,[3] you think,[4] they (*masc.*) play,[5] they (*fem.*) dance.[6] 3. I shall give[7] him these flowers which please[8] (to) him. 4. Go *and* (to) see him. 5. You believe[9] that I wish to recompense[10] her. 6. We have read the review of your book. 7. I consent[11] to it; I speak[12] of him; he has some of them; we come[13] from that place.[14] 8. I will show[15] it to you; don't show it to her.

Disjunctive pronouns. 1. It is he; it was[16] I; speak[17] to them (*masc.*); remember[18] them (*fem.*) 2. Far[19] from thee; go[20] with them; let us go[21] there ourselves; they do everything[22] themselves (*fem.*). 3. One should never speak[23] of one's self. 4. They flatter[24] themselves. 5. I who was there (*I*) know[25] it better than he.

SECTION II.

DEMONSTRATIVE PRONOUNS.

97. Demonstrative pronouns are used to point out the person or thing spoken of: *Mon cheval est plus grand que* **celui-ci** (=my horse is higher than this one).

98. The demonstrative pronouns are the following:

SINGULAR.   PLURAL.
Ce, celui, celle (=this, that, it).   **ceux, celles** (=these, those.)

99. We have seen (§ 82) that the adverb **ci** is added to the demonstrative adjective to point out an object *close to* us, and the adverb **là** to indicate another object *far from* us. Those two adverbs are also, and for the same purpose, joined to the demonstrative pronouns **ce** (but without a hyphen): **ceci** (=this); **cela** (=that); **celui** (with a hyphen) =*celui*-**ci**, *celle*-**ci**, *celui*-**là**, *celle* **là**; *ceux*-**ci**, *ceux*-**là**, etc.

100. Ce is a pronoun—

1. When it accompanies a verb: **Ce** *doit être son frère* (=it must be his brother); *est-***ce** *lui!* (=is it he?).

2. When it is placed before the pronouns *qui* (=who), *que* (=whom), *quoi* (=what), *dont* (=whose): *J'irai voir* **ce** *qui est arrivé* (=I will go and see what has happened); *je ferai* **ce** *que vous me demandez* (=I will do what you ask me).

But placed before a noun **ce** is an adjective: **Ce** *livre* (=this book); **ce** *chapeau* (=that hat).

Celui qui = he who, the one who; *celui que* = he whom, the one whom.

Exercise 21.

1. Mon livre et celui de mon frère. 2. Ma chaise et celle de ma cousine. 3. Ses crayons et ceux de Guillaume. 4. Vos offres et celles de votre ami. 5. Préférez-vous ce couteau-ci ou celui-là? 6. Gardez ces bottes-là; je choisis celles-ci. 7. Ceci mérite attention. 8. Cela ne vaut rien. 9. Quel est ce monsieur? Ce doit être son colonel. 10. Est-ce bien lui?

[1] préfère, [2] qui faites, [3] commode, [4] mais, [5] ne vaut rien, [6] paire (f.), [7] choisis, [8] parce que ce doit être, [9] ouvrage (m.), [10] récompense (f.).

1. I prefer[1] these boots to those. 2. Is it you who make[2] these offers? 3. Give me this or that. 4. Your chairs are not so comfortable[3] as those of your friend. 5. These knives are excellent, but[4] this one is good for nothing.[5] 6. Of several pairs[6] of boots, this one or that one? these or those? 7. I choose[7] this book, because it must be[8] an excellent work.[9] 8. Your brother's attention deserves a reward.[10] 9. I do not like that. 10. The one that I show you.

SECTION III.

POSSESSIVE PRONOUNS.

101. Possessive pronouns take the place of the noun, and at the same time denote possession: *Mon chapeau est meilleur que le* **vôtre** (=my hat is better than yours); *ton cheval est plus noir que* **le sien** (=thy horse is blacker than his). **Le vôtre, le sien** are possessive pronouns—*pronouns*, because they are used to avoid the repetition of the noun which represents the object, and *possessive*, because they indicate, at the same time, to whom the object belongs.

When one object possessed by **only one** person is spoken of (as *mon chapeau est meilleur que* **le tien**), the possessive pronouns are:

		SINGULAR.	PLURAL.	
1st Person	Masc.	le mien	les miens	} mine
	Fem.	la mienne	les miennes	
2nd Person	Masc.	le tien	les tiens	} thine
	Fem.	la tienne	les tiennes	
3rd Person	Masc.	le sien	les siens	his, its
	Fem.	la sienne	les siennes	hers, its.

Mien, tien, sien are softened forms of *mon, ton, son*. In the Middle-Ages the pronouns *mien, tien, sien* could be used as adjectives, that is to say, placed between the article and the name of the possessed object; people said indiscriminately either *mon frère* (=my brother), *ton vassal* (=thy vassal), or *le* **mien** *frère, le* **tien** *vassal,* etc. This rule soon disappeared, but some remains of it are still found in the modern expressions: *un* **mien** *cousin* (=a cousin of mine), *le* **tien** *propre* (=thine own), *une* **sienne** *tante* (=an aunt of his), etc.

When an object possessed by **several** persons at the same time is spoken of (as *leur cheval est moins beau que le* **nôtre** =their horse is not so fine as ours), the possessive pronouns are:

		SINGULAR.		PLURAL.	
1st Person	Masc.	le nôtre	... ...	} les nôtres	=ours
	Fem.	la nôtre	... ...		
2nd Person	Masc.	le vôtre	... ...	} les vôtres	=yours
	Fem.	la vôtre	... ...		
3rd Person	Masc.	le leur	... ...	} les leurs	=theirs.
	Fem.	la leur	... ...		

Exercise 22.

1. Votre fusil est plus lourd que le mien. 2. J'aime votre maison, mais je n'aime pas la leur. 3. Est-il à ma place ou à la sienne? 4. Voici mes patins; montrez-moi les vôtres. 5. Donnez-moi un morceau de ton gâteau, le mien n'est pas encore arrivé.

6. Quels jolis enfants! Sont-ce les vôtres? 7. Le domestique m'a apporté mes lettres et les leurs. 8. Il a parlé à mon colonel et au sien. 9. Je vois souvent vos amis et les siens. 10. Je trouve mon pays meilleur que le vôtre.

¹ domestique (m.), ² n'est pas encore arrivé, ³ canif (m.), ⁴ pays (m.), ⁵ Angleterre (f.), ⁶ confiance (f.), ⁷ joli, ⁸ étang (m.).

1. Your servant[1] is here, but mine has not arrived yet.[2] 2. My colonel's gun is heavier than yours. 3. Is that your pen-knife[3]? No; it is his. 4. (The) France is my country[4]; (the) England[5] is yours. 5. My friend deserves your confidence[6] and theirs. 6. His skates and thine. 7. He speaks to your pretty[7] children and to mine. 8. Your gloves and hers. 9. This pond[8] is smaller than ours. 10. I have read your book and his.

SECTION IV.

RELATIVE PRONOUNS.

102. Relative pronouns are those which connect the noun or pronoun they stand for with the part of the sentence which follows them: *Le chêne* **qui** *ombrage notre cour est très-vieux* (=the oak which overshades our yard is very old); *le livre* **que** *vous m'avez prêté est intéressant* (=the book [which] you have lent me is interesting).

103. The word represented by the relative pronoun is called the **antecedent.** In the above examples *chêne* and *livre* are the antecedents of *qui* and of *que*.

The French word *antécédent* comes from the Latin *antecedentem* (= preceding), because it is placed before the relative pronoun.

104. The relative pronouns are—

1. **qui** = who, which (applied to persons and things);
   de qui = whose, of or from whom ⎫ applied to
   à qui = to whom ⎭ persons only;
2. **que**[*] = whom, which, what (persons and things);
3. **quoi** = what (things only) in exclamation and after prepositions;
4. **dont** = whose, of or from whom *or* which (persons and things);
5. **lequel** = who, which, what (persons and things).

[*] *Que* is spelt *qu'* before a vowel; *qui* is never shortened.

RELATIVE PRONOUNS.

The relative pronouns *qui, que, quoi, dont* are **invariable**, but *lequel* is **variable**:—

SINGULAR.

MASC.	FEM.	
lequel	*laquelle*	= who, which, what
duquel	*de laquelle*	= of *or* from whom, which, what
auquel	*à laquelle*	= to whom, which, what.

PLURAL.

lesquels	*lesquelles*	= who, which, what
desquels	*desquelles*	= of whom, which, what
auxquels	*auxquelles*	= to whom, which, what.

105. REMARK.—**Que**, pronoun, must not be mistaken for *que* adverb or *que* conjunction. *Que* is a pronoun when *lequel, laquelle, lesquels, lesquelles* can be used in its place, as: *la rose* **que** *j'ai cueillie ce matin est fanée* (= the rose I gathered this morning is faded) = **laquelle** *j'ai cueillie.*—*Que* is an adverb when it means *how many*, as: **que** *de belles roses j'ai cueillies!* (= how many beautiful roses I have plucked!) And, lastly, *que* is a conjunction when it means neither *lequel* nor *combien*, as: *J'espère* **que** *vous réussirez dans votre entreprise* (= I hope [that] you will succeed in your undertaking).

NOTE that the relative pronouns are often understood in English, but must always be expressed in French.

106. The relative pronouns are also used in interrogative sentences, in which case they are called **interrogative pronouns: Qui** *êtes-vous?* (= who are you?) **que** *demandez-vous?* (= what do you ask for?) *à* **quoi** *cela est-il bon?* (= what is the use of that?) *voici deux accusés*, **lequel** *est coupable?* (= here are two accused persons, which is the guilty one?).

REMARK.—Interrogative pronouns *have no antecedent.*

Dont is never used as an interrogative pronoun: **De qui** (not *dont*) *parlez-vous?* (= whom are you speaking of?).

107. Besides the interrogative pronouns proper, there is the **interrogative adjective** *quel*, which precedes a noun or pronoun: **Quel** *âge arez-vous?* (=what is your age, *or* how old are you?) **quelle** *heure est-il?* (= what o'clock is it?) *j'ai des nouvelles à vous apprendre.*—**Quelles** *sont-elles?* (= I have some news to tell you.—What is it?).

103. Quel is variable:—

masc. sing.	*quel*	masc. plur.	*quels*
fem. sing.	*quelle*	fem. plur.	*quelles.*

Exercise 23.

1. La personne qui vous connaît. 2. Le marchand que vous avez vu. 3. La bataille dont je parle. 4. En quoi vous ai-je trompé? 5. L'affaire à laquelle il a donné ses soins. 6. Quel âge a cet enfant? 7. De qui vous a-t-il parlé? 8. À quoi vous occupez-vous? 9. La rose que j'ai cueillie. 10. La loi qui est votée.

[1] marchand, [2] parlais hier, [3] failli, [4] s'applique-t-il, [5] cassé, [6] vaisseau (m.), [7] acheté part demain, [8] poème (m.), [9] tout le monde, [10] ministre (m.), [11] bonté, [12] doit, [13] tigre (m.), [14] habitent, [15] dessin, [16] consacre, [17] traité (m.), [18] lisez, [19] plein, [20] idée (f.)

1. Have you seen the merchant[1] of whom I spoke yesterday[2]? 2. In what have you failed[3]? 3. To what does he apply himself[4]? 4. Which of my fans has he broken[5]? 5. The ship[6] (which) he has bought sails to-morrow[7]. 6. The poem[8] of which everybody[9] speaks is by Victor Hugo. 7. The minister[10] to whose kindness[11] he owes[12] his place (f.). 8. The lions (m.) and tigers[13] which inhabit[14] the desert (m.). 9. (The) drawing[15] is an art (m.) to which I devote[16] myself. 10. The treatise[17] you are reading[18] is full[19] of original ideas.[20]

SECTION V.

INDEFINITE PRONOUNS.

109. Indefinite pronouns denote persons or things in a general, vague, and indeterminate manner: *Quelqu'un est venu* (= somebody came); *on nous l'a dit* (= some one told us so); *ne faites pas de mal à autrui* (= do no harm to others).

INDEFINITE PRONOUNS.

The indefinite pronouns are—

autrui	= other people, others	quelqu'un	= somebody		
chacun	= every one,	rien	= something		
on (*or* l'on)	= people, one, they	rien ne	= nothing		
personne	= somebody	l'un l'autre	= one another		
personne ne	= nobody	l'un et l'autre	= both		
quiconque	= whoever	l'un ou l'autre	= either		
		ni l'un ni l'autre	= neither		

110. Personne (from Latin *persona*) is a **pronoun** (and of the *masculine* gender) when it is not accompanied by an article or adjective, as: **Personne** *n'est venu* (= no one came); **personne** *a-t-il jamais parlé comme vous?* (= has any one ever spoken like you?). In all other cases **personne** is a *feminine* **substantive**: *Cette* **personne** *est très-obligeante* (= this person [either *man* or *woman*] is very obliging).

2. **Rien** is a **pronoun** when not accompanied by an article or an adjective: *Je n'ai* **rien** *vu* (= I have not seen anything). Otherwise, it is a *masculine* **noun**: *Un songe, un* **rien**, *tout lui fait peur* (= a dream, a trifle, everything frightens him). (LA FONTAINE, *Fables*, viii. 11.)

121. Some **indefinite adjectives** may be used by themselves, *i.e.* without being placed before a substantive, and are therefore considered as **indefinite pronouns**. Such are **nul, plusieurs, tout**: **Nul** *n'est irréprochable* (= no one is blameless); **plusieurs** *ont pleuré* (= several shed tears); **tout** *est perdu* (= all [everything] is lost), etc.

The following adjectives may be used as pronouns: *autre, certains, nul, plusieurs, tel, tout.*

REMARK.—**Certain** is an **indefinite pronoun** *in the plural* when it means *quelques-uns* (= some persons), as: *Certains l'affirment* (= some persons affirm this).

In answers, **rien** and **personne** do not require the *ne*: *Qu'avez-vous vu?* **rien** (= what have you seen? nothing).

Exercise 24.

1. Quelqu'un est venu vous voir. 2. Ne dites jamais du mal d'autrui. 3. Chacun pense que la guerre sera déclarée. 4. Quiconque ouvrira cette porte, sera puni. 5. On dit qu'un incendie a détruit le palais du roi. 6. Ils se sont mordus l'un l'autre. 7. Je n'ai rien entendu. 8. Voici deux bons fouets, prenez l'un ou l'autre. 9. J'aime l'un et l'autre. 10. Chacun a fait son devoir.

[1] bonheur (*m.*), [2] rend, [3] heureux, [4] toujours gai, [5] société (*f.*), [6] se calomnient, [7] porte (*f.*), [8] fermé, [9] plaît, [10] coûté plusieurs, [11] mordu, [12] pauvre, [13] sévèrement, [14] erreur (*f.*), [15] il y avait, [16] qu'y avait-il.

1. The happiness[1] of others makes[2] me happy.[3] 2. One is always merry[4] in your society.[5] 3. They calumniate[6] one another. 4. Either of these doors[7] shall be closed.[8] 5. Neither of these whips pleases[9] me. 6. Each one of these palaces has cost several[10] millions. 7. Whoever has bitten[11] that poor[12] child shall be severely[13] punished. 8. I have seen nothing of the fire. 9. Each one has his opinion. 10. No one is exempt from error.[14] 11. There was[15] nobody; what was there?[16] Nothing; there was nothing.

QUESTIONS FOR EXAMINATION.

1. Define a *pronoun*.
2. What is the rule for the agreement of pronouns?
3. How many kinds of pronouns are there?
4. Define a *personal pronoun*.
5. Give a list of the personal pronouns, and say where you place the conjunctive; and where the disjunctive?
6. When is *vous* used instead of *tu*?
7. State the difference between, *le, la, les*, articles, and *le, la, les*, pronouns;—between *leur*, adjective, and *leur*, pronoun;—between *en*, pronoun, and *en*, adverb;—between *y*, pronoun, and *y*, adverb.
8. Mention a *compound* pronoun.
9. Give a table of the demonstrative pronouns.
10. When is *ce* a pronoun?—When is it an adjective?
11. Give a list of the *possessive* pronouns.
12. What is meant by a *relative* pronoun?
13. What is an *antecedent*?
14. Remark on the word *que*.
15. What are the *interrogative* pronouns?—What is *quel*?
16. What is the difference between *qui* and *que*, 1° as relative, 2° as interrogative pronouns?
17. Write a table of the *indefinite* pronouns.
18. Remark on *personne*;—on *rien*.
19. Name the indefinite adjectives used as pronouns.

CHAPTER V.

OF THE VERB.

112. The **verb** is a word which expresses the idea of an *action* or of a *state* which can be ascribed to a person or to a thing: *Le cheval est docile* (=the horse is docile); *le loup mange l'agneau* (=the wolf eats the lamb).

113. When we say, *le loup mange l'agneau*, the word *mange* (=eats), which indicates the action performed by the wolf, is called the **verb**; the word *loup* (=wolf), indicating the animal which performs the action, is called the **subject**; the word *agneau* (=lamb), pointing out the animal eaten by the wolf, is called the **complement** (or **object**).

114. The word *agneau* (=lamb) is called the **complement** (or **object**) because it *completes* the idea which the verb *mange* (=eats) commences, by indicating what animal the wolf is eating. There are two kinds of complements: the **direct** and the **indirect**.

115. The **direct** *complement* is that which completes the meaning of the verb in a *direct* manner, that is to say, without the aid of any other word: *il aime son père* (=he loves his father). *Son père* is a direct complement.

116. The **indirect** *complement* is that which completes *indirectly* the meaning of the verb, that is to say, with the aid of certain words, such as *à, de*, etc. (=to, of, etc.), which are called **prepositions**: *il obéit à son père, il dépend de son père* (=he obeys his father, he depends on his father), *à son père, de son père* are indirect complements.

There is only one verb properly so called, namely the verb *être*, which expresses existence, and is designated as *substantive verb*; all the other verbs are called *adjective verbs*, because, in addition to the idea of existence, they also describe a *quality*, a manner of being of the subject: thus, *je dors* (=I sleep) is the same as *je suis* (=*I am*, denoting existence) **dormant** (=*sleeping*, denoting the quality, the manner of being).

117. In studying verbs, we must examine *the stem, the termination, the number, the person, the mood, the tense.*

1. Stem.—2. Termination.

118. The verb is always formed of two distinct parts: 1st. A part which does not change, called the **stem** (or **root**) of the verb. 2nd. A changeable and variable part, which is called the **termination**. Thus in *je march*e, *nous mar*ch**ons**, *vous march*erez (=I walk, we walk, you will walk), the stem *march* expresses the action of walking; and the syllables **e, ons, erez**, which follow the stem and mark the different shades of the meaning, are the terminations.

3. Numbers.

119. Verbs, like nouns, have two **numbers**: the singular, relating to one person and thing alone: **je** *marche,* **tu** *lis,* **il** *mange* (=I walk, thou readest, he eats); the plural, when several are alluded to: **nous** *lisons,* **vous** *marchez,* **ils** *finissent* (=we read, you walk, they finish).

4. Persons.

120. The action expressed by the verb can be performed by the person who speaks: **je** *marche,* **nous** *mangeons* (=I walk, we eat); by the person to whom we speak: **tu** *marches,* **vous** *mangez* (=thou walkest, you eat), or by the person of whom we speak: **il** *lit,* **ils** *marchent* (=he reads, they walk). The French language marks these changes of persons, both in the singular and in the plural, by adding for each of them a new termination (**e, ons, ez,** etc.) to the stem of the verb. These different terminations are called in grammar the **persons** of the verb.

5. Moods.

121. The *mood* is the *manner* in which the verb presents the state or action which it expresses.

Mode (= mood) is from the Latin *modus* (*manière* = manner).

There are in French five *moods*: the **indicative**, the **imperative**, the **conditional**, the **subjunctive**, and the **infinitive**.

1. The **indicative** mood merely *indicates* that the action takes place: *je marche, tu lis* (= I walk, thou readest).

2. The **imperative** mood expresses *command*: *marchez, lisons* (= walk, let us read).

3. The **conditional** mood shows that the action would take place, if a certain condition were fulfilled: *je sortirais, s'il faisait beau* (= I should go out, if the weather were fine).

4. The **subjunctive** mood presents the action in a doubtful and uncertain manner, because it always depends upon another action: *je veux que tu viennes* (= I wish you to come). *Que tu viennes* is governed by the verb *je veux*, and depends on it.

5. The **infinitive** mood presents the action simply in a vague, *indefinite* manner, without any distinction of number or person: *lire, faire, remplir* (= to read, to do, to fill).

REMARK.—The *infinitive mood*, which takes no notice of persons, is called the *impersonal mood*; the other moods, which indicate the persons, are called *personal moods*.

6. Tenses.

122. The *tense* is the form assumed by the verb to show at what *time*, at what *moment* the action alluded to takes place.

There are three principal tenses: the **past**, the **present**, the **future**.

123. The **present** shows that the action occurs at the time when we are speaking (as, *je lis* = I read); the **past** shows that the action is already performed at the time when we are speaking (as, *j'ai marché* = I have walked); the **future** shows that the action will be performed at some future time (as, *je marcherai* = I shall walk).

124. There is only one *present*, but there are several *past* and several *future* tenses, because every action can be more or less past, more or less future.

125. There are five kinds of *past* or *perfect* tenses: the *imperfect*, the *preterite* or *past definite*, the *past indefinite*, the *past anterior*, and the *pluperfect*.

1. The **imperfect** expresses an action actually performed, but which was not so, when another action took place: *il* **lisait** *lorsque j'entrai* (=he was reading when I came in).

It is also used when speaking of a state or action which was habitual or characteristic: *il* **venait** *tous les jours* (=he came [used to come] every day).

2. The **preterite** or **past definite** shows that a thing has been done at a *definite*, determined epoch, which has completely passed at the time when we are speaking: *je chantai hier toute la soirée* (=I sang all last evening).

3. The **past indefinite** expresses an action which has taken place at a vague, indefinite epoch: *j'***ai lu** *ce livre autrefois* (=I have read that book formerly).

4. The **pluperfect** (*j'***avais** **lu** *quand vous êtes entré* = I had read when you entered) is thus called because it doubly expresses the past, by marking that a certain thing was done before another one took place in a past time.

5. The **preterite anterior** marks that the circumstance occurred immediately *before* another one which took place in a past time: *quand j'***eus lu** *ce journal, je sortis* (=as soon as I had read that newspaper, I went out).

126. There are two kinds of *future*: the future *simple*, and the future *anterior*.

1. The **future simple** indicates that the thing in question shall be, or shall take place: *je* **chanterai** *demain* (=I shall sing to-morrow).

2. The **future anterior** indicates that the thing in question will take place before another one: *quand j'***aurai lu** *ce journal, je sortirai* (=when I have read that newspaper, I shall go out).

AUXILIARY VERBS.

127. The verbs *avoir* and *être* are called **auxiliary** verbs, because they help in the conjugation of others: *je suis venu* (=I have come), *j'ai dormi* (=I have slept).

128. Simple tenses are those which are conjugated without the auxiliary *avoir* or *être*: *j'aime, j'aimais, que j'aime* (= I love, I loved, that I may love).

The simple tenses are formed by merely adding a termination to the stem.

129. Compound tenses are those which are conjugated with the auxiliary *avoir* or *être*: **j'ai** *aimé*, **j'aurai** *aimé*, **que j'eusse** *aimé* (= I have loved, I shall have loved, that I might have loved).

Conjugation.

130. The union of all the tenses of the same verb, with all their numbers and all their persons, is called its **conjugation.**

131. There are in French **four** conjugations, which are distinguished by the termination of the infinitive.

> The infinitive of the **first** conjugation ends in **-er**, as *aimer* (= to love).
>
> The **second** conjugation has **-ir** for the termination of the infinitive, as *finir* (= to finish); and the imperfect of the indicative ends in **iss-ais**, *je fin-iss-ais* (= I finished).

The verbs in **ir** really include two conjugations: the one, as *finir*, the imperfect of which ends in *issais*, as *je finissais*; the other, as *sentir* (= to feel), the imperfect of which ends in *-ais*, as *je sentais*. We give here the first of these conjugations, which includes more than *three hundred* French verbs, reserving for the chapter on irregular verbs the notice of the second conjugation in **-ir**, which includes only *twenty-eight* verbs.

> The **third** conjugation terminates in the infinitive in **-oir**, as *recevoir* (= to receive).
>
> The **fourth** conjugation has for the ending of the infinitive **-re**, as *rompre* (= to break).

The French language includes (if we take the *Dictionnaire de l'Académie* as an authority) about 4000 simple verbs (leaving out the compound ones); of these, 3600 end in **-er**; 330 in **-ir** (with the imperfect in *-issais*): 28 in **-ir** (with the imperfect in *-ais*); 10 verbs in **-oir**; and 50 verbs in **-re**. We thus see that the first conjugation in **-er** includes in itself nine-tenths of the French verbs.

As we shall see (Section 10) the French language creates new verbs with the help of substantives and adjectives, by adding to the former the termination -er: *fête, fêter*; *gant, ganter*; *lard, larder*; *camp, camper* (=holiday, to make holiday; glove, to put gloves on; bacon, to lard; camp, to camp); and to the latter the termination -ir: *maigre, maigrir*; *cher, chérir*; *bleu, bleuir*; *pâle, pâlir* (=thin, to become thin; dear, to cherish; blue, to make blue; pale, to become pale).

The first conjugation, in -er, forms new verbs with *substantives*; the second conjugation, in -ir, with *adjectives*. We may, then, designate them as *living* conjugations (*des conjugaisons* **vivantes**), inasmuch as they are constantly used for the purpose of new formations.

The conjugations in -oir, -re (and the second in -ir) are, on the contrary, incapable of being used to form new verbs, and since the origin of their language, the French have not added one *single verb* in -oir or in -re to the small number of those bequeathed by the Latin language. These conjugations, which have remained, so to say, barren, can with good reason be called *dead* conjugations (*des conjugaisons* **mortes**).

This simple distinction of the conjugations into *dead* and *living* shows us at once why 3900 French verbs (out of 4000) are in -er and in -ir, whilst the three other conjugations put together only include about 90 verbs.

SECTION L.

AUXILIARY VERBS.

132. Avoir and **être** are auxiliaries only when they serve to conjugate another verb, that is to say, when they are followed by a past participle; they have no claim to that designation when they are conjugated by themselves, as: *j'ai un cheval* (=I have a horse); *je* **suis** *roi* (=I am king).

I. Conjugation of the Auxiliary Verb AVOIR (=*to have*).

INDICATIVE.

PRESENT.	PERFECT.
(*I have*)	(*I have had*)
J'ai	J'ai eu
tu as	tu as eu
il *or* elle a	il *or* elle a eu
nous avons	nous avons eu
vous avez	vous avez eu
ils *or* elles ont	ils *or* elles ont eu.

IMPERFECT.
(I had)
J'avais
tu avais
il *or* elle avait
nous avions
vous aviez
ils *or* elles avaient

PLUPERFECT.
(I had had)
J'avais eu
tu avais eu
il *or* elle avait eu
nous avions eu
vous aviez eu
ils *or* elles avaient eu.

PAST DEFINITE.
(I had)
J'eus
tu eus
il *or* elle eut
nous eûmes
vous eûtes
ils *or* elles eurent

PAST ANTERIOR.
(I had had)
J'eus eu
tu eus eu
il *or* elle eut eu
nous eûmes eu
vous eûtes eu
ils *or* elles eurent eu.

FUTURE.
(I shall have)
J'aurai
tu auras
il *or* elle aura
nous aurons
vous aurez
ils *or* elles auront

FUTURE ANTERIOR.
(I shall have had)
J'aurai eu
tu auras eu
il *or* elle aura eu
nous aurons eu
vous aurez eu
ils *or* elles auront eu.

CONDITIONAL.

PRESENT.
(I should have)
J'aurais
tu aurais
il *or* elle aurait
nous aurions
vous auriez
ils *or* elles auraient

ANTERIOR.
(I should have had)
J'aurais eu
tu aurais eu
il *or* elle aurait eu
nous aurions eu
vous auriez eu
ils *or* elles auraient eu.

IMPERATIVE.

PRESENT.
(Have [thou])
. . . . .
Aie
. . . . .
ayons
ayez
. . . . .

PERFECT.
(Have [thou] had)
. . . . .
Aie eu
. . . . .
ayons eu
ayez eu
. . . . .

SUBJUNCTIVE.

PRESENT.

(That I may have)

Que j'aie
que tu aies
qu'il *or* qu'elle ait
que nous ayons
que vous ayez
qu'ils *or* qu'elles aient

PERFECT.

(That I may have had)

Que j'aie eu
que tu aies eu
qu'il *or* qu'elle ait eu
que nous ayons eu
que vous ayez eu
qu'ils *or* qu'elles aient eu.

IMPERFECT.

(That I might have)

Que j'eusse
que tu eusses
qu'il *or* qu'elle eût
que nous eussions
que vous eussiez
qu'ils *or* qu'elles eussent

PLUPERFECT.

(That I might have had)

Que j'eusse eu
que tu eusses eu
qu'il *or* qu'elle eût eu
que nous eussions eu
que vous eussiez eu
qu'ils *or* qu'elles eussent eu.

INFINITIVE.

PRESENT.

Avoir *(to have)*

PERFECT.

Avoir eu *(to have had)*.

PARTICIPLE PRESENT.

Ayant *(having)*

PERFECT.

Ayant eu *(having had)*.

PAST (VARIABLE).

Eu, *fem.* eue.

Exercise 25.

Indicatif présent.—J'ai un chapeau neuf. Tu as une robe neuve. Nous avons une grande maison. Vous avez de l'ambition. Ils ont un cheval noir.

Imparfait.—J'avais un bon maître. Tu avais une belle bibliothèque. Elle avait une voiture élégante. Nous avions des chagrins. Vous aviez perdu votre temps. Elles avaient des tiroirs pleins de jouets.

Passé défini.—J'eus un grand jardin. Il eut un morceau de pain. Nous eûmes une récompense. Ils eurent de la joie.

Futur.—J'aurai six paires de bas. Tu auras des raisins. Nous aurons des poires délicieuses. Vous aurez trop de plaisir.

Conditionnel présent.—J'aurais un billet pour le convoi de Paris. Elle aurait une robe et un chapeau neuf. Nous aurions un habile jardinier. Ils auraient une récompense.

Impératif.—Aie du courage. Ayons un peu de patience. Ayez plus de persévérance.

Subjonctif présent.—Que j'aie mon déjeûner. Que tu aies tes lettres. Que vous ayez votre fusil chargé.

Imparfait.—Que j'eusse mon épée et mes pistolets. Que tu eusses un grand pouvoir. Qu'elle eût une nombreuse famille. Que nous eussions des embarras. Que vous eussiez des billets de banque. Qu'elles eussent une chambre petite mais propre.

Temps composés.—Mon frère a eu une bonne place. Elle avait eu des oiseaux. J'eus eu des fleurs. J'aurai eu mon argent. Nous aurions eu un été magnifique. Que tu aies eu de la prudence. Qu'elles eussent eu une bouteille de vin.

Infinitif.—Avoir de l'esprit. Ayant eu du succès.

[1] persévérance (*f.*), [2] place (*f.*), [3] cour (*f.*), [4] poire (*f.*), [5] chapeau (*m.*), [6] comédie (*f.*), [7] choix (*m.*), [8] main (*f.*), [9] laborieux, [10] congé (*m.*), [11] éperon (*m.*), [12] aiguille (*f.*), [13] boîte (*f.*) à ouvrage, [14] loisir (*m.*), [15] lorgnon (*m.*), [16] consentement (*m.*), [17] tasse (*f.*), [18] théière (*f.*), [19] rideau (*m.*), [20] chandelier (*m.*), [21] rhume (*m.*), [22] citron (*m.*), [23] malheur (*m.*), [24] dîner (*m.*), [25] verger (*m.*), [26] inquiétude (*f.*), [27] manteau (*m.*), [28] bonheur (*m.*), [29] écharpe (*f.*), [30] argent, [31] nourriture (*f.*), [32] couronne (*f.*).

Indicative present.—I have a sword and (some) pistols. Thou hast very little (of) patience (*f.*). She has prudence (*f.*). We have more (of) perseverance.[1]

Imperfect.—I had two large gardens. Thou hadst a bottle of wine. He had a good situation[2] at (the) court.[3] We had some delicious pears.[4] They had new bonnets.[5]

Perfect.—She had a pair of stockings. We had a ticket for the play.[6] My gardener, who was in the train, had an accident (*m.*).

Future.—I shall have lost my time. You will have an elegant carriage. They will have their reward.

Conditional present.—I should have my choice.[7] Thou wouldst have a small room. He would have some bank-notes. We should have some difficulty. You would have some new skates. They would have a quire[8] of paper.

Imperative.—Have (thou) a more industrious[9] pupil. Let us have our holidays.[10] Have (ye) some melons (*m.*).

Subjunctive present.—That I may have a pair of spurs.[11] That thou may'st have some needles.[12] That she may have a work-box.[13] That we may have leisure.[14] That you may have more (of) confidence. That they may have eye-glasses.[15]

Imperfect.—That I might have your consent.[16] That thou mightest have a cup [17] and a tea-pot.[18] That he might have jewels. That she might have curtains [19] in her room. That we might have a candlestick.[20] That you might have a cold.[21] That they might have lemons.[22]

Compound tenses.—I have had a misfortune.²³ Thou hadst had a good dinner.²⁴ She had had a large orchard.²⁵ We shall have had much (of) anxiety.²⁶ You would have had a cloak.²⁷ That this merchant may have had luck.²⁸ That she might have had a scarf.²⁹

Infinitive.—To have money ³⁰ is not always to be happy. Having food.³¹ Having had a crown.³²

II. Conjugation of the Auxiliary Verb ÊTRE (= *to be*).

INDICATIVE.

PRESENT.

(*I am*)
Je suis
tu es
il *or* elle est
nous sommes
vous êtes
ils *or* elles sont

PERFECT.

(*I have been*)
J'ai été
tu as été
il *or* elle a été
nous avons été
vous avez été
ils *or* elles ont été.

IMPERFECT.

(*I was*)
J'étais
tu étais
il *or* elle était
nous étions
vous étiez
ils *or* elles étaient

PLUPERFECT.

(*I had been*)
J'avais été
tu avais été
il *or* elle avait été
nous avions été
vous aviez été
ils *or* elles avaient été.

PAST DEFINITE.

(*I was*)
Je fus
tu fus
il *or* elle fut
nous fûmes
vous fûtes
ils *or* elles furent

PAST ANTERIOR.

(*I had been*)
J'eus été
tu eus été
il *or* elle eut été
nous eûmes été
vous eûtes été
ils *or* elles eurent été.

FUTURE.

(*I shall be*)
Je serai
tu seras
il *or* elle sera
nous serons
vous serez
ils *or* elles seront

FUTURE ANTERIOR.

(*I shall have been*)
J'aurai été
tu auras été
il *or* elle aura été
nous aurons été
vous aurez été
ils *or* elles auront été.

CONDITIONAL.

PRESENT.	ANTERIOR.
(I should be)	*(I should have been)*
Je serais	J'aurais été
tu serais	tu aurais été
il *or* elle serait	il *or* elle aurait été
nous serions	nous aurions été
vous seriez	vous auriez été
ils *or* elles seraient	ils *or* elles auraient été.

IMPERATIVE.

PRESENT.	PERFECT.
(Be [thou])	*(Have [thou] been)*
. . . . .	. . . . .
Sois	Aie été
. . . . .	. . . . .
soyons	Ayons été
soyez	Ayez été
. . . . .	. . . . .

SUBJUNCTIVE.

PRESENT.	PERFECT.
(That I may be)	*(That I may have been)*
Que je sois	Que j'aie été
que tu sois	que tu aies été
qu'il *or* qu'elle soit	qu'il *or* qu'elle ait été
que nous soyons	que nous ayons été
que vous soyez	que vous ayez été
qu'ils *or* qu'elles soient	qu'ils *or* qu'elles aient été.

IMPERFECT.	PLUPERFECT.
(That I might be)	*(That I might have been)*
Que je fusse	Que j'eusse été
que tu fusses	que tu eusses été
qu'il *or* qu'elle fût	qu'il *or* qu'elle eût été
que nous fussions	que nous eussions été
que vous fussiez	que vous eussiez été
qu'ils *or* qu'elles fussent	qu'ils *or* qu'elles eussent été.

INFINITIVE.

PRESENT.	PERFECT.
Être *(to be)*	Avoir été *(to have been)*.

PARTICIPLE PRESENT.	PERFECT.
Étant *(being)*	Ayant été *(having been)*.

PAST (INVARIABLE).
Été *(been)*.

AUXILIARY VERBS.

Exercise 26.

Indicatif présent.—Je suis malade. Tu es savant. Il est malheureux. Elle est joyeuse. Nous sommes laborieux. Vous êtes modestes. Ils sont oisifs. Elles sont oisives.

Imparfait.—J'étais prudent. Tu étais timide. Il était honteux. Elle était honteuse. Nous étions discrètes. Vous étiez studieux. Ils étaient jaloux. Vos sœurs étaient jalouses.

Passé défini.—Je fus son ami intime. Tu fus mon plus grand ennemi. Elle fut excellente musicienne. Nous fûmes généreux. Vous fûtes ingrats. Elles furent cruelles.

Futur.—Je serai général en chef. Il sera mis à mort. Elle sera estimée. Nous serons fidèles à notre pays. Vous serez dans des craintes continuelles. Ils seront inquiets.

Conditionnel présent.—Je serais prêt. Tu serais turbulent. Il serait défiant. Elle serait fière. Nous serions fermes. Vous seriez frivoles. Ils seraient entêtés. Elles seraient soigneuses.

Impératif.—Sois tranquille. Soyez charitables. Soyons amis. Soyez obéissants. Soyons libres. Soyez gaies.

Subjonctif présent.—Que je sois moins impatient. Que tu sois un bon citoyen. Qu'il soit toujours puissant. Qu'elle soit soumise à ses parents. Que nous soyons sobres. Que vous soyez crédules. Qu'ils soient opiniâtres.

Imparfait.—Que je fusse ferme et courageux. Que tu fusses économe. Qu'il fût modéré. Que nous fussions hospitaliers. Que vous fussiez trompés. Qu'elles fussent satisfaites.

Temps composés.—Tu as été trop prompt. Elle avait été prise. Nous eûmes été invités. Vous aurez été moqueurs. Ils auraient été plus généreux. Que j'aie été volé. Qu'elles eussent été précoces.

Infinitif.—Pour être heureux il faut avoir la conscience tranquille. Étant battu, je me retire.

☞ *The pupil must be careful to observe here the rules for the place of adjectives*; see § 64, Note.

[1]indiscret, [2]obstiné, [3]ridicule, [4]capricieux, [5]reconnaissant, [6]emporté, [7]appliqué, [8]moqueur, [9]sage, [10]humain, [11]malhonnête, [12]infirme, [13]content, [14]compatissant, [15]bienveillant, [16]timide, [17]suffisant, [18]découragé, [19]faible, [20]posé, [21]battu, [22]prudent à l'avenir, [23]ennuyeux, [24]soupçonné, [25]conquis, [26]trompé, [27]tué, [28]chagrin, [29]commandé, [30]devint, [31]réservé.

Indicative present.—I am obedient. Thou art ready. He is charitable. She is impatient. We are moderate. You are in continual fears. They are inconsiderate.[1]

Imperfect.—I was *a* distrustful *man.* Thou wast obstinate.[6] She was firm. We were ridiculous.[3] You were whimsical.[4] These soldiers were brave.

Past definite.—I was jealous. Thou wast grateful.[5] He was studious. We were hasty.[6] You were attentive. My sisters were diligent.[7]

Future.—I shall be sarcastic.[8] Thou wilt be a rich man. She will be *a* wise [9] *woman.* We shall be humane.[10] You will be unpolite.[11] They will be ridiculous.

Conditional present.—I should be firm. Thou wouldst be cruel. She would be infirm.[12] We should be pleased.[13] You would be discreet. They would be kind.

Imperative.—Be indulgent. Let us be compassionate.[14] Let us be benevolent.[15]

Subjunctive present.—That I may be very timid.[16] That thou may'st be too conceited.[17] That she may be discouraged.[18] That we may be weak.[19] That you may be steady.[20] That they may be dumb.

Imperfect.—That I might be beaten.[21] That he might be respectable. That he might be cautious for the future.[22] That they might be tedious.[23]

Compound tenses.—I have been absent. Thou hadst been suspected.[24] She had been quiet. We shall have been conquered.[25] You would have been deceived.[26] That I may have been happy. That he might have been killed.[27]

Infinitive.—To be sorrowful.[28] Being the master, I order [29] here. Having been deceived, he became [30] more reserved.[31]

QUESTIONS FOR EXAMINATION.

1. Define the *verb,* the *subject,* the *direct complement* or *object,* the *indirect complement* or *object.*
2. What is the *substantive* verb? What is meant by an *adjective* verb?
3. What is the *stem*? the *termination*?
4. When is the verb put in the singular? when in the plural?
5. How many persons are there? how many moods?
6. Explain the force of every one of the moods?
7. What is meant by a *personal* mood?
8. What is an *impersonal* mood?
9. How many kinds of *perfect* are there? What is expressed by the *imperfect,* the *past definite,* etc.?
10. How many kinds of *future* are there?
11. Define a *simple* tense;—a *compound* tense.
12. Give a list of the French conjugations, and explain how they are distinguished from each other.
13. When are *avoir* and *être* auxiliary verbs?

SECTION II.

ACTIVE VERBS.

133. There are in French five kinds of verbs: the *active* verb, the *neuter* verb, the *passive* verb, the *reflective* verb, and the *impersonal* verb.

134. The **active** verb expresses the action performed by the subject, and is followed by a direct object: *J'***aime** *votre frère* (= I love your brother).

The active verb is also called *transitive* (from the Latin *transire* = to pass over from one place to another), because the action is *transmitted* from the subject to the object: *Le loup* **mange** *l'agneau* (= the wolf eats the lamb), *je* **récompense** *cet enfant* (= I reward this child).

135. We now give a model of the four conjugations of French verbs, taking care to point out, by different types, the stem from the termination.

I. First Conjugation.—Verb AIMER (=to love).

Stem, **aim**; *termination*, **er**.

INDICATIVE.

PRESENT.

(*I love*)
J'aime
tu aimes
il *or* elle aime
nous aimons
vous aimez
ils *or* elles aim**ent**.

PAST INDEFINITE.

(*I have loved*)
J'ai aimé
tu as aimé
il *or* elle a aimé
nous avons aimé
vous avez aimé
ils *or* elles ont aimé.

IMPERFECT.

(*I was loving*)
J'aimais
tu aimais
il *or* elle aimait
nous aimions
vous aimiez
ils *or* elles aimaient.

PLUPERFECT.

(*I had loved*)
J'avais aimé
tu avais aimé
il *or* elle avait aimé
nous avions aimé
vous aviez aimé
ils *or* elles avaient aimé.

ACTIVE VERBS.

PAST DEFINITE.
(*I loved*)
J'aim**ai**
tu aim**as**
il *or* elle aim**a**
nous aim**âmes**
vous aim**âtes**
ils *or* elles aim**èrent**

PAST ANTERIOR.
(*I had loved*)
J'eus aimé
tu eus aimé
il *or* elle eut aimé
nous eûmes aimé
vous eûtes aimé
ils *or* elles eurent aimé.

FUTURE.
(*I shall love*)
J'aim*er*ai
tu aim*er*as
il *or* elle aim*er*a
nous aim*er*ons
vous aim*er*ez
ils *or* elles aim*er*ont

FUTURE ANTERIOR.
(*I shall have loved*)
J'aurai aimé
tu auras aimé
il *or* elle aura aimé
nous aurons aimé
vous aurez aimé
ils *or* elles auront aimé.

CONDITIONAL.

PRESENT.
(*I should love*)
J'aim*er*ais
tu aim*er*ais
il *or* elle aim*er*ait
nous aim*er*ions
vous aim*er*iez
ils *or* elles aim*er*aient

ANTERIOR.
(*I should have loved*)
J'aurais *or* j'eusse aimé
tu aurais *or* tu eusses aimé
il *or* elle aurait *or* eût aimé
nous aurions *or* eussions aimé
vous auriez *or* eussiez aimé
ils *or* elles auraient *or* eussent aimé.

IMPERATIVE.

PRESENT.
(*Love thou*)

Aime

aimons
aimez

PERFECT.
(*Have [thou] loved*)

Aie aimé

ayons aimé
ayez aimé

SUBJUNCTIVE.

PRESENT.
(*That I may love*)
Que j'aime
que tu aimes
qu'il *or* qu'elle aime
que nous aimions
que vous aimiez
qu'ils *or* qu'elles aiment

PERFECT.
(*That I may have loved*)
Que j'aie aimé
que tu aies aimé
qu'il *or* qu'elle ait aimé
que nous ayons aimé
que vous ayez aimé
qu'ils *or* qu'elles aient aimé.

ACTIVE VERBS.

IMPERFECT.	PLUPERFECT.
(That I might love)	*(That I might have loved)*
Que j'aimasse	Que j'eusse aimé
que tu aimasses	que tu eusses aimé
qu'il *or* qu'elle aimât	qu'il *or* qu'elle eût aimé
que nous aimassions	que nous eussions aimé
que vous aimassiez	que vous eussiez aimé
qu'ils *or* qu'elles aimassent	qu'ils *or* qu'elles eussent aimé

INFINITIVE.

PRESENT.	PERFECT.
Aimer *(to love)*	Avoir aimé *(to have loved)*.

PARTICIPLE PRESENT.	PERFECT.
Aimant *(loving)*	Ayant aimé *(having loved)*.

PAST (VARIABLE).
Aimé, *fem.* aimée *(loved)*.

Exercise 27.

Indicatif présent.—J'aime mon père. Tu adores Dieu. Il alarme le pays. Elle danse très-bien. Nous apportons de bonnes nouvelles. Vous arrosez le jardin. Ils attaquent l'ennemi.

Imparfait.—Je balayais l'école. Il bassinait le lit. Elle brodait sa robe. Nous cachetions la lettre. Vous trouviez votre thème. Ils condamnaient ma conduite.

Passé défini.—Je récompensai le domestique. Tu donnas ta parole. Il discuta la question. Elle consola sa mère. Nous contentâmes notre maître. Vous remarquâtes les fautes. Ils décachetèrent la lettre.

Futur.—Je déciderai la question. Tu tueras un canard. Il déclarera la guerre. Elle déjeûnera avec vous. Nous aimerons les bons. Vous détromperez ma sœur. Ils différeront la punition.

Conditionnel présent.—Je fréquenterais la bonne compagnie. Tu dévoilerais le complot. Il graverait ce tableau. Elle humilierait votre orgueil. Nous imprimerions une grammaire. Vous oublieriez mes torts envers vous. Ils réformeraient leurs lois.

Impératif.—Sacrifie ton intérêt au bien public. Débrouillez cette affaire. Terminons ce livre. Apaisez sa colère. Evitons le danger.

Subjonctif présent.—Que je donne ce joujou à votre fils. Que tu blâmes sa conduite. Qu'il propose un avis salutaire. Que nous admirions la beauté de ce paysage. Que vous pensiez à mes malheurs. Qu'ils oublient une circonstance essentielle.

Imparfait.—Que je surmontasse les obstacles. Que tu consolasses les pauvres. Qu'il renforçât le parti. Que nous fermassions les volets. Que vous racontassiez cette charmante histoire. Qu'ils surveillassent ce méchant homme.

Infinitif.—Trop parler nuit. Il faut avoir traversé le désert.

Participes.—En patinant hier, il s'est cassé la jambe.

Temps composés.—J'ai chanté deux airs. Tu avais montré trop de talent. Il eut fermé la porte. Nous aurons dépensé trois mille francs. Vous auriez passé la journée chez des amis. Que j'aie hésité à vous défendre. Que tu eusses manqué à tous tes devoirs.

[1] trouve, [2] fortifier, [3] débrouiller, [4] offense (*f.*), [5] punition (*f.*), [6] un avis salutaire, [7] dévoiler, [8] complot (*m.*), [9] vertueux, [10] proposer, [11] planche (*f.*), [12] de musée (*m.*), [14] oie (*f.*), [15] armer, [16] les pauvres, [17] trop, [18] voler, [19] juste, [20] moyen d'être, [21] glace (*f.*), [22] à travers, [23] col (*m.*), [24] surveiller, [25] départ (*m.*).

Indicative present.—I speak (the) French. Thou skatest very well. He shows much (of) talent. Our troops [1] strengthen [2] your party (*m.*). We print a grammar. You unravel [3] my affairs (*f.*).

Imperfect.—I thought of your misfortunes. Thou wast crossing the wilderness. He related a charming history. We were shutting the shutters (*m.*). You were mending your conduct. He was discussing the question (*f.*).

Past definite.—Your sister sang yesterday. I forgot all your offences.[4] Thou avoidedst a great danger. We spent more (of) money than you. You forgot your punishment.[5]

Future.—I shall give you some sound advice.[6] Thou wilt undeceive my sister. He will expose [7] the plot.[8] You will frequent the company of (the) virtuous [9] men. They will propose [10] three questions.

Conditional present.—I would sweep the school. Thou shouldst alarm the camp (*m.*). He would give these toys to my children. We would water their flower-beds [11] in the garden. You should love your parents. He should engrave the best pictures in [12] the museum.[13]

Imperative.—Worship God. Let us notice the mistakes in this exercise. Shut your books.

Subjunctive present.—That I may kill a goose.[14] That thou may'st warm the bed. That she may think of us when she is in France. That we may breakfast this morning with our friends. That you may arm [15] all the troops. That you may visit the poor.[16]

Imperfect.—That I might condemn her conduct. That thou mightest satisfy thy kind mother. That she might scold her servants. That we might spend too much.[17] That you might steal [18] my letter. That they might weep.

Infinitive.—To sing in tune [19] is an essential quality. To have confessed one's faults is the best means of being [20] pardoned.

Participles.—I have seen you breaking the ice [21] in the garden. Passing through [22] the camp.

Compound tenses.—I have avoided this wicked man. Thou hadst embroidered my collar.[23] He had watched over [24] that child. We shall have dined. You would have postponed your departure.[25] That they may have observed all the circumstances. That I might have admired the landscape.

II. Second Conjugation.—Verb FINIR (= *to finish*).

Stem, fin; termination, ir.

INDICATIVE.

PRESENT.	PAST INDEFINITE.
(*I finish*)	(*I have finished*)
Je finis	J'ai fini
tu finis	tu as fini
il *or* elle finit	il *or* elle a fini
nous finissons	nous avons fini
vous finissez	vous avez fini
ils *or* elles finissent	ils *or* elles ont fini

IMPERFECT.	PLUPERFECT.
(*I was finishing*)	(*I had finished*)
Je finissais	J'avais fini
tu finissais	tu avais fini
il *or* elle finissait	il *or* elle avait fini
nous finissions	nous avions fini
vous finissiez	vous aviez fini
ils *or* elles finissaient	ils *or* elles avaient fini

PAST DEFINITE.	PAST ANTERIOR.
(*I finished*)	(*I had finished*)
Je finis	J'eus fini
tu finis	tu eus fini
il *or* elle finit	il *or* elle eut fini
nous finîmes	nous eûmes fini
vous finîtes	vous eûtes fini
ils *or* elles finirent	ils *or* elles eurent fini

FUTURE.	FUTURE ANTERIOR.
(*I shall finish*)	(*I shall have finished*)
Je finirai	J'aurai fini
tu finiras	tu auras fini
il *or* elle finira	il *or* elle aura fini
nous finirons	nous aurons fini
vous finirez	vous aurez fini
ils *or* elles finiront	ils *or* elles auront fini

CONDITIONAL.

PRESENT.
(I should finish)
Je fin*ir*ais
tu fin*ir*ais
il *or* elle fin*ir*ait
nous fin*ir*ions
vous fin*ir*iez
ils *or* elles fin*ir*aient

ANTERIOR.
(I should have finished)
J'aurais *or* j'eusse fini
tu aurais *or* tu eusses fini
il *or* elle aurait *or* eût fini
nous aurions *or* eussions fini
vous auriez *or* eussiez fini
ils *or* elles auraient *or* eussent fini

IMPERATIVE.

PRESENT.
(Finish [thou])

Finis

fin*iss*ons
fin*iss*ez

PERFECT.
(Have [thou] finished)

Aie fini

ayons fini
ayez fini

SUBJUNCTIVE.

PRESENT.
(That I may finish)
Que je fin*iss*e
que tu fin*iss*es
qu'il *or* qu'elle fin*iss*e
que nous fin*iss*ions
que vous fin*iss*iez
qu'ils *or* qu'elles fin*iss*ent

PERFECT.
(That I may have finished)
Que j'aie fini
que tu aies fini
qu'il *or* qu'elle ait fini
que nous ayons fini
que vous ayez fini
qu'ils *or* qu'elles aient fini.

IMPERFECT.
(That I might finish)
Que je fin**isse**
que tu fin**isses**
qu'il *or* qu'elle fin**ît**
que nous fin**issions**
que vous fin**issiez**
qu'ils *or* qu'elles fin**issent**

PLUPERFECT.
(That I might have finished)
Que j'eusse fini
que tu eusses fini
qu'il *or* qu'elle eût fini
que nous eussions fini
que vous eussiez fini
qu'ils *or* qu'elles eussent fini.

INFINITIVE.

PRESENT.
Fin**ir** *(to finish)*

PERFECT.
Avoir fini *(to have finished)*.

PARTICIPLE PRESENT.
Fin*iss*ant *(finishing)*

PERFECT.
Ayant fini *(having finished)*.

PAST (VARIABLE).
Fini, *fem.* finie *(finished)*.

Exercise 28.

Indicatif présent.—Je punis les coupables. Il adoucit le cœur. Vous applaudissez à ce qu'il dit.

Imparfait.—J'avertissais votre frère de son danger. Nous bannissions les méchants de notre société.

Passé défini.—Tu réussis dans ton entreprise. Vous désobéîtes à votre maître. Ils envahirent le pays.

Futur.—Je finirai mon ouvrage ce soir. Il garnira cette chambre de tableaux. Nous jouirons des plaisirs de la campagne.

Conditionnel présent.—Tu trahirais mes intérêts. Nous enrichirions notre famille. Elles compâtiraient à nos malheurs.

Impératif.—Polis ces cuillers. Attendrissez ce cœur inflexible.

Subjonctif présent.—Que j'établisse ma réputation. Qu'il affaiblisse son parti. Que vous renchérissiez ces marchandises.

Imparfait.—Que tu les affermisses dans leur devoir. Que nous abolissions ces impôts. Qu'ils asservissent les nations étrangères.

Infinitif.—Je puis fournir ce travail. Avoir assorti ces couleurs.

Participes.—En punissant les coupables, j'ai rempli un véritable devoir.

Temps composés.—Tu as appauvri ces enfants. Ce cheval avait henni. Vous auriez accompli cette tâche.

[1] chérir, [2] droits (m.), [3] société (f.), [4] répartir, [5] fléchir, [6] coup (m.), [7] tonnerre (m.), [8] retentir, [9] fournir, [10] de charbon, [11] rôtir, [12] gigot (m.), [13] Espagne (f.), [14] aplanir, [15] répartir, [16] paroisse (f.), [17] échelle (f.), [18] chagrin (m.), [19] accomplir, [20] subir, [21] approfondir, [22] tiroir, [23] musique (f.).

Indicative present.—Thou cherishest[1] thy parents. We abolish the duties[2] on those goods. You strengthen them in their duty.

Imperfect.—I finished this book. She enjoyed the pleasures of (the) society.[3] We distributed[4] the provisions (f.).

Past definite.—He bent[5] under the blow.[6] The thunder[7] resounded.[8] You supplied[9] our house with coal.[10]

Future.—Thou wilt betray the party. We shall roast[11] a leg[12] of mutton. They will invade (the) Spain.[13]

Conditional present.—I would smooth[14] the difficulties. He would assess[15] the taxes of the parish.[16] They would establish their reputation.

Imperative.—Polish all the forks. Strengthen this ladder.[17]

Subjunctive present.—That thou mayest enslave the nation. That we may soften his grief.[18] That the fruit may rise in price.

Imperfect.—That I might discharge[19] my duty. That she might undergo[20] the punishment. That you might unfurnish the room.

Infinitive.—To finish this book before a month is impossible.

Participles.—By examining into[21] this question, you will find that the laws have been established.

Compound tenses.—I have filled these drawers.[22] We shall have applauded that beautiful music.[23] That he might have been warned.

III. Third Conjugation.—Verb RECEVOIR (= *to receive*).

Stem, **recev**; *termination,* **oir.**

INDICATIVE.

PRESENT.	PERFECT.
(*I receive*)	(*I have received*)
Je reçois	J'ai reçu
tu reçois	tu as reçu
il *or* elle reçoit	il *or* elle a reçu
nous recevons	nous avons reçu
vous recevez	vous avez reçu
ils *or* elles reçoivent	ils *or* elles ont reçu.

IMPERFECT.	PLUPERFECT.
(*I was receiving*)	(*I had received*)
Je recevais	J'avais reçu
tu recevais	tu avais reçu
il *or* elle recevait	il *or* elle avait reçu
nous recevions	nous avions reçu
vous receviez	vous aviez reçu
ils *or* elles recevaient	ils *or* elles avaient reçu.

PAST DEFINITE.	PAST ANTERIOR.
(*I received*)	(*I had received*)
Je reçus	J'eus reçu
tu reçus	tu eus reçu
il *or* elle reçut	il *or* elle eut reçu
nous reçûmes	nous eûmes reçu
vous reçûtes	vous eûtes reçu
ils *or* elles reçurent	ils *or* elles eurent reçu.

FUTURE.	FUTURE ANTERIOR.
(*I shall receive*)	(*I shall have received*)
Je recevr ai	J'aurai reçu
tu recevr as	tu auras reçu
il *or* elle recevr a	il *or* elle aura reçu
nous recevr ons	nous aurons reçu
vous recevr ez	vous aurez reçu
ils *or* elles recevr ont	ils *or* elles auront reçu.

CONDITIONAL.

PRESENT.
(I should receive)
Je recevrais
tu recevrais
il *or* elle recevrait
nous recevrions
vous recevriez
ils *or* elles recevraient

ANTERIOR.
(I should have received)
J'aurais *or* j'eusse reçu
tu aurais *or* tu eusses reçu
il *or* elle aurait *or* eût reçu
nous aurions *or* eussions reçu
vous auriez *or* eussiez reçu
ils *or* elles auraient *or* eussent reçu.

IMPERATIVE.

PRESENT.
(Receive [thou])

Reçois

recevons
recevez

PERFECT.
(Have [thou] received)

Aie reçu

ayons reçu
ayez reçu

SUBJUNCTIVE.

PRESENT.
(That I may receive)
Que je reçoive
que tu reçoives
qu'il *or* qu'elle reçoive
que nous recevions
que vous receviez
qu'ils *or* qu'elles reçoivent

PERFECT.
(That I may have received)
Que j'aie reçu
que tu aies reçu
qu'il *or* qu'elle ait reçu
que nous ayons reçu
que vous ayez reçu
qu'ils *or* qu'elles aient reçu.

IMPERFECT.
(That I might receive)
Que je reçusse
que tu reçusses
qu'il *or* qu'elle reçût
que nous reçussions
que vous reçussiez
qu'ils *or* qu'elles reçussent

PLUPERFECT.
(That I might have received)
Que j'eusse reçu
que tu eusses reçu
qu'il *or* qu'elle eût reçu
que nous eussions reçu
que vous eussiez reçu
qu'ils *or* qu'elles eussent reçu.

INFINITIVE.

PRESENT.
Recevoir *(to receive)*

PERFECT.
Avoir reçu *(to have received).*

PARTICIPLE PRESENT.
Recevant *(receiving)*

PERFECT.
Ayant reçu *(having received).*

PAST (VARIABLE).
Reçu, *fem.* reçue *(received).*

Exercise 29.

Indicatif présent.—Je conçois comment cela est arrivé. Il aperçoit votre intention. Nous redevons le loyer de notre maison.

Imparfait.—Tu recevais tes livres. Vous déceviez ses espérances. Ils percevaient mes revenus.

Passé défini.—Je reçus une visite de votre oncle. Elle conçut un grand projet. Nous aperçûmes le voleur.

Futur.—Tu recevras demain une lettre de mon ami. Vous concevrez un nouveau projet. Ils apercevront aisément si le thème est bien fait.

Conditionnel présent.—Il recevrait les arrérages. Je devrais écrire ce devoir. Vous apercevriez son erreur.

Impératif.—Conçois l'importance de cette affaire. Recevez mes remercîments de toutes vos bontés.

Subjonctif présent.—Qu'il perçoive l'intérêt de cet argent. Que nous recevions son télégramme. Qu'elles redoivent le montant du billet.

Imparfait.—Que je redusse une bagatelle. Que vous déçussiez mes plus chères espérances. Que nous reçussions ce tribut d'estime.

Infinitif.—Apercevoir des défauts dans autrui est chose facile.

Participes.—En recevant cette demande, le roi a fait un acte de justice. Les impôts sont perçus.

Temps composés.—Je l'ai reçu hier. Il a aperçu mon frère. Vous auriez aperçu le clocher de l'église. Que tu eusses conçu l'étendue de ses projets.

[1] gouvernement (*m.*), [2] profondeur (*f.*), [3] trahison (*f.*), [4] cargaison (*f.*), [5] politesse (*f.*), [6] dessein (*m.*), [7] bouquet (*m.*), [8] tout à fait, [9] désirer, [10] montrer, [11] juste, [12] mériter, [13] billet (*m.*), [14] tache (*f.*), [15] drap (*m.*).

Indicative present.—I perceive your mistake. You collect the taxes for the government.[1] They receive a tribute (in) money.

Imperfect.—He perceived his situation. We owed again a sum of seventy francs. They deceived my fondest hopes.

Past definite.—I conceived the depth[2] of his treachery.[3] You received a cargo[4] of goods. We perceived the steeple of the church.

Future.—Thou wilt owe many (of) thanks to thy friend. She will receive your message (*m.*). They will conceive a plan (*m.*).

Conditional present.—I should receive him with politeness.[5] Thou wouldst receive a telegram. We should perceive the house.

Imperative.—Receive my sincere thanks. Let us conceive a better design.[6]

ACTIVE VERBS. 89

Subjunctive present.—That we may receive the nosegay.[7] That he may collect the arrears. That they may owe less.

Imperfect.—That I might understand my lesson thoroughly.[8] I wished[9] that you might perceive your danger. That we might conceive the importance of his duties.

Infinitive.—To receive this man is to show[10] one's contempt of what is right.[11]

Participles.—In deceiving me you have deserved[12] to be punished.

Compound Tenses.—I had received your note.[13] She had perceived his intentions. That I might have perceived a stain[14] on that cloth.[15]

IV. Fourth Conjugation.—Verb ROMPRE (= to break).

Stem, romp; *termination,* re.

INDICATIVE.

PRESENT.	PERFECT.
(I break)	*(I have broken)*
Je romps	J'ai rompu
tu romps	tu as rompu
il *or* elle rompt	il *or* elle a rompu
nous rompons	nous avons rompu
vous rompez	vous avez rompu
ils *or* elles rompent	ils *or* elles ont rompu.

IMPERFECT.	PLUPERFECT.
(I was breaking)	*(I had broken)*
Je rompais	j'avais rompu
tu rompais	tu avais rompu
il *or* elle rompait	il *or* elle avait rompu
nous rompions	nous avions rompu
vous rompiez	vous aviez rompu
ils *or* elles rompaient	ils *or* elles avaient rompu.

PAST DEFINITE.	PAST ANTERIOR.
(I broke)	*(I had broken)*
Je rompis	J'eus rompu
tu rompis	tu eus rompu
il *or* elle rompit	il *or* elle eut rompu
nous rompîmes	nous eûmes rompu
vous rompîtes	vous eûtes rompu
ils *or* elles rompirent	ils *or* elles eurent rompu.

ACTIVE VERBS.

FUTURE.
(I shall break)
Je romp**rai**
tu romp**ras**
il *or* elle romp**ra**
nous romp**rons**
vous romp**rez**
ils *or* elles romp**ront**

FUTURE ANTERIOR.
(I shall have broken)
J'aurai rompu
tu auras rompu
il *or* elle aura rompu
nous aurons rompu
vous aurez rompu
ils *or* elles auront rompu.

CONDITIONAL.

PRESENT.
(I should break)
Je romp**rais**
tu romp**rais**
il *or* elle romp**rait**
nous romp**rions**
vous romp**riez**
ils *or* romp**raient**

ANTERIOR.
(I should have broken)
J'aurais *or* j'eusse rompu
tu aurais *or* tu eusses rompu
il *or* elle aurait *or* eût rompu
nous aurions *or* eussions rompu
vous auriez *or* eussiez rompu
ils *or* elles auraient *or* eussent rompu.

IMPERATIVE.

PRESENT.
(Break [thou])
. . . .
Romps
. . . .
rompons
rompez
. . . .

PERFECT.
(Have [thou] broken)
. . . .
Aie rompu
. . . .
ayons rompu
ayez rompu
. . . .

SUBJUNCTIVE.

PRESENT.
(That I may break)
Que je rompe
que tu rompes
qu'il *or* qu'elle rompe
que nous romp**ions**
que vous romp**iez**
qu'ils *or* qu'elles rompent

PERFECT.
(That I may have broken)
Que j'aie rompu
que tu aies rompu
qu'il *or* qu'elle ait rompu
que nous ayons rompu
que vous ayez rompu
qu'ils *or* qu'elles aient rompu.

IMPERFECT.
(That I might break)
Que je rompisse
que tu rompisses
qu'il *or* qu'elle rompît
que nous romp**issions**
que vous romp**issiez**
qu'ils *or* qu'elles romp**issent**

PLUPERFECT.
(That I might have broken)
Que j'eusse rompu
que tu eusses rompu
qu'il *or* qu'elle eût rompu
que nous eussions rompu
que vous eussiez rompu
qu'ils *or* qu'elles eussent rompu.

ACTIVE VERBS.

INFINITIVE.

PRESENT.
Rompre (*to break*)

PERFECT.
Avoir rompu (*to have broken*)

PARTICIPLE PRESENT.
Rompant (*breaking*)

PERFECT.
Ayant rompu (*having broken*)

PAST (VARIABLE).
Rompu, *fem.* rompue (*broken*).

Exercise 30.

Indicatif présent.—J'attends de la compagnie aujourd'hui. Il répond correctement. Vous défendez votre patrie.

Imparfait.—Tu suspendais ton jugement. Ce chien mordait tout le monde. Vous prétendiez à sa place.

Passé défini.—Il condescendit à ses désirs. Nous fondîmes le plomb. Ils tendirent leurs bras.

Futur.—Je répondrai à votre lettre. Il entendra ce qu'ils disent. Elles vendront leur maison de campagne.

Conditionnel présent.—Tu tordrais la corde. Nous confondrions leur orgueil. Ils prendraient leurs chapeaux dans le vestiaire.

Impératif.—Entends leur justification. Attendons l'arrivée du bateau à vapeur.

Subjonctif présent.—Que tu vendes ces fruits trop cher. Que vous répandiez l'eau sur le tapis. Qu'ils tendent cette corde.

Imparfait.—Que je tendisse au même but. Que nous fendissions la presse. Que vous entendissiez le bruit du tonnerre.

Infinitif.—Prétendre savoir toutes choses est ridicule.

Participes.—En fendant ce morceau de bois, je me suis blessé. La cause entendue, le président prononça la sentence.

Temps composés.—J'ai vendu tous mes livres. Vous aviez confondu ces deux règles. Il aura répondu à mon appel.

[1] immédiatement, [2] régulièrement, [3] tendre à, [4] but (*m.*), [5] défendre, [6] usage (*m.*), [7] correspondre, [8] séance (*f.*), [9] linge (*m.*), [10] terres (*f.*), [11] chapeau (*m.*), [12] convention (*f.*), [13] fendre, [14] toute la journée, [15] répandre, [16] chemin (*m.*), [17] ne devriez pas, [18] bruit (*m.*) [19] confondre, [20] raison (*f.*), [21] larme (*f.*), [22] grand escalier (*m.*)

Indicative present.—I am coming down immediately.[1] He answers my letters very regularly.[2] We are aiming at[3] a difficult end.[4]

Imperfect.—I was forbidding[5] him the use[6] of it. She was writing. You were confounding this rule with another.

Past definite.—He corresponded[7] with your friends. We suspended the meeting.[8] She wrung the linen[9] in the garden.

Future.—I shall sell all my estates.[10] She will take her bonnet.[11] You will break the agreement.[12]

Conditional present.—Thou wouldst answer my letters. We should recast the poem. They would hear us.

Imperative.—Split [13] the wood. Let us hang up our coats in the cloak room.

Subjunctive present.—That I may wait all day long.[14] That we should sell all the jewels. That you should stretch this rope.

Imperfect.—That she might shear the sheep. That I might scatter [15] flowers on his path.[16] That they might defend their interests.

Infinitive.—You should not [17] sell your goods so dear.

Participles.—Hearing this rumour [18] I went out. His insolence (*f.*) was brought to confusion.[19]

Compound tenses.—I had heard his reasons.[20] We should have melted into tears.[21] Thou wouldst have waited. That I might have come down by the principal staircase.[22]

SECTION III.

CONJUGATION OF VERBS. 1. Interrogatively; 2. Negatively; 3. Interrogatively with a negative.

136. If we wish to conjugate these verbs *interrogatively* we have only to displace the pronoun, putting it (in the simple tenses) after the verb: *aimez-***vous**? (=do you love?), or in the compound tenses, between the auxiliary and the past participle: *ai-***je** *aimé* (=have I loved?), *avais-***je** *aimé* (=had I loved?), *aurai-***je** *aimé* (=shall I have loved?) etc.

137. If the first person singular ends in an *e* mute (*j'aime*=I love; *que je puisse*=that I may be able), that *e* mute is replaced by a close **é**: *aimé-***je** (=do I love?) *puissé-***je** (=may I?).

138. When the third person singular ends with a vowel, as is the case for the first conjugation (*il aime*=he loves; *il va*=he goes) a **t**, called euphonic, is placed between the verb and the pronoun (*aime-***t**-*il*, *va-***t**-*il?* =does he love, does he go?)

The old French always had a *t* at the end of the third person, and said il *aimet*, il *vat*, without sounding the *t*. This letter, being mute, disappeared from the direct conjugation; but it persisted in the interrogative one, on account of the following vowel. This *t*, which is called *euphonic t*, and which is joined to the verb by a hyphen, was therefore really, in former times, part of the verb.

139. **Est-ce que** (=is it that) is also used in asking questions, especially with verbs of one syllable: **est-ce que** *je vends?* (=do I sell?) **est-ce que** *vous aimez cette ville?* (=do you like this town?). Then the verb is put in the affirmative.

In sentences like: You see it, do you not? You will do it, will you not? You have not done it, have you? the interrogation is in every case expressed in French by **n'est-ce pas?** *Vous le voyez*, **n'est-ce pas?** *Vous le ferez*, **n'est-ce pas?** *Vous ne l'avez pas fait*, **n'est-ce pas?**

140. When in a question the verb has a noun for the subject, as: Is your friend here? the noun is placed first, as in the affirmation, and the pronoun (of the same gender, number, and person as the noun) is placed after the verb to show that the sentence is interrogative: **Votre ami** *est-il ici?* (=is your friend here?) **Vos amis** *sont-ils ici?* (=are your friends here?).

141. In order to conjugate the verbs in the *negative* form (with the negative *ne...pas*, *ne...point*), it suffices that we should place *ne* between the pronoun and the verb, and *pas* after the verb, for the simple tenses: *je* **ne** *veux* **pas** (=I do not wish); *tu* **ne** *veux* **pas** (=thou dost not wish) etc. In the compound tenses, the word *pas* is placed between the auxiliary and the participle: *je* **n'ai** **pas** *voulu*=(I have not wished); *je* **n'aurais pas** *voulu* (=I would not have wished) etc. With the infinitive, *pas* generally comes before the verb: *pour* **ne pas** *faire cela* (=not to do that).

142. To conjugate a verb *interrogatively with a negative*, *ne* is placed before the verb and *pas* after the pronoun following the verb: **ne** *vois-je* **pas**? (=do I not see?). In the compound tenses *ne* comes before the auxiliary, and *pas* after the pronoun following the auxiliary: **n'ai je pas** *vu?* (=have I not seen?)

☞ *A table of these conjugations will be found at page* 156.

Exercise 31.

Indicatif présent.—Préféré-je cet ouvrage? Il ne finit pas ses devoirs. Ne recevons-nous pas son avis avec reconnaissance?

Imparfait.—Demeurais-tu à Londres? Il ne renchérissait pas ses marchandises. N'entendaient-ils pas le bruit de la voiture? Vous aimiez cette ville, n'est-ce pas?

Passé défini.—Conçut-elle toute l'importance de cette démarche? N'aima-t-il pas son séjour à la campagne? Vous ternîtes votre gloire par votre cruauté.

Futur.—Est-ce que nous ne profiterons pas d'une occasion aussi favorable? Vous ne réussirez jamais à le persuader. Vos amis ne vendront-ils pas leur propriété?

Conditionnel présent.—Je n'agirais pas contre ma conscience. Choisiriez-vous ce cheval? Ne recevriez-vous pas du monde demain?

Impératif.—Ne reçois jamais de ses lettres.

Subjonctif présent.—Que je ne rende compte à personne.

Imparfait.—Que ce chemin n'aboutit pas au château.

Infinitif.—Ne pas me répondre est une preuve d'impertinence.

Participes.—N'ayant pas trahi sa patrie, il est plein de confiance.

Temps composés.—Avez-vous chanté ce matin? Il n'avait pas démoli cette chaumière. N'eurent-ils pas aperçu le vaisseau dans le port? Je n'aurais jamais condescendu à une telle demande. N'auront-ils ni livres ni papiers? Qu'elle n'ait pas d'argent. Que nous ne fussions pas dénués de ressources.

[1] cave (*f.*), [2] revendre, [3] voiture (*f.*), [4] autrefois, [5] projet (*m.*), [6] négliger, [7] réussir, [8] réfléchir à, [9] proposition (*f.*), [10] rendre, [11] arc (*m.*), [12] ternir, [13] céder, [14] louer, [15] cloche (*f.*), [16] honorablement, [17] tromper, [18] critiquer, [19] sévèrement.

Indicative present.—Do you answer (to) his letter? He does not finish his picture. Do they not dine?

Imperfect.—Was I going down into the cellar[1]? We did not resell[2] this carriage.[3] Did they not correspond formerly[4]?

Perfect definite.—I had no money. She did not burst into tears. Did he not perceive my design[5]?

Future.—I shall never neglect[6] my duties. They will succeed,[7] will they not? Will you recast your work?

Conditional.—I would not disobey. Would your friend reflect on[8] that proposal[9]? Would they negotiate that treaty?

Imperative.—Do not return[10] (to) him his letter.

Subjunctive present.—That I may not owe this sum.

Imperfect.—That they might not stretch that bow.[11]

Infinitive.—Not to sully[12] your reputation (*f.*), confess your fault.

Participles.—Not having yielded,[13] he was praised[14] by the journal.

Compound tenses.—I have not heard the bell.[15] Wast thou acting honourably?[16] Did she not sell her estates? I shall not have received this dangerous man. Would she not have rewarded the merit of that pupil? That they may not have deceived[17] you. That we might not have criticised[18] him too severely.[19]

SECTION IV.

REMARKS ON THE FORMATION OF THE TENSES.

143. Notice that in the first person of the present indicative the verbs in -**er** do not take an *s* (*je chante*), while the other conjugations do (*je finis, je romps*).

This exception is a vestige of the Old French language: the first person formerly never took an *s*: *j'aime, je voi, je rend* (= I love, I see, I restore); about the beginning of the sixteenth century, an *s* was added, by analogy with the *s* of the second person *tu chantes, tu lis, tu vois* (= thou singest, thou readest, thou seest); but the first conjugation escaped this assimilation, and even in the case of the other conjugations, the forms without *s* still remained for a long time in the language of poetry. Thus we find in the seventeenth century: *je voi, je li, je croi*. (LA FONTAINE, MOLIÈRE, CORNEILLE.)

144. The imperfect is the same in all conjugations (-*ais*, -*ais*, -*ait*, -*ions*, -*iez*, -*aient*), always remembering that the conjugation in -**ir** interpolates the particle -**iss** between the root and the termination: *je fin-iss-ais*, *tu fin-iss-ais*.

Before the time of Voltaire, the imperfect was always written with the syllable *ois* (*j'aimois, je chantois*, etc.) instead of *ais*. It was he who first wrote: *j'aimais, je chantais*, etc. This orthographical modification was only adopted by the Academy in 1835. A century before Voltaire, in 1675, an obscure lawyer, Nicolas Bérain, had already asked for this reform.

145. The future is formed throughout all the conjugations in the same manner, that is to say, by adding to the infinitive of the verb the indicative present of the verb *avoir* (*ai, as, a*, etc.).

Je chanterai is therefore exactly equivalent to *j'ai à chanter*; hence: *aimerai, as, a*. In the plural, however, the syllable *av* is struck out: *aimer-* (av) *ons, aimer-* (av) *ez, aimer-ont*. The third conjugation is an exception to this rule, as the termination *oir* is shortened into **r**: *je recev-r-ai*.

The conditional present is formed in the same way from the imperfect indicative, the syllable *av* being suppressed: *j'aimer-* (av) *ais*.

146. It will be observed that all the persons of the imperative are borrowed from the corresponding persons of the indicative present. The only exception is in the first conjugation, which has *chante* without an *s*, whilst *finis, reçois, romps* retain the *s* of the indicative (*tu finis, tu reçois, tu romps*). But the *s* of *chante* is expressed, and reappears when the imperative is placed before a word beginning with a vowel, such as *y* or *en: chantes-en une partie* (= sing part of it), *vas-y voir* (= go there and see), etc.

147. The tenses of the verbs are divided into **primitive** and **derivative.** From the five primitive tenses all the others are formed in the following manner:—

The Present Infinitive forms	1. The *future*, see § 145. 2. The *conditional*, see § 145.
The Present Participle ,,	1. The *plural* of the *present indicative*: aimant, aimons, aimez, aiment. 2. The *imperfect indicative*: finissant, finissais, etc. 3. The *present subjunctive* finissant, finisse, finisses, except the 3rd conjugation, in which *oi* reappears: *recevant, reçoive.*
The Past Participle ,,	All the *compound tenses* with the auxiliary *avoir* or *être*.
The Present Indicative ,,	the *imperative*, see § 146.
The Past Definite ,,	The *imperfect subjunctive*, by adding *se* to the second person singular: *tu aimas, aimasse.*

148. Idiomatic tenses.—Besides the tenses given in the models for the four conjugations, the French use others which are made up with the verbs *aller* (= to go), *venir* (= to come), and *devoir* (= to owe, to be obliged, must). Here is a list of these tenses:—

1. PAST JUST ELAPSED.
   (*I have just spoken*)

Je viens de parler
tu viens de parler
il vient de parler
nous venons de parler
vous venez de parler
ils viennent de parler.

2. PAST DEFINITE ANTERIOR.
   (*I had just spoken*)

Je venais de parler
tu venais de parler
il venait de parler
nous venions de parler
vous veniez de parler
ils venaient de parler.

3. FUTURE PROXIMATE.

(I am going to speak)

Je vais parler
tu vas parler
il va parler
nous allons parler
vous allez parler
ils vont parler.

4. FUTURE DEFINITE.

(I am to, or I must, or I intend to speak)

Je dois parler
tu dois parler
il doit parler
nous devons parler
vous devez parler
ils doivent parler.

5. FUTURE IMPERFECT ANTERIOR.

(I was going to speak)

J'allais parler
tu allais parler
il allait parler
nous allions parler
vous alliez parler
ils allaient parler.

6. CONDITIONAL IMPERFECT.

(I was to, or I intended to speak)

Je devais parler
tu devais parler
il devait parler
nous devions parler
vous deviez parler
ils devaient parler.

7. CONDITIONAL FUTURE.*

(I ought to, or I should speak)

Je devrais parler
tu devrais parler
il devrait parler
nous devrions parler
vous devriez parler
ils devraient parler.

8. CONDITIONAL ANTERIOR.*

(I ought to, or I should have spoken)

J'aurais dû parler
tu aurais dû parler
il aurait dû parler
nous aurions dû parler
vous auriez dû parler
ils auraient dû parler.

There is also a past tense with *devoir*, expressing either obligation or supposition—

J'ai dû parler } = I have had to speak, *or* must (surely) have
tu as dû parler }   thou hadst to speak, &c.   [spoken.

The verb *faire* (= to do, to make), is frequently used as an auxiliary, and is also followed (like the above) by the present infinitive: *il a fait faire un habit* (= he has ordered, caused to be made, a coat, *or* he has had a coat made).

---

* In translating into French any sentence in which *shall, will, should, would, may, might* are used, the pupil should be very careful to distinguish whether those words simply express a future or a subjunctive, or whether they express a duty, a strong intention, or a capacity; in the latter case they must be translated literally into French, *shall, should* by **devoir**; *will, would* by **vouloir** and *may, might*, by **pouvoir**, according to the examples given above.

QUESTIONS FOR EXAMINATION.

1. How many kinds of verbs are there?
2. What is an *active* verb?— By what other name is it known?
3. Write the subjunctive present of *aimer, chanter, devoir, rendre*; the past definite of *agir, recevoir, vendre*; the conditional past of *parler* and *bénir*.
4. How is a verb conjugated interrogatively?
5. Remark on the following moods and tenses: the *indicative present*, the *imperfect indicative*, the *future*, the *conditional*, the *imperative*.
6. Conjugate negatively the future simple of *parler, douter, recevoir*; the conditional past of *gémir, devoir, chanter*.
7. Conjugate: 1 interrogatively; 2. interrogatively with a negative, the indicative present of *agir*; the past definite of *devoir*.
8. What are the primitive tenses, and what tenses do they form?
9. Give a list of the idiomatic tenses.

SECTION V.

PASSIVE VERBS.

149. The passive verb expresses an action suffered by the subject: *l'agneau* **a été mangé** *par le loup* (=the lamb has been eaten by the wolf).

Every active verb can become passive, that is to say, it can be employed in the passive form. *Manger* (=to eat) is active in *le chat* **mange** *la souris* (=the cat eats the mouse); it becomes passive in *la souris* **est mangée** *par le chat* (=the mouse is eaten by the cat).

NOTE.—The French seldom use the passive verb. They employ instead the active verb with an indefinite pronoun for subject: **on vend** *le sucre quarante centimes la livre* (=sugar is sold at forty centimes a pound), or they use the reflective verb. (See § 160.)

150. There is only one form of conjugation for the passive verbs; it consists of the auxiliary **être**, followed (in all its moods, tenses, and persons) by the *past participle* of the verb we wish to conjugate: **je suis** *mordu* (=I am bitten); **j'ai été** *mordu* (=I have been bitten); **je serai** *mordu* (=I shall be bitten), etc.

151. Care must be taken to make the past participle *always* agree with the subject of the verb: **il** *est mord***u** (=he is bitten); **elle** *est mordu***e** (=she is bitten); **ils** *sont mordu***s** (=they are bitten), etc.

Conjugation of the Passive Verb ÊTRE AIMÉ
(= to be loved).

INDICATIVE.

PRESENT.

(*I am loved*)

Je suis
tu es } aimé or aimée
il or elle est

nous sommes
vous * êtes } aimés or aimées
ils or elles sont

PAST INDEFINITE.

(*I have been loved*)

J'ai été
tu as été } aimé or aimée
il or elle a été

nous avons été
vous avez été } aimés or aimées
ils or elles ont été

IMPERFECT.

(*I was loved*)

J'étais
tu étais } aimé or aimée
il or elle était

nous étions
vous étiez } aimés or aimées
ils or elles étaient

PLUPERFECT.

(*I had been loved*)

J'avais été
tu avais été } aimé or aimée
il or elle avait été

nous avions été
vous aviez été } aimés or aimées
ils or elles avaient été

PAST DEFINITE.

(*I was loved*)

Je fus
tu fus } aimé or aimée
il or elle fut

nous fûmes
vous fûtes } aimés or aimées
ils or elles furent

PAST ANTERIOR.

(*I had been loved*)

J'eus été
Tu eus été } aimé or aimée
il or elle eut été

nous eûmes été
vous eûtes été } aimés or aimées
ils or elles eurent été

FUTURE.

(*I shall be loved*)

Je serai
tu seras } aimé or aimée
il or elle sera

nous serons
vous serez } aimés or aimées
ils or elles seront

FUTURE ANTERIOR.

(*I shall have been loved*)

J'aurai été
tu auras été } aimé or aimée
il or elle aura été

nous aurons été
vous aurez été } aimés or aimées
ils or elles auront été

* When *vous* (= *you*) is used, out of politeness, instead of *tu* (= *thou*), the past participle remains, of course, in the *singular* either *masculine* or *feminine*.

CONDITIONAL.

PRESENT.
(I should be loved)

Je serais
tu serais } aimé or aimée
il or elle serait
nous serions
vous seriez } aimés or aimées.
ils or elles seraient

ANTERIOR.
(I would have been loved)

J'aurais été
tu aurais été } aimé or aimée
il or elle aurait été
nous aurions été
vous auriez été } aimés or aimées
ils or elles auraient été

IMPERATIVE.

PRESENT.
(Be loved)

Sois aimé or aimée

Soyons } aimés or aimées.
Soyez

PERFECT.
(Have [thou] been loved)

Aie été aimé or aimée

Ayons été } aimés or aimées.
Ayez été

SUBJUNCTIVE.

PRESENT.
(That I may be loved)

Que je sois
que tu sois } aimé or aimée
qu'il or qu'elle soit
que nous soyons
que vous soyez } aimés or aimées
qu'ils or qu'elles soient

PERFECT.
(That I might have been loved)

Que j'aie été
que tu aies été } aimé or aimée
qu'il or qu'elle ait été
que nous ayons été
que vous ayez été } aimés or aimées
qu'ils or qu'elles aient été

IMPERFECT.
(That I might be loved)

Que je fusse
que tu fusses } aimé or aimée
qu'il or qu'elle fût
que nous fussions
que vous fussiez } aimés or aimées
qu'ils or qu'elles fussent

PLUPERFECT.
(That I might have been loved)

Que j'eusse été
que tu eusses été } aimé or aimée
qu'il or qu'elle eût été
que nous eussions été
que vous eussiez été } aimés or aimées
qu'ils or qu'elles eussent été

INFINITIVE.

PRESENT.
(To be loved)
Être aimé or aimée

PERFECT.
(To have been loved)
Avoir été aimé or aimée.

PARTICIPLE PRESENT.
(Being loved)
Étant aimé or aimée

PERFECT.
(Having been loved)
Ayant été aimé or aimée.

PAST (VARIABLE).
Aimé, fem. aimée (loved).

Exercise 32.

Write *affirmatively* in the passive voice: the indicative present of *aimer, recevoir, vendre, finir;* the subjunctive present of *travailler, devoir, répandre, définir.*

Write *negatively* in the same voice: the imperfect subjunctive of *concevoir, répandre, éblouir, montrer;* the conditional present of *entendre, critiquer, obéir, concevoir.*

Write *interrogatively* in the same voice: the perfect definite of *consoler, nourrir, apercevoir, confondre;* the future anterior of *rendre, décevoir, munir, tourmenter.*

Write *interrogatively with a negative* in the same voice: the pluperfect indicative of *tromper, désobéir, recevoir, rendre;* the conditional past of *décevoir, obéir, blâmer, fondre.*

QUESTIONS FOR EXAMINATION.

1. What is a *passive* verb?
2. Describe the formation of a passive verb.
3. How many conjugations of passive verbs are there?
4. Remark on the participle of passive verbs.
5. Write the subjunctive present, the conditional past, and the future anterior of the passive verbs: *être trompé, être béni, être reçu, être battu.*
6. What do the French often use instead of the passive verb?

SECTION VI.

NEUTER VERBS.

152. A **neuter** verb is one which expresses the state or the action of the subject, but which has no direct complement or object: *Je tombe* (= I fall), *nous languissons* (= we languish).

The neuter verb is also called *intransitive,* because it does not transmit the action to a complement.

153. The *simple* tenses of the neuter verbs are the same as those of the active ones. The compound tenses of the neuter verbs are formed, sometimes with the help of the auxiliary **être**: *Je suis arrivé* (= I have arrived), sometimes with the help of the auxiliary **avoir**: *j'ai dormi* (= I have slept).

There are only twelve neuter verbs which are conjugated with the auxiliary **être**. They are the following: *aller* (= to go); *arriver* (= to arrive); *décéder* (= to die); *échoir* (= to fall due); *éclore* (= to be hatched); *entrer* (= to enter); *mourir* (= to die); *naître* (= to be born); *partir* (= to go away); *sortir* (= to go out); *tomber* (= to fall, and its compound *retomber* = to fall again); *venir* (= to come, and its compounds: *devenir* [= to become]; *intervenir* [= to interfere]; *parvenir* [= to succeed]; *revenir* [= to come back]; *survenir* [= to arrive unexpectedly]).

154. When the neuter verbs are conjugated with the auxiliary **être**, the participle always agrees with the subject or nominative: **il** *est arrivé* (= he has arrived), **elle** *est arrivée* (= she has arrived), **ils** *sont arrivés* (= they have arrived), etc.

Conjugation of the verb **TOMBER** (= *to fall*).
Stem, **tomb** ; *termination*, **er**.

INDICATIVE.

PRESENT.
(*I fall*)
Je tombe
tu tombes
il *or* elle tombe
nous tomb**ons**
vous tombez
ils *or* elles tomb**ent**

PERFECT.
(*I have fallen*)
Je suis ⎫
tu es ⎬ tombé *or* tombée
il *or* elle est ⎭
nous sommes ⎫
vous êtes ⎬ tombés *or*
ils *or* elles sont ⎭ tombées

IMPERFECT.
(*I was falling*)
Je tomb**ais**
tu tomb**ais**
il *or* elle tomb**ait**
nous tomb**ions**
vous tomb**iez**
ils *or* elles tomb**aient**

PLUPERFECT.
(*I had fallen*)
J'étais ⎫
tu étais ⎬ tombé *or*
il *or* elle était ⎭ tombée
nous étions ⎫
vous étiez ⎬ tombés *or*
ils *or* elles étaient ⎭ tombées

PAST DEFINITE.
(*I fell*)
Je tombai
tu tombas
il *or* elle tomba
nous tombâmes
vous tombâtes
ils *or* elles tomb**èrent**

PAST ANTERIOR.
(*I had fallen*)
Je fus ⎫
tu fus ⎬ tombé *or* tombée
il *or* elle fut ⎭
nous fûmes ⎫
vous fûtes ⎬ tombés *or*
ils *or* elles furent ⎭ tombées

FUTURE.
(I shall fall)
Je tomberai
tu tomberas
il *or* elle tombera
nous tomberons
vous tomberez
ils *or* elles tomberont.

FUTURE ANTERIOR.
(I shall have fallen)
Je serai ⎫
tu seras ⎬ tombé *or* tombée
il *or* elle sera ⎭
nous serons ⎫
vous serez ⎬ tombés *or* tombées
ils *or* elles seront ⎭

CONDITIONAL.

PRESENT.
(I should fall)
Je tomberais
tu tomberais
il *or* elle tomberait
nous tomberions
vous tomberiez
ils *or* elles tomberaient.

ANTERIOR.
(I should have fallen)
Je serais ⎫
tu serais ⎬ tombé *or* tombée
il *or* elle serait ⎭
nous serions ⎫
vous seriez ⎬ tombés *or* tombées
ils *or* elles seraient ⎭

IMPERATIVE.

PRESENT.
Fall [thou]
· · · · ·
Tombe
· · · · ·
tombons
tombez
· · · · ·

PERFECT.
(Have [thou] fallen)
· · · · ·
Sois tombé *or* tombée
· · · · ·
soyons ⎱ tombés *or* tombées.
soyez ⎰
· · · · ·

SUBJUNCTIVE.

PRESENT.
(That I may fall)
Que je tombe
que tu tombes
qu'il *or* qu'elle tombe
que nous tombions
que vous tombiez
qu'ils *or* qu'elles tombent.

PERFECT.
(That I may have fallen)
Que je sois ⎫
que tu sois ⎬ tombé *or* tombée
qu'il *or* qu'elle soit ⎭
que nous soyons ⎫
que vous soyez ⎬ tombés *or* tombées
qu'ils *or* qu'elles soient ⎭

IMPERFECT.
(That I might fall)
Que je tombasse
que tu tombasses
qu'il *or* qu'elle tombât
que nous tombassions
que vous tombassiez
qu'ils *or* qu'elles tombassent.

PLUPERFECT.
(That I might have fallen)
Que je fusse ⎫
que tu fusses ⎬ tombé *or* tombée
qu'il *or* qu'elle fût ⎭
que nous fussions ⎫
que vous fussiez ⎬ tombés *or* tombées
qu'ils *or* qu'elles fussent ⎭

INFINITIVE.

PRESENT.
(To fall)
Tomber

PERFECT.
(To have fallen)
Être tombé *or* tombée.

PARTICIPLE PRESENT.
(Falling)
Tombant

PERFECT.
(Having fallen)
Étant tombé *or* tombée.

PAST (VARIABLE).
Tombé, *fem.* tombée *(fallen).*

QUESTIONS FOR EXAMINATION.

1. What is a *neuter* verb?
2. Under what other name is it known?
3. How are the compound tenses of neuter verbs formed?
4. Name the neuter verbs conjugated with the auxiliary *être.*
5. Remark on the past participle of neuter verbs conjugated with the auxiliary *être.*
6. Write out the subjunctive present of *tomber*, negatively; and the conditional past of the same verb interrogatively.

SECTION VII.

REFLEXIVE VERBS.

155. Whenever the subject at the same time performs and bears the action, as *je me mords, je me flatte* (=I bite myself, I flatter myself), the verb is called **reflexive**, because the action which the subject performs is likewise *reflected* by it.

This verb has likewise been called *pronominal*, on account of its being conjugated with two pronouns.

156. Reflexive verbs are divided into two classes: 1. The verbs reflexive by nature, *s'écrouler* (=to fall to pieces); *se cabrer* (=to rear); *s'évanouir* (=to faint). 2. The active verbs, as *laver* (=to wash), or neuter verbs, as *nuire* (=to injure), employed in a reflexive form: *je me suis lavé* (=I have washed myself); *je me suis nui* (=I have injured myself).

157. Reflexive verbs are conjugated in all tenses with two pronouns, viz., the *subject* **je**, and the *complement* **me**; these pronouns must always belong to the same person, because the action is both performed and suffered by the subject: *je* **me** *lave, tu* **te** *nuis,* etc.

158. The compound tenses of reflexive verbs are formed with the auxiliary *être*.

159. When the verb is reflexive by nature, the participle agrees: *ils se sont repent***is** (=they have repented);* when, on the other hand, the verb is only used reflexively, the participle agrees, if the verb is active, and *preceded by its direct object: ils se sont aim***és** (=they have loved one another); but it remains invariable, if the verb is neuter: *elles se sont pl***u** (=they have pleased one another); or if the verb, being active, is *followed by its direct object: ils se sont* **dit** *des injures* (=they have insulted each other).

160. The reflexive verb is often used in French, when the passive is used in English: *Le sucre* **se vend** *quarante centimes la livre* (=sugar is sold at forty centimes a pound); *ce légume* **se mange** *cru* (=this vegetable is eaten raw, uncooked).

Conjugation of the Reflexive Verb SE REPOSER
(= to rest).

Stem, **repos**; termination, **er**.

INDICATIVE.

PRESENT.

(I rest)

Je me repose
tu te reposes
il *or* elle se repose
nous nous reposons
vous vous reposez
ils *or* elles se reposent

PAST INDEFINITE.

(I have rested)

Je me suis ⎫ reposé or
tu t'es ⎬
il *or* elle s'est ⎭ reposée

nous nous sommes ⎫ reposés or
vous vous êtes ⎬
ils *or* elles se sont ⎭ reposées

IMPERFECT.

(I was resting)

Je me reposais
tu te reposais
il *or* elle se reposait
nous nous reposions
vous vous reposiez
ils *or* elles se reposaient

PLUPERFECT.

(I had rested)

Je m'étais ⎫ reposé or
tu t'étais ⎬
il *or* elle s'était ⎭ reposée

nous nous étions ⎫ reposés or
vous vous étiez ⎬
ils *or* elles s'étaient ⎭ reposées

---

* The reflexive verb *s'arroger* (=to assume [for oneself]) is an exception to the rule, as the personal pronoun is always the *indirect object*.

REFLEXIVE VERBS.

PAST DEFINITE.
(I rested)

Je me reposa**i**
tu te reposa**s**
il *or* elle se repos**a**
nous nous repos**âmes**
vous vous repos**âtes**
ils *or* elles se repos**èrent**

PAST ANTERIOR.
(I had rested)

Je me fus ⎫
tu te fus ⎬ reposé *or*
il *or* elle se fut ⎭ reposée

nous nous fûmes ⎫
vous vous fûtes ⎬ reposées *or*
ils *or* elles se furent ⎭ reposéos

FUTURE.
(I shall rest)

Je me reposer**ai**
tu te reposer**as**
il *or* elle se reposer**a**
nous nous reposer**ons**
vous vous reposer**ez**
ils *or* elles se reposer**ont**

FUTURE ANTERIOR.
(I shall have rested)

Je me serai ⎫
tu te seras ⎬ reposé *or*
il *or* elle sera ⎭ reposée

nous nous serons ⎫
vous vous serez ⎬ reposés *or*
ils *or* elles se seront ⎭ reposées

CONDITIONAL.

PRESENT.
(I should rest)

Je me repos *er* **ais**
tu te repos *er* **ais**
il *or* elle se repos *er* **ait**
nous nous repos *er* **ions**
vous vous repos *er* **iez**
ils *or* elles se repos *er* **aient**

ANTERIOR.
(I should have rested)

Je me serais ⎫
tu te serais ⎬ reposé *or*
il *or* elle se serait ⎭ reposée

nous nous serions ⎫
vous vous seriez ⎬ reposés *or*
ils *or* elles se seraient ⎭ reposées

IMPERATIVE.

PRESENT.
(Rest)

. . . . . .
Repose-toi
. . . . . .
repos**ons**-nous
repos**ez**-vous
. . . . . .

PERFECT.

(Never used.)

SUBJUNCTIVE.

PRESENT.
(That I may rest)

Que je me repose
que tu te repos**es**
qu'il *or* qu'elle se repose
que nous nous repos**ions**
que vous vous repos**iez**
qu'ils *or* qu'elles se repos**ent**

PERFECT.
(That I may have rested)

Que je me sois ⎫
que tu te sois ⎬ reposé
qu'il *or* qu'elle se soit ⎭ *or* reposée

que nous nous soyons ⎫
que vous vous soyez ⎬ reposés *or* reposées
qu'ils *or* qu'elles se soient ⎭

IMPERFECT.

(That I might rest)
Que je me reposasse
que tu te reposasses
qu'il *or* qu'elle se reposât
que nous nous reposassions
que vous vous reposassiez
qu'ils *or* qu'elles se reposassent

PLUPERFECT.

(That I might have rested)
Que je me fusse ⎫ reposé
que tu te fusses ⎬ *or*
qu'il *or* qu'elle se fût ⎭ reposée
que nous nous fussions
que vous vous fussiez ⎫ reposés
qu'ils *or* qu'elles se fussent ⎭ *or* reposées

INFINITIVE.

PRESENT.
(To rest)
Se reposer

PERFECT.
(To have rested)
S'être reposé *or* reposée.

PARTICIPLE PRESENT.
(Resting).
Se reposant

PERFECT.
(Having rested)
S'étant reposé *or* reposée

PAST (VARIABLE).
Reposé, *fem.* reposée *(rested).*

☞ *The interrogative and negative conjugation of reflexive verbs will be found at page* 164.

QUESTIONS FOR EXAMINATION.

1. Define a *reflexive* verb.
2. Under what other name is it known?
3. Describe the various classes of reflexive verbs.
4. What auxiliary is used in the compound tenses of reflexive verbs?
5. For what purpose do the French often use the reflexive verb?
6. Write the future anterior, the past indefinite, and the imperfect subjunctive of the verb *se reposer*.

Exercise 33.

Indicatif présent.—Je m'habille. Il ne se repose pas. Vous vous tourmentez en vain. Ils se baignent tous les étés.

Imparfait.—Je me proposais de vous écrire. Votre frère ne s'imaginait-il pas que vous aviez tort? Nous ne nous abonnions pas au cabinet de lecture.

Parfait défini.—Je ne me fâchai jamais sans motif. Nous enorgueillîmes-nous de cet avantage? Vous ne vous dépêchâtes pas.

Futur.—T'apercevras-tu de son dessein? Il s'empressera de le faire. Ne nous acquitterons-nous pas de nos compliments? Elles s'enrhumeront.

Conditionnel présent.—Je ne me déciderais jamais aussi imprudemment. Ne s'appliquerait-elle pas au dessin? Votre sœur ne se tromperait-elle pas? Ces élèves ne s'habitueraient pas au travail.

Impératif.—Repose-toi. Dépêchons-nous. Attendez-vous à recevoir de nos nouvelles? Ne nous fatiguons pas trop.

Subjonctif présent.—Il désire que je me porte mieux. Qu'il ne s'amuse pas à mes dépens. Que nous nous précipitions dans le danger. Que ces fleurs ne se flétrissent pas.

Imparfait.—J'exigeais que tu te nourrisses avec soin. Que nous nous détournassions du droit chemin. Que vous vous confondissiez en excuses. Qu'ils ne s'enorgueillissent pas d'un avantage insignifiant.

Infinitif.—Ne se reposer qu'à de longs intervalles. Ne s'être jamais trompé.

Participes.—Ne me fiant qu'à un honnête homme, je ne crois m'être aperçu d'aucune fraude.

Temps composés.—Je me suis esquivé. Tu ne t'étais pas rendu à discrétion. Elle ne se fut pas réjouie de cette nouvelle. Vous seriez-vous dégradés dans l'opinion publique? Que je me sois décidé à rester. Que tu ne te fusses pas égaré dans la forêt. Que cette propriété ne se fut pas vendue si cher.

[1] se rendre, [2] raison (f.), [3] jouir de, [4] santé (f.), [5] s'enorgueillir, [6] léger avantage (m.), [7] s'offenser, [8] de poisson, [9] se détromper, [10] s'emparer, [11] en vain, [12] se réunir, [13] se réjouir de, [14] se précipiter, [15] fortune (f.), [16] se tromper, [17] s'égarer, [18] se rétracter, [19] s'apercevoir de, [20] s'évanouir, [21] s'esquiver, [22] se recueillir, [23] surprenant, [24] s'acquitter de, [25] avouer, [26] se condamner, [27] se moquer de, [28] se décider, [29] se déshonorer, [30] se vanter.

Indicative present.—I yield[1] to his reasons.[2] Dost thou not enjoy[3] better health[4]? We trust an honest man.

Imperfect.—He boasted[5] of a trifling advantage.[6] Were you not offended[7]? They feed on fish.[8]

Perfect definite.—She undeceived[9] herself. Thou didst not perceive my plan. They took possession[10] of the farm.

Future.—I shall subscribe to the circulating library. He will torment himself uselessly.[11] You will not meet[12] here.

Conditional present.—Thou wouldst catch cold. We should rejoice at[13] your success. They would rush[14] into (the) danger (m.).

Imperative.—Make haste. Let us not trust too much to his good luck.[15] Do not make a mistake.[16]

Subjunctive present.—That I may not lose myself[17] in the wood. That she may not retract.[18] That we may not wound ourselves.

Imperfect.—That thou might perceive[19] the force of this argument. That she might not faint away.[20] That they might steal away.[21]

Infinitive.—To collect one's thoughts²³ is often necessary. To have perceived this error is not wonderful.²³

Participles.—Going to Paris, I shall perform²⁴ your commissions with pleasure. Having made a mistake, he confessed ²⁵ it.

Compound tenses.—I have condemned ²⁶ myself. Thou hadst not trusted thy father. We shall not have laughed at ²⁷ him. You would not have made up your mind ²⁸ to remain. That they may have disgraced ²⁹ themselves. That I might have boasted³⁰ of it.

SECTION VIII.

IMPERSONAL VERBS.

161. An **impersonal** verb expresses an action which cannot be ascribed to any special subject or *person*, such as the verbs *neiger* (= to snow), and *pleuvoir* (= to rain).

162. Impersonal verbs are used only in the third person singular, and are preceded by the pronoun **il**, which refers to no subject, and has merely a vague and indefinite sense.

The pronoun *il* of the impersonal verbs is not the same as the pronoun *il* of the active verbs; this latter one stands for a distinct person; the former signifies *cela* (= that), and has only a vague, indeterminate sense.

163. Besides the verbs which are naturally impersonal (as *il pleut, il neige*), we can employ both active and neuter verbs impersonally: *Il tombe de l'eau* (= water is falling); *il fait beau* (= the weather is fine); *il convient d'obéir* (= it is proper to obey), etc.

These verbs having *only one person*, are called *unipersonal*.

Conjugation of the Impersonal Verb NEIGER (= *to snow*).

Stem, **neig**; *termination* **er**.

INDICATIVE.

PRESENT.
Il neige (*it snows*)

PAST INDEFINITE.
Il a neigé (*it has snowed*).

IMPERFECT.
Il neigeait (*it was snowing*)

PLUPERFECT.
Il avait neigé (*it had snowed*).

PAST DEFINITE.   PAST ANTERIOR.
Il neigea (*it snowed*)   Il eut neigé (*it had snowed*).

FUTURE.   FUTURE ANTERIOR.
Il neigera (*it will snow*)   Il aura neigé (*it will have snowed*).

CONDITIONAL.

PRESENT.   ANTERIOR.
Il neigerait (*it would snow*)   Il aurait neigé (*it would have snowed*).

SUBJUNCTIVE.

PRESENT.   PERFECT.
Qu'il neige (*that it may snow*)   Qu'il ait neigé (*that it may have snowed*).

IMPERFECT.   PLUPERFECT.
Qu'il neigeât (*that it might snow*)   Qu'il eût neigé (*that it might have snowed*).

INFINITIVE.

PRESENT.   PERFECT.
Neiger (*to snow*)   Avoir neigé (*to have snowed*).

PARTICIPLE PAST (INVARIABLE).
Neigé (*snowed*).

NOTE the use of *avoir* with the adverb **y** (=there), as an impersonal verb:

Present Ind.—Il **y** a (= there is), etc.

SECTION IX.

IRREGULAR AND DEFECTIVE VERBS.

164. Every verb is called *irregular* which, in the formation of its simple tenses, deviates from the rules we have explained above.

165. A verb may be irregular in one of two ways. 1. It may lack one or more of the moods, tenses, or persons of regular verbs, and then it is called a *defective verb* (from the Latin *defectivus* = defective, imperfect); or, 2. It may possess all these moods, tenses, or persons, but at the same time vary, so far as their formation is concerned, from the prescribed rules; it is, then, an *irregular verb* properly so called.

The main characteristic which distinguishes the regular from the irregular verbs, is that in the former the stem remains invariable, whilst the endings *alone* change with the moods, tenses, and persons: *chant-er, chant-ons, chant-erai*; whereas, in the irregular verbs the stem is not uniformly written throughout all the tenses of the conjugation: *ten-ir, je* **tiens**; *voul-oir, veuillez, je* **veux**; *sav-oir,* **sus, sache,** etc.

1. First conjugation: ER.

166. Verbs like *mener* (=to lead), *lever* (=to raise), which have a mute *e* in the last syllable but one, take a grave accent over that *e* whenever it is followed by a mute syllable: *je mène* (=I lead), *il lèvera* (=he will raise). See § 24.

Most verbs, however, in *eler, eter,* like *appeler* (=to call), *jeter* (=to throw), double the **l** or **t** : *j'appelle* (=I call), *il jette* (=he throws). See § 24.

But *acheter* (=to buy), *celer* (=to conceal), *geler* (=to freeze), *modeler* (=to fashion), *peler* (=to peel), etc., take the grave accent, *j'achète* (=I buy), *il pèlera* (=he will peel).

The verbs having a close *é* before the final syllable change it into an open *è* before a consonant followed by an *e* mute, as *céder* (=to yield), *je cède* (=I yield), but those ending in *éger* keep the close *é*, as *protéger* (=to protect), *il me protége* (=he protects me).

167. The verbs ending in **cer** and **ger**, such as *percer* (=to pierce), *tracer* (=to trace), *manger* (=to eat), *loger* (=to lodge), keep their *c* and *g* soft before *a* and *o*, the former by taking a cedilla under the *c*: *nous perçons* (=we pierce), *il traça* (=he traced), the latter by adding an *e* mute after the *g*: *nous mangeons* (=we eat), *nous logeons* (=we lodge).

168. Verbs ending in **yer** change *y* into *i* before *e* mute: *essuyer* (=to wipe), *j'essuie* (=I wipe), *envoyer* (=to send), *ils envoient* (=they send).

For verbs ending in **ayer**, like *payer* (=to pay), *balayer* (=to sweep), the change is optional, but the *y* is more generally retained: *je paye* (=I pay).

169. The first conjugation has really only two irregular verbs: *aller* (= to go), and *envoyer* (= to send).

Aller (= to go).

Prim. Tenses.	Aller, allant, allé, je vais, j'allai.
Ind. Pres.	Je vais, tu vas, il *or* elle va, nous allons, vous allez, ils *or* elles vont.
Imperf.	J'allais, etc., nous allions, etc.
Past Def.	J'allai, tu allas, il *or* elle alla, nous allâmes, vous allâtes, ils *or* elles allèrent.
Fut.	J'irai, tu iras, il *or* elle ira, nous irons, vous irez, ils *or* elles iront.
Cond. Pres.	J'irais, tu irais, il *or* elle irait, nous irions, vous iriez, ils *or* elles iraient.
Imper.	Va, allons, allez.
Subj. Pres.	Que j'aille, etc., que nous allions, que vous alliez, qu'ils *or* qu'elles aillent.
Imperf.	Que j'allasse, etc., que nous allassions, etc.
Infin.	Aller.
Part.	Allant, allé.

Conjugated with the auxiliary **être**.

S'en aller (= to go away) is conjugated in the same manner:—

Je m'en vais, tu t'en vas, etc. The compound tenses, *je m'en suis allé, que je m'en fusse allé,* etc., ought to be thoroughly acquired by the pupils.

Envoyer (= to send).

Prim. Tenses. Envoyer, envoyant, envoyé, j'envoie, j'envoyai.
Future. J'enverrai; *conditional,* j'enverrais.

Conjugated with the auxiliary **avoir**.

2. Second conjugation in IR with Imperfect in ISSAIS.

170. This conjugation has but one irregular verb, and that only in the past participle. It is the verb **bénir**, the past participle of which can be spelt, according to the meaning, *bénit* or *béni: bénit*, in the case of things consecrated by the church, and *béni* in all other instances: *pain bénit* (= consecrated bread), *nation bénie* (= blessed nation).

Fleurir (= to blossom, to flourish), has two forms, the one regular, *fleurissais, fleurissant;* the other irregular, *florissais, florissant;—florissais, florissant* are the remains of the old verb *florir*.

Haïr (= to hate) takes no diæresis in the indicative present singular, and in the imperative (second person singular): *je hais, tu hais, il hait; hais.*

3. Second (direct) conjugation in IR.

171. We have seen (§ 131) that there are two regular conjugations in **ir**: the one (consisting of more than three hundred verbs) which places **iss** between the stem and the termination (*fin*-**iss**-*ais*); the other (composed only of about twenty verbs) which merely adds the simple termination *directly* to the stem (*je sent*-**ais**); we have left this latter one entirely aside in studying the formation of the simple tenses; we shall now study in detail each one of the verbs of which it consists, and we designate this conjugation by the name of *direct* conjugation in **ir**.

172. The verbs constituting the direct conjugation in **ir** are divided into three classes, according to the form of their past definite; *dormir* (= to sleep), *courir* (= to run), and *tenir* (= to hold), have for their respective past definites: *je dorm*-**is**, *je cour*-**us**, *je* **tins**. Accordingly, the first class comprises all the verbs whose past definite is in **is**, the second is characterised by the ending of the same tense in **us**, and the third forms the past definite with the help of the root of the verb: *ten*-**ir**, *je tin*-**s**, *ven*-**ir**, *je vin*-**s**.

The irregular verbs of the second conjugation are as follows:—

Acquérir (= to acquire).

Prim. Tenses. Acquérir, acquérant, acquis, j'acquiers, j'acquis.
Ind. Pres. J'acquiers, tu acquiers, il *or* elle acquiert, nous acquérons, vous acquérez, ils *or* elles acquièrent.
Imperf. J'acquérais, etc., nous acquérions, etc.
Past Def. J'acquis, etc., nous acquîmes, etc.
Fut. J'acquerrai, tu acquerras, il *or* elle acquerra, nous acquerrons, vous acquerrez, ils *or* elles acquerront.
Cond. Pres. J'acquerrais, etc., nous acquerrions, etc.

I

Imper.   Acquiers, acquérons, acquérez.
Subj. Pres.   Que j'acquière, que tu acquières, qu'il *or* qu'elle acquière, que nous acquérions, que vous acquériez, qu'ils *or* qu'elles acquièrent.
Imperf.   Que j'acquisse, etc., que nous acquissions, etc.
Infin.   Acquérir.
Part.   Acquérant, acquis, acquise.

Conjugated with the auxiliary **avoir**.

Acquérir, *mourir* and *courir* have for their future respectively, acquerrai, mourrai, courrai; as *saillir* has in the future *saillera*, side by side with *saillira*, so, instead of *acquerirai*, *mourirai*, *courirai*, the old French had *acquérerai*, *mourerai*, *courerai*; then, later on, the *e* mute disappeared, and the contracted forms acquerrai, mourrai, courrai, prevailed. This explains also why the two r's must be pronounced strongly.

Bouillir (= to boil).

Prim. Tenses. Bouillir, bouillant, bouilli, je bous, je bouillis.
Ind. Pres.   Je bous, tu bous, il *or* elle bout, nous bouillons, vous bouillez, ils *or* elles bouillent.
Imperf.   Je bouillais, etc., nous bouillions, etc.
Past Def.   Je bouillis, etc., nous bouillîmes, etc.
Fut.   Je bouillirai, etc., nous bouillirons, etc.
Cond. Pres.   Je bouillirais, nous bouillirions, etc.
Imp.   Bous, bouillons, bouillez.
Subj. Pres.   Que je bouille, que tu bouilles, qu'il *or* qu'elle bouille, que nous bouillions, que vous bouilliez, qu'ils *or* qu'elles bouillent.
Imperf.   Que je bouillisse, etc., que nous bouillissions, etc.
Infin.   Bouillir.
Part.   Bouillant, bouilli, bouillie.

Conjugated with the auxiliary verb **avoir**.

N.B.—*Bouillir* is essentially a neuter verb, and *to boil*, used actively, is rendered by the verb *faire* (= to make) and *bouillir*, as : boil these vegetables = **faites bouillir** ces *légumes*.

Courir (= to run).

Prim. Tenses. Courir, courant, couru, je cours, je courus.
Ind. Pres.   Je cours, tu cours, il *or* elle court, nous courons, vous courez, ils *or* elles courent.
Imperf.   Je courais, etc., nous courions, etc.
Past Def.   Je courus, etc., nous courûmes, etc.
Fut.   Je courrai, tu courras, il *or* elle courra, nous courrons, vous courrez, ils *or* elles courront.
Cond. Pres.   Je courrais, etc., nous courrions, etc.
Imp.   Cours, courons, courez.

IRREGULAR AND DEFECTIVE VERBS. 115

Subj. Pres.	Que je coure, que tu coures, qu'il *or* qu'elle coure, que nous courions, que vous couriez qu'ils *or* qu'elles courent.
Imperf.	Que je courusse, etc., que nous courussions, etc.
Infin.	Courir.
Part.	Courant, couru, courue.

Conjugated with the auxiliary **avoir.**

Besides *courir*, the old French had also the form *courre*, which still exists in the expression *chasse à courre* (*chassé à courir* = hunting); for the future *courrai*, see above, *acquérir*.

Couvrir (=to cover).

Prim. Tenses. Couvrir, couvrant, couvert, je couvre, je couvris.
See *offrir*. *Conjugated with the auxiliary* **avoir.**

Cueillir (=to pluck).

Prim. Tenses. Cueillir, cueillant, cueilli, je cueille, je cueillis.

Ind. Pres.	Je cueille, tu cueilles, il *or* elle cueille, nous cueillons, vous cueillez, ils *or* elles cueillent.
Imperf.	Je cueillais, etc., nous cueillions, etc.
Past Def.	Je cueillis, etc., nous cueillimes, etc.
Fut.	Je cueillerai, etc., nous cueillerons, etc.
Cond. Pres.	Je cueillerais, etc., nous cueillerions, etc.
Imper.	Cueille, cueillons, cueillez.
Sub. Pres.	Que je cueille, etc., que nous cueillions, etc.
Imperf.	Que je cueillisse, etc., que nous cueillissions, etc.
Infin.	Cueillir.
Part.	Cueillant, cueilli, cueillie.

Conjugated with the auxiliary **avoir.**
For the future *cueillerai*, see *acquérir*.

Dormir (=to sleep).

Prim. Tenses. Dormir, dormant, dormi, je dors, je dormis.
See *mentir*. *Conjugated with the auxiliary* **avoir.**

Faillir (=to fail).

Several tenses of this verb, such as the *Indicative Present, Imperfect, and Future,* are seldom used.

Prim. Tenses. Faillir, faillant, failli, je faux, je faillis.

Ind. Pres.	Je faux, tu faux, il *or* elle faut, nous faillons, vous faillez, ils *or* elles faillent.
Imperf.	Je faillais, tu faillais, il *or* elle faillait, nous faillions, vous failliez, ils *or* elles faillaient.
Past Def.	Je faillis, etc., nous faillimes, etc.

116 IRREGULAR AND DEFECTIVE VERBS.

Fut.	Je faillirai, etc., nous faillirons, etc.
Cond. Pres.	Je faillirais, etc., nous faillirions, etc.
Imper.	Faille, . . faillez.
Subj. Pres.	Que je faille, etc., que nous faillions, etc.
Imperf.	Que je faillisse, etc., que nous faillissions, etc.
Infin.	Faillir.
Part.	Faillant, failli.

Conjugated with the auxiliary **avoir**.

The first three persons of the singular, *je faux, tu faux, il faut* have fallen almost entirely into disuse; the expression is, however, still met with: *le cœur me faut* (*me manque*) = my heart fails me. The *Pres. Part.* also is obsolete.

Férir (= to strike) has preserved only the past participle *féru*.

It survives in the expression *sans coup férir* (= without striking a blow): *d'Harcourt prit Turin sans coup férir* (= d'Harcourt took Turin without striking a blow).

Fuir (= to flee).

Prim. Tenses.	Fuir, fuyant, fui, je fuis, je fuis.
Ind. Pres.	Je fuis, tu fuis, il *or* elle fuit, nous fuyons, vous fuyez, ils *or* elles fuient.
Imperf.	Je fuyais, etc., nous fuyions, etc.
Past Def.	Je fuis, etc., nous fuîmes, etc.
Fut.	Je fuirai, etc., nous fuirons, etc.
Cond. Pres.	Je fuirais, etc., nous fuirions, etc.
Imper.	Fuis, fuyons, fuyez.
Subj. Pres.	Que je fuie, etc., que nous fuyions, que vous fuyiez, qu'ils *or* qu'elles fuient.
Imperf.	Que je fuisse, etc., que nous fuissions, etc.
Infin.	Fuir.
Part.	Fuyant, fui, fuie.

Conjugated with the auxiliary **avoir**.

Gésir (*être couché* = to lie down).

This verb is no longer used in the infinitive; the following are the only parts employed: Il gît, nous gisons, il gisent; il gisait, gisant. *Ci-gît* (= here lies) is used in epitaphs.

Mentir (= to tell lies).

Prim. Tenses.	Mentir, mentant, menti, je mens, je mentis.
Ind. Pres.	Je mens, tu mens, il *or* elle ment, nous mentons, vous mentez, ils *or* elles mentent.
Imperf.	Je mentais, etc., nous mentions, etc.
Past Def.	Je mentis, etc., nous mentîmes, etc.
Fut.	Je mentirai, etc., nous mentirons, etc.

IRREGULAR AND DEFECTIVE VERBS. 117

Cond. Pres.   Je mentirais, etc., nous mentirions, etc.
Imper.   Mens, mentons, mentez.
Subj. Pres.   Que je mente, etc., que nous mentions, etc.
Imperf.   Que je mentisse, etc., que nous mentissions, etc.
Infin.   Mentir.
Part.   Mentant, menti.

Conjugated with the auxiliary **avoir.**

Mourir (= to die).

Prim. Tenses. Mourir, mourant, mort, je meurs, je mourus.

Indic. Pres.   Je meurs, tu meurs, il *or* elle meurt, nous mourons, vous mourez, ils *or* elles meurent.
Imperf.   Je mourais, etc., nous mourions, etc.
Past Def.   Je mourus, etc., nous mourûmes, etc.
Fut.   Je mourrai, etc., nous mourrons, etc.
Cond. Pres.   Je mourrais, etc., nous mourrions, etc.
Imper.   Meurs, mourons, mourez.
Subj. Pres.   Que je meure, etc., que nous mourions, que vous mouriez, qu'ils meurent.
Imperf.   Que je mourusse, etc., que nous mourussions, etc.
Infin.   Mourir.
Part.   Mourant, mort, morte.

Conjugated with the auxiliary **être.**

For the future *mourrai*, see above *acquérir*.

Offrir (= to offer).

Prim. Tenses. Offrir, offrant, offert, j'offre, j'offris.

Ind. Pres.   J'offre, tu offres, il *or* elle offre, nous offrons, vous offrez, ils *or* elles offrent.
Imperf.   J'offrais, etc., nous offrions, etc.
Past Def.   J'offris, etc., nous offrîmes, etc.
Fut.   J'offrirai, etc., nous offrirons, etc.
Cond. Pres.   J'offrirais, etc., nous offririons, etc.
Imper.   Offre, offrons, offrez.
Subj. Pres.   Que j'offre, etc., que nous offrions, etc.
Imperf.   Que j'offrisse, etc., que nous offrissions, etc.
Infin.   Offrir.
Part.   Offrant, offert, offerte.

Conjugated with the auxiliary **avoir.**

Ouïr (= to hear).

This verb is used only in the *Inf. Pres.*, ouïr; the *Part. Past,* ouï; the *Past Def.*, j'ouïs, tu ouïs, etc.; the *Imperf. Subj.* que j'ouïsse, que tu ouïsses, etc. *Conjugated with the auxiliary* **avoir.**

The past participle subsists in law language: *ouïe la lecture de l'arrêt (la lecture de l'arrêt entendue)* = the reading of the sentence being heard.

Ouvrir (= to open).

Prim. Tenses. Ouvrir, ouvrant, ouvert, j'ouvre, j'ouvris.
　See *offrir*. *Conjugated with the auxiliary* **avoir**.

Partir (= to set out).

Prim. Tenses. Partir, partant, parti, je pars, je partis.
　See *mentir*. *Conjugated with the auxiliary* **être**.

Saillir (= to jump, to gush) is conjugated like *finir*, but when it means *to jut out* it has :—

Prim. Tenses. Saillir, saillant, sailli, il saille, and the future is *saillera*.
　See *tressaillir*. *Conjugated with the auxiliary* **avoir**.

Sentir (= to feel).

Prim. Tenses. Sentir, sentant, senti, je sens, je sentis.
　See *mentir*. *Conjugated with the auxiliary* **avoir**.

Servir (= to serve).

Prim. Tenses. Servir, servant, servi, je sers, je servis
　See *mentir*. *Conjugated with the auxiliary* **avoir**.

Sortir (= to go out).

Prim. Tenses. Sortir, sortant, sorti, je sors, je sortis.
　See *mentir*. *Conjugated with the auxiliary* **être**.

Souffrir (= to suffer).

Prim. Tenses. Souffrir, souffrant, souffert, je souffre, je souffris.
　See *offrir*. *Conjugated with the auxiliary* **avoir**.

Tenir (= to hold).

Prim. Tenses. Tenir, tenant, tenu, je tiens, je tins.
　See *venir*. *Conjugated with the auxiliary* **avoir**.

Tressaillir (= to start).

Prim. Tenses. Tressaillir, tressaillant, tressailli, je tressaille, je tressaillis.
Ind. Pres.　Je tressaille, tu tressailles, il tressaille, nous tressaillons, vous tressaillez, ils tressaillent.
Imperf.　Je tressaillais, etc., nous tressaillions, etc.
Past Def.　Je tressaillis, etc., nous tressaillîmes, etc.
Fut.　Je tressaillirai, etc., nous tressaillirons, etc.
Cond. Pres.　Je tressaillirais, etc., nous tressaillirions, etc.
Imper.　Tressaille, tressaillons, tressaillez.

IRREGULAR AND DEFECTIVE VERBS. 119

Subj. Pres. Que je tressaille, etc., que nous tressaillions, etc.
Imperf. Que je tressaillisse, etc., que nous tressaillissions, etc.
Infin. Tressaillir.
Part. Tressaillant, tressailli.

  Conjugated with the auxiliary **avoir**.

Venir (= to come).

Prim. Tenses. Venir, venant, venu, je viens, je vins.
Ind. Pres. Je viens, tu viens, il *or* elle vient, nous venons, vous venez, ils *or* elles viennent.
Imperf. Je venais, etc., nous venions, etc.
Past. Def. Je vins, etc., nous vînmes, etc.
Fut. Je viendrai, etc., nous viendrons, etc.
Cond. Pres. Je viendrais, etc., nous viendrions, etc.
Imper. Viens, venons, venez.
Subj. Pres. Que je vienne, etc., que nous venions, que vous veniez, qu'ils *or* qu'elles viennent.
Imperf. Que je vinsse, etc., que nous vinssions, etc.
Infin. Venir.
Part. Venant, venu, venue.

  Conjugated with the auxiliary **être**.

Vêtir (= to clothe).

Prim. Tenses. Vêtant, vêtu, je vêts, je vêtis.
Ind. Pres. Je vêts, tu vêts, il *or* elle vêt, nous vêtons, vous vêtez, ils *or* elles vêtent.
Imperf. Je vêtais, etc., nous vêtions, etc.
Past Def. Je vêtis, etc., nous vêtîmes, etc.
Fut. Je vêtirai, etc., nous vêtirons, etc.
Cond. Pres. Je vêtirais, etc., nous vêtirions, etc.
Imper. Vêts, vêtons, vêtez.
Subj. Pres. Que je vête, etc., que nous vêtions, etc.
Imperf. Que je vêtisse, etc., que nous vêtissions, etc.
Infin. Vêtir.
Part. Vêtant, vêtu, vêtue.

  Conjugated with the auxiliary **avoir**.

4. Third Conjugation: OIR.

173. The irregular verbs in *oir* are subdivided into two classes:—

1. The first forms its past definite in **us**, and its participle in **u**: *ra*loir (= to be worth), *va*lus, *va*lu.

2. The second class comprises the two verbs *asseoir* (= to sit), and *voir* (= to see), forming their past definite

in *is* (*assis*, *vis*), but differing from each other in the past participle (*assis*, *vu*).

174. The irregular verbs of the third conjugation are the following:—

Asseoir (= to seat, to place, to sit).

Prim. Tenses. Asseoir, asseyant, assis, j'assieds, j'assis.

Ind. Pres. J'assieds, tu assieds, il assied, nous asseyons, vous asseyez, ils asseyent.
Imperf. J'asseyais, etc., nous asseyions, etc.
Past Def. J'assis, etc., nous assîmes, etc.
Fut. J'assiérai, etc., nous assiérons, etc.; the French also say: j'asseyerai, etc., nous asseyerons, etc.
Cond. Pres. J'assiérais, etc., nous assiérions, etc.; also: j'asseyerais, etc., nous asseyerions, etc.
Imper. Assieds, asseyons, asseyez.
Subj. Pres. Que j'asseye, etc., que nous asseyions, que vous asseyiez, qu'ils asseyent.
Imperf. Que j'assisse, etc., que nous assissions, etc.
Infin. Asseoir.
Part. Asseyant, assis, assise.

The verb *asseoir* is also conjugated as follows:—

Ind. Pres. J'assois, tu assois, il assoit, nous assoyons, vous assoyez, ils assoient.
Imperf. J'assoyais, etc.

But this manner is not used in written language.

The verb *surseoir* (= to postpone) follows this second form.

Conjugated with the auxiliary **avoir**; *but it takes the auxiliary* **être** *when used as a reflexive verb:* *s'asseoir* (= to sit down).

Choir (*tomber* = to fall).

Employed only in the infinitive, and in a limited number of instances.

In the old French it was conjugated throughout (*chois, chéais, cherrai, chut, chéant, chu*). Even as late as the seventeenth century we find the future *cherrai*: *Tirez la chevillette, et la bobinette* **cherra** (= pull the peg and the bobbin will fall). PERRAULT.

The past participle *chu* (= *tombé*) has given the feminine substantive *chute*, just as the past participles *entrée, revue, battue* have given, respectively, the substantives: *une entrée, une revue, une battue*.

Déchoir (= to decay, fall).

Prim. Tenses. Déchoir, déchu, je déchois, je déchus.
Ind. Pres. Je déchois, tu déchois, il déchoit, nous déchoyons, vous déchoyez, ils déchoient.
Imperf. Je déchoyais, etc., nous déchoyions, etc.
Past Def. Je déchus, etc., nous déchûmes, etc.
Fut. Je décherrai, etc., nous décherrons, etc.
Cond. Pres. Je décherrais, etc., nous décherrions, etc.
Imper. Déchois, déchoyons, déchoyez.
Subj. Pres. Que je déchoie, etc., que nous déchoyions, que vous déchoyiez, qu'ils déchoient.
Imperf. Que je déchusse, etc., que nous déchussions, etc.
Infin. Déchoir.
Part. (no *Pres. Part.*) déchu, déchue.

Conjugated with avoir when it expresses an action, and with être when it denotes a state.

Échoir (= to fall due).

Prim. Tenses: échoir, échéant, échu, il échoit, j'échus.

Conjugated as *déchoir*.—Used only in the *Part. Pres.*, échéant; the *Part. Past*, échu; the *Indic. Pres.*, *third person singular*, il échoit (pronounced and often written échet); the *Past Def.*, j'échus, etc.; the *Fut.*, j'écherrai, etc.; the *Cond. Pres.*, j'écherrais, etc.; the *Imperf. Subj.*, que j'échusse, etc.

See *déchoir*. Conjugated *with* avoir or être.

From the Pres. Part. *échéant* comes the feminine substantive *échéance*, just as *vengeant*, *surveillant* have formed *vengeance*, *surveillance*. (See § 44.)

Falloir (= to be necessary).

Prim. Tenses. Falloir, fallu, il faut, il fallut.

Ind. Pres. Il faut.
Imperf. Il fallait.
Past Def. Il fallut.
Fut. Il faudra.
Cond. Pres. Il faudrait.
Imper. (None.)
Subj. Pres. Qu'il faille.
Imperf. Qu'il fallût.
Infin. Falloir.
Part. (no *Pres. Part.*) fallu.

Conjugated with the auxiliary avoir

Mouvoir (= to move).

Prim. Tenses. Mouvoir, mouvant, mû, je meus, je mus.
Ind. Pres. Je meus, tu meus, il meut, nous mouvons, **vous** mouvez, ils meuvent.
Imperf. Je mouvais, etc., nous mouvions, etc.
Past Def. Je mus, etc., nous mûmes, etc.
Fut. Je mouvrai, etc., nous mouvrons, etc.
Cond. Pres. Je mouvrais, etc., nous mouvrions, etc.
Imper. Meus, mouvons, mouvez.
Subj. Pres. Que je meuve, que tu meuves, qu'il meuve, que nous mouvions, que vous mouviez, qu'ils meuvent.
Imperf. Que je musse, etc., que nous mussions, etc.
Infin. Mouvoir.
Part. Mouvant, mû, mue.

Conjugated with the auxiliary **avoir.**

Pleuvoir (= to rain).

Prim. Tenses. Pleuvoir, pleuvant, plu, il pleut, il plut.
Ind. Pres. Il pleut.
Imperf. Il pleuvait.
Past Def. Il plut.
Fut. Il pleuvra.
Cond. Pres. Il pleuvrait.
Subj. Pres. Qu'il pleuve.
Imperf. Qu'il plût.
Infin. Pleuvoir.
Part. Pleuvant, plu.

Conjugated with the auxiliary **avoir.**

Pouvoir (= to be able).

Prim. Tenses. Pouvoir, pouvant, pu, je peux or je puis, je pus.
Ind. Pres. Je peux or je puis*, tu peux, il peut, nous **pouvons,** vous pouvez, ils peuvent.
Imperf. Je pouvais, etc., nous pouvions, etc.
Past Def. Je pus, etc., nous pûmes, etc.
Fut. Je pourrai, etc., nous pourrons, etc.†
Cond. Pres. Je pourrais, etc., nous pourrions, etc.†
Imper. (None).
Subj. Pres. Que je puisse, etc., que nous puissions, etc.
Imperf. Que je pusse, etc., que nous pussions, etc.
Infin. Pouvoir.
Part. Pouvant, pu.

Conjugated with the auxiliary **avoir.**

Puis is the only form used in the interrogative conjugation (*for the first person*). *Puis-je?* (=can I?)

† The two r's sounded only as one, whilst in *acquerrai*, etc., both are sounded strongly.

Savoir (= to know).

Prim. Tenses. Savoir, sachant, su, je sais, je sus.

Ind. Pres.	Je sais, tu sais, il sait, nous savons, vous savez, ils savent.
Imperf.	Je savais, etc., nous savions, etc.
Past Def.	Je sus, etc., nous sûmes, etc.
Fut.	Je saurai, etc., nous saurons, etc.
Cond. Pres.	Je saurais, etc., nous saurions, etc.
Imper.	Sache, sachons, sachez.
Subj. Pres.	Que je sache, etc., que nous sachions, etc.
Imperf.	Que je susse, etc., que nous sussions, etc.
Infin.	Savoir.
Part.	Sachant, su, sue.

Conjugated with the auxiliary **avoir**.

In the Old French, *savoir* was *saver*, from the Latin *sapere*. This form *saver* gave the future *saver-ai*, which, contracted later into *savrai* (as *recevoir* into *recevrai*, *devoir* into *devrai*, etc.), became in the fourteenth century *saurai*, as *habere* has given *aver-ai*, then *avrai*, and finally *aurai*.

Seoir.

In the sense of to be seated (= *être assis*) this verb is obsolete. It is sometimes used in the present participle, *séant*, and the past participle, *sis, sise*. When meaning to be becoming (= *être convenable*) it is still used in certain tenses, and always in the third person singular or plural : *il sied, ils siéent, il seyait, il siéra*.

Valoir (= to be worth).

Prim. Tenses. Valoir, valant, valu, je vaux, je valus.

Ind. Pres.	Je vaux, tu vaux, il vaut, nous valons, vous valez, ils valent.
Imperf.	Je valais, etc., nous valions, etc.
Past Def.	Je valus, etc., nous valûmes, etc.
Fut.	Je vaudrai, etc., nous vaudrons, etc.
Cond. Pres.	Je vaudrais, nous vaudrions, etc.
Imper.	Vaux, valons, valez.
Subj. Pres.	Que je vaille, que tu vailles, qu'il vaille, que nous valions, que vous valiez, qu'ils vaillent.
Imperf.	Que je valusse, etc., que nous valussions, etc.
Infin.	Valoir.
Part.	Valant, valu.

Conjugated with the auxiliary **avoir**.

The compounds of this verb are conjugated in the same manner, with the exception of *prévaloir* (= to prevail), whose *Subj. Pres.* is: *que je prévale*, etc., *que nous prévalions*, etc.

Voir (= to see).

Prim. Tenses.	Voir, voyant, vu, je vois, je vis.
Ind. Pres.	Je vois, tu vois, il voit, nous voyons, vous voyez, ils voient.
Imperf.	Je voyais, etc., nous voyions, etc.
Past Def.	Je vis, etc., nous vîmes, etc.
Fut.	Je verrai, etc., nous verrons,* etc.
Cond. Pres.	Je verrais, etc., nous verrions,* etc.
Imper.	Vois, voyons, voyez.
Subj. Pres.	Que je voie, etc., que nous voyions, etc.
Imperf.	Que je visse, etc., que nous vissions, etc.
Infin.	Voir.
Part.	Voyant, vu, vue.

Conjugated with the auxiliary **avoir**.

N.B.—*Pourvoir* (= to provide), and *prévoir* (= to foresee), make in the *Fut.* and *Cond.*: je pourvoirai, je pourvoirais, and je prévoirai, je prévoirais. Besides, the *Past. Def.* and *Imperf. Subj.* of *pourvoir* are je pourvus, que je pourvusse.

Conjugated with the auxiliary **avoir**.

Vouloir (= to will, to be willing).

Prim. Tenses.	Vouloir, voulant, voulu, je veux, je voulus.
Ind. Pres.	Je veux, tu veux, il veut, nous voulons, vous voulez, ils veulent.
Imperf.	Je voulais, etc., nous voulions, etc.
Past Def.	Je voulus, etc., nous voulûmes, etc.
Fut.	Je voudrai, etc., nous voudrons, etc.
Cond. Pres.	Je voudrais, etc., nous voudrions, etc.
Imper.	Veuille, veuillons, veuillez. (The *Imper.* proper, veux, voulons, voulez, is seldom used).
Subj. Pres.	Que je veuille, etc., que nous voulions, que vous vouliez, qu'ils veuillent.
Imperf.	Que je voulusse, etc., que nous voulussions, etc.
Infin.	Vouloir.
Part.	Voulant, voulu, voulue.

Conjugated with the auxiliary **avoir**.

5. Fourth Conjugation: RE.

175. The irregular verbs in **re** may be subdivided into two classes according to the formation of the past definite: 1. Verbs with the past definite in **is**: *craindre* (= to fear), *craignis*; 2. Verbs with the past definite in **us**: *connaître* (= to know), *connus*.

* See Note on *pourvoir*.

176. The irregular verbs in **re** are the following:—

Absoudre (= to absolve).

Prim. Tenses. Absoudre, absolvant, absous (*fem.* absoute), j'absous; no *Past Definite.* See *résoudre*.

Conjugated with the auxiliary **avoir.**

Boire (= to drink).

Prim. Tenses. Boire, buvant, bu, je bois, je bus.

Ind. Pres.	Je bois, tu bois, il boit, nous buvons, vous buvez, ils boivent.
Imperf.	Je buvais, etc., nous buvions, etc.
Past Def.	Je bus, etc., nous bûmes, etc.
Fut.	Je boirai, etc., nous boirons, etc.
Cond. Pres.	Je boirais, etc., nous boirions, etc.
Imper.	Bois, buvons, buvez.
Subj. Pres.	Que je boive, etc., que nous buvions, que vous buviez, qu'ils boivent.
Imperf.	Que je busse, etc., que nous bussions, etc.
Infin.	·Boire.
Pa.t.	Buvant, bu, bue.

Conjugated with the auxiliary **avoir.**

Braire (= to bray).

This verb, according to the *Académie*, is used only in the *Infinitive*, and in the third person of the *Present Indicative*, *Future*, and *Conditional*: braire, il brait, ils braient, il braira, ils brairont, il brairait, ils brairaient.

Conjugated with the auxiliary **avoir.**

Braire, in the old language, had the general sense of *crier* (= to shout), and was applied to men as well as to animals; it is only at a comparatively recent period that the meaning was limited to the noise made by an ass.

Bruire (= to roar, rattle, resound).

This verb has only the following forms: bruire, il bruit, il bruyait, ils bruyaient. Bruyant now is rather an adjective than a present participle.

Conjugated with the auxiliary **avoir.**

Clore (= to close).

Used only in the *Past Participle*, clos, close; the three persons singular of the *Ind. Pres.*, je clos, tu clos, il clôt; the *Fut.*, je clorai, tu cloras, etc.; the *Cond. Pres.*, je clorais, etc.; the *Imper.* singular, clos; *Subj. Pres.*, que je close; and all compound tenses.

Conjugated with the auxiliary **avoir.**

Conclure (= to conclude).

Prim. Tenses. Conclure, concluant, conclu, je conclus, je conclus.
Ind. Pres. Je conclus, tu conclus, il conclut, nous concluons, vous concluez, ils concluent.
Imperf. Je concluais, etc., nous concluions, etc.
Past Def. Je conclus, etc., nous conclûmes, etc.
Fut. Je conclurai, etc., nous conclurons, etc.
Cond. Pres. Je conclurais, etc., nous conclurions, etc.
Imper. Conclus, concluons, concluez.
Subj. Pres. Que je conclue, etc., que nous concluions, que vous concluiez, qu'ils concluent.
Imperf. Que je conclusse, etc., que nous conclussions, etc.
Infin. Conclure.
Part. Concluant, conclu, conclue.

Conjugated with the auxiliary **avoir**.

Conduire (= to conduct).

Prim. Tenses. Conduire, conduisant, conduit, je conduis, je conduisis.

See *nuire*. Conjugated with the auxiliary **avoir**.

Confire (= to pickle).

Prim. Tenses. Confire, confisant, confit, je confis, je confis.
Ind. Pres. Je confis, tu confis, il confit, nous confisons, vous confisez, ils confisent.
Imperf. Je confisais, etc., nous confisions, etc.
Past Def. Je confis, etc., nous confîmes, etc.
Fut. Je confirai, etc., nous confirons, etc.
Cond. Pres. Je confirais, etc., nous confirions, etc.
Imper. Confis, confisons, confisez.
Subj. Pres. Que je confise, etc., que nous confisions, etc.
Imperf. (None.)
Infin. Confire.
Part. Confisant, confit, confite.

Conjugated with the auxiliary **avoir**.

Connaître (= to know).

Prim. Tenses. Connaître, connaissant, connu, je connais, je connus.
Ind. Pres. Je connais, tu connais, il connaît, nous connaissons, vous connaissez, ils connaissent.
Imperf. Je connaissais, etc., nous connaissions, etc.
Past Def. Je connus, etc., nous connûmes, etc.
Fut. Je connaîtrai, etc., nous connaîtrons, etc.

IRREGULAR AND DEFECTIVE VERBS. 127

Cond. Perf.   Je connaîtrais, etc., nous connaîtrions, etc.
Imper.   Connais, connaissons, connaissez.
Subj. Pres.   Que je connaisse, etc., que nous connaissions, etc.
Imperf.   Que je connusse, etc., que nous connussions, etc.
Infin.   Connaitre.
Part.   Connaissant, connu, connue.

Conjugated with the auxiliary **avoir**.

N.B.—Whenever the vowel **i** is followed by **t** in this verb, it takes the circumflex accent: connaît, connaîtrai, etc.

Coudre (= to sew).

Prim. Tenses.   Coudre, cousant, cousu, je couds, je cousis.
Ind. Pres.   Je couds, tu couds, il coud, nous cousons, vous cousez, ils cousent.
Imperf.   Je cousais, etc., nous cousions, etc.
Past Def.   Je cousis, etc., nous cousîmes, etc.
Fut.   Je coudrai, etc., nous coudrons, etc.
Cond. Pres.   Je coudrais, etc., nous coudrions, etc.
Imper.   Couds, cousons, cousez.
Subj. Pres.   Que je couse, etc., que nous cousions, etc.
Imperf.   Que je cousisse, etc., que nous cousissions, etc.
Infin.   Coudre.
Part.   Cousant, cousu, cousue.

Conjugated with the auxiliary **avoir**.

Craindre (= to fear).

Prim. Tenses.   Craindre, craignant, craint, je crains, je craignis.
Ind. Pres.   Je crains, tu crains, il craint, nous craignons, vous craignez, ils craignent.
Imperf.   Je craignais, etc., nous craignions, etc.
Past Def.   Je craignis, etc., nous craignîmes, etc.
Fut.   Je craindrai, etc., nous craindrons, etc.
Cond. Pres.   Je craindrais, etc., nous craindrions, etc.
Imper.   Crains, craignons, craignez.
Subj. Pres.   Que je craigne, etc., que nous craignions, que vous craigniez, qu'ils craignent.
Imperf.   Que je craignisse, etc., que nous craignissions, etc.
Infin.   Craindre.
Part.   Craignant, craint, crainte.

Conjugated with the auxiliary **avoir**.

Croire (= to believe).

Prim. Tenses.   Croire, croyant, cru, je crois, je crus.
Ind. Pres.   Je crois, tu crois, il croit, nous croyons, vous croyez, ils croient.
Imperf.   Je croyais, etc., nous croyions, etc.

Past. Def.	Je crus, etc., nous crûmes, etc.
Fut.	Je croirai, etc., nous croirons, etc.
Cond. Pres.	Je croirais, etc., nous croirions, etc.
Imper.	Crois, croyons, croyez.
Subj. Pres.	Que je croie, etc., que nous croyions, que vous croyiez, qu'ils croient.
Imperf.	Que je crusse, etc., que nous crussions, etc.
Infin.	Croire.
Part.	Croyant, cru, crue.

Conjugated with the auxiliary **avoir.**

Croître (= to grow).

Prim. Tenses.	Croître, croissant, crû, je croîs, je crus.
Ind. Pres.	Je croîs, tu croîs, il croît, nous croissons, vous croissez, il croissent.
Imperf.	Je croissais, etc., nous croissions, etc.
Past Def.	Je crûs, etc., nous crûmes, etc.
Fut.	Je croîtrai, etc., nous croîtrons, etc.
Cond. Pres.	Je croîtrais, etc., nous croîtrions, etc.
Imper.	Croîs, croissons, croissez.
Subj. Pres.	Que je croisse, etc., que nous croissions, etc.
Imperf.	Que je crusse, etc., que nous crussions, etc.
Infin.	Croître.
Part.	Croissant, crû, crue.

Conjugated with the auxiliary **avoir.**

N.B.—See *connaître.*

Dire (= to say).

Prim. Tenses.	Dire, disant, dit, je dis, je dis.
Ind. Pres.	Je dis, tu dis, il dit, nous disons, vous dites, ils disent.
Imperf.	Je disais, etc., nous disions, etc.
Past Def.	Je dis, etc., nous dîmes, etc.
Fut.	Je dirai, etc., nous dirons, etc.
Cond. Pres.	Je dirais, etc., nous dirions, etc.
Imper.	Dis, disons, dites.
Subj. Pres.	Que je dise, etc., que nous disions, etc.
Imperf.	Que je disse, etc., que nous dissions, etc.
Infin.	Dire.
Part.	Disant, dit, dite.

Conjugated with the auxiliary **avoir.**

N.B.—All the compounds of *dire* make *disez* in the second person plural of the *Pres. Indic.*, with the exception of *redire* (= to repeat), and *maudire* (= to curse), which make *redites, maudissez.*

Éclore (= to be hatched, to open, to dawn).
Limited to the following forms:—

Ind. Pres.	Il éclôt, ils éclosent.
Fut.	Il éclôra, ils éclôront.
Cond. Pres.	Il éclôrait, ils éclôraient.
Subj. Pres.	Qu'il éclose, qu'ils éclosent.
Infin.	Éclore.
Part. Past.	Éclosant, éclos, éclose.

Conjugated with the auxiliary **être.**

Écrire (= to write).

Prim. Tenses.	Écrire, écrivant, écrit, j'écris, j'écrivis.
Ind. Pres.	J'écris, tu écris, il écrit, nous écrivons, vous écrivez, ils écrivent.
Imperf.	J'écrivais, etc., nous écrivions, etc.
Past Def.	J'écrivis, etc., nous écrivîmes, etc.
Fut.	J'écrirai, etc., nous écrirons, etc.
Cond. Pres.	J'écrirais, etc., nous écririons, etc.
Imper.	Écris, écrivons, écrivez.
Subj. Pres.	Que j'écrive, etc., que nous écrivions, etc.
Imperf.	Que j'écrivisse, etc., que nous écrivissions, etc.
Infin.	Écrire.
Part.	Écrivant, écrit, écrite.

Conjugated with the auxiliary **avoir.**

Faire (= to make *or* to do).

Prim. Tenses.	Faire, faisant, fait, je fais, je fis.
Ind. Pres.	Je fais, tu fais, il fait, nous faisons, vous faites, ils font.
Imperf.	Je faisais, etc., nous faisions, etc.
Past Def.	Je fis, etc., nous fîmes, etc.
Fut.	Je ferai, etc., nous ferons, etc.
Cond. Pres.	Je ferais, etc., nous ferions, etc.
Imper.	Fais, faisons, faites.
Subj. Pres.	Que je fasse, etc., que nous fassions, etc.
Imperf.	Que je fisse, etc., que nous fissions, etc.
Infin.	Faire.
Part.	Faisant, fait, faite.

Conjugated with the auxiliary **avoir.**

Frire (= to fry).

This verb, besides the *Infin. Pres.*, has also the three persons singular of the *Ind. Pres.*, je fris, tu fris, il frit; the *Fut.*, je

K

frirai, etc.; the *Cond. Pres.*, je frirais, etc.; the second person singular of the *Imper.*, fris; the *Part. Past*, frit, frite.

The tenses of this verb are more generally made up by placing the verb *faire* before the infinitive *frire*: nous faisons frire, vous faites frire.

Conjugated with the auxiliary **avoir.**

Joindre (= to join).

Prim. Tenses. Joindre, joignant, joint, je joins, je joignis.
See *craindre*. *Conjugated with the auxiliary* **avoir.**

Lire (= to read).

Prim. Tenses. Lire, lisant, lu, je lis, je lus.

Ind. Pres.	Je lis, tu lis, il lit, nous lisons, vous lisez, ils lisent.
Imperf.	Je lisais, etc., nous lisions, etc.
Past Def.	Je lus, etc., nous lûmes, etc.
Fut.	Je lirai, etc., nous lirons, etc.
Cond. Pres.	Je lirais, etc., nous lirions, etc.
Imper.	Lis, lisons, lisez.
Subj. Pres.	Que je lise, etc., que nous lisions, etc.
Imperf.	Que je lusse, etc., que nous lussions, etc.
Infin.	Lire.
Part.	Lisant, lu, lue.

Conjugated with the auxiliary **avoir.**

Luire (= to shine).

Prim. Tenses. Luire, luisant, lui, je luis, je luisis.

Ind. Pres.	Je luis, tu luis, il luit, nous luisons, vous luisez ils luisent.
Imperf.	Je luisais, etc., nous luisions, etc.
Past Def.	Je luisis, etc., nous luisîmes, etc.*
Fut.	Je luirai, etc., nous luirons, etc.
Cond. Pres.	Je luirais, etc., nous luirions, etc.
Imper.	Luis, luisons, luisez.
Subj. Pres.	Que je luise, etc., que nous luisions, etc.
Imperf.	Que je luisisse, etc., que nous luisissions etc.
Infin.	Luire.
Part.	Luisant, lui.

Conjugated with the auxiliary **avoir.**

* This tense, which the *Académie* does not give, is very seldom used. It is to be found in Bossuet.

Mettre (=to place, to put).

Prim. Tenses. Mettre, mettant, mis, je mets, je mis.
Ind. Pres. Je mets, tu mets, il met, nous mettons, vous mettez, ils mettent.
Imperf. Je mettais, etc., nous mettions, etc.
Past Def. Je mis, etc., nous mîmes, etc.
Fut. Je mettrai, etc., nous mettrons, etc.
Cond. Pres. Je mettrais, etc., nous mettrions, etc.
Imper. Mets, mettons, mettez.
Subj. Pres. Que je mette, etc., que nous mettions, etc.
Imperf. Que je misse, etc., que nous missions, etc.
Infin. Mettre.
Part. Mettant, mis, mise.

Conjugated with the auxiliary **avoir.**

Moudre (=to grind).

Prim. Tenses. Moudre, moulant, moulu, je mouds, je moulus.
Ind. Pres. Je mouds, tu mouds, il moud, nous moulons, vous moulez, ils moulent.
Imperf. Je moulais, etc., nous moulions, etc.
Past Def. Je moulus, etc., nous moulûmes, etc.
Fut. Je moudrai, etc., nous moudrons, etc.
Cond. Pres. Je moudrais, etc., nous moudrions, etc.
Imper. Mouds, moulons, moulez.
Subj. Pres. Que je moule, etc., que nous moulions, etc.
Imperf. Que je moulusse, etc., que nous moulussions, etc.
Infin. Moudre.
Part. Moulant, moulu, moulue.

Conjugated with the auxiliary **avoir.**

Naitre (=to be born).

Prim. Tenses. Naitre, naissant, né, je nais, je naquis.
Ind. Pres. Je nais, tu nais, il nait, nous naissons, vous naissez, ils naissent.
Imperf. Je naissais, etc., nous naissions, etc.
Past Def. Je naquis, etc., nous naquimes, etc.
Fut. Je naitrai, etc., nous naitrons, etc.
Cond. Pres. Je naitrais, etc., nous naitrions, etc.
Imper. Nais, naissons, naissez.
Subj. Pres. Que je naisse, etc., que nous naissions, etc.
Imperf. Que je naquisse, etc., que nous naquissions, etc.
Infin. Naitre.
Part. Naissant, né, née.

See *connaitre.* *Conjugated with the auxiliary* **être.**

Nuire (= to injure, to be hurtful).

Prim. Tenses.	Nuire, nuisant, nui, je nuis, je nuisis.
Ind. Pres.	Je nuis, tu nuis, il nuit, nous nuisons, vous nuisez, ils nuisent.
Imperf.	Je nuisais, etc., nous nuisions, etc.
Past Def.	Je nuisis, etc., nous nuisîmes, etc.
Fut.	Je nuirai, etc., nous nuirons, etc.
Cond. Pres.	Je nuirais, etc., nous nuirions, etc.
Imper.	Nuis, nuisons, nuisez.
Subj. Pres.	Que je nuise, etc., que nous nuisions, etc.
Imperf.	Que je nuisisse, etc., que nous nuisissions, etc.
Infin.	Nuire.
Part.	Nuisant, nui.

Conjugated with the auxiliary **avoir.**

Oindre (= to anoint).

Prim. Tenses.	Oindre, oignant, oint, j'oins, j'oignis.
Ind. Pres.	J'oins, etc., nous oignons, etc.
Imperf.	J'oignais, etc., nous oignions, etc.
Past Def.	J'oignis, etc., nous oignîmes, etc.
Fut.	J'oindrai, etc., nous oindrons, etc.
Cond. Pres.	J'oindrais, etc., nous oindrions, etc.
Imper.	Oins, oignons, oignez.
Subj. Pres.	Que j'oigne, etc., que nous oignions, etc.
Imperf.	Que j'oignisse, etc., que nous oignissions, etc.
Infin.	Oindre.
Part.	Oint, ointe.

Conjugated with the auxiliary **avoir.**

This verb is seldom used, except in the *Pres. Infin.*, the *Participles*, and the *Future*.

Paître (= to graze).

Prim. Tenses.	Paître, paissant, —, je pais, —.
Ind. Pres.	je pais, tu pais, il paît, nous paissons, vous paissez, ils paissent.
Imperf.	Je paissais, etc., nous paissions, etc.
Fut.	Je paîtrai, etc., nous paîtrons, etc.
Cond. Pres.	Je paîtrais, etc., nous paîtrions, etc.
Imper.	Pais, paissons, paissez.
Subj. Pres.	Que je paisse, etc., que nous paissions, etc.
Infin.	Paître.
Part.	Paissant.

This verb has neither *Past Def.*, *Imperf. Subjunctive*, nor *Past Participle*.

Repaître

Repaître is conjugated like *paître*; but it has both a *Past Def.*: je repus, and a *Past Participle*: repu.

The simple participle **pu** is still used as a term of falconry: *un faucon qui a pu* (=a hawk which has been fed).

Paraître (=to appear).

Prim. Tenses. Paraître, paraissant, paru, je parais, je parus.
See *connaître*.

Peindre (=to paint).

Prim. Tenses. Peindre, peignant, peint, je peins, je peignis.
See *craindre*.

Plaire (=to please).

Prim. Tenses.	Plaire, plaisant, plu, je plais, je plus.
Ind. Pres.	Je plais, tu plais, il plaît, nous plaisons, vous plaisez, ils plaisent.
Imperf.	Je plaisais, etc., nous plaisions, etc.
Past Def.	Je plus, etc., nous plûmes, etc.
Fut.	Je plairai, etc., nous plairons, etc.
Cond. Pres.	Je plairais, etc., nous plairions, etc.
Imper.	Plais, plaisons, plaisez.
Subj. Pres.	Que je plaise, etc., que nous plaisions, etc.
Imperf.	Que je plusse, etc., que nous plussions, etc.
Infin.	Plaire.
Part.	Plaisant, plu.

Conjugated with the auxiliary **avoir.**

Prendre (=to take).

Prim. Tenses.	Prendre, prenant, pris, je prends, je pris.
Ind. Pres.	Je prends, tu prends, il prend, nous prenons, vous prenez, ils prennent.
Imperf.	Je prenais, etc., nous prenions, etc.
Past Def.	Je pris, etc., nous prîmes, etc.
Fut.	Je prendrai, etc., nous prendrons, etc.
Cond. Pres.	Je prendrais, etc., nous prendrions, etc.
Imper.	Prends, prenons, prenez.
Subj. Pres.	Que je prenne, etc., que nous prenions, que vous preniez, qu'ils prennent.
Imperf.	Que je prisse, etc., que nous prissions, etc.
Infin.	Prendre.
Part.	Prenant, pris, prise.

Conjugated with the auxiliary **avoir.**

Résoudre (= to resolve).

Prim. Tenses. Résoudre, résolvant, résolu, je résous, je résolus.
Ind. Pres. Je résous, tu résous, il résout, nous résolvons, vous résolvez, ils résolvent.
Imperf. Je résolvais, etc., nous résolvions, etc.
Past Def. Je résolus, etc., nous résolûmes, etc.
Fut. Je résoudrai, etc., nous résoudrons, etc.
Cond. Pres. Je résoudrais, etc., nous résoudrions, etc.
Imper. Résous, résolvons, résolvez.
Subj. Pres. Que je résolve, etc., que nous résolvions, etc.
Imperf. Que je résolusse, etc., que nous résolussions, etc.
Infin. Résoudre.
Part. Résolvant, résolu, résolue: *or* résous ; we still say, *brouillard* **résous en pluie** (= a fog resolved into rain).

Conjugated with the auxiliary **avoir**.

Rire (= to laugh).

Prim. Tenses. Rire, riant, ri, je ris, je ris
Ind. Pres. Je ris, tu ris, il rit, nous rions, vous riez, ils rient.
Imperf. Je riais, etc., nous riions, etc.
Past Def. Je ris, etc., nous rîmes, etc.
Fut. Je rirai, etc., nous rirons, etc.
Cond. Pres. Je rirais, etc., nous ririons, etc.
Imper. Ris, rions, riez.
Subj. Pres. Que je rie, que tu ries, qu'il rie, que nous riions, que vous riiez, qu'ils rient.
Imperf. Que je risse, etc., que nous rissions, etc.
Infin. Rire.
Part. Riant, ri.

Conjugated with the auxiliary **avoir**.

Suivre (= to follow).

Prim. Tenses. Suivre, suivant, suivi, je suis, je suivis.
Ind. Pres. Je suis, tu suis, il suit, nous suivons, vous suivez, ils suivent.
Imperf. Je suivais, etc., nous suivions, etc.
Past Def. Je suivis, etc., nous suivîmes, etc.
Fut. Je suivrai, etc., nous suivrons, etc.
Cond. Pres. Je suivrais, nous suivrions, etc.
Imper. Suis, suivons, suivez.
Subj. Pres. Que je suive, etc., que nous suivions, etc.
Imperf. Que je suivisse, etc., que nous suivissions, etc.
Infin. Suivre.
Part. Suivant, suivi, suivie.

Conjugated with the auxiliary **avoir**.

Taire (= to keep silent, to conceal).

Prim. Tenses. Taire, taisant, tû, je tais, je tus.
   See *plaire*. *Conjugated with the auxiliary* **avoir**.

Se taire (= to hold one's tongue), being a reflexive verb, is conjugated with *être* in its compound tenses.

Traire (= to milk).

Prim. Tenses. Traire, trayant, trait, je trais, no *Past Def.*

Ind. Pres.	Je trais, tu trais, il trait, nous trayons, vous trayez, ils traient.
Imperf.	Je trayais, etc., nous trayions, etc.
Fut.	Je trairai, etc., nous trairons, etc.
Cond. Pres.	Je trairais, etc., nous trairions, etc.
Imper.	Trais, trayons, trayez.
Subj. Pres.	Que je traie, etc., que nous trayions, que vous trayiez, qu'ils traient.
Infin.	Traire.
Part.	Trayant, trait, traite.

This verb has neither *Past Def.*, nor *Imperf. Subj.*
Conjugated with the auxiliary **avoir**.

Vaincre (= to conquer).

Prim. Tenses. Vaincre, vainquant, vaincu, je vaincs, je vainquis.

Ind. Pres.	Je vaincs, tu vaincs, il vainc, nous vainquons, vous vainquez, ils vainquent.
Imperf.	Je vainquais, etc., nous vainquions, etc.
Past Def.	Je vainquis, etc., nous vainquîmes, etc.
Fut.	Je vaincrai, etc., nous vaincrons, etc.
Cond. Pres.	Je vaincrais, etc., nous vaincrions, etc.
Imper.	Vaincs, vainquons, vainquez.
Subj. Pres.	Que je vainque, etc., que nous vainquions, etc.
Imperf.	Que je vainquisse, etc., que nous vainquissions, etc.
Infin.	Vaincre.
Part.	Vainquant, vaincu, vaincue.

Conjugated with the auxiliary **avoir**.

Vivre (= to live).

Prim. Tenses. Vivre, vivant, vécu, je vis, je vécus.

Ind. Pres.	Je vis, tu vis, il vit, nous vivons, vous vivez, ils vivent.
Imperf.	Je vivais, etc., nous vivions, etc.
Past Def.	Je vécus, etc., nous vécûmes, etc.
Fut.	Je vivrai, etc., nous vivrons, etc.

Cond. Pres.	Je vivrais, etc., nous vivrions, etc.
Imper.	Vis, vivons, vivez.
Subj. Pres.	Que je vive, etc., que nous vivions, etc.
Imperf.	Que je vécusse, etc., que nous vécussions, etc.
Infin.	Vivre.
Part.	Vivant, vécu.

Conjugated with the auxiliary **avoir**.

QUESTIONS FOR EXAMINATION.

1. What is the difference between an irregular and a defective verb?
2. Give the future of *mener*, and the indicative present of *appeler*.
3. Give the present participle of *effacer*, and the past participle of *percer*.
4. Write the imperfect of *ranger*, the past participle of *bénir*, and the future of *aller* and *envoyer*.
5. Write the following verbs in the subjunctive present :—*acquérir, bouillir, courir, cueillir*.
6. Write the following verbs in the future :—*mourir, saillir, tenir, venir, braire*.
7. Write the following verbs in the indicative present :—*dormir, faillir, gésir*.
8. Write the following verbs in the conditional :—*asseoir, seoir, échoir, falloir, mouvoir, pleuvoir, pouvoir, choir, savoir, valoir, voir, vouloir*.
9. Write the following verbs in the indicative present, and past definite :—*coudre, dire, éclore, faire, frire, naître, prendre, résoudre, traire, vaincre*.

Exercise 34.

Première conjugaison.

1. Je vais à la poste. 2. Vas-tu lire ce livre? 3. Ce cheval ne va pas vite. 4. Ne vont-ils pas tous les jours à leur bureau? 5. J'irai dimanche matin à l'église. 6. N'iriez-vous pas au concert? 7. Ne croyez pas que j'aille à Paris l'été prochain. 8. Je ne voudrais pas qu'il allât se compromettre. 9. Quand m'enverrez-vous mon argent? 10. Nous vous enverrions ces livres si nous les avions. 11. Je me lève tous les matins à six heures. 12. J'achèterais cette maison de campagne. 13. Il m'appellera quand il sera prêt. 14. Traçons un tableau complet de la situation. 15. En rangeant ma bibliothèque, j'ai trouvé votre lettre.

[1] morceau (m.), [2] penser, [3] se lever, [4] de bonne heure, [5] tous les matins, [6] bureau (m.), [7] menacer, [8] revue (f.), [9] achever, [10] cacheter.

1. I shall send you some books. 2. Would you go to the concert? 3. Let us eat a piece[1] of bread. 4. I do not think[2] that he gets up[3] early.[4] 5. This child goes to (the) school every morning.[5] 6. Will you go to your office[6]? 7. Let us threaten[7] him. 8. He will call you to-morrow. 9. We went yesterday *to* see a review.[8] 10. You would send too little (of) money. 11. That they might protect that bad man. 12. Finish[9] this book. 13. That he may seal[10] the letter.

Seconde conjugaison.

1. Béni soit-il pour toute sa générosité. 2. J'ai mangé du pain bénit. 3. Les sciences et les arts florissaient sous le règne de Louis XIV. 4. Nous haïssons les méchants, mais il hait les hommes vertueux. 5. Il acquiert de jour en jour plus de réputation. 6. Nous accourûmes à sa voix. 7. Ci-gît le meilleur des rois. 8. Je me suis enquis de votre ami partout. 9. Il fuirait les flatteurs. 10. Cueillerai-je ces jolies fleurs ? 11. Croyez-vous qu'il m'en offrît, si j'allais le voir ? 12. Je me meurs. 13. Les forces lui défaillent. 14. Il mourut de chagrin. 15. J'ai très-bien dormi. 16. Je requiers votre secours. 17. Faites bouillir un peu d'eau. 18. Je pars ce soir pour la France. 19. Vous ressentiriez les effets de sa colère. 20. Il ne concourra pas pour ce prix. 21. Avez-vous ouï dire qu'il mente jamais ? 22. Il viendra si vous le souffrez.

[1] consentir, [2] mariage (m), [3] pressentir, [4] malheur (m.), [5] malade, [6] dormir, [7] mourir, [8] l'année dernière, [9] assaillir, [10] retranchement (m.), [11] se vêtir, [12] tressaillir, [13] de, [14] requérir, [15] rouvrir, [16] malle (f.), [17] entr'ouvrir, [18] obtenir, [19] disconvenir de, [20] dit, [21] devenir, [22] haïr, [23] gésir, [24] pays (m.), [25] bénir, [26] prêtre, [27] pendant.

1. I consent[1] to the marriage[2] of my son. 2. I apprehend[3] some misfortunes.[4] 3. The patient[5] slept[6] very well yesterday. 4. He died[7] last year.[8] 5. Shall we not assault[9] the enemy to-morrow in his intrenchments[10]? 6. That you might clothe yourself[11] a little better. 7. That she might start[12] with[13] fear. 8. He would request[14] a favour from you. 9. I shall open again[15] that trunk.[16] 10. They would half open[17] the window. 11. I shall obtain[18] the consent of my parents. 12. I disowned[19] what he said.[20] 13. Would you not become[21] learned if you worked a little more ? 14. We hate[22] (the) hypocrites. 15. Here lies[23] a man who has served his country[24] with zeal. 16. This water has been consecrated[25] by the priest.[26] 17. (The) commerce flourished (*imperfect*) in our country during[27] his reign.

Troisième conjugaison.

1. Tu ne vaux pas mieux que ton frère. 2. C'est un ressort très-ingénieux qui meut la machine. 3. Il faut pratiquer la vertu si l'on veut être heureux. 4. Nous pouvons vous être utiles. 5. Vous ne savez pas votre leçon. 6. Il pleuvait hier. 7. Vous prévaliez sur nous. 8. Nous prévîmes toutes les conséquences de cette affaire. 9. Ils s'assirent sur le pont du navire. 10. Vous pourvûtes à la sûreté de la ville. 11. Cette robe vous sied à merveille.

12. Vous verrez mieux d'ici. 13. Cette réponse équivaudrait à un refus. 14. Je ne pense pas qu'il faille lui demander pardon. 15. Qu'ils sachent que je ne les oublie pas. 16. Si je pouvais lui parler, j'obtiendrais ce que je demande. 17. Cette lettre de change écherra lundi. 18. Je crains qu'il ne pleuve. 19. Elle émut le cœur de cet homme insensible.

[1] valoir, [2] guinée, [3] seoir, [4] vouloir, [5] émouvoir, [6] il faut, [7] savoir, [8] chemin (m.), [9] grand, [10] prévoir, [11] pourvoir, [12] à, [13] besoin (m.), [14] chaise (f.), [15] équivaloir, [16] insulte (f.), [17] prévaloir, [18] lettre de change, [19] échoir, [20] falloir, [21] proposition (f.).

1. This horse is worth[1] two hundred guineas.[2] 2. Has he moved the spring of the machine? 3. We shall see if this dress becomes[3] (to) her. 4. If you wish[4] to move[5] the heart of that unfeeling man, you must[6] be useful to him. 5. It was raining yesterday. 6. You will not know[7] your way[8] in this large[9] town. 7. Did you foresee[10] the consequences of the battle? 8. I shall provide[11] for[12] your wants.[13] 9. Sit down, gentlemen, here are some chairs.[14] 10. Do you think that his answer is equivalent[15] to an insult[16]? 11. I shall prevail[17] upon him. 12. When will your bill[18] fall due?[19] 13. We did not suppose that it was necessary[20] to accept his proposal.[21] 14. These colours will never become you. 15. He knows his lesson wonderfully well. 16. Do you see this magnificent landscape?

Quatrième conjugaison.

1. Je buvais un verre d'eau. 2. Il écrivit à ses enfants. 3. Croyez-vous qu'il comprenne votre remarque? 4. Je ferai tout mon possible pour vous servir. 5. S'il vous connaissait mieux, il vous croirait. 6. Permettez-moi de vous accompagner chez vous. 7. Je désirerais que vous lussiez ce bel ouvrage. 8. Ces enfants souriaient. 9. Ils se plurent beaucoup dans votre société. 10. Je veux qu'il prenne un parti énergique. 11. Je le suivrais partout. 12 Nous apprendrions ces règles avec facilité. 13. Il vécut heureux et mourut à un âge avancé. 14. Ils trayaient leurs vaches. 15. Il me nuisit dans toutes les occasions. 16. Pourquoi n'absoudrions-nous pas ce pauvre homme? 17. Il défit les ennemis à deux reprises différentes. 18. Ils abattirent le mur. 19. Ne déplurent-ils pas à leur maître? 20. Poursuis ton chemin. 21. Faites votre devoir. 22. Ils se repurent de chimères. 23. Cet arbre croîtrait rapidement s'il était arrosé. 24. Il éteignit les chandelles. 25. Ne plaignaient-ils pas vos malheurs? 26. Ils disparurent bientôt. 27. Enjoignez-lui de terminer cette affaire.

¹ boire, ² écrire, ³ croire, ⁴ comprendre, ⁵ suivre, ⁶ à travers, ⁷ tous les, ⁸ abattre, ⁹ absoudre, ¹⁰ disparaître, ¹¹ croître, ¹² se plaindre, ¹³ se repaître de, ¹⁴ chimère (f.), ¹⁵ vivre, ¹⁶ défaire, ¹⁷ aucun, ¹⁸ atteindre, ¹⁹ balle (f.), ²⁰ traire, ²¹ vache, ²² sourire, ²³ éteindre, ²⁴ lampe (f.), ²⁵ joindre, ²⁶ réduire, ²⁷ reconduire, ²⁸ feindre, ²⁹ enfreindre, ³⁰ naître, ³¹ sujet, ³² se dédire de, ³³ coudre, ³⁴ traduire, ³⁵ se résoudre à, ³⁶ plaindre, ³⁷ émoudre, ³⁸ légume (m.), ³⁹ confire, ⁴⁰ vinaigre.

1. I never drink¹ wine. 2. Have you written² to your father? 3. I thought³ that you understood⁴ me. 4. I shall follow⁵ him through⁶ every⁷ obstacle. 5. They were felling⁸ a tree. 6. I absolve⁹ you. 7. When did he disappear¹⁰? 8. These trees have grown¹¹ a great deal lately. 9. I shall complain¹² of you. 10. Do not feed on¹³ idle dreams.¹⁴ 11. This stupid poem will never live.¹⁵ 12. I shall defeat¹⁶ the enemy without any¹⁷ difficulty. 13. He has been struck¹⁹ by a bullet.¹⁹ 14. I do not believe you. 15. Have you milked²⁰ the cows²¹? 16. He is always smiling.²² 17. Put out²³ the lamp.²⁴ 18. If you join²⁵ your efforts, you will succeed. 19. Would he drive²⁶ you to (the) despair? 20. I shall take you back²⁷ in my carriage. 21. He pretended²⁸ to be ill. 22. Will they not infringe²⁹ the laws? 23. We are born³⁰ liable³¹ to many (of) infirmities. 24. We would withdraw³² our accusation. 25. They will sew³³ on this button. 26. She translated³⁴ her letter. 27. Let them resolve³⁵ to suffer much. 28. That they may pity³⁶ his fall. 29. I have ground³⁷ your knives. 30. These vegetables³⁸ are pickled³⁹ in (some) vinegar.⁴⁰

SECTION X.

FORMATION OF THE VERBS.

177. New French verbs are formed by placing before them: 1. a noun: **main***tenir* (=to maintain [properly *tenir avec la main* =to hold with the hand]);—2. an adjective employed adverbially or an adverb: **mal** traiter, traiter **mal** (=to ill-use);—3. a prefix: **dé***faire* dé... and *faire* (=to undo); **sur***monter*, *sur* and *monter* (=to surmount).

The most important of the prefixes are the following: 1. **contre** (=against), *dire*, **contre***dire* (=to say, to contradict); *signer*, **contre***signer* (=to sign, to countersign); 2. **entre** (=between), *voir*, **entre***voir* (=to see, to have a glimpse of); *ouvrir*, **entr'***ouvrir* (=to open, to half-open); *aider*, *s'***entr'***aider*, (=to help, to help one another); *dévorer*, *s'***entre**-*dévore*

(=to devour, to devour one another); 3. **bien** (=well), *faire*, **bien***faire* (=to do, to do good); 4. **mal** (=ill), *traiter*, **mal***traiter* (=to treat, to ill-treat); *mener*, **mal***mener* (=to lead, to treat roughly); 5. **més**, prefix of depreciation, Eng. *mis*, *allier*, **més***allier* (=to match, to mis-match); *user*, **més***user* (=to use, to misuse); 6. **re**, prefix of return and repetition, *changer*, **re***changer* (=to change, to change over again); *venir*, **re***venir* (=to come, to come again); *blanchir*, **re***blanchir* (=to whiten, to whiten over again); 7. **sur** (=above, over), *mener*, **sur***mener* (=to drive, to overdrive); *chauffer*, **sur***chauffer* (=to heat, to overheat); this prefix implies excess.

New verbs are moreover formed in French by adding to substantives the termination **er** of the first conjugation. Thus *barricade* (=a barricade), *fourrage* (=forage), *chemin* (=path, road), *crayon* (=pencil), *frisson* (=shudder), give *barricader*, *fourrager*, *cheminer*, *crayonner*, *frissonner* (=to barricade, to forage, to journey, to sketch, to shudder). But the most recent words are generally formed with the termination **iser**: *german***iser**, *napoléon***iser**, *bonapart***iser** (=to make German, to win over to the cause of Napoleon or Bonaparte).

178. The French language makes up new verbs from *adjectives*, sometimes by the addition of the termination **ir**: *jaune*, *bleu*, *gros* (=yellow, blue, big), give *jaunir*, *bleuir*, *grossir* (=to become yellow, blue, big); sometimes by adding the termination **ir** and prefixing **a**: *grand*, **a**-*grand*-**ir** (=great, to enlarge), *mince*, **a**-*minc*-**ir** (=thin, to make thin), *maigre*, **a**-*maigr*-**ir** (=lean, to become or make lean), etc.

179. The French language creates new verbs with the help of *verbs* already existing, by introducing the three diminutive suffixes: **ot, on, asse,** which give to the words a depreciative sense: *cligner*, *clign*-**ot**-*er* (=to wink, to wink repeatedly); *trembler*, *trembl*-**ot**-*er* (=to tremble, to shiver); *chanter*, *chant*-**onn**-*er* (=to sing, to hum); *griffer*, *griff*-**onn**-*er* (=to scratch, to scribble); *rêver*, *rêv*-**ass**-*er* (=to dream, to muse).

SECTION XI.

RULES FOR THE AGREEMENT OF THE VERB WITH ITS SUBJECT.

180. Every verb must be in the same number and person as its subject: *Je* **lis** (=I read), *vous* **chantez** (=you sing).

Lis is in the first person singular, because its subject *je* is in the first person singular; *chantez* is in the second person plural, because its subject *vous* is in the second person plural.

181. When a verb has two subjects in the singular, it is put in the plural: *Paul et Marie* **lisent** (=Paul and Mary read).

182. When the subjects are of different persons, the verb is put in the first, if there is a pronoun of the first person in the sentence, otherwise it is put in the second: *vous, lui et moi, nous* **sommes** *heureux* (=you, he, and I, we are happy); *vous et lui, vous* **êtes** *sages* (=you and he are wise). The pronoun *nous* or *vous* is generally expressed before the verb.

QUESTIONS FOR EXAMINATION.

1. How are new verbs formed in French?
2. Give a list of the prefixes used in connection with the verb.
3. Write a list of suffixes added to the substantive;—to the adjective.
4. Name a few diminutive verbs.
5. How does the verb agree with its subject?
6. In what number is the verb put when there are two subjects?
7. In what person is the verb put when the subjects are of different persons?

Exercise 35.

1. Form new verbs from the following ones, preceded with: (1) a noun (*main*); 2. an adverb (*mal*); 3. a prefix (a. *contre*; b. *entre*; c. *re*; d. *sur*): 1. *tenir*; 2. *mener, traiter, verser*; 3. (a) *dire, faire, carrer*; (b) *prendre, larder, mettre*; (c) *lancer, trancher, vêtir, voir, prendre*; (d) *veiller, seoir, nager, passer, prendre*.

2. Form new verbs of the first conjugation from the following substantives: *ménage, chant, apostrophe, cri*.

3. Form new verbs of the second conjugation (a) from the following adjectives: *bleu, jaune, gros, rouge, sale, verd* (old

spelling of *vert*); (*b*) from the following adjectives, together with the prefix *a: maigre, mince, faible, fade, doux, brute*.

4. Form new verbs from the following ones by placing between the stem and the ending one of the suffixes: (a) *ot*, (b) *on*, (c) *asse*; (a) *cligner, taper*; (b) *chanter, griffer*; (c) *rêver*.

Give in every case the English meaning of the verb, and write out the verbs in the following tenses:—
1. Subjunctive present, conditional past, perfect definite;
2. Indicative present, imperfect subjunctive, conditional present;
3. Future anterior, imperative, imperfect indicative;
4. Pluperfect subjunctive, past anterior, pluperfect indicative.

CHAPTER VI.

OF THE PARTICIPLE.

183. The participle is a word which *participates* at once in the nature of the verb, because it marks a tense: **lisant, ayant** *lu* (=reading, having read); and in that of the adjective, because it can serve to qualify a noun: *un homme* **charmant** (=a charming man), *une romance* **chantée** (=a ballad sung).

Participe comes from the Latin accusative *participem* (=that which takes a part, which participates).

184. There are two kinds of participles, the *participle present* and the *participle past*.

The present participle marks an action, and is always invariable: *il est doux de voir des enfants* **aimant** *leur mère et lui* **obéissant** *avec empressement* (=it is pleasant to see children loving their mother and obeying her with eagerness).

The same word becomes an *adjective* when it expresses the quality of a person or thing, in which case it agrees with the noun: *ces enfants sont* **aimants** *et* **obéissants** (=these children are affectionate and obedient).

185. When the present participle is *employed as an adjective*, it agrees in gender and number with the noun to which it refers: *un homme* **aimant** (=an affectionate man), *des eaux* **courantes** (=running waters).

186. The same rule applies to the past participle: *un roi* **honoré** (=an honoured king), *une maison* **meublée** (=a furnished house), *des champs* **cultivés** (=cultivated fields).

QUESTIONS FOR EXAMINATION.

1. What is a *participle?* Explain the meaning of the word.
2. How many kinds of participles are there?
3. When is the present participle invariable?
4. How can the present participle be distinguished from the adjective?
5. State the rule of agreement for the present participle used as an adjective.
6. What is the rule of agreement for the past participle?

Exercise 36.

1. Un père obligeant. 2. Une demoiselle obligeante. 3. Cette femme est obligeante, prévenant tout le monde. 4. Des rumeurs alarmant la ville entière. 5. La plainte de ce pauvre esclave est touchante. 6. Une porte battante. 7. Des jeunes gens prévenants. 8. Une attitude suppliante. 9. Un ouvrage terminé. 10. Des fleurs arrachées de leur tige. 11. Des fruits cueillis.

[1] bruit (*m.*), [2] alarmer, [3] obliger, [4] offre (*f.*), [5] en, [6] mériter, [7] flétrir, [8] chaleur (*f.*) [9] composer, [10] vivre, [11] obéir, [12] billet (*m.*), [13] supplier, [14] offensant.

1. These rumours[1] are alarming.[2] 2. An obliging[3] offer.[4] 3. By[5] obliging your friends, you will deserve[6] their friendship. 4. The flowers have been withered[7] by the heat.[8] 5. (The) society is composed[9] of men living[10] under the same laws. 6. Pupils obeying[11] (to) their master. 7. A finished house. 8. My two notes[12] are written. 9. A mother loving her children. 10. Slaves entreating[13] the judge. 11. Offensive words.[14]

CHAPTER VII.

OF THE ADVERB.

187. The **adverb** is a word which serves to modify the significations of the verb, the adjective, or another adverb: *Le cheval court* **vite** (=the horse runs fast), *cette rose est* **très-belle** (=this rose is very beautiful), *cet enfant marche* **très-***lentement* (=that child walks very slowly).

Adverb comes from the Latin *adverbium*, which means *near the verb*, because that word is usually placed near the verb.

OF THE ADVERB.

188. There are in French eight kinds of adverbs: the adverbs of *place*, of *time*, of *manner*, of *quantity*, of *interrogation*, of *affirmation*, of *negation*, and of *doubt*.

189. The principal **adverbs of place** are: *ici* (=here), *là* (=there), *y* (=here or there), *où* (=where), *en* (=in), *loin* (=far), *ailleurs* (=elsewhere), *deçà* (=on this side), *delà* (=on that side), *partout* (=everywhere), *çà* (=here), *dessus* (=above), *dessous* (=beneath), *dedans* (=within), *dehors* (=without), *devant* (=before), *derrière* (=behind), etc. *Je partirai d'***ici** *pour aller* **partout où** *tu voudras* (=I shall start from hence to go wherever thou wilt), *restez* **là** (=remain there), *allons* **ailleurs** (=let us go elsewhere).

Adverbs of place are either expressed by one word, as *là, y, où, en*; or compounded of two, as *dedans* (from *de* and *dans*), *partout* (from *par* and *tout*), *dessous* (from *de* and *sous*).

190. The principal **adverbs of time** are: *quand* (=when), *puis* (=then), *depuis* (=since), *souvent* (=often), *toujours* (=always), *maintenant* (=now), *jamais* (=ever), *aujourd'hui* (=to-day), *demain* (=to-morrow), *hier* (=yesterday), *jadis* (=formerly), *lors*, *alors* (=then), *longtemps* (=for a long time), *enfin* (=at last), etc. *J'irai* **demain** *et aussi* **souvent** *que tu le voudras* (=I shall go to-morrow, and as often as thou wilt).

These adverbs are either expressed by a single word, as *hier, lors, quand, puis;* or compounded of two words, as *longtemps* (from *long* and *temps*), *aussitôt* (from *aussi* and *tôt*), *ensuite* (from *en* and *suite*).

191. The **adverbs of manner** are formed by adding the termination **ment** to a feminine adjective: *Il mourut courageuse***ment**, i.e., *il mourut d'une* **manière** *courageuse* (=he died courageously); *il vécut sage***ment**, i.e., *il vécut d'une* **manière** *sage* (=he lived wisely).

EXCEPTIONS:

A. If the feminine adjective ends with two vowels, the last one is cut off · *hardie* (=bold), *hardiment* (=boldly).

B. The following adjectives form their adverbs by placing an **acute accent** over the **e** preceding the termination **-ment**:—

aveugle	= blind	*aveuglément*	= blindly
commun	= common	*communément*	= commonly
conforme	= conformable	*conformément*	= conformably
confus	= confused	*confusément*	= confusedly
diffus	= diffuse	*diffusément*	= diffusely
énorme	= enormous	*énormément*	= enormously
exprès	= express	*expressément*	= expressly
immense	= immense	*immensément*	= immensely
impuni	= unpunished	*impunément*	= with impunity
obscur	= dark	*obscurément*	= darkly
opiniâtre	= obstinate	*opiniâtrément*	= obstinately
précis	= precise	*précisément*	= precisely
profond	= deep	*profondément*	= deeply
uniforme	= uniform	*uniformément*	= uniformly.

N.B.—The **è open** of the feminine adjective *complète* (=complete) becomes **é close** in the adverb *complétement* (=completely).

C. *Brièvement* (=briefly) and *traîtreusement* (=treacherously), commonly used as the adverbs of the adjectives *bref* (=short), and *traître* (=treacherous), are formed in the regular manner from the old feminine adjectives *brière* and *traîtreuse*.

D. The final **l** of *gentil* (=pretty) not being pronounced, the adverb is spelt *gentiment* (=prettily).

192. The adjectives ending in **ent, ant** form their adverbs in **em**ment, **am**ment: *prud*ent (=prudent), *prud***emment** (=prudently); *oblig*eant (=obliging), *oblige***amment** (=obligingly).

Exceptions :—

A. *Lent* (=slow) and *véhément* (=vehement, violent) form their adverbs *lent***ement** (=slowly), *véhément***ement** (=vehemently), according to the general rule. (See § 191.)

B. The adverbs *notamment* (=especially), *nuitamment* (=by night), and *sciemment* (=knowingly), were formed from the Old French adjectives *notant, nuitant,* and *scient,* which are now obsolete.

L

193. Adverbs of quality are also formed in French by the occasional use of the *simple adjective: chanter* **juste** (= to sing in tune), *voir* **clair** (= to see distinctly), *parler* **bas** (= to speak in a low voice), etc.

194. The adverbs of manner in *ment* have, like their corresponding adjectives, the three degrees of comparison: *clairement,* **plus** *clairement,* **très-***clairement.*

The *adjectives* employed as adverbs of quality have likewise the three degrees of comparison: *chanter* **juste**, **plus** *juste,* **très-***juste.*

The adverbs of quality, **bien, mal,** form their degrees of comparison irregularly: **bien** makes *mieux* in the comparative, *le mieux* in the superlative relative, and *très-bien* in the superlative absolute; **mal** makes *pis* or *plus mal* in the comparative, and *le pis* in the superlative relative, or *très-mal* in the superlative absolute.

In the same way, the adverbs *loin* (= far), *près* (= near), *tôt* (= soon), *tard* (= late), *vite* (= quickly), *volontiers* (= willingly), make **plus** *loin,* **très-***loin,* **plus** *près,* **très-***près,* etc.

NOTE.—Adverbs are generally placed after the verb: *Il parle* **clairement** (= he speaks clearly).

195. The principal **adverbs of quantity** are *assez* (= enough), *trop* (= too much), *peu* (= little), *beaucoup* (= much), *très* (= very), *tant* (= so much), etc.

N.B.—*Peu* makes *moins* in the comparative, *le moins* in the superlative relative, and *très-peu* in the superlative absolute.

Adverbs of quantity generally take **de** after them. *Très, environ, davantage* are exceptions; *bien* requires **des**.

196. The principal **adverbs of interrogation** are: *pourquoi* (= why), *comment* (= how), *quand* (= when), *combien* (= how much), etc.

197. The principal **adverbs of affirmation** are: *oui* (= yes), *certes* (= certainly), *vraiment* (= truly), etc.

Oui was *oïl* in the Old French (*see* Introduction, p. 3). This *oïl* had for its corresponding negative expression *nenil*, which has become in modern French *nenni*, just as *oïl* has become *oui*.

198. The principal **adverbs of negation** are: *non, ne, pas, goutte, personne, rien,* etc.: **non,** *je* **ne** *veux* **pas** (= no, I will not).

The French have really only two adverbs of negation: *non* and *ne;* the other words, such as *pas, point, goutte,* are mere substantives: *un pas* (=a step), *un point* (=a point), *une goutte* (=a drop), used adverbially as terms of comparison. Every one knows that, in order to give greater strength to the expression of our judgments, we readily support them by a comparison: **pauvre** *comme Job* (=as poor as Job), **fort** *comme un lion* (=as strong as a lion), **féroce** *comme un tigre* (=as fierce as a tigre), etc.; or by using an estimation: *Cet objet ne vaut pas un* **sou** (=this object is not worth a penny). In like manner, the adverbial locutions *pas, mie, goutte, point,* etc., were originally employed in a matter-of-fact manner—they were placed, we mean, in a comparison where they had a distinctive signification: *Je ne marche* **pas** (=I do not walk a step), *je ne vois* **point** (=I do not see a point), *je ne mange* **mie** (=I do not eat a crumb), *je ne bois* **goutte** (=I do not drink a drop), etc.

199. The principal **adverbs of doubt** are: *peut-être* (=perhaps), *probablement* (=probably): *Il sera* **probablement** *ici demain* (=he will probably be here to-morrow).

Peut-être is elliptical for *cela peut être,* and this accounts for the fact that it can be followed by *que* : *Peut-être* **que** *je viendrai,* i.e. *cela peut être* **que** *je viendrai* (=it may be that I shall come).

200. A combination of words having the force of an adverb is called an **adverbial locution.** Thus: *à l'envi* (=vying with each other), *au delà* (=beyond), *en deçà* (=on this side of), *tout à fait* (=quite), *point du tout* (=not at all).

QUESTIONS FOR EXAMINATION.

1. What is an *adverb?*—Explain the meaning of the word.
2. How many kinds of adverbs are there?
3. Name the adverbs of *place;*—of *time.*
4. What is the comparative of *bien?*—of *mal?*—of *peu?*
5. Give a list of the adverbs of *quantity—interrogation—affirmation—negation—doubt.*
6. How do you form adverbs of *manner?*
7. What is meant by an adverbial locution?
8. Name a few adjectives used adverbially.

Exercise 37.

1. Il dit toujours la vérité. 2. Elle vient quelquefois. 3. Nous réussirons tôt ou tard. 4. Je suis allé hier à Brighton. 5. Voyez-vous cette maison là-bas? 6. Il est tard; vous devriez venir plus tôt. 7. Parlez peu, mais parlez à propos. 8. Ce que l'on conçoit bien s'énonce clairement, et les mots pour le dire arrivent aisément. 9. Il ne se moquera pas de moi impunément. 10. Ne lui aviez-

vous pas expressément défendu de prendre votre fusil ? 11. Puisque vous le voulez, j'y consens. 12. Je me tiendrai dorénavant sur mes gardes. 13. Cette demoiselle ne chante pas juste. 14. Ces élèves étudient à l'envi. 15. Il entra tout à coup.

¹ arriver, ² guerrier (m.), ³ action (f.), ⁴ entreprise (f.), ⁵ périr, ⁶ gagner, ⁷ en retard, ⁸ se rencontrer, ⁹ paraitre, ¹⁰ de, ¹¹ se conduire, ¹² se rappeler.

1. This event happened [1] suddenly. 2. Whence comes this warrior [2] ? 3. How many shares [3] have you bought in this undertaking [4] ? 4. We shall certainly perish [5] together. 5. The general has already won [6] two battles. 6. He often loses his money, and he is always late [7] for the train (m.). 7. When shall we meet [8] again ? 8. Your daughter seemed [9] quite surprised at [10] my offer. 9. The citadel was obstinately attacked by the enemy. 10. I have seen that man everywhere. 11. I went to the Crystal Palace yesterday. 12. Above all, tell him to meet me to-morrow in the park. 13. This child behaves [11] very well. 14. I remember [12] the details of the catastrophe confusedly.

CHAPTER VIII.

OF THE PREPOSITION.

201. The **preposition** is an invariable word which serves to unite two words by showing the relation in which the one stands to the other: *Le livre* **de** *Paul* (=Paul's book) ; *utile* **à** *l'homme* (=useful to man); *de* and *à* are prepositions.

Preposition comes from the Latin accusative *præpositionem*, from *præ* (=before), and *positionem* (=position).

202. The relations expressed by prepositions are *five* in number: 1. time: *avant* (=before), *après* (=after), *depuis* (=since), etc. ; 2. place: *à* (=to, at), *vers* (=towards), *dans* (=in), *chez* (=at or in the house of), *devant* (=before), *derrière* (=behind), etc. ; 3. manner or means : *par* (=by), *avec* (=with), *sans* (=without), *selon* (=according to), etc. ; 4. origin or cause : *de* (=of), *par* (=by), *pour* (=for) ; 5. tendency towards *or* remoteness from : *envers* (=towards), *pour* (=for), *contre* (=against), *à* (=to), *de* (of), etc.

203. The prepositions sometimes consist of one word, as *à, de, dans, pour, par, sur,* and are then called simple prepositions; sometimes they are made up of two or more words, as *quant à*, (=as for), *à cause de* (=on account of), *vis-à-vis de* (=opposite), *au-dessus de* (=above, upon), *à l'égard de* (=with regard to), etc., and are then designated as **prepositive locutions.**

204. REMARK 1.—The preposition **à** must not be confounded with **a**, third person singular of the verb *avoir*; **à**, preposition, takes the grave accent: *il monte* **à** *cheval* (=he goes on horseback); **a**, verb, has no accent: *il* **a** *un livre* (=he has a book).

2. **Dès**, preposition, takes the grave accent: *il se lève* **dès** *l'aurore* (=he rises with the dawn); **des** (=of the), genitive plural of the definite article, takes no accent: *les feuilles* **des** *arbres* (=the leaves of the trees).

SECTION I.

FORMATION OF SIMPLE PREPOSITIONS.

205. The French language has formed new prepositions with the help of:—

1. **Substantives**: *malgré*, from the old French adjective **mal** (=*mauvais*=bad), and the substantive **gré** (=will=in spite of).

2. **Adjectives**: *sauf* (still found in *sain et sauf* [=safe and sound] =except, but): *Sauf mes intérêts* (=my interests excepted), *sauf Jean* (=John excepted).

3. **Imperative of verbs**: *voici* (=here is, here are), *voilà* (there is, there are).

These words are compounded of the adverb *ci* and *là* and of *voi*, the old imperative of *voir*. *Voici le loup* (=here is the wolf), means therefore really: *voyez ici le loup* (=see here the wolf), or *le loup est ici*; *voyez-le* (=the wolf is here; see him).

4. **Past participles**: *passé* (=over), *vu* (=considering), *excepté* (=except, save), *attendu* (=considering), *passé ce moment* (=the moment being over), *excepté cet homme* (=with the exception of that man), *vu le danger que nous courons* (=considering the danger we are running), *attendu son infirmité* (=considering his infirmity).

We must add to this list *hormis* (=except), spelt in Old French *hor-mis*, that is to say, *mis hors* (=placed outside). In this locution the participle *mis* (*missus*) was variable; the French of the thirteenth century said: *Cet homme a perdu tous ses enfants, hors mise sa fille* (=this man has lost all his children, with the exception of his daughter). In the fifteenth century the participle *mis* was joined on to the adverb *hors*, and the expression *hors mis* became in its turn a preposition.

5. **Present participles**: *durant, pendant, suivant, concernant, touchant* (from *durer, pendre, suivre, concerner, toucher*). *L'avocat mourut pendant le procès* = *tandis que le procès était pendant* (=the barrister died whilst the lawsuit was pending), *durant sa vie* = *sa vie durant* (=as long as his life lasts), *durant le jour* = *pendant que le jour dure* (=whilst the day lasts).

SECTION II.

FORMATION OF PREPOSITIVE LOCUTIONS.

206. They are formed chiefly with the help either of substantives or of adverbs followed by the preposition **de**. Thus nouns, such as *face, force, cause, faute, milieu*, etc., give the prepositive locutions: *en face de* (=opposite), *à force de* (=by dint of), *à cause de* (=on account of), *faute de* (=for want of), *au milieu de* (=in the midst of), etc.; and adverbs, such as *loin, autour, devant*, etc., give *loin de* (=far from), *autour de* (=around), *au devant de* (=in front of), etc.

Vis-à-vis is a compound of the same kind. The Old French *vis* (from the Latin *visus*) = *visage* (=the face); hence the locution *vis-à-vis*, which is literally equivalent to *face à face* (=face to face). *Vis* is also found in the word *visière* (=visor); the visor was originally the part of the helmet intended to protect the face = *vis*.

SECTION III.

GOVERNMENT OF PREPOSITIONS.

207. 1. Prepositions usually govern the accusative;
    2. Prepositive locutions generally govern the genitive;
    3. The following prepositions and prepositive locutions govern the dative:—

Jusqu'à, jusques à, (=as far as, until), *quant à* (=as for, as to), *par rapport à* (=with regard to).

GOVERNMENT OF PREPOSITIONS.

208. The prepositions are always placed, in French, immediately before the object: *De quoi parlez-vous?* (=what are you speaking of?).

209. The prepositions must be repeated before every word which they govern: *Il ira à Paris et à Londres* (=he will go to Paris and London).

210. The verb governed by a preposition must be put in the infinitive, except in the case of *en*, which governs the present participle: *Ne partez pas sans venir me voir* (=do not start without coming to see me), *il tremble en parlant* (=he trembles whilst speaking).

QUESTIONS FOR EXAMINATION.

1. What is *a preposition?*
2. State the difference between *a*, verb, and *à*, preposition;— between *des*, article, and *des* preposition.
3. What is a prepositive locution?
4. Name the *present* and *past participles* used as prepositions.
5. How are *prepositive locutions* formed with the help (a) of nouns, (b) of adverbs?
6. Name the prepositions which govern substantives (a) in the genitive, (b) in the dative, (c) in the accusative.
7. What preposition governs the verb in the present participle?
8. Where are prepositions placed?

Exercise 33.

1. Ne va-t-il pas à Paris? 2. Il a été ingrat envers son bienfaiteur. 3. Mon chapeau est dans la chambre. 4. Venez chez moi. 5. Vers le nord, la nature présente un aspect triste et sauvage. 6. Dès aujourd'hui je renonce à le voir. 7. En agissant ainsi vous avez manqué à toutes les convenances. 8. Mettez vos livres sur la table. 9. Irez-vous jusqu'à Berlin? 10. Quant à moi, je meurs de faim. 11. Êtes-vous hors d'affaire? 12. Attendu sa jeunesse, nous ne le punirons pas. 13. Il demeure près de l'église.

[1] près de, [2] offense (f.), [3] doux, [4] orage (m.), [5] éclater, [6] dès.

1. He is going to Paris. 2. I live near[1] the railway. 3. In absolving this man, justice has not been done. 4. Never be ungrateful towards your parents. 5. Considering the nature of the offence,[2] the punishment is extremely mild.[3] 6. During the ceremony, a thunderstorm[4] burst[5] over the town. 7. The troops are out of danger. 8. As for my books, they are in your room. 9. Towards the river you will find a pretty country-house. 10. The book shall be sent to the printer's as early as[6] to-morrow morning. 11. The laws are the same in France and Algeria.

CHAPTER IX.

OF THE CONJUNCTION.

211. The conjunction is an invariable word which serves to unite together two words or two propositions: *Pierre* **et** *Paul sont frères* (= Peter and Paul are brothers), *aimons Dieu* **puisqu'**il *est bon* (= let us love God, since He is good); **et, puisque** are conjunctions.

Conjunction is from the Latin accusative *conjunctionem* (= conjunction, properly *union*).

212. The conjunctions are sometimes one single word, as *et, ou, si, mais,* etc., and are then called **simple conjunctions**; sometimes they are formed of two or more words: *tandis que, bien que, parce que,* and are then designated as **conjunctive locutions**.

213. The principal **simple conjunctions** are: *car* (= for), *comme* (= as), *donc* (= then, therefore), *et* (= and), *mais* (= but), *or* (= now, but), *ou* (= or), *que* (= that), *quand* (= though, even though), *ni* (= nor), *si* (= if), each of which is really only one word.

To the above list we must add the conjunctions such as *plutôt* (= rather), *puisque* (= since), *néanmoins* (= nevertheless), *cependant* (= meanwhile), *lorsque* (= when), which are really compounded of two distinct words (*plus-tôt, puis-que, néant-moins, ce-pendant, lors-que*), combined into one by modern orthography.

214. The principal **conjunctive locutions** are: *au contraire,* (= on the contrary), *au moins* (= at least), *tandis que* (= whilst), *alors que* (= when, now that), *sans que* (= without), *dès que* (= as soon as), *avant que* (= before that), *après que* (= after that), etc.

215. REMARK.—1. **Que** is a relative pronoun when used instead of *lequel, laquelle;* it is an adverb when used instead of *combien;* it is a conjunction when it serves to unite two clauses of a sentence: *Je crois* **que** *Dieu est saint* (= I believe that God is holy).

2. **Où**, adverb (=where, when), points out a place or a time, and takes the grave accent; *ou*, conjunction (=or) takes no accent: *Mon frère* **ou** *moi* (=my brother or I).

3. **Si** is an adverb when it can be used instead of *tant, tellement* (=so, so much); in all other cases, it is a conjunction: *Je sortirai* **si** *le temps est beau* (=I shall go out if the weather is fine).

216. Conjunctions followed by *de* take the verb in the infinitive. (For the use of the indicative or subjunctive after conjunctions, *see* Syntax of prepositions).

QUESTIONS FOR EXAMINATION.

1. What is a *conjunction*?
2. Distinguish between *simple conjunctions*, and *conjunctive locutions*.
3. When is *que* an adverb?
4. When is *où* an adverb?
5. Distinguish between *si*, adverb, and *si*, conjunction.
6. In what mood is the verb placed after a conjunction followed by *de*.

Exercise 39.

1. Vous et moi, lui ou elle. 2. J'ai fait mon thème, mais je n'ai pas appris ma leçon. 3. Soyez tranquille, car le maitre est là. 4. Puisque vous ne voulez pas m'accompagner, je ne sortirai pas. 5. Il ferait cela plutôt que de vous le proposer. 6. Le roi a rejeté cette mesure comme trop violente. 7. Il ne sait ni lire, ni écrire. 8. Il a perdu beaucoup d'argent, néanmoins il persiste à jouer. 9. Quoiqu'il aille à Londres, il ne verra pas son ami.

[1] pourvu que. [2] réussir. [3] grandeur (*f.*). [4] quoique, [5] parce que, [6] indisposé. [7] dire. [8] tandis que, [9] déguiser, [10] que, [11] à moins que, [12] ne changiez, [13] abandonner, [14] part (*f.*).

1. Provided[1] you are* attentive, you will succeed.[2] 2. Neither gold nor greatness[3] make a man happy. 3. You and I shall go together. 4. Although[4] I do* all (that which) I can, I do not succeed. 5. If we do not succeed, it will not be our fault. 6. I cannot come because[5] I am unwell.[6] 7. We speak[7] the truth, whereas[8] your friend always disguises[9] it. 8. Whether[10] I was* hungry or not, you should have kept the dinner on the table. 9. Unless[11] you alter [12]* your plans, I shall give up[13] my share[14] in the business.

* These verbs must be put in the subjunctive.

CHAPTER X

OF THE INTERJECTION.

217. The **interjection** is a cry, an exclamation expressing the sudden impulse of the mind: *Ah! Oh! Fi! Hélas!*

Interjection comes from the Latin accusative *interjectionem*, which means literally the action of throwing into the middle (of the sentence).

Principal interjections.

Joy:	*Bon! Vive la joie!*	Surprise:	*Quoi! Vraiment!*
Grief:	*Hélas! Aïe! Ah! Ouf!*	Silence:	*Chut! Paix!*
Fear:	*Ha! Hé! Ho!*	Calling:	*Holà! Ho! Hem!*
Aversion:	*Fi! Fi donc!*	Warning:	*Gare!*
Admiration:	*Oh!*	Attention:	*Tenez! Voilà!*
Encouraging:	*Allons! Courage!*	Disbelief:	*Ah! bah!*

Ciel! Bis! Bravo! Tout beau (= softly), are also used in various exclamations.

218. The interjections are formed either with the help of nouns: *paix!* (=silence), *courage!* (=cheer up!), *patience!* (=have patience!), or of verbs: *soit!* (=be it so!), *allons!* (=come on!), *suffit!* (=enough! that will do!). Sometimes they are mere exclamations: *ah! oh!* etc.

Hélas, written in Old French in two words: *hé! las!* is formed of the interjection *hé!* and the adjective *las* (*lassus*), which formerly meant *malheureux* = unhappy. The French of the thirteenth century said: *Cette mère est* **lasse** *de la mort de son fils* (=this mother is unhappy at the death of her son). *Hé!* **las!** *que je suis* (=Ah! unhappy that I am!). It was only in the fifteenth century that the two words coalesced, and that *hélas* became inseparable. At the same time, *las* lost all its primitive energy, and changed the meaning of *grief* for that of *weariness* or *fatigue*, just as it had happened in the words *gêne* (=inconvenience) and *ennui* (=weariness), which originally meant *torture* and *hatred*, respectively.

Dame! which must not be confounded with the feminine substantive *dame* (= lady), is the abbreviation of *Dame-Dieu*, an Old French exclamation equivalent to *Seigneur Dieu* (= Lord God). We constantly find in medieval texts: *que* **Dame-Dieu** *nous aide!* (= the Lord God help us!). *Dame-Dieu*, and simply *Dame* (that is to say, Lord God), was used as an interjection; and the exclamation *Ah! dame* (= ah! well), which, nowadays, has lost all meaning, signifies really *Ah! Seigneur!* (= ah! Lord!). The word *dame* is still found in the geographical names *Dammartin*, *Dampierre*, etc., which signify *the Lord* Martin, *the Lord* Peter, etc.

QUESTIONS FOR EXAMINATION.

1. What is an *interjection*?
2. Name the principal interjections.
3. How are interjections formed?
4. Explain the original meaning of *Hélas!* and *Dame!*

The following table will complete and resume all the details given in Section III.

Conjugation of the auxiliary verb **avoir** (= to have), *negatively, interrogatively, and interrogatively with a negation.*

N.B.—The same scheme is applicable to any transitive verb, and to all neuter verbs conjugated with the auxiliary **avoir**.

INFINITIVE MOOD.
Negatively.

PRESENT.—**Ne pas** avoir *or* **n'**avoir **pas**, *not to have.*
PAST.—**N'**ayant **pas** eu, *not to have had.*

PARTICIPLES.
Negatively.

PRESENT.—**N'**ayant **pas**, *not having.*
PAST.—**N'**ayant **pas** eu, *not having had.*
FUTURE.—**Ne** devant **pas** avoir, *not about to have.*

INDICATIVE MOOD.
PRESENT TENSE.

Negatively.	*Interrogatively.*	*Interrog. with a neg.*
I have not, etc.	*Have I? etc.*	*Have I not? etc.*
Je **n'**ai **pas**	ai-*je*? *	**n'**ai-*je* **pas**? †
tu **n'**as **pas**	as-*tu*?	**n'**as-*tu* **pas**?
il **n'**a **pas**	a-*t-il*?	**n'**a-*t-il* **pas**?
nous **n'**avons **pas**	avons-*nous*?	**n'**avons-*nous* **pas**?
vous **n'**avez **pas**	avez-*vous*?	**n'**avez-*vous* **pas**?
ils **n'**ont **pas**	ont-*ils*?	**n'**ont-*ils* **pas**?

* Aimé-*je*? Est-ce que *je* romps?
† N'aimé-*je* **pas**? Est-ce que *je* **ne** romps **pas**?

CONJUGATION OF VERBS.

PAST INDEFINITE.

I have not had, etc.	Have I had? etc.	Have I not had? etc.
Je n'ai pas eu	Ai-je * eu?	N'ai-je pas eu?
tu n'as pas eu	as-tu eu?	n'as-tu pas eu?
il n'a pas eu	a-t-il eu?	n'a-t-il pas eu?
nous n'avons pas eu	avons-nous eu?	n'avons-nous pas eu?
vous n'avez pas eu	avez-vous eu?	n'avez-vous pas eu?
ils n'ont pas eu	ont-ils eu?	n'ont-ils pas eu?

IMPERFECT.

I had not, etc.	Had I? etc.	Had I not? etc.
Je n'avais pas	Avais-je?	N'avais-je pas?
tu n'avais pas	avais-tu?	n'avais-tu pas?
il n'avait pas	avait-il?	n'avait-il pas?
nous n'avions pas	avions-nous?	n'avions-nous pas?
vous n'aviez pas	aviez-vous?	n'aviez-vous pas?
ils n'avaient pas	avaient-ils?	n'avaient-ils pas?

PLUPERFECT.

I had not had, etc.	Had I had? etc.	Had I not had? etc.
Je n'avais pas eu	avais-je eu?	N'avais-je pas eu?
tu n'avais pas eu	avais-tu eu?	n'avais-tu pas eu?
il n'avait pas eu	avait-il eu?	n'avait-il pas eu?
nous n'avions pas eu	avions-nous eu?	n'avions-nous pas eu?
vous n'aviez pas eu	aviez-vous eu?	n'aviez-vous pas eu?
ils n'avaient pas eu	avaient-ils eu?	n'avaient-ils pas eu?

PAST DEFINITE or PRETERPERFECT.

I had not, etc.	Had I? etc.	Had I not? etc.
Je n'eus pas	Eus-je?	N'eus-je pas?
tu n'eus pas	eus-tu?	n'eus-tu pas?
il n'eut pas	eut-il?	n'eut-il pas?
nous n'eûmes pas	eûmes-nous?	n'eûmes-nous pas?
vous n'eûtes pas	eûtes-vous?	n'eûtes-vous pas?
ils n'eurent pas	eurent-ils?	n'eurent-ils pas?

* The e of je is not dropped in the interrogation before a vowel.

PAST ANTERIOR.

I had not had, etc.	Had I had? etc.	Had I not had? etc.
Je n'eus **pas** eu	Eus-*je* eu?	N'eus-*je* **pas** eu?
tu n'eus **pas** eu	eus-*tu* eu?	n'eus-*tu* **pas** eu?
il n'eut **pas** eu	eut-*il* eu?	n'eut-*il* **pas** eu?
nous n'eûmes **pas** eu	eûmes-*nous* eu?	n'eûmes-*nous* **pas** eu?
vous n'eûtes **pas** eu	eûtes-*vous* eu?	n'eûtes-*vous* **pas** eu?
ils n'eurent **pas** eu	eurent-*ils* eu?	n'eurent-*ils* **pas** eu?

FUTURE.

I shall not have, etc.	Shall I have? etc.	Shall I not have? etc.
Je n'aurai **pas**	Aurai-*je*?	N'aurai-*je* **pas**?
tu n'auras **pas**	auras-*tu*?	n'auras-*tu* **pas**?
il n'aura **pas**	aura-*t-il*?	n'aura-*t-il* **pas**?
nous n'aurons **pas**	aurons-*nous*?	n'aurons-*nous* **pas**?
vous n'aurez **pas**	aurez-*vous*?	n'aurez-*vous* **pas**?
ils n'auront **pas**	auront-*ils*?	n'auront-*ils* **pas**?

FUTURE ANTERIOR.

I shall not have had, etc.	Shall I have had? etc.	Shall I not have had? etc.
Je n'aurai **pas** eu	Aurai-*je* eu?	N'aurai-*je* **pas** eu?
tu n'auras **pas** eu	auras-*tu* eu?	n'auras-*tu* **pas** eu?
il n'aura **pas** eu	aura-*t-il* eu?	n'aura-*t-il* **pas** eu?
nous n'aurons **pas** eu	aurons-*nous* eu?	n'aurons-*nous* **pas** eu?
vous n'aurez **pas** eu	aurez-*vous* eu?	n'aurez-*vous* **pas** eu?
ils n'auront **pas** eu	auront-*ils* eu?	n'auront-*ils* **pas** eu?

CONDITIONAL PRESENT.

I should not have, etc.	Should I have? etc.	Should I not have? etc.
Je n'aurais **pas**	Aurais-*je*?	N'aurais-*je* **pas**?
tu n'aurais **pas**	aurais-*tu*?	n'aurais-*tu* **pas**?
il n'aurait **pas**	aurait-*il*?	n'aurait-*il* **pas**?
nous n'aurions **pas**	aurions-*nous*?	n'aurions-*nous* **pas**?
vous n'auriez **pas**	auriez-*vous*?	n'auriez-*vous* **pas**?
ils n'auraient **pas**	auraient-*ils*?	n'auraient-*ils* **pas**?

CONDITIONAL PAST.

I should not have had, etc.	Should I have had? etc.	Should I not have had, etc.
Je n'aurais pas eu	Aurais-je eu?	N'aurais-je pas eu?
tu n'aurais pas eu	aurais-tu eu?	n'aurais-tu pas eu?
il n'aurait pas eu	aurait-il eu?	n'aurait-il pas eu?
nous n'aurions pas eu	aurions-nous eu?	n'aurions-nous pas eu?
vous n'auriez pas eu	auriez-vous eu?	n'auriez-vous pas eu?
ils n'auraient pas eu	auraient-ils eu?	n'auraient-ils pas eu?

or

Je n'eusse pas eu	Eussé-je eu?	N'eussé-je pas eu?
tu n'eusses pas eu	eusses-tu eu?	n'eusses-tu pas eu?
il n'eût pas eu	eût-il eu?	n'eût-il pas eu?
nous n'eussions pas eu	eussions-nous eu?	n'eussions-nous pas eu?
vous n'eussiez pas eu	eussiez-vous eu?	n'eussiez-vous pas eu?
ils n'eussent pas eu	eussent-ils eu?	n'eussent-ils pas eu?

IMPERATIVE MOOD.

Negatively.

PRESENT.	PAST.
Have not	Have not had.
N'aie pas	N'aie pas eu
n'ayons pas	n'ayons pas eu
n'ayez pas	n'ayez pas eu

SUBJUNCTIVE MOOD.

Negatively.

PRESENT or FUTURE.	PAST.
That I may not have, etc.	That I may not have had, etc.
Que je n'aie pas	Que je n'aie pas eu
que tu n'aies pas	que tu n'aies pas eu
qu'il n'ait pas	qu'il n'ait pas eu
que nous n'ayons pas	que nous n'ayons pas eu
que vous n'ayez pas	que vous n'ayez pas eu
qu'ils n'aient pas	qu'ils n'aient pas eu

IMPERFECT.	PLUPERFECT.
That I might not have, etc.	*That I might not have had, etc*
Que je n'eusse pas	Que je n'eusse pas eu
que tu n'eusses pas	que tu n'eusses pas eu
qu'il n'eût pas	qu'il n'eût pas eu
que nous n'eussions pas	que nous n'eussions pas eu
que vous n'eussiez pas	que vous n'eussiez pas eu
qu'ils n'eussent pas	qu'ils n'eussent pas eu

Conjugation of the auxiliary verb **être** *(= to be), negatively, interrogatively, and interrogatively with a negation.*

INFINITIVE MOOD.

Negatively.

PRESENT.—**Ne pas** être *or* **n'être pas,** *not to be.*
PAST.—**N'**avoir **pas** été, *not to have been.*

PARTICIPLES.

Negatively.

PRESENT.—**N'**étant **pas,** *not being.*
PAST.—**N'**ayant **pas** été, *not having been.*
FUTURE.—**Ne** devant **pas** être, *not about to be.*

INDICATIVE MOOD.

PRESENT TENSE.

Negatively.	*Interrogatively.*	*Interrog. with a neg.*
I am not, etc.	*Am I? etc.*	*Am I not? etc.*
Je ne suis pas	Suis-je ?	Ne suis-je pas ?
tu n'es pas	es-tu ?	n'es-tu pas ?
il n'est pas	est-il ?	n'est-il pas ?
nous ne sommes pas	sommes-nous ?	ne sommes-nous pas ?
vous n'êtes pas	êtes-vous ?	n'êtes-vous pas ?
ils ne sont pas	sont-ils ?	ne sont-ils pas ?

PAST INDEFINITE.

I have not been, etc. *Have I been? etc.* *Have I not been? etc.*

Je n'ai pas été   Ai-je été?   N'ai-je pas été?
tu n'as pas été   as-tu été?   n'as-tu pas été?
il n'a pas été   a-t-il été?   n'a-t-il pas été?
nous n'avons pas été   avons-nous été?   n'avons-nous pas été?
vous n'avez pas été   avez-vous été?   n'avez-vous pas été?
ils n'ont pas été   ont-ils été?   n'ont-ils pas été?

IMPERFECT.

I was not, etc. *Was I? etc.* *Was I not? etc.*

Je n'étais pas   Etais-je?   N'étais-je pas?
tu n'étais pas   étais-tu?   n'étais-tu pas?
il n'était pas   était-il?   n'était-il pas?
nous n'étions pas   étions-nous?   n'étions-nous pas?
vous n'étiez pas   étiez-vous?   n'étiez-vous pas?
ils n'étaient pas   étaient-ils?   n'étaient-ils pas?

PLUPERFECT.

I had not been, etc. *Had I been? etc.* *Had I not been? etc.*

Je n'avais pas été   Avais-je été?   N'avais-je pas été?
tu n'avais pas été   avais-tu été?   n'avais-tu pas été?
il n'avait pas été   avait-il été?   n'avait-il pas été?
nous n'avions pas été avions-nous été?   n'avions-nous pas été?
vous n'aviez pas été   aviez-vous été?   n'aviez-vous pas été?
ils n'avaient pas été avaient-ils été?   n'avaient-ils pas été?

PAST DEFINITE or PRETERPERFECT.

I was not, etc. *Was I? etc.* *Was I not? etc.*

Je ne fus pas   Fus-je?   Ne fus-je pas?
tu ne fus pas   fus-tu?   ne fus-tu pas?
il ne fut pas   fut-il?   ne fut-il pas?
nous ne fûmes pas   fûmes-nous?   ne fûmes-nous pas?
vous ne fûtes pas   fûtes-vous?   ne fûtes-vous pas?
ils ne furent pas   furent-ils?   ne furent-ils pas?

PAST ANTERIOR.

I had not been, etc.	Had I been? etc.	Had I not been? etc.
Je n'eus pas été	Eus-je été?	N'eus-je pas été?
tu n'eus pas été	eus-tu été?	n'eus-tu pas été?
il n'eut pas été	eut-il été?	n'eut-il pas été?
nous n'eûmes pas été	eûmes-nous été?	n'eûmes-nous pas été?
vous n'eûtes pas été	eûtes-vous été?	n'eûtes-vous pas été?
ils n'eurent pas été	eurent-ils été?	n'eurent-ils pas été?

FUTURE.

I shall not be, etc.	Shall I be? etc.	Shall I not be? etc.
Je ne serai pas	Serai-je?	Ne serai-je pas?
tu ne seras pas	seras-tu?	ne seras-tu pas?
il ne sera pas	sera-t-il?	ne sera-t-il pas?
nous ne serons pas	serons-nous?	ne serons-nous pas?
vous ne serez pas	serez-vous?	ne serez-vous pas?
ils ne seront pas	seront-ils?	ne seront-ils pas?

FUTURE ANTERIOR.

I shall not have been, etc.	Shall I have been? etc.	Shall I not have been? etc.
Je n'aurai pas été	Aurai-je été?	N'aurai-je pas été?
tu n'auras pas été	auras-tu été?	n'auras-tu pas été?
il n'aura pas été	aura-t-il été?	n'aura-t-il pas été?
nous n'aurons pas été	aurons-nous été?	n'aurons-nous pas été?
vous n'aurez pas été	aurez-vous été?	n'aurez-vous pas été?
ils n'auront pas été	auront-ils été?	n'auront-ils pas été?

CONDITIONAL PRESENT.

I should not be, etc.	Should I be? etc.	Should I not be? etc.
Je ne serais pas	Serais-je?	Ne serais-je pas?
tu ne serais pas	serais-tu?	ne serais-tu pas?
il ne serait pas	serait-il?	ne serait-il pas?
nous ne serions pas	serions-nous?	ne serions-nous pas?
vous ne seriez pas	seriez-vous?	ne seriez-vous pas?
ils ne seraient pas	seraient-ils?	ne seraient-ils pas?

CONDITIONAL PAST.

I should not have been, etc.	*Should I have been? etc.*	*Should I not have been? etc.*
Je n'aurais pas été	Aurais-je été ?	N'aurais-je pas été ?
tu n'aurais pas été	aurais-tu été ?	n'aurais-tu pas été ?
il n'aurait pas été	aurait-il été ?	n'aurait-il pas été ?
nous n'aurions pas été	aurions-nous été ?	n'aurions-nous pas été ?
vous n'auriez pas été	auriez-vous été ?	n'auriez-vous pas été ? [été ?
ils n'auraient pas [été	auraient-ils été ?	n'auraient-ils pas

or

Je n'eusse pas été	Eussé-je été ?	N'eussé-je pas été ?
tu n'eusses pas été	eusses-tu été ?	n'eusses-tu pas été ?
il n'eût pas été	eût-il été ?	n'eût-il pas été ?
nous n'eussions pas été	eussions-nous été ?	n'eussions-nous pas été ?
vous n'eussiez pas été	eussiez-vous été ?	n'eussiez-vous pas été ? [été ?
ils n'eussent pas été	eussent-ils été ?	n'eussent-ils pas

IMPERATIVE MOOD.
Negatively.

PRESENT.	PAST.
Do thou not be.	*Have not been.*
Ne sois pas	N'aie pas été
ne soyons pas	n'ayons pas été
ne soyez pas	n'ayez pas été.

SUBJUNCTIVE MOOD.
Negatively.

PRESENT or FUTURE.	PAST.
That I may not be, etc.	*That I may not have been, etc.*
Que je ne sois pas	Que je n'aie pas été
que tu ne sois pas	que tu n'aies pas été
qu'il ne soit pas	qu'il n'ait pas été
que nous ne soyons pas	que nous n'ayons pas été
que vous ne soyez pas	que vous n'ayez pas été
qu'ils ne soient pas	qu'ils n'aient pas été

IMPERFECT.	PLUPERFECT.
That I might not be.	*That I might not have been.*
Que je ne fusse pas	Que je n'eusse pas été
que tu ne fusses pas	que tu n'eusses pas été
qu'il ne fût pas	qu'il n'eût pas été
que nous ne fussions pas	que nous n'eussions pas été
que vous ne fussiez pas	que vous n'eussiez pas été
qu'ils ne fussent pas	qu'ils n'eussent pas été.

164 REFLEXIVE VERBS.

Models of Reflexive Verbs conjugated negatively, interrogatively, a interrogatively with a negation.

INFINITIVE MOOD.
PRESENT.
Negatively.

Ne pas se réjouir, *not to rejoice*	ne pas s'apercevoir, *not to perceive*	ne pas se perdre, *no lose one's self.*

PAST.

Ne pas s'être réjoui, *not to have rejoiced*	ne pas s'être aperçu, *not to have perceived*	ne pas s'être perdu, *to have lost one's se*

PARTICIPLES.
PRESENT.
Negatively.

Ne se réjouissant pas, *not rejoicing*	ne s'apercevant pas, *not perceiving*	ne se perdant pas, *osing one's self.*

PAST.

Réjoui, -ie, -is, or -ies, *rejoiced*	aperçu, -ue, -us, *or* -ues, *perceived*	perdu, -ue, -us, *or* -u *lost*
ne s'étant pas réjoui, *not having rejoiced*	ne s'étant pas aperçu, *not having perceived*	ne s'étant pas perdu, *having lost one's se*

FUTURE.

Ne devant pas se réjouir, *not about to rejoice*	ne devant pas s'apercevoir, *not about to perceive*	ne devant pas se perd *not about to lose o se'f.*

INDICATIVE MOOD.
PRESENT TENSE.

Negatively.	*Interrogatively.*	*Interrog. with a ne*
I do not rejoice, etc.	*Do I perceive ? etc.*	*Do I not lose myself ?*
Je ne me réjouis pas	M'aperçois-je ?	Est-ce que je ne perds pas ?
tu ne te réjouis pas	t'aperçois-tu ?	ne te perds-tu pas ?
il ne se réjouit pas	s'aperçoit-il ?	ne se perd-il pas ?
nous ne nous réjouissons pas	nous apercevons-nous ?	ne nous perdons-nc pas ?
vous ne vous réjouissez pas	vous apercevez-vous ?	ne vous perdez-vc pas ?
ils ne se réjouissent pas	s'aperçoivent-ils ?	ne se perdent-ils pa

REFLEXIVE VERBS.

PAST INDEFINITE.

I have not rejoiced, etc.	Have I perceived? etc.	Have I not lost myself? etc.
Je ne me suis pas réjoui	Me suis-je aperçu?	Ne me suis-je pas perdu?
tu ne t'es pas réjoui	t'es-tu aperçu?	ne t'es-tu pas perdu?
il ne s'est pas réjoui	s'est-il aperçu?	ne s'est-il pas perdu?
nous ne nous sommes pas réjouis	nous sommes-nous aperçus?	ne nous sommes-nous pas perdus?
vous ne vous êtes pas réjouis	vous êtes-vous aperçus?	ne vous êtes-vous pas perdus? [dus?
ils ne se sont pas réjouis	se sont-ils aperçus?	ne se sont-ils pas per-

IMPERFECT.

I was not rejoicing, etc.	Was I perceiving? etc.	Was I not losing myself? etc.
Je ne me réjouissais pas	M'apercevais-je?	Ne me perdais-je pas?
tu ne te réjouissais pas	t'apercevais-tu?	ne te perdais-tu pas?
il ne se réjouissait pas	s'apercevait-il?	ne se perdait-il pas?
nous ne nous réjouissions pas	nous apercevions-nous?	ne nous perdions-nous pas?
vous ne vous réjouissiez pas [pas	vous aperceviez-vous?	ne vous perdiez-vous pas?
ils ne se réjouissaient	s'apercevaient-ils?	ne se perdaient-ils pas?

PLUPERFECT.

I had not rejoiced, etc.	Had I perceived? etc.	Had I not lost myself? etc.
Je ne m'étais pas réjoui	M'étais-je aperçu?	Ne m'étais-je pas perdu?
tu ne t'étais pas réjoui	t'étais-tu aperçu?	ne t'étais-tu pas perdu?
il ne s'était pas réjoui	s'était-il aperçu?	ne s'était-il pas perdu?
nous ne nous étions pas réjouis	nous étions-nous aperçus?	ne nous étions-nous pas perdus?
vous ne vous étiez pas réjouis [jouis	vous étiez-vous aperçus?	ne vous étiez-vous pas perdus? [dus?
ils ne s'étaient pas ré-	s'étaient-ils aperçus?	ne s'étnient-ils pas per-

PAST DEFINITE OR PRETERPERFECT.

I did not rejoice, etc.	Did I perceive? etc.	Did I not lose myself? etc.
Je ne me réjouis pas	M'aperçus-je?	Ne me perdis-je pas?
tu ne te réjouis pas	t'aperçus-tu?	ne te perdis-tu pas?
il ne se réjouit pas	s'aperçut-il?	ne se perdit-il pas?
nous ne nous réjouîmes pas [pas	nous aperçûmes-nous?	ne nous perdîmes-nous pas? [pas?
vous ne vous réjouîtes	vous aperçûtes-vous?	ne vous perdîtes-vous
ils ne se réjouirent pas	s'aperçurent-ils?	ne se perdirent-ils pas?

PAST ANTERIOR.

I had not rejoiced, etc.	*Had I perceived? etc.*	*Had I not lost myself? etc.*
Je ne me fus pas réjoui	Me fus-je aperçu ?	Ne me fus-je pas perdu ?
tu ne te fus pas réjoui	te fus-tu aperçu ?	ne te fus-tu pas perdu ?
il ne se fut pas réjoui	se fut-il aperçu ?	ne se fut-il pas perdu ?
nous ne nous fûmes pas réjouis	nous fûmes-nous aperçus ?	ne nous fûmes-nous pas perdus ?
vous ne vous fûtes pas réjouis [réjouis	vous fûtes-vous aperçus ?	ne vous fûtes-vous pas perdus ? [perdus ?
ils ne se furent pas	se furent-ils aperçus ?	ne se furent-ils pas

FUTURE.

I shall not rejoice, etc.	*Shall I perceive ? etc.*	*Shall I not lose myself ? etc.*
Je ne me réjouirai pas	M'apercevrai-je ?	Ne me perdrai-je pas ?
tu ne te réjouiras pas	t'apercevras-tu ?	ne te perdras-tu pas ?
il ne se réjouira pas	s'apercevra-t-il ?	ne se perdra-t-il pas ?
nous ne nous réjouirons pas [pas	nous apercevrons-nous ?	ne nous perdrons-nous pas ? [pas ?
vous ne vous réjouirez	vous apercevrez-vous ?	ne vous perdrez-vous
ils ne se réjouiront pas	s'apercevront-ils ?	ne se perdront-ils pas ?

FUTURE ANTERIOR.

I shall not have rejoiced, etc.	*Shall I have perceived ? etc.*	*Shall I not have lost myself ? etc.*
Je ne me serai pas réjoui	Me serai-je aperçu ?	Ne me serai-je pas perdu ?
tu ne te seras pas réjoui	te seras-tu aperçu ?	ne te seras-tu pas perdu ?
il ne se sera pas réjoui	se sera-t-il aperçu ?	ne se sera-t-il pas perdu ?
nous ne nous serons pas réjouis	nous serons-nous aperçus ?	ne nous serons-nous pas perdus ?
vous ne vous serez pas réjouis [réjouis	vous serez-vous aperçus ?	ne vous serez-vous pas perdus ? [dus ?
ils ne se seront pas	se seront-ils aperçus ?	ne se seront-ils pas per-

CONDITIONAL MOOD.

PRESENT.

I should not rejoice, etc.	*Should I perceive ? etc.*	*Should I not lose myself ? etc.*
Je ne me réjouirais pas	M'apercevrais-je ?	Ne me perdrais-je pas ?
tu ne te réjouirais pas	t'apercevrais-tu ?	ne te perdrais-tu pas ?
il ne se réjouirait pas	s'apercevrait-il ?	ne se perdrait-il pas ?
nous ne nous réjouirions pas	nous apercevrions-nous ?	ne nous perdrions-nous pas ?
vous ne vous réjouiriez pas [pas	vous apercevriez-vous ?	ne vous perdriez-vous pas ? [pas ?
ils ne se réjouiraient	s'apercevraient-ils ?	ne se perdraient-ils

REFLEXIVE VERBS.

PAST.

I should not have rejoiced, etc.	Should I have perceived? etc.	Should I not have lost myself? etc.
Je ne me serais pas réjoui	Me serais-je aperçu ?	Ne me serais-je pas perdu ? [du ?
tu ne te serais pas réjoui	te serais-tu aperçu ?	ne te serais-tu pas perdu ?
il ne se serait pas réjoui	se serait-il aperçu ?	ne se serait-il pas perdu ?
nous ne nous serions pas réjouis	nous serions-nous aperçus ?	ne nous serions-nous pas perdus ?
vous ne vous seriez pas réjouis [réjouis	vous seriez-vous aperçus ?	ne vous seriez-vous pas perdus ? [perdus ?
ils ne se seraient pas	se seraient-ils aperçus ?	ne se seraient-ils pas

or

je ne me fusse pas réjoui	me fussé-je aperçu ?	ne me fussé-je pas perdu ? [du ?
tu ne te fusses pas réjoui	te fusses-tu aperçu ?	ne te fusses-tu pas perdu ?
il ne se fût pas réjoui	se fût-il aperçu ?	ne se fût-il pas perdu ?
nous ne nous fussions pas réjouis	nous fussions-nous aperçus ?	ne nous fussions-nous pas perdus ?
vous ne vous fussiez pas réjouis	vous fussiez-vous aperçus ?	ne vous fussiez-vous pas perdus ?
ils ne se fussent pas réjouis	se fussent-ils aperçus ?	ne se fussent-ils pas perdus ?

IMPERATIVE MOOD.
Negatively.
PRESENT.

Do not rejoice, etc.	Do not perceive, etc.	Do not lose thyself, etc.
Ne te réjouis pas [pas	Ne t'aperçois pas [pas	Ne te perds pas
Ne nous réjouissons	Ne nous apercevons	Ne nous perdons pas
Ne vous réjouissez pas	Ne vous apercevez pas	Ne vous perdez pas

PAST.

Have not rejoiced, etc.	Have not perceived, etc.	Have not lost thyself, etc.
Ne te sois pas réjoui	Ne te sois pas aperçu	Ne te sois pas perdu
Ne nous soyons pas réjouis [jouis	Ne nous soyons pas aperçus [çus	Ne nous soyons pas perdus [dus
Ne vous soyez pas ré-	Ne vous soyez pas aper-	Ne vous soyez pas per-

SUBJUNCTIVE MOOD.
Negatively.
PRESENT or FUTURE.

That I may not rejoice, etc.	That I may not perceive, etc.	That I may not lose myself, etc.
Que je ne me réjouisse pas [pas	Que je ne m'aperçoive pas [pas	Que je ne me perde pas
que tu ne te réjouisses	que tu ne t'aperçoives	que tu ne te perdes pas
qu'il ne se réjouisse pas	qu'il ne s'aperçoive pas	qu'il ne se perde pas

que nous ne **nous** ré-
jouissions pas
que vous ne **vous** ré-
jouissiez pas [pas
qu'ils ne **se** réjouissent

que nous ne **nous** aper-
cevions pas
que vous ne **vous** aper-
ceviez pas [pas
qu'ils ne **s'**aperçoivent

que nous ne **nous** per-
dions pas
que vous ne **vous** per-
diez pas
qu'ils ne **se** perdent pas

PAST.

*That I may not have re-
joiced, etc.*

Que je ne **me** sois pas
réjoui
que tu ne **te** sois pas réjoui
qu'il ne **se** soit pas réjoui
que nous ne **nous**
soyons pas réjouis
que vous ne **vous** soyez
pas réjouis
qu'ils ne **se** soient pas
réjouis

*That I may not have per-
ceived, etc.*

Que je ne **me** sois pas
aperçu
que tu ne **te** sois pas
aperçu
qu'il ne **se** soit pas aperçu
que nous ne **nous**
soyons pas aperçus
que vous ne **vous** soyez
pas aperçus
qu'ils ne **se** soient pas
aperçus

*That I may not have lost
myself, etc.*

Que je ne **me** sois pas
perdu
que tu ne **te** sois pas
perdu
qu'il ne **se** soit pas perdu
que nous ne **nous**
soyons pas perdus
que vous ne **vous** soyez
pas perdus
qu'ils ne **se** soient pas
perdus

IMPERFECT.

*That I might not rejoice,
etc.*

Que je ne **me** réjouisse
pas [pas
que tu ne **te** réjouisses
qu'il ne **se** réjouît pas
que nous ne **nous** réjou-
issions pas
que vous ne **vous** réjou-
issiez pas [pas
qu'ils ne **se** réjouissent

*That I might not per-
ceive, etc.*

Que je ne **m'**aperçusse
pas [pas
que tu ne **t'**aperçusses
qu'il ne **s'**aperçût pas
que nous ne **nous** aper-
çussions pas
que vous ne **vous** aper-
çussiez pas [pas
qu'ils ne **s'**aperçussent

*That I might not lose
myself, etc.*

Que je ne **me** perdisse
pas [pas
que tu ne **te** perdisses
qu'il ne **se** perdît pas
que nous ne **nous** per-
dissions pas
que vous ne **vous** per-
dissiez pas [pas
qu'ils ne **se** perdissent

PLUPERFECT.

*That I might not have
rejoiced, etc.*

Que je ne **me** sois pas
réjoui
que tu ne **te** sois pas réjoui
qu'il ne **se** soit pas réjoui
que nous ne **nous**
soyons pas réjouis
que vous ne **vous** soyez
pas réjouis
qu'ils ne **se** soient pas
réjouis

*That I might not have
perceived, etc.*

Que je ne **me** sois pas
aperçu
que tu ne **te** sois pas
aperçu
qu'il ne **se** soit pas aperçu
que nous ne **nous**
soyons pas aperçus
que vous ne **vous** soyez
pas aperçus
qu'ils ne **se** soient pas
aperçus

*That I might not have
lost myself, etc.*

Que je ne **me** sois pas
perdu
que tu ne **te** sois pas
perdu
qu'il ne **se** soit pas perdu
que nous ne **nous**
soyons pas perdus
que vous ne **vous** soyez
pas perdus
qu'ils ne **se** soient pas
perdus

INDEX.

The numbers refer to the paragraphs when the word page is not expressed.

able (suffix), 73.
accents, 6, 20; tonic, 24.
active verbs, 134; used impersonally, 163.
ade (suffix), 40, 44.
adjective, 49; qualifying, 50; determinative, 50, 77; indefinite, 50; formation of fem. in, 52 and foll.; formation of, 69 and foll.; derivative, 70 and foll.; agreement of, 74 and foll.; numeral, 78 and foll.; demonstrative, 82; possessive, 83; indefinite, 84, 111; interrogative, 107; used as adverb, 193.
adverb, 187; of place, 189; of time, 190; of manner, 191; how formed, 191, 192; adjectives used as, 193; comparison of, 194; of quantity, 195; of interrogation, 196; of affirmation, 197; of negation, 198; of doubt, 199.
adverbial locutions, 200.
age (suffix), 40, 44.
aille (suffix), 42.
ain (suffix), 40, 71.
aller, 169; s'en aller, 169.
alphabet, page 7.
ance (suffix), 44.
anti (prefix), 69.
apostrophe, 21.
après (prefix), 39.
archi (prefix), 69.
ard (suffix), 40, 73.
arrière (prefix), 39.
article, 45; definite, 46 and foll.; indefinite, 48; used in French when *some* or *any* is meant in English, 48.

as (suffix), 42.
asse (suffix), in verbs, 179.
at (suffix), 40.
âtre (suffix), 72.
aud (suffix), 72.
auxiliary verbs, 127, 132; with neuter verbs, 153; with reflexive verbs, 158.
avoir, 132; y avoir, page 110.
avant (prefix), 39.

Basque, page 1.
bénir, 170.
bien (prefix), 69.
bis (prefix), 24.
Breton (Bas-), page 1.
Burgundian, pages 1, 3.

cardinal adjectives, 79, 81.
Catalonian, page 1.
ce, 100.
cedilla, 22.
Celtic, page 4.
celui qui, 100.
cer, verbs ending in, 167.
collective numbers, 81.
comparative in adjectives, 66; irregular, 67; in adverbs, 194.
complement, 113, 114; direct, 115; indirect, 116.
conditional mood, 121.
conjugation, 130, 131; first, page 79; second, page 83; third, page 86; fourth, page 82; interrogative, 136 and foll.; negative, 141; interrogative and negative, 142; passive, page 99; neuter, page 102; reflexive, page 105; im-

personal, page 109; observations on first conj., 166 and foll.; on second conj., with imperfect in *issais*, 170; on 2nd (direct) conj., 171; irregular, page 112 and foll.
conjunction, 211 and foll.; government of, 216.
conjunctive locutions, 214.
consonants, 3, 11 and foll.
contre (prefix), 39.

defective verbs, 165.
demi (prefix), 69.
demonstrative, see adjective and pronoun.
derivative tenses, 147.
determinative, see adjective and pronoun.
devoir, page 97, note.
diæresis, 21.
diphthong, 9.

é, ée (suffix), 40, 71.
eau, elle (suffix), 42.
éser (verbs ending in), 166.
eler (verbs ending in), 166.
elet (suffix), 72.
en (pronoun), 92.
entre (prefix), 39.
envoyer, 169.
er, ier (suffix), 40, 71.
esse (suffix), 40, 43.
et (suffix), 42, 72.
eter (verbs ending in), 166.
être, page 75; with neuter verbs, 153.
eur (suffix), 44.
eux (suffix), 71.

feminine (formation of) in nouns, 30 and foll.; in adjectives, 52 and foll.
Flemish, page 1.
fleurir, 170.
foreign words, page 5.
French patois, page 2; dialect, page 3; learned, page 5; popular, page 5.
future tense, 125, 126.

Gascon, pages 2, 4.
gender, 29; formation of fem in nouns, 30 and foll.; in adjectives, 52 and foll.
ger (verbs ending in), 167.
grammar (definition), page 5.

haïr, 170.
hyphen, 23.

idiomatic tenses, 148.
ie (erie) (suffix), 40, 43.
if (suffix), 73.
imperative mood, 121.
imperfect tense, 125.
impersonal verbs, 161; their pronoun subject, 162; active or neuter verbs used as impersonal, 163.
in (prefix), 69; (suffix), 71.
indefinite, see adjective and pronoun.
indicative mood, 121.
infinitive mood, 121.
interjection, 217; how formed, 218.
interrogative, see adjective and pronoun.
irregular verbs, 165; 1st conj., 166 and foll.; 2nd conj. with imperfect in *issais*, 170; 3rd. conj. (direct), 171.
is (suffix), 44.
ise (suffix), 43.
ison (suffix) 44.
isseur (suffix), 44.
iste (suffix), 40.
Italian, page 3.

Languedocian, pages 2, 4.
Latin (popular), pages 2, 3, 4; classical, 2.
leur, 92.
Limousin, pages 2, 4.
locutions, adverbial, 200; prepositive, 203; how formed, 206; conjunctive, 214.
Lorrain, page 1.

mal (prefix), 69.
ment (suffix), 44.
mi (prefix), 39.
moods, 121.

neuter verbs, 152; their auxiliary, 153; used impersonally, 163.
non (prefix), 39.
Norman, pages 1, 3.
noun, *see* substantive.
number, 31; formation of plur. in nouns, 32 and foll.; in adjectives, 62 and foll.; in verbs, 119.
numbers, 81.
numeral adjectives, 78, 81.

object, 113; direct, 115; indirect, 116.
Oc (langue d') pages 3, 4.
Oïl (langue d'), pages 3, 4.
oir (suffix), 44.
on (suffix), 42, 44; in verbs, 179.
ordinal adjectives, 80, 81.
orthographic signs, 29.
ot (suffix), 42, 72; in verbs, 179.

participle, 183; present, 184; used as an adjective, 185.
passive verbs, 149 and foll.; the reflexive used instead, 149, 160.
past anterior, 125.
past definite, 125.
past indefinite, 125.
past participle of passive verbs, 151; of neuter verbs, 154; of reflexive verbs, 159; used as an adjective, 186.
past tense, 123.
personal pronouns, *see* pronouns.
persons in verbs, 120.
Picard, pages 1, 3.
pluperfect, 125.

plural (formation of) in nouns, 32 and foll.; in adjectives, 62 and foll.
positive, 65.
possessive, how expressed in French, 48; *see* adjective and pronoun.
pouvoir, page 97, note.
prefixes, 39.
prepositions, 201 and foll; how formed, 205; government of, 207, 210; their place, 208; repetition of, 209.
prepositive locutions, 203, 206.
present participle, 184; used as an adjective, 185.
present tense, 123.
preterite, *see* past.
primitive tenses, 147.
pronouns, 85; personal, 89; conjunctive, 89; where placed, 90, 92; disjunctive, 93; used as subject, 94; used as object, 95; reflective, 96; demonstrative, 97 and foll.; possessive, 101; relative, 102 and foll.; interrogative, 105 and foll.; indefinite, 109 and foll.
Provençal, pages 2, 4; Patois, page 2.

qualifying adjectives, *see* adjectives.
que, 104, 105, 106.
qui, 104, 106.

reflexive verbs, 155; how conjugated, 157; their auxiliary, 158; their past participle, 159; instead of the passive, 149, 160.
Romance language, pages 3, 5.

sans (prefix), 39.
some, translated by *du*, &c., 48.

sous (prefix), 39, 69.
Spanish, page 3.
speech (parts of), 25.
stem, 118.
subject, 113; agreement of verb with, 180 and foll.
subjunctive mood, 121.
substantive, 26 and foll.; formation of the fem., 29 and foll.; of the plural, 31 and foll.; formation of substantives, 37; derivative, 38; compound, 39; formed from adjectives, 43; from verbs, 44.
suffixes, 40; diminutive, 41, 42.
superlative, 68.
sur (prefix), 69.
syllable, 19; tonic, 24.

té (suffix), 43.
tenses, 122; simple, 128; compound, 129; formation of, 143 and foll.; primitive and derivative, 147; idiomatic, 148.

termination (of verbs), 118.
trait d'union, 23.
tréma, 21.

u (suffix), 71.
ultra (prefix), 69.
ure (suffix), 43, 44.

verb, 112, auxiliary, 127, 132; active, 134; passive, 149 and foll.; neuter, 152 and foll.; reflexive, 155 and foll.; impersonal, 161; irregular, 164; defective, 165; formation of, 177 and foll.; agreement with the subject, 180 and foll.
vice (prefix), 39.
vouloir, page 97, note.
vowels, 3 and foll.

y (pronoun), 92.
y avoir, page 110.
yer (verbs ending in), 168.

FRENCH-ENGLISH VOCABULARY.

A

À, *prep.*, at, to
a, *v.a.*, avoir, (*page* 71)
abattement, *s.m.*, prostration
abattre, *v.a.*, to cast down
abolir, *v.a.*, to abolish
abonner (s') *v.r.*, to subscribe to
abonnement, *s.m.*, subscription
aboucher, *v.a.*, to bring together
aboutir, *v.n.*, to lead
abreuver, *v.a.*, to water
abreuvoir, *s.m.*, horsepond, watering-place
abrutir, *v.a.*, to make a brute of, to stultify, to besot
absoudre, *v.a.*, to absolve
absurde, *adj.*, absurd
absurdité, *s.f.*, absurdity
acajou, *s.m.*, mahogany
accabler, *v.a.*, to weigh down
accablement, *s.m.*, despondency, dejection
accident, *s.m.*, accident
accompagner, *v.a.*, to accompany
accomplir, *v.a.*, to accomplish
accomplissement, *s.m.*, accomplishment, fulfilment

accourir, *vn.*, to run
acheter, *v.a.*, to buy
acheteur, *s.m.*, buyer, purchaser
acide, *adj.*, acid
acidité, *s.f.*, acidity
acier, *s.m.*, steel
aciérie, *s.f.*, steel work
acolyte, *s.m.*, acolyte, clerk
acquéreur, *s.m.*, buyer, purchaser
acquérir, *v.a.*, to acquire
acquitter, (s') *v.r.*, to perform
âcre, *adj.*, acrid, sour
acreté, *s.f.*, acridness, sourness
acteur, *s.m.*, actor
actrice, *s.f.*, actress
admirateur, -trice, *s.m.f.*, admirer
admirer, *v.a.*, to admire
adorateur, -trice, *s.m.f.*, worshipper, adorer
adorer, *v.a.*, to adore, to worship
adoucir, *v.a.*, to soften
adresser (s'), *v.r.*, to apply, to address, to speak to
affadir, *v.a.*, to make tasteless
affaiblir, *v.a.*, to weaken
affaire *s.f.*, affair, business, difficulty
affaisser, *v.a.*, to sink

affaissement, *s.m.*, sinking
affermir, *v.a.*, to strengthen
Afrique, *s.f.*, Africa
africain, *s.m.*, African
âge, *s.m.*, age
âgé, e, *adj.*, old, aged
agencer, *v.a.*, to dispose
agencement, *s.m.*, arrangement
agile, *adj.*, nimble
agilité, *s.f.*, nimbleness, agility
agir, *v.n.*, to act
agrandir, *v.a.*, to enlarge
agrandissement, *s.m.*, enlargement
aïeul, *s.m.*, grand-father, ancestor
aigle, *s.m.*, eagle
aiglon, *s.m.*, eaglet
aigre, *adj.*, sour
aigrelet, *adj.*, sourish
aiguille, *s.f.*, needle
aiguillon, *s.m.*, goad
aile, *s.f.*, wing
ailé, e, *adj.*, winged
aileron, *s.m.*, pinion, fin
aimable, *adj.*, kind, amiable, gentle
aimant, aimé, aiment, *l'art.pres.*; *part.past*; *ind. pr.* of
aimer, *v.a*, to like, to love, to be fond of
ainsi, *adv.*, thus, so

nisément, *adv.*, easily, readily
alarmer, *v.a.*, to alarm
allée, *s.f.*, path, alley, going
aller, *v.n.*, to go
allure, *s.f.*, gait
amaigrir, *v.a.*, to make thin
amande, *s.f.*, almond
amandier, *s.m.*, almond-tree
ambition, *s.f.*, ambition
amener, *v.a.*, to bring, to bring along
Amérique, *s.f.*, America
américain, *s.m.*, American
ami, *s.m.*, friend
amincir, *v.a.*, to make thin
amiral, *s.m.*, admiral
amollir, *v.a.*, to soften
amollissement, *s.m.*, softening
amuser, *v.a.*, to amuse
amuser (s'), *v.r.*, to amuse one's self
amusement, *s.m.*, amusement
analyse, *s.f.*, analysis, parsing, outline
ancien, -ne, *adj.*, ancient
ancienneté, *s.f.*, antiquity, seniority
ancre, *s.f.*, anchor
ancrage, *s.m.*, anchorage
âne, *s.m.*, ass
ânon, *s.m.*, young ass
anglais, *s.m.*, Englishman, Briton
annexion, *s.f.*, annexion
antiféebrile, *adj.*, antifebrile
anti-monarchique, *adj.*, anti-monarchical
anti-religieux, *adj.*, anti-religious
antisocial, *adj.*, antisocial

août, *s.m.*, August
apaiser, *v.a.*, to appease, to calm, to soothe
apercevoir, *v.a.*, to perceive, to see
s'apercevoir, *v.r.*, to perceive one's self, to see each other
s'apercevoir, *v.r.* [de], to notice, to discover
aperçu, *s.m.*, glimpse
apôtre, *s.m.*, apostle
apostrophe, *s.f.*, apostrophe, address, reproach
apostropher, *v.a.*, to apostrophise, to address (roughly)
appauvrir, *v.a.*, to impoverish
appauvrissement, *s.m.*, impoverishment
appeler, *v.a.*, to call
appel, *s.m.*, call
applaudir, *v.a.*, to applaud
applaudissement, *s.m.*, applause
appliquer, (s'), *v.r.*, to apply one's self
apporter, *v.a.*, to bring
âpre, *adj.*, rough, sour, eager
âpreté, *s.f.*, roughness, tartness, eagerness
après, *prep.*, after
après-coup, *loc. adv.*, when too late, afterwards
après-demain, *loc. adv.*, the day after to-morrow
après-dîner, *s.m.*, after dinner, evening
après-midi, *s.f.*, afternoon
arc, *s.m.* arc
arcade, *s.f.*, arcade
archidiaconal, *adj.*, archidiaconal
archidiaconal, *adj.*, archducal

archiépiscopal, *adj.*, archiepiscopal
archi fou, *adj.*, stark mad
argent, *s.m.*, silver, money
argenterie, *s.f.*, plate
armée, *s.f.*, army
arracher, *v.a.*, to tear
arranger, *v.a.*, to put in order, to arrange
arrérages, *s.m.*, arrears
arrêter, *v.a.*, to arrest
arrêt, *s.m.*, stoppage, decree
arrière-boutique, *s.f.*, back-shop
arrière-garde, *s.f.*, rear-guard, rear
arrière-neveu, *s.m.*, grand nephew
arrière-pensée, *s.f.*, mental reservation
arrière-saison, *s.f.*, latter end of the season, autumn, decline (of life)
arrivée, *s.f.*, arrival
arriver, *v.n.*, to arrive
arroser, *v.a.*, to water
arsenal, *s.m.*, arsenal
art, *s.m.* art
artiste, *s.m.*, artist
aspect, *s.m.*, aspect
assassin, *s.m.*, murderer
assassinat, *s.m.*, assassination
asseoir (s'), *v.r.*, to sit down
asservir, *v.a.*, to enslave, to subdue
assiéger, *v.a.*, to besiege
assiégeant, *s.m.*, besieger
assiette, *s.f.*, plate
assiettée, *s.f.*, plateful
assistance, *s.f.*, assistance
assistant, *s.m.*, assistant, bystander
assister, *v.a.n.*, to assist, to be present
assortir, *v.a.*, to match, to sort, to suit

attabler, v.a., to sit at table
attaquer, v.a., to attack
attendre, v.a., to wait for, to expect
s'attendre, v.r., to expect
attendu, prep., considering
attendrir, v.a., to soften, to move
attentif, adj., attentive
attention, s.f., attention
attirail, s.m., implements, apparatus, train
atitude, s.f., attitude
aubade, s.f., morning serenade
aube, s.f., dawn
auberge, s.f., inn
aubergiste, s.m., innkeeper
aucun,-e, adj, any, no, none
aujourd'hui, adv., to-day
autre, adj. and pr. ind., other
autrui, pr. ind., others, our neighbour
Auvergne, s.f., Auvergne
auvergnat, s.m., native of Auvergne
avancé, -e, adj., advanced, forward, clear
avancer, v.a.n., to advance
avant, prep., before
avantage, s.m., advantage
avant-coureur, s.m., forerunner
avant-goût, s.m., foretaste
avant-poste, s.m., outpost
avant-propos, s.m., preface
avertir, v.a., to warn
avide, adj., greedy
avidité, s.f., greediness
avis, s.m., advice, opinion
avoine, s.f., oats
avoir, v. aux. and act., to have
avoir, s.m., property

B

Bagatelle, s.f., trifle
baigner (se), v.a., to bathe
baigneur, -euse, s.m.f., bather
bail, s.m., lease
bailler, v.n., to yawn
baillement, s.m., yawning
baillon, s.m., gag
bal, s.m., ball (dancing)
balancer, v.a., to balance
balançoire, s.f., swing, see-saw
balayer, v.a., to sweep
balle, s.f., ball
ballon, s.m., balloon
ballot, s.m., package
balustrade, s.f., railing
balustre, s.f., railing
bambou, s.m., bamboo
banal, adj., trite
banalité, s.f., commonplace saying
bandage, s.m., bandage
bande, s.f., band
bandelette, s.f., bandlet
bannir, v.a., to banish, to exile
barbare, adj., barbarous, barbarian
barbarie, s.f., barbarity, rudeness
barbe, s.f., beard
barbier, s.m., barber
barbouiller, v.a., to besmear
barbu, -e, adj., bearded
barbue, s.f., brill
barre, s.f., bar, cross-bar
barreau, s.m., (small bar, grating
bas, s.m., stocking
bassiner, v.a., to warm
bât, s.m., pack-saddle
bâté, -e, adj., pack saddled; un âne bâté, a downright ass

bataille, s.f., battle
bateau, s.m., boat
batelier, s.m., boatman
battant, -e, adj., porte battante, slamming door
battre, v.a., to beat
bavard, adj., talkative
baver, v.n., to slobber
beau, bel (m.), belle (f.), adj., beautiful, handsome, fine
beaucoup, adv., much
beauté, s.f., beauty
bellâtre adj., of insipid beauty
bénir, v.a., to bless
berger, s.m., shepherd
bergerie, s.f., fold
Berlin, n.p., Berlin
beurre, s.m., butter
bible, s.f., bible
bibliothèque, s.f., library book-case
bien, adv., well, very much, really
bien, s.m., good, property, wealth
bien-aimé, adj., well beloved, dearest
bienfaisant, adj., beneficent
bienfaiteur, -rice, s.m.f., benefactor (m.), benefactress (f.)
bienheureux, -se, adj., blessed
bijou, -x, s.m., jewel
bijouterie, s.f., jewellery
bille, s.f., ball
billard, s.m., billiards
billot, s.m., block, clog
billet, s.m., ticket ; billet de banque, bank-note
bisaïeul, s.m., great grandfather
bissac, s.m., wallet
blâmer, v.a., to blame
blanc, -che, adj., white
blanchir, v.a., to whiten

blanchisseur, *s.m.*, bleacher
blé, *s.m.*, corn, wheat
blesser, *v.a.*, to wound
blessure, *s.f.*, wound
bleu, *adj.*, blue
bleuir, *v.n.*, to become blue
bocal, *s.m.*, glass jar, glass globe
boire, *v.a.*, to drink
boire, *s.m.*, drink, drinking
bois, *s.m.*, wood
boiserie, *s.f.*, wainscot
boiteux, -se, *adj.*, lame, crippled
bombarde, *s.f.*, bombard
bombe, *s.f.*, bomb
bon, *adj.*, good, kind; les bons, the good
bord, *s.m.*, edge
bordage, *s.m.*, planking
border, *v.a.*, to hem
bordure, *s.f.*, edging, border, frame
bosse, *s.f.*, lump, hunch
bossu, -e, *adj.*, lump-backed, hunch-backed
botte, *s.f.*, boot
bottier, *s.m.*, bootmaker
bouche, *s.f.*, mouth
bouchée, *s.f.*, mouthful
boucher, *s.m.*, butcher; boucherie, butcher's shop
boucher, *v.a.*, to stop
bouchon, *s.m.*, cork
boucle, *s.f.*, buckle, tie, ring
bouffée, *s.f.*, puff
bouffer, *v.n.*, to swell
bouffir, *v.n.*, to swell out
bouffissure, *s.f.*, swelling, bombast
bouillir, *v.n.*, to boil, *page 114*
boulanger, *s.m.*, baker
boulangerie, *s.f.*, bakery
boule, *s.f.*, ball

boulet, *s.m.*, cannon ball
boulette, *s.f.*, ball (of bread or paper)
bourg, *s.m.*, borough, market-town
bourgade, *s.f.*, small market-town, village
bourrade, *s.f.*, blow (with the but end of a musket)
bourre, *s.f.*, flock, wad
bourse, *s.f.*, purse
boursier, *s.m.*, bursar, treasurer, stock-jobber
bouteille, *s.f.*, bottle
boutique, *s.f.*, shop
bracelet, *s.m.*, bracelet
branchage, *s.m.*, branches, boughs
branche, *s.f.*, branch
branchu, -e, *adj.*, branched, branchy
bras, *s.m.*, arm
brigand, *s.m.*, brigand
brigandage, *s.m.*, brigandage
broche, *s.f.*, brooch
brochette, *s.f.*, skewer
broder, *v.a.*, to embroider
brouillard, *adj.*, for blotting; papier-bouillard, blotting-paper
brouiller, *v.a.*, to mix together, to upset
brouillon, *s.m.*, rough draft, blunderer
bruit, *s.m.*, noise, fame, rumour
brume, *s.f.*, mist, fog
brute, *s.f.*, brute
brute, *adj.*, brutish
bruyant, *adj.*, noisy; *see* bruire, *p.* 125
bûche, *s.f.*, log of wood
bûcher, *s.m.*, log-house, stake
bûcheron, *s.m.*, woodcutter
bûchette, *s.f.*, small log of wood

bureau, *s.m.*, office
but, *s.m.*, aim, end

C

cache, *s.f.*, hiding place
cachette, *s.f.*, hiding place
cabine, *s.f.*, cabin
cabinet, *s.m.*, cabinet, closet, study
cacheter, *v.a.*, to seal
cahier, *s.m.*, copy-book
caillou, *s.m.*, flint, pebble
caisse, *s.f.*, case
caisson, *s.m.*, waggon
camail, *s.m.*, camail
camp, *s.m.*, camp
campagne, *s.f.*, country
campagnard, *s.m.*, countryman
canal, *s.m.*, canal, channel
canard, *s.m.*, duck
canne, *s.f.*, cane, stick
cannelle, *s.f.*, cinnamon
capital, *s.m.*, main point, capital, stock
capitaliste, *s.m.*, capitalist
car, *conj.*, for
caractère, *s.m.*, character, temper
carafe, *s.f.*, flaggon
carafon, *s.m.*, decanter
cardinal, *s.m.*, cardinal
cardinalat, *s.m.*, cardinalate
carnaval, *s.m.*, carnival
carpe, *s.f.*, carp
carpillon, *s.m.*, little carp
carrosse, *s.m.*, carriage
carrossier, *s.m.*, carriage or coachmaker
cascade, *s.f.*, cascade, waterfall, fall
cause, *s.f.*, cause
cave, *s.f.*, cellar, win vault
caveau, *s.m.*, cellar, burial vault

ce, cet, *m.*, cette, *f.*, ces, *pl.*, *adj.dem.*, this, these, that, those
ce, c', *pr.dem.*, 1, he, she, they; 2, it; 3, *expletive*, ce qui, ce que, what
cela, *pr.dem.*, that
celui, (*m.*), celle, (*f.*), ceux, celles, *pl. Pr. dem. subj.*, he, she, one; *pl.*, they or those; *obj.*, him, her, the one; *pl.*, those
celui-ci, (*m.*), celle-ci, (*f.*), ceux-ci, celles-ci, (*m.f.pl.*) *pr. dem.*, (*see page 58*)
celui-là, (*m.*), celle-là, (*f.*), ceux-là, celles-là, (*m.f.pl.*) *pr. dem.*, (*see page 58*)
ceinture, *s.f.*, girdle
ceinturon, *s.m.*, belt
céleste, *adj.*, heavenly, celestial
cendre, *s.f.*, ashes
cendrier, *s.m.*, fender
cent, *adj. num.*, hundred
centaine, *s.f.*, about a hundred
cerise, *s.f.*, cherry
cerisier, *s.m.*, cherry-tree
certain, -e, *adj.*, sure, certain; (*ind.*) one, some
cerveau, *s.m.*, cerebellum
cervelas, *s.m.*, saveloy
chacal, *s.m.*, jackal
chagrin, *s.m.*, sorrow
chaîne, *s.f.*, chain
chaînette, *s.f.*, little chain
chaise, *s.f.*, chair, seat
chaleur, *s.f.*, heat
chambre, *s.f.*, room
champ, *s.m.*, field
chandelle, *s.f.*, candle

change, *s.m.*, exchange, change; lettre de change, bill of exchange, bill
chanoine, *s.m.*, canon, prebendary
chanoinesse, *s.f.*, canoness
chant, *s.m.*, song, singing
chanter, *v.a.n.*, to sing
chanteur, -euse, *s.m.f.*, singer; cantatrice, a professional singer
chantonner, *v.n.*, to hum
chape, *s.f.*, cope
chapeau, *s.m.*, hat
chaperon, *s.m.*, hood, chaperon
chaque, *adj. ind.*, each
charger, *v.a.*, to load
charitable, *adj.*, charitable
Charles, *s.m.*, Charles
Charlot, *s.m.*, Charlie
charmant, *adj.*, charming, delightful
charrue, *s.f.*, plough
chasse, *s.f.*, hunting, sporting
châsse, *s.f.*, shrine
chasseur, *s.m.*, hunter, sportsman
châtaigne, *s.f.*, chestnut
châtaignier, *s.m.*, chestnut-tree
châtelain, -e, *adj.*, ; le seigneur châtelain, the lord of the manor; la dame châtelaine, the lady of the manor; chaîne châtelaine, or châtelaine, chain
châtelet, *s.m.*, little castle
chaumière, *s.f.*, cottage
chausser, *v.a.*, to shoe
chaussure, *s.f.*, boots, shoes
chemin, *s.m.*, way, road
chemise, *s.f.*, shirt
cher, *adj.*, dear, (*adv.*) dear, dearly

cheval, *s.m.*, horse
chevalier, *s.m.*, knight
chevelure, *s.f.*, hair
chèvre, *s.f.*, goat
chevreau, *s.m.*, kid
chez, *prep.*, at or to the house of; allons chez moi, chez nous, let us go home
chien, *s.m.*, dog
chimère, *s.f.*, idle dream
chimie, *s.f.*, chemistry
chimiste, *s.m.*, chemist
chômer, *v.n.*, to be without work
chômage, *s.m.*, want of work, rest
chœur, *s.m.*, chorus, choir
choisir, *v.a.*, to choose, to select
chose, *s.f.*, thing
chrétien, -ne, *adj.*, christian
chrétienté, *s.f.*, christendom
chute, *s.f.*, fall
ci, *adv.*, here; ci-gît, here lies
cible, *s.f.*, target
cinquante, *adj.num.*, fifty
cinquantaine, *s.f.*, about fifty
circonstance, *s.f.*, circumstance
citoyen, *s.m.*, citizen
citron, *s.m.*, citron, lemon
citronelle, *s.f.*, balm
clairement, *adv.*, clearly
cligner, *v.a.*, to half close (the eyes)
clignoter, *v.n.*, to wink (repeatedly)
cliqueter, *v.n.*, to clack
cliquetis, *s.m.*, din, clang
cloche, *s.f.*, bell
clocher, *s.m.*, bell-tower, steeple
cœur, *s.m.*, heart
coffre, *s.m.*, coffer
coffret, *s.m.*, little coffer

colère, s.f., anger
colombe, s.f., dove
colombier, s.m., dove-cot
colonel, s.m., colonel
colonnade, s.f., colonnade
colonne, s.f., column
colorer, v.a., to colour
coloris, s.m., colouring
combattre, v.a., to combat
combattant, s.m., combatant
combinaison, s.f., combination
combiner, v.a., to combine
comédien, s.m., comedian, actor
commander, v.a.n., to command
commandant, s.m., commander
comme, adv., how
comme, conj., as
comment, adv., how
commercer, v.n., to trade
commerçant, s.m., trader
compagnie, s.f., company, society
comparable, adj., comparable
comparaison, s.f., comparison
comparer, v.a., to compare
compatir, v.n., to sympathise (with)
complet, -ète, adj., complete
compliment, s.m., compliment, congratulation
complot, s.m., plot
composer (se), v.r., to be composed
comprendre, v.a., to understand, to comprehend
compromettre (se), v.r., to compromise one's self
compte, s.m., account

compter, v.a., to reckon
compteur, s.m., meter (gas)
Comte, s.m., Count, Earl
comté, s.m., earldom, county
Comtesse, s.f., Countess
concert, s.m., concert
concevoir, v.a., to conceive
concourir, v.n., (à), to concur (in); concourir pour, to compete for
condamner, v.a., to condemn
condescendre, v.n., to condescend
conducteur, -trice, s.m.f., conductor, guide, driver
conduire, v.a., to lead
conduite, s.f., conduct, behaviour
confiance, s.f., confidence, trust
confier, v.a., to entrust
confondre, v.a., to confound; se confondre, to be blended; se confondre en excuses, to be lost in apologies
conjugaison, s.f., conjugation
conjuguer, v.a., to conjugate
connaître, v.a., to know
conquérant, s.m., conqueror
conquérir, v.a., to conquer
conscience, s.f., conscience
consentir, v.n., to consent
conséquence, s.f., consequence
consoler, v.a., to console
consul, s.m., consul
consulat, s.m., consulate
contenir, v.a., to contain

contenter, v.a., to content
contenu, s.m., contents
continuel, -le, adj., continual
contre, prep., against
contre-amiral, s.m., rear admiral
contre-coup, s.m., rebound, consequence
contre-maître, s.m., foreman
contre-marque, s.f. countermark, check
contre-sens, s.m., mistranslation
contrecarrer, v.a., to thwart
contredire, v.a., to contradict
contrefaire, v.a., to imitate
convenance, s.f., fitness, (pl.), propriety; manquer aux convenances, to be guilty of impropriety
convenir, v.n., to agree to, to fit
convoi, s.m., funeral, convoy, train
copie, s.f., copy
copiste, s.m., copyist
coquet, -te, adj., coquettish, elegant
coquetterie, s.f., coquetry, flirtation
coquillage, s.m., shell-fish
coquille, s.f., shell
corail, s.m., coral
cordage, s.m., cordage, rope
corde, s.f., cord
cordeau, s.m., cord
corder, v.a., to cord
corderie, s.f., rope-making
cordier, s.m., rope-maker
cordon, s.m., string
correctement, adv., correctly

côte, s.f., rib, cost
côtelette, s.f., cutlet, chop
cotte, s.f., petticoat
cotillon, s.m., under-petticoat
couleur, s.f., colour
coupable, adj., guilty
couple, s.m., couple
couplet, s.m., verse (of a song)
coup, s.m., blow, stroke, knock; tout-à-coup, all at once
couper, v.a., to cut
coupon, s.m., coupon
coupure, s.f., cut
courage, s.m., courage
courageux, -se, adj., courageous
coureur, s.m., runner
court, adj., short
cousin, s.m., cousin
coussin, s.m., cushion
coussinet, s.m., little cushion
couteau, s.m., knife
coutelier, s.m., cutler
couvée, s.f., brood
couver, v.a., to hatch
cracher, v.n., to spit
crachoir, s.m., spittoon
craignez, v.a., (see craindre, p. 127)
craindre, v.a., to fear
crainte, s.f., fear
cravate, s.f., cravat, necktie
crayon, s.m., pencil
crédule, adj., credulous
crédulité, s.f., credulity
cri, s.m., cry
crier, v.n., to cry
cristal, s.m., crystal
critiquer, v.a., to criticise
croc, s.m., hook
crochet, s.m., little hook
croire, v.a.n., to believe
crois, -croit, ind.pres. of croire
croisée, s.f., window

croître, v.n., to grow
croix, s.f., cross; croisillon, cross-bar
croquer, v.a., to crunch, to sketch
croquis, s.m., sketch
croûte s.f., crust
croyance, s.f., belief
croyant, v.a., p.pr. of croire
croyant, s.m., believer
croyez, imp. of croire
cru, v., p.past of croire
cru, adj., raw, crude
crû, v., p.past of croître
crû, s.m., growth, growing
cruauté, s.f., cruelty
cruel, -le, adj., cruel, unkind
cueillir, v.a., to gather, to pluck
cuiller, s.f., spoon
cuillerée, s.f., spoonful
cuir, s.m., leather
cuisine, s.f., kitchen
cuisinier, s.m., cook
cyprès, s.m., cypress

D

danger, s.m., danger
dans, prep., in, into
danser, v.a.n., to dance
danseur, -se, s.m.f., dancer
dame, s.f., lady
dame, int., indeed, well
de, prep., of
de, art., def. or part, (instead of du, de la, des), some, any
déclinaison, s.f., declension
décliner, v.a., to decline
déballer, v.a., to unpack
débat, s.m., debate
débattre, v.a., to discuss
débitant, s.m., retailer
débiter, v.a., to retail
débrouiller, v.a., to unravel

début, s.m., beginning
débuter, v.n., to begin
décacheter, v.a., to open (a letter)
décevoir, v.a., to deceive
décider, v.a., to decide
se décider, v.r., to come to a decision, to make up one's mind
déclarer, v.a., to declare
défaillir, v.n., to fall, to decay, to faint
défaire, v.a., to undo, to defeat, to rout
défaut, s.m., defect, fault
défendre, v.a., to forbid, to defend
défendeur, s.m., -eresse, s.f., defendant
défiant, adj., distrustful
définir, v.a., to define
dégât, s.m., damage, waste
dégrader (se), v.r., to degrade or disgrace one's self
déjeûner, v.n. to breakfast
déjeûner, s.m., breakfast
délateur, s.m., délatrice, s.f., informer
délicieux, -se, adj., delicious
délivrance, s.f., deliverance
délivrer, v.a., to deliver
démarche, s.f., step, proceeding
demain, adv., to-morrow
demande, s.f., request, question
demander, v.a., to ask
demeure, s.f., abode, dwelling
demeurer, v.n., to live, to remain, to stay
demi-fermé, adj., half-closed, partly closed
demi-fin, adj., half-fine
demi-mort, adj., half-dead

demi-nu, *adj.*, half-naked
démolir, *v.a.*, to demolish, to pull down
dent, *s.f.*, tooth
dentelle, *s.f.*, lace
dentier, *s.m.*, set of teeth
dentiste, *s.m.*, dentist
dénué, -e, *adj.*, destitute, devoid
dépêcher (se), *v.r.*, to hasten
dépendance, *s.f.*, dependance
dépendre, *v.n.*, to depend
dépens, *s.m.pl.*, expense, cost, charge; à mes dépens, at my expense
dépenser, *v.a.* to spend
déplaire, *v.n.*, to displease
déranger, *v.a.*, to disturb
des, *art.pl.*, of the, of; from the, from; some, any
désir, *s.m.*, desire, wish
désirer, *v.a.*, to desire, to wish for
désobéir, *v.n.*, to disobey
dessein, *s.m.*, design, project
dessin, *s.m.*, drawing
détail, *s.m.*, detail, *pl.* details, particulars
détourner (se), to go out of one's way, to turn away
détromper, *v.a.*, to undeceive
détruire, *v.a.*, to destroy
deuil, *s.m.*, mourning
deux, *adj.card.*, two
dévoiler, *v.a.*, to reveal
devoir, *v.a.*, to owe
devoir, *s.m.*, duty
diable, *s.m.*, devil
diaconal, -e, *adj.*, diaconal
dictionnaire, *s.m.*, dictionary
Dieu, *s.m.*, God
différent, *adj.*, different, various

différer, *v.a.*, to defer, to postpone
dimanche, *s.m.*, Sunday
dinde, *s.f.*, turkey-hen
dindon, *s.m.*, turkey
dîner, *v.n.*, to dine
dîner, *s.m.*, dinner
diocèse, *s.m.*, diocese
diocésain, *s.m.*, diocesan
dire, *v.a.*, to say
dire, *s.m.*, saying, statement
disent, dit, dites, *v.a.*, (from dire p. 128)
directeur, *s.m.*, director, manager
directrice, *s.f.*, directrix
discret, -ète, *adj.*, discreet
discrétion, *s.f.*, discretion
discuter, *v.a.*, to discuss
disparaître, *v.n.*, to disappear
diviser, *v.a.*, to divide
diviseur, *s.m.*, divisor
dix, *adj.n.*, ten
dizaine, *s.f.*, about ten
docile, *adj.*, docile
docilité, *s.f.*, docility
doigt, *s.m.*, finger
doigté, *s.m.*, fingering
domestique, *s.m.s.f.*, manservant; woman servant
donner, *v.a.*, to give; donner la parole, to give leave to speak
dont, *pr. relat.* (par. 103 to 106)
dorénavant, *adv.*, henceforth
dormir, to sleep
douane, *s.f.*, custom-house
douanier, *s.m.*, custom-house officer
douceâtre, *adj.*, sweetish, insipidly sweet
doux, -ce, *adj.*, sweet, fresh, soft, mild
douze *adj.num.*, twelve

douzaine, *s.f.*, about twelve, or a dozen
droit, *adj.*, straight, right
drôle, *adj.*, droll, funny
drôlerie, *s.f.*, drollery
du (instead of de le) of the, of; from the, from some, any
dû, *s.m.*, due
ducal, *adj.*, ducal
dur, *adj.*, hard
dureté, *s.f.*, hardness

E

Eau, *s.f.*, water
ébarber, *v.a.*, to strip (quills)
ébène, *s.f.*, ebony
ébénier, *s.m.*, ebony-tree
ébéniste, *s.m.*, cabinet-maker
ébénisterie, *s.f.*, cabinet-making
éblouir, *v.a.*, to dazzle
échafaud, *s.m.*, scaffold
échafaudage, *s.m.*, scaffolding
échappée, *s.f.*, vista, prank
échapper, *v.n.*, to escape
échoir, *v.n.*, to fall, to befall, to fall due
éclaircir, *v.a.*, to enlighten
éclaircissement, *s.m.*, explanation
école, *s.f.*, school
écolier, *s.m.*, school-boy
économat, *s.m.*, stewardship
économe, *adj.*, thrifty, saving
économe, *s.m.*, steward
écrire, *v.a.*, to write
écrit, *s.m.*, writing
écriteau, *s.m.*, bill, board
écrivain, *s.m.*, writer
écrivassier, *s.m.*, scribbler

écueil, s.m., rock, reef
écuelle, s.f., bowl
écuellée, s.f., bowl-full
écureuil, s.m., squirrel
édenté, adj., toothless
édifice, s.m., edifice
effacer, v.a., to efface
effet, s.m., effect
égal, adj., equal
égarer (s'), v.r., to lose one's self, to go astray
église, s.f., church
élargir, v.a., to enlarge, to widen
élargissure, s.f., piece put in to widen
élégant, adj., elegant
élève, s.2y., pupil
élever, v.a., to raise
élire, v.a., to elect
élu, s.m., elect
émail, s.m., enamel
emballer, v.a., to pack up
embarras, s.m., encumbrance, trouble
emboucher, v.a., to put (a wind instrument) to one's mouth
embouchure, s.f., mouth of a river
embrassade, s.f., embrace
embrasser, v.a., to embrace
émigrant, s.m., emigrant
émigrer, v.n., to emigrate
émouvoir, v.a., to move
empresser (s'), v.r., to hasten
en, prep., in, into
en, adv., from thence
en, pr.pers. (page 56)
enchanteur, s.m., enchanter
enchanteresse, s.f., enchantress
enchérir, v.a., to raise (prices)
enchérisseur, s.m., bidder

encore, adv., still, yet, again
encre, s.f., ink
encrier, s.m., inkstand
endenté, adj., with teeth
énergique, adj., energetic
enfant, s.m., infant, baby, child
enfantin, adj., childish
enfiler, v.a., to thread
enfilade, s.f., suite of rooms, long string
enjamber, v.a., to stride
enjambée, s.f., stride
enjoindre, v.a., to enjoin, to direct
ennemi, s.m., enemy, foe
ennui, s.m., wearisomeness, care
énoncer, v.a., to express; s'énoncer, to express one's-self, to be expressed
enorgueillir (s'), v.r., to boast
enquérir (s'), to inquire, to ask
enrhumer (s'), to catch a cold
enrichir, v.a., to enrich
entabler, v.a., to entable
entablement, s.m., entablature
entendre, v.a.n., to hear, to understand
entêté, adj., obstinate
entre-côte, s.m., meat between the ribs
entrelarder, v.a., to interlard
entremets, s.m., side-dish
entremettre, v.a., to interpose
entrepont, s.m., between the decks
entreprendre, v.a., to undertake
entreprise, s.f., enterprising, undertaking

entrée, s.f., entrance
entrer, v.n., to enter
entresol, s.m., mezzanine
envahir, v.a., to invade
envers, pr., towards, to
envi (à l'), adv., in emulation of each other, vying with each other
envie, s.f., envy, wish, longing
envoyer, v.a., to send
épais, -se, adj., thick
épanchement, s.m., discharge, overflow, (fig.) overflow, outburst
épancher, v.a., to pour out, (fig.) to vent, to discharge
épée, s.f., sword
épiscopal, adj., episcopal
épître, s.f., epistle
équestre, adj., equestrian
équivaloir, v.n., to be equivalent, to be tantamount
ermite, s.m., hermit
ermitage, s.m., hermitage
erreur, s.f., error, mistake
esclavage, s.m., slavery
esclave, s.m.f., slave
espérance, s.f., hope
espiègle, adj., frolicsome
espièglerie, s.f., frolic
esprit, s.m., wit; avoir de l'esprit, to be witty
esquiver (s'), v.r., to steal away
essentiel, -le, adj., essential
estime, s.m., esteem
estimer, v.a., to esteem
établir, v.a., to establish
établissement, s.m., establishment
été, s.m., summer
éteindre, v.a., to extinguish, to put out

étendre, v.c., to extend
étendue, s.f., extent
étoile, s.f., star
étranger,-ère,adj.,foreign
étroit, adj., narrow, light
européen, adj., European
éventail, s.m., fan
éviter, v.a., to avoid
excellent, adj., excellent
excès, s.m., excess, abuse
excuse, s.f., excuse, apology
exemple, s.m., example
exhaler, v.a., to exhale, to emit
exigeant, adj., particular, unreasonable
exiger, v.a., to exact, to require
exigu, -üe, adj., small, slender, slight
expédient,adj.,expedient, advisable
expédient, s.m., expedient, device
expédicr, v.a., from expédier, to dispatch
exposer, v.a., to expose
exprès, s.m., express, courier
exprès,-esse, adj., express
exprès, adv., purposely
expressément, adv., expressly
externat,s.m., day-school
externe, s.m., day-pupil

F

Façade, s.f., front (of a building)
face, s.f., face
facette, s.f., facet
fâcher(se)v.r.,to get angry
facile, adj., easy
facilité, s.f., facility
façon, s.f., fashion, way
fade, adj., tasteless
faible, adj., weak, feeble

faiblesse, s.f., weakness, feebleness
fainéant, adj., idle, lazy
fainéantise, s.f., idleness, laziness
faire, v.a.n., to do, to make
falloir, v.imp., to be necessary
famille, s.f., family
fatal, adj., fatal
fatiguer (se), v.r., to fatigue or to tire one's self
faucheur, -euse, s.m.f., mower; (fem.) a mowing machine
faute, s.f., fault, mistake
fauteuil, s.m., arm-chair
favorable, adj., favourable
favori, -te, adj., favourite
fébrile, adj., febrile
félon, adj., felonious
félonie, s.f., treason
fendre, v.a., to split; fendre la presse, to squeeze through the throng
fermage, s.m., rent (of a farm)
ferme, s.f., farm
ferme, adj., firm
fermeté, s.f., firmness
fermer, v.a., to close
fermier, s.m., farmer
fermoir, s.m., clasp
féroce, adj., fierce, ferocious
ferrer, v.a., to put iron to, to shoe (a horse)
ferrure, s.f., iron-work
festin, s.m., feast, banquet
fête, s.f., feast, festival
feu, s.m., fire
feuillage, s.m., foliage
feuille, s.f., leaf
feuillet, s.m., leaflet
fidèle, adj., faithful
fier, adj., proud
figure, s.f., figure, face

fier, (se), v.r., (à, snr. en) to trust, to confide (in), to rely (on)
fil, s.m., thread
filasse, s.f., tow
fille, s.f., daughter, child
filleul, s.m., godson, godchild
fils, s.m., son, boy
fin, adj., fine, sharp, shrewd
finaud, adj., artful, cunning
finir, v.a., to finish, to end
flâner, v.n., to lounge
flâneur, s.m., lounger
flatteur, -se, s.m.f., flatterer, adj., flattering
flétrir, (se) v.r., to wither
flétrissure,s.f.,withering, disgrace
fleur, s.f., flower
fleurir, v.n., to blossom, to flourish
fleuriste, s.m., flower-seller, flower-maker, flower gardener, florist
fonction, s.f., duty, function
fondateur, -trice, s.m.f., founder
fondement, s.m., foundation
fondre, v.a., to melt
forêt, s.f., forest
forme, s.f., shape, mould
format, s.m., size (of a book)
fortune, s.f., fortune, wealth
fou, fol, folle, adj., mad, foolish; follet,-te, playful, foolish
foudre, s.f., lightning, thunder, thunderbolt
foudroyant, adj., thundering, thunder-striking

fouet, *s.m.*, whip
fourbe, *s.m.*, knave, cheat
fourberie, *s.f.*, knavery
fourche, *s.f.*, pitchfork
fourchette, *s.f.*, fork
fournir, *v.a.*, to furnish
fournisseur, *s.m.*, purveyor
frais, fraîche, *adj.*, fresh, cool
Français, *s.m.*, Frenchman
franc, -che, *adj.*, free, frank
franchise, *s.f.*, freedom, frankness, franchise
frande, *s.f.*, fraud, deceit
frémir, *v.n.*, to shudder, to quiver
frémissement, *s.m.*, shudder, thrill
fréquenter, *v.a.*, to frequent
frère, *s.m.*, brother
frivole, *adj.*, frivolous
froment, *s.m.*, wheat
fruiterie, *s.f.*, fruitery
fuir, *v.a.n.*, to flee, to fly
fumer, *v.a.*, to smoke
fumée, *s.f.*, smoke
fusil, *s.m.*, gun
fusillade, *s.f.*, firing, volley of musketry
fût, *s.m.*, cask
futaille, *s.f.*, small cask
fuyard, *adj.*, fugitive

G

Gâcher, *v.a.*, to mix (mortar), to make a mess of
gâchis, *s.m.*, mess
gagner, *v.a.*, to gain, to win
gai, -e, *adj.*, gay
galop, *s.m.*, gallop
galoper, *v.n.*, ot gallop
garçon, *s.m.*, boy, servant, waiter
garde, *s.f.*, guard; se tenir sur ses gardes, to be on one's guard
garde, *s.m.*, guard, guardian
garder, *v.a.*, to keep, to guard
gardien, *s.m.*, keeper, guardian
garnir, *v.a.*, to fill, to trim
garnison, *s.f.*, garrison
Gascogne, *s.f.*, Gascony
Gascon, *s.adj.*, Gascon
gâteau, *s.m.*, cake
géant, *s.m.*, giant
gémir, *v.n.*, to groan, to lament
gendarme, *s.m.*, gendarme
gendarmerie, *s.f.*, gendarmery
gêne, *s.f.*, trouble, uneasiness
général, *s.m.*, general
généreux, -se, *adj.*, generous
générosité, *s.f.*, generosity
gens, *s.m.*, folks, persons, men; les jeunes gens, young people
gésir, *v.n.*, to lie
gibier, *s.m.*, game
glace, *s.f.*, ice
glaçon, *s.m.*, icicle
glissade, *s.f.*, slip
glisser, *v.n.*, to glide, to slip
golfe, *s.m.*, gulf
gomme, *s.f.*, gum
gommier, *s.m.*, gum-tree
gorger, *v.a.*, to gorge, to glut
gorgée, *s.f.*, mouthful (of a liquid), draught

gourmand, -e, *adj.*, greedy
goût, *s.m.*, taste
goûter, *v.a*, to taste
goûter, *s.m.*, lunch
goutte, *s.f.*, drop
gouttelette, *s.f.*, little drop
gouvernail, *s.m.*, rudder helm
grammaire, *s.f.*, grammar
graver, *v.a.*, to engrave
grand, -e, *adj.*, great, large, wide
gravure, *s.f.*, engraving
grec, -que, *adj.*, Greek
grenade, *s.f.*, pomegranate, grenade
grenadier, *s.m.*, pomegranate-tree, grenadier
griffer, *v.a.*, to claw, to scratch
griffonner, *v.n.*, to scribble
grillade, *s.f.*, broiled meat
grillage, *s.m.*, wire-work
grille, *s.f.*, grating
griller, *v.a.*, to broil
grogner, *v.n.*, to grumble
grognon, *s.m.*, grumbler
gros, -se, *adj.*, big
groseille, *s.f.*, currant
groseillier, *s.m.*, currant-tree
grossir, *v.n.*, to become big
guérir, *v.a.*, to cure
guérison, *s.f.*, recovery
guerre, *s.f.*, war
guerrier, *s.m.*, warrior
guêtre, *s.f.*, gaiter
guide, *s.m.*, guide
guidon, *s.m.*, guidon, sight of a gun, flag, cornet
Guillaume, *s.p.m.*, William

H

Habile, *adj.*, clever, skilful, able
habiller, *v.a.*, to dress; s'habiller, to dress oneself
habit, *s.m.*, clothes, coat, dress-coat
habiter, *v.a.n.*, to inhabit
habitant, *s.m.*, inhabitant
habitation, *s.f.*, habitation, abode
habituer, (s'), *v.r.*, to accustom one's self
hache, *s.f.*, axe, hatchet
hacher, *v.a.*, to mince
hachis, *s.m.*, hash
hagard, *adj.*, haggard, wild
haie, *s.f.*, hedge, row, line
haine, *s.f.*, hatred
haïr, *v.a.*, to hate
hardi, *adj.*, bold
hardiesse, *s.f.*, boldness
hasard, *s.m.*, chance, hazard
haut, *adj.*, high
hautesse, *s.f.*, highness
hélas! *int.*, alas! ah!
hennir, *v.n.*, to neigh
herbe, *s.f.*, herb
herbage, *s.m.*, herbage
héritier, *s.m.*, heir
heur, *s.m.*, luck
heure, *s.f.*, hour
heureux, -se *adj.*, happy, lucky, fortunate
hibou, *s.m.*, owl
hier, *adv.*, yesterday
histoire, *s.f.*, history
hiver, *s.m.*, winter
hommage, *s.m.*, homage
homme, *s.m.*, man
honnête, *adj.*, honest
honnêteté, *s.f.*, honesty
honteux, -se. *adj. m.f.*, ashamed, shameful
horloge, *s.f.*, clock
horloger, *s.m.*, clockmaker
hors, *prep.*, out
hospitalier, *adj.*, hospitable
hôte, *s.m.*, host
houille, *s.f.*, coal
houiller, *adj.*, containing coal; bassin houiller, coal-basin
huile, *s.f.*, oil
huilier, *s.m.*, oil-cruet
huit, *adj.num.*, eight
huitaine, *s.f.*, about a week, or a week
humilier, *v.a.*, to humble

I

Ici, *adv.*, here
île, *s.f.*, island
îlot, *s.m.*, islet
imaginer, (s'), *v.r.*, to imagine
immense, *adj.*, immense
immensité, *s.f.*, immensity
impatient, *adj.*, impatient
impertinence, *s.f.*, impertinence
importance, *s.f.*, importance
impôt, *s.m.*, tax
imprimer, *v.a.*, to print
imprudemment, *adv.*, imprudently
impunément, *adv.*, with impunity
incendie, *s.m.*, fire, conflagration
inconstant, *adj.*, inconstant, inconsistent
indifférent, *adj.*, indifferent
infirme, *adj.*, infirm
infirmerie, *s.f.*, infirmary
inflexible, *adj.*, inflexible
ingénieux, -se *adj.*, ingenious, clever
ingrat, *adj.*, ungrateful
inquiet, -ète, *adj.*, uneasy
insensible, *adj.*, insensible, unfeeling
insignifiant, *adj.*, insignificant
instituteur, *s.m.*, founder, tutor, schoolmaster
institutrice, *s.f.*, governess, school-mistress
insuffisant, *adj.*, insufficient
intendant, *s.m.*, steward
intention, *s.f.*, intention, design
intéressant, *adj.*, interesting
intérêt, *s.m.*, interest
interne, *s.m.*, boarder
internat, *s.m.*, boarding-school
intervalle, *s.m.*, interval; *loc.*, à de longs intervalles, at long intervals
intime, *adj.*, intimate
intimité, *s.f.*, intimacy
invariable, *adj.*, invariable
inviter, *v.a.*, to invite
invité, *adj.*, invited
irai, *v.n.*, see aller, p. 112
Italien, *s.m.*, Italian

J

Jaloux, -se, *adj.*, jealous
jalousie, *s.f.*, jealousy
jamais, *adv.*, ever; ne... jamais, never
jambage, *s.m.*, stroke (of a pen), jamb
jambe, *s.f.*, leg
jambon, *s.m.*, ham
jardin, *s.m.*, garden
jardinage, *s.m.*, gardening
jardiner, *v.n.*, to garden
jardinier, *s.m.*, gardener
jatte, *s.f.*, bowl

jatée, s.f., bowl-full
jaune, adj., yellow
jaunir, v.n., to become yellow
je, j', pr.pers., I
jeune, adj., young
jeûne, s.m., fast, fasting
joie, s.f., joy
joli, -e, adj., pretty
jouet, s.m., toy, plaything
joueur, s.m., player (fem. joueuse)
joujou, s.m., toy
jour s.m., day ; loc., de jour en jour, from day to day
journal, s.m., journal, newspaper
journaliste, s.m., journalist
joûte, s.f., joust, tilt, fight
joyeux, -se, adj., joyous, joyful
jugement, s.m., judgment
juillet, s.m., July
jumeau, s.m., twin
jumeau, adj.m. (fem. jumelle), twin
jupe, s.f., skirt
jupon, s.m. petticoat
jurer, v.a.n., to swear
juron, s.m., oath
jusque (à), pr., to, as far as
juste, adj., just, correct, (adv.) chanter juste, to sing in tune
justesse, s.f., justness, accuracy, propriety
justice, s.f., justice
justification, s.f., justification

K

Kilomètre, s.m., kilometer

L

La, l', art.f., the
la, pr.pers.reg.dir., her, it

là, adv., there, thither; là-bas, yonder
laborieux, -se adj., laborious, industrious
lait, s.m., milk
laiterie, s.f., dairy
laite, s.f., soft-roe
laité, -e, adj., soft-roed
lancer, v.a., to dart, to throw, to cast
langage, s.m., language
langue, s.f., tongue
languette, s.f., tongue
lard, s.m., bacon
lardon, s.m., slice of bacon
Latin, s.m., Latin
latiniste, s.m., Latin scholar
lavage, s.m., washing
laver, v.a., to wash
laveur, s.m., washer ; laveuse, s.f., washerwoman
lavis, s.m., wash (drawing)
le, l', art.m., the
le, l', pr.pers. masc. reg. dir., him, it
leçon, s.f., lesson
lecteur, s.m., reader, lecturer
lectrice, s.f., reader
lecture, s.f., reading ; cabinet de lecture, reading-rooms
légèreté, s.f., lightness
les, art.pl., the
les, pr.pers.reg.dir.pl., them
lettre, s.f., letter
lever (se), v.r., to rise
liaison, s.f., union, joining
libre, adj., free
lier, v.a., to tie
ligne, s.f., line
lignage, s.m., lineage
limon, s.m., lemon
limonade, s.f., lemonade
limonier, s.m., lemon-tree
lion, s.m., lion

liquide, s.m., and adj., liquid
lire, v.a., to read
lit, s.m., bed
livre, s.m., book
livre, s.f., pound
livret, s.m., little book
loger, v.a.n., to lodge
logis, s.m., dwelling
loi, s.f., law
Londres, n.p., London
louage, s.m., letting out, hire
Louis, s.m., Lewis
lourd, -e, adj., heavy
louve, s.f., she-wolf
loyal, -e, adj., loyal
loyer, s.m., rent
lu, past part., of lire
luxe, s.m., luxury

M

Mâcher, v.a., to chew
mâchoire, s.f., jaw
machine, s.f., machine
machiniste, s.m., machinist
magasin, s.m., shop
magasinage, s.m., warehousing
magicien, s.m., magician
magnifique, adj., magnificent
maigre, adj., thin
maille, s.f., stitch, mesh, mail
maillot, s.m., swaddling clothes
maint, -e, adj., many
maintenir, v.a., to maintain
maison, s.f., house
maître, s.m., master
mal, s.m., evil
malade, adj., ill, sick
malformé, adj., badly made. ill-shaped
malhabile, adj., awkward

malheur, *s.m.*, misfortune
malheureux, -se, *adj.*, unhappy
malin, maligne, *adj.*, malicious
malintentionné, *adj.*, evilminded
malmener, *v.a.*, to ill-treat
malsain, *adj.*, unhealthy
maltraiter, *v.a*, to ill-treat
malverser, *v.n.*, to be guilty of malversations
mangeoire, *s.f.*, manger
manger, *v.a.*, to eat
manger, *s.m.*, eating
manquer, *v.n.*, to fail, to miss ; manquer à, to be deficient or wanting (in), to fall short of
manteau, *s.m.*, mantle
mantelet, *s.m.*, mantlet
marbre, *s.m.*, marble
marbrerie, *s.f.*, marble-cutting, marble yard
marchand, -e, *adj.*, saleable, trading
marchand, *s.m.*, dealer, tradesman, merchant
marchandise, *s.f.*, merchandise, goods
maréchal, *s.m.*, farrier, marshal
mari, *s.m.*, husband
mariage, *s.m.*, marriage
marin, *s.m.*, seaman, sailor
Maroc, *s.m.*, Morocco
Marocain, *s.m.*, native of Morocco
marque, *s.f.*, mark
marquis, *s.m.*, marquis
marquisat, *s.m*, marquisate
marteau, *s.m.*, hammer
martelet, *s.m.*, little hammer

martyr, *s.m.*, martyr
matin, *s.m.*, morning
matinée, *s.f.*, morning, forenoon
méchanceté, *s.f.*, wickedness
méchant, *adj.*, wicked, bad, naughty
méchant, *s.m.*, wicked (person)
médaille, *s.f.*, medal
médailler, *v.a.*, to give a medal to
médaillier, *s.m.*, cabinet of medals
médailliste, *s.m.*, medallist
médaillon, *s.m.*, medallion
médiocre, *adj.*, middling, indifferent
médiocre, *s.m.*, mediocrity
médire, *v.n.*, to speak ill
médisance, *s.f.*, slander
même, *adj.* (see paragraph 84)
même, *adv.*, even
ménage, *s.m.*, household, housekeeping, husbandry
ménager, *v.a.*, to husband, to take care of
mendier, *v.a.*, to beg
mendiant, *s.m.*, beggar
mener, *v.a.*, to lead
mensonge, *s.m.*, falsehood, story, lie
mensonger, -ère, *adj.*, untrue, delusive
mentir, *v.n.*, to lie, to tell a falsehood
menton, *s.m.*, chin
mer, *s.f.*, sea
mercier, *s.m.*, haberdasher, mercer
mériter, *v.a.*, to deserve, to merit
message, *s m.*, message

messager- ère, *s.m.f.*, messenger, courier; *adj.*, le pigeon messager (Béranger)
mesure, *s.f.*, measure
mets, *s.m.*, dish
meurtrir, *v.a.*, to bruise
meurtrissure, *s.f.*, bruise
merveille, *s.f.*, wonder, marvel ; à merveille, wonderfully well
mieux, *adv.*, better
midi, *s.m.*, noon, midday
mie, *s.f.*, crumb
miette, *s.f.*, crumb
mi-jambe (à), half-way up the leg
mi-juillet, *s f.*, middle of July
mince, *adj.*, thin
minuit, *s.m.*, midnight
mi-partie, *s.f.*, half
mirer, *v.n.*, to aim
miroir, *s.m.*, looking-glass
mis, *past part.* of mettre, to put
mode, *s.f.*, fashion
modiste, *s.f.*, milliner
modéré, -e, *adj.*, moderate
modeste, *adj.*, modest
moi, *pron.*, *pers.*, 1. subject, I ; 2. object (instead of à moi), to me, me
moindre, *adj.comp.*, lesser, less (with the *def. art.*), the least
moins, *adv.*, less ; le moins, the least
moisir, *v.n.*, to mould
moisissure, *s.f.*, mouldiness
mollesse, *s.f.*, softness, indolence
mollet, -ette, *dim.adj.*, soft ; pain mollet, roll
mon, ma, mes, *adj.poss.*, my

monarchie, *s.f.*, monarchy; monarchique, monarchical
monarchiste, *s.m.*, monarchist
monde, 1. *s.m.*, world, people, company; 2. tout le monde, *pr.ind.*, everybody
mondain, *adj.*, worldly, mundane
monotone, *adj.*, monotonous
monotonie, *s.f.*, monotony
monsieur, *s.m.*,(*pl.* messieurs) sir, gentleman
montagne, *s.f.*, mountain
montagnard, *s.m.*, mountaineer, highlander
montant, *s.m.*, amount
monter, *v.n.*, to mount
montée, *s.f.*, ascent, rise
montre, *s.f.*, watch
montrer, *v.a.*, to show
moquer (se), *v.r.* (do), to laugh (at)
moqueur, -se, *adj.*, sarcastic
morale, *s.f.*, morals
moraliste, *s.m.*, moralist
morceau, *s.m.*, bit, piece, morsel; *lit.*, passage
mordre, *v.a.*, to bite
mort, *s.f.*, death
mot, *s.m.*, word
moteur, motrice, *s.m.f.*, mover, moving-power
motif, *s.m.*, motive
mou, mol, molle, *adj.*, soft
mouche, *s.f.*, fly
moucher, *v.a.*, to blow one's nose
moucheron, *s.m.*, gnat
mouchoir, *s.m.*, handkerchief
mouiller, *v.a.*, to wet
moule, *s.m.*, shape, mould
moulage, *s.m.*, moulding

mourir, *v.n.*, to die; se mourir (*ref.*) to be dying
moût, *s.m.*, must, unfermented wine
moutarde, *s.f.*, mustard
moutardier, *s.m.*, mustard-pot
mouvoir, *v.a.*, to move
munir, *v.a.*, to provide
mur, *s.m.*, wall; muraille, thick wall
mûr, *adj.*, ripe
musicien, -ne, *s.m.f.*, musician

N

Nager, *v.n.*, to swim
nageoire, *s.f.*, fin
nageur, *s.m.*, swimmer
naître, *v.n.*, to be born
naissance, *s.f.*, birth
nation, *s.f.*, nation, people
nature, *s.f.*, nature
navigation, *s.f.*, navigation
navire, *s.m.*, ship
ne, *adv.*, 1. before or after aucun, rien, jamais, etc.; no, not. 2. instead of ne pas; not. 3. ne.... pas, ne.... point; not, *loc.* ne.... que, but, only
néanmoins, *adv.*, nevertheless
nègre, *s.m.*, negro
négresse, *s.f.*, negress
négrillon, -ne, *s.m.f.*, negro-boy; negro-girl
net, nette, *adj.*, clean, clear, plain
netteté, *s.f.*, cleanness, clearness, plainness
nettoyer, *v.a.*, to clean
nettoiement, nettoyage, *s.m.*, cleaning, clearing
neuf, *adj.*, new; nine

neveu, *s.m.*, nephew
ni, *conj.*, neither, nor
niche, *s.f.*, niche, kennel
nichée, *s.f.*, brood
nœud, *s.m.*, knot
noir, *adj.* black
noirâtre, *adj.*, blackish
noiraud, *adj.*, dark, (complexion) darkish
noix, *s.f.*, walnut, nut
nombreux, -se, *adj.*, numerous
non-payement, *s.m.*, want of payment
non-sens, *s.m.*, nonsense
non-valeur, *s.f.*, thing without value
nord, *s.m.*, north
Normand, *s.m.*, Norman
notre, nos, *adj.*, our
nôtre (le, la) *pr.poss.*, ours
nourrir, *v.a.*, to nourish, to feed
se nourrir, *v.r.*, to feed, to live
nouvelle, *s.f.*, news, tidings, intelligence
nuire, *v.n.*, to injure, to harm, to do harm
nuit, *s.f.*, night
nul, nulle, *adj.* and *pr. ind.*, no, none

O

Obéir, *v.n.*, to obey
obéissance, *s.f.*, obedience
obéissant, -e, *adj.*, obedient
obliger, *v.a.*, to oblige
obligeance, *s.f.*, kindness
obstacle, *s.m.*, obstacle
occasion, *s.f.*, occasion, opportunity
occuper, (s'), *v.r.*, to occupy one's self
œil, *s.m.*, eye
œillade, *s.f.*, glance, ogle
œuf, *s.m.*, egg

officier, s.m., officer
offre, s.f., offer, tender
oiseau, s.m., bird
oisif, -ve, adj., idle
ombre, s.f., shade, shadow
ombrelle, s.f., parasol
oncle, s.m., uncle
opiniâtre, adj., obstinate
opinion, s.f., opinion
orange, s.f., orange
orangé, adj., orange-colour
orangeade, s.f., orangeade
orangeat, s.m., cand.ied orange-peel
oranger, s.m., orange-tree
orangerie, s.f., orange-house
oreille, s.f., ear
oreiller, s.m., pillow
orgueil, s.m., pride
orme, s.m., elm
ormeau, s.m. young elm, elm
orphelin, s.m., orphan, (boy)
où, adv., where, whither
ou, conj., or
oubli, s.m., forgetfulness
oublier, v.a., to forget
œuvre, s.2g., work
ouïr, v.a., to hear; ouïr dire, to hear (it said)
ours, s.m., bear
ouvrer, v.a., to work
ouvrage, s.m., work
ouvrier, s.m., workman

P

Pain, s.m., bread
pair, s.m., equal, fellow, peer
pair, adj., equal
paire, s.f., pair
palais, s.m., palace
pâle, adj., pale
palot, -te, adj., palish
paperasse, s.f., waste paper

papier, s.m., paper
parade, s.f., parade, show
pardon, s.m., pardon
parents, s.pl., parents. relations
parenté, s.f., relationship
parer, v.a., to adorn
parler, v.a.n., to speak
parloir, s.m., parlour
parole, s.f., word
parti, s.m., party, decision
partie, s.f., part, portion
partir, v.n., to set out
partout, adv., everywhere
pas, adv., not; see ne
passage, s.m., passage
passager, -ère, adj., passing, short-lived, transitory
passer, v.n., to pass
passant, s.m., passer-by
pâté, s.m., pie
pâte, s.f., paste
pâtée, s.f., paste, mess
patience, s.f., patience
patin, s.m., skate
pauvre, adj., poor; les pauvres, the poor
pauvreté, s.f., poverty
payement, s.m., payment
pays, s.m., country, birth-place
paysage, s.m., landscape
paysagiste, s.m., landscape painter
paysan, s.m., peasant, countryman
péage, s.m., toll, tollhouse
péager, s.m., toll-gatherer
taxe-péagère, tax, toll
pêche, s.f., peach
pêcher, s.m., peach-tree
pêcher, v.a.n., to fish
pécher, v.n., to sin
pêcheur, s.m., fisherman
pécheur, s.m., sinner
peigner, v.a., to comb
peignoir, s.m., dressing-gown (lady's)

pèlerin, s.m., pilgrim
pèlerinage, s.m., pilgrimage
penchant, s.m., leaning
pencher, v.n., to lean
pendant, pr., during
pendre, v.a., to hang
pendu, s.m., hanged man
pensée, s.f., thought
penser, v.a.n., to think
pensif, -ve, adj., pensive, thoughtful
percevoir, v.a., to gather in, to collect
percher, v.n., to perch
perchoir, s.m., roost
perdrix, s.f., partridge
perdue, p.p fem. of perdre, to lose
père, s.m., father
perfide, adj., perfidious, treacherous
perfidie, s.f., perfidy, treacherousness
péril, s.m., peril, danger
période, s.2g., period
permettre, v.a., to allow, to permit to suffer
persévérance, s.f., perseverance
persister, v.n., to persist
personne, s.f., person, (pl.) people, persons; loc., une jeune personne, a young lady
personne, pr.ind., page 64
perte, s.f., loss
petit, adj., small, little
petitesse, s.f., littleness, meanness
peu, adv., little, few
peu, s.m., a little, a few
peuple, s.m., people
peuplade, s.f., tribe
pierraille, s.f., broken stone
pierre, s.f., stone
pierreux, -se, adj., stony
pillage, s.m., plunder
pillard, adj., plundering

iller, v.a., to plunder
is, adv.comp., worse
is, sup., the worst
istolet, s.m., pistol
itié, s.f., pity
lace, s.f., place
laindre, v.a., to pity
lainte, s.f., complaint
laire, v.n., to please
e plaire, v.r., to please one's self or each other, to take delight, to be delighted
laisir, s.m., pleasure
lancher, s.m., floor, ceiling
lat, s.m., dish
lateau, s.m., wooden basin, tray
lein, -e, adj., full
leurer, v.a., to mourn over
leurer, v.n., to weep, to cry
leuvoir, v.i., to rain
li, s.m., fold
linge, s.m., folding
lier, v.a., to fold
lomb, s.m., lead
lombier, s.m., plummer
louger, v.a.n., to plunge
longeon, s.m., diver (bird)
plumage, s.m., plumage
lumassier, s.m., feather-seller
lumasserie, s.f., feather-trade
lume, s.f., feather, pen
lumée, s.f., ponful
lumeau, s.m., feather-broom
lumer, v.a., to pluck the feathers
lumet, s.m., plumet
lumetis, s.m., needle-embroidery
lus, adv., more (p.40,11)
lutôt, adv., (que), rather (than)

plusieurs, adj.ind., several
poète, s.m., poet
pointe, s.f., point, top
pointu, adj., pointed, sharp
poire, s.f., pear
poirier, s.m., pear-tree
pois, s.m., pea
poivrade, s.f., pepper sauce
poivre, s.m., pepper
poivrer, v.a., to pepper
poivrier, s.m., pepper-tree
poivrière, s.f., pepper-box
pôle, s.m., pole
polir, v.a., to polish
polisseur, s.m., polisher
polissure, s.f., polishing
pomme, s.f., apple
pommeau, s.m., pommel
pommier, s.m., apple-tree
pont, s.m., bridge, deck
porcelaine, s.f., china, porcelain; de or en porcelaine, china (adj.)
port, s.m., port, harbour
porter, v.a., to bear, to carry, to wear
se porter, v.r., to be, to do; comment vous portez-vous? how do you do? je me porte assez bien, I am pretty well
porte, s.f., door
portier, s.m., door-keeper
possible, adj., possible
possible, s.m., possibility, what is possible; je ferai tout mon possible, I will do my utmost, all I can
poste, s.f., post-house, post, post-office
poste, s.m., post, guard-house, station
potage, s.m., soup
potager, -ère, adj., jardin-potager, kitchen garden

poularde, s.f., fat poulet
poule, s.f., hen
poulet, s.m., chicken
pour, prep., for (before a infinitive), to, in order to
pourquoi? conj. and adv., why? wherefore? what ...for?
poursuivre, v.a., to pursue
pourvoir, v.n., to provide
poussée, s.f., push
pousser, v.a., to push
pouvoir, v.a.n., to be able (to do)
pouvoir, s.m., power
prairie, s.f., meadow
pratiquer, v.a., to practice
précipiter, (se), v.r., to fling one's self headlong, to run headlong.
précipiter, v.a., to precipitate
précipité, s.m., precipitate
précoce, adj., precocious
préférer, v.a., to prefer
préfet, s.m., prefect
prendre, v.a., to take
près, prep. (de), near
presbytère, s.m., parsonage, vicarage
présent, s.m., present, gift
présent, adj., present
présenter, v.a., to present, to offer
président, s.m., president
présider, v.n., to preside
presque, adv., almost, nearly
prêt, adj., ready
prétendre, v.a.n., to pretend, to pretend to, to claim
preuve, s.f., proof
prévaloir, v.n., to prevail
prévenir, v.a., to precede, to prevent, to anticipate

prévenant, *adj.*, complaisant
prévoir, *v.a.*, to foresee
prévoyance, *s.f.*, foresight
prévôt, *s.m.*, provost
prévôté, *s.f.*, provostship
prince, *s.m.*, prince
princesse, *s.f.*, princess
prise, *p.p.fem.*, *of* prendre, to take
procéder, *v.n.*, to proceed
procédé, *s.m.*, proceeding, operation
prochain, *adj.*, near, nearest, next
proche, *adj.*, near, nigh
proches, *s.m.pl.*, kindred
profiter, *v.n.*, to profit
projet, *s.m.*, project
promener, (se), *v.r.*, to walk
promenoir, *s.m.*, place for walking
prompt, -e, *adj.*, prompt, quick
prononcer, *v.a.*, to pronounce
prophète, *s.m.*, prophet
propos, *s.m.*, speech, talk, tattle, purpose; à propos, to the purpose
proposer, *v.a.*, to propose
proposer, (se), *v.r.*, to purpose
propre, *adj.*, clean, own, proper
propriété, *s.f.*, property
protester, *v.a.n.*, to protest
protestant, *s.m.*, protestant
prudence, *s.f.*, prudence
prudent, -e, *adj.*, prudent
prune, *s.f.*, plum
pruneau, *s.m.*, small plum, French plum
prunelle, *s.f.*, sloe, eyeball

public (publique, *f.*), public
publicain, *s.m.*, publican
puis, *v.a.n.*, *ind.pres.* of pouvoir, to be able
puisque, *conj.*, since
puissant, *adj.*, powerful
punir, *v.a.*, to punish
punissable, *adj.*, punishable
punition, *s.f.*, punishment
pureté, *s.f.*, purity

Q

Quand, *adv.*, when
quand, *conj.*, though
quant (à), *adv.*, with, in regard to, as to
quarante, *adj.n.*, forty;
quarantaine, *s.f.*, about forty, or quarantine
quatre, *adj.*, four
quatrain, *s.m.*, quatrain
que, *p.rel.*, whom, that, which, (*interr.*) what?
que, *conj.*, that, than, as
que, *adv.*, how, how much, how many, why
quel, quelle, *adj.*, what (*parag.* 107)
quelconque, *adj. ind.*, whatever, whatsoever
quelquefois, *adv.*, sometimes
question, *s.f.*, question
queue, *s.f.*, tail, end
qui, *pr.rel.sub.*, who, that; *obj.*, whom, that, which; *interr.*, who, whom, which
quille, *s.f.*, keel, skittle
quinze, *adj.*, fifteen
quinzaine, *s.f.*, about fifteen or a fortnight
quoique, *conj.*, though, although

R

Rabat, *s.m.*, band (for the neck)
rabattre, *v.a.*, to beat down
rabot, *s.m.*, plane
raboteux, *adj.*, uneven, rugged
raconter, *v.a.*, to relate
raffiner, *v.a.*, to refine; raffinage, refining
rail, *s.m.*, rail
raisin, *s.m.*, grapes
rallonger, *v.a.*, to lengthen
rallonge, *s.f.*, lengthening piece, leaf of a table
ramer, *v.n.*, to row
rameur, *s.m.*, rower
rang, *s.m.*, rank
rangée, *s.f.*, row
ranger, *v.a.*, to put in a row
râpe, *s.m.*, rasp
râper, *v.a.*, to rasp
rapidement, *adv.*, rapidly
rayon, *s.m.* ray, beam, shelf
rebuter, *v.a.*, to repel, to rebuff
rebut, *s.m.*, refuse
recevoir, *v.a.*, to receive
récompenser, *v.a.*, to reward, to recompense
reconnaître, *v.a.*, to recognise
reconnaissance, *s.f.*, gratitude
recul, *s.m.*, recoil
reculade, *s.f.*, backing, retreat
redevoir, *v.a.*, to owe still
réduire, *v.a.*, to reduce
réduit, *s.m.*, small habitation
réformer, *v.a.*, to reform
refus, *s.m.*, refusal
régal, *s.m.* (*pl.* régals), entertainment, feast, treat

régir, v.a., to administer
régisseur, s.m., administrator, steward
règle, s.f., rule
règne, s.m., reign
reine, s.f., queen
rejet, s.m., rejection, shoot
rejeter, v.a., to throw again, to throw back or away, to reject, to set aside
rejeton, s.m., sprout, scion, offspring
réjouir, (se), v.r., to rejoice
relancer, v.a., to start anew
relier, v.a., to bind
relieur, s.m., binder
religieux, -se, adj., religious
remarque, s.f., remark
remarquer, v.a., to remark, to notice
remerciement, s. m., thanks
remontrer, v.a., to remonstrate
remontrance, s.f., remonstrance
remplir, v.a., to fill again, to fill up; remplir un devoir, to fulfil a duty
remplumer, v.a., to feather again
renard, s.m., fox
enchérir, v.a., to raise the price of
rencontrer v.a., to meet
rendre, v.a., to render, to give back
se rendre, v.r., 1. to repair, to betake one's self; 2. to yield; 3. to give one's self up, to surrender
renforcer, v.a., to strengthen, to reinforce
renommer, v.a., to name again
renommée, s.f., fame

renoncer, v.n., to renounce
repaître, (se), v.r., (de) to feed on
répandre, v.a., to pour, to spill, to spread
répondre, v.a., to answer
reposer, v.n., reposer, (se), v.r., to rest
repousser, v.a., to repulse
repoussoir, s.m., driving bolt
reprendre, v.a., to resume
reprise, s.f., retaking, renewal; à deux reprises différentes, two several times
république, s.f., republic
républicain, s.m., republican
répugner, v.n., to be repugnant
répugnance, s.f., repugnance
réputation, s.f., reputation, fame
requérir, v.a., to request, to demand, to require
requête, s.f., request, petition
réserver, v.a., to reserve
réservoir, s.m., reservoir, cistern
ressemblance, s.f., likeness
ressembler, v.n., to resemble
ressentir, v.a., to feel, to resent
ressort, s.m., spring
ressource, s.f., resource
rester, v.n., to stay, to remain
retirer (se), v.r., to retire, to withdraw
retrancher, v.a., to retrench
réussir, v.n., to succeed
revenir, v.n., to come back

revenu, s.m., income, revenue
rêver, v.a.n., to dream; rêvasser, v.n., to muse
revers, s.m., back, reverse
revêtir, v.a., to clothe again
revoir, v.a., to see again
revue, s.f., review
riche, adj., rich, wealthy
richesse, s.f., riches, wealth
ridicule, adj., ridiculous
rien, s. and pr., (page 64)
rieur, s.m., laugher
rire, v.n., to laugh
rire, s.m., laughter
rivage, s.m., shore, bank
robe, s.f., dress
roc, s.m., rock
rocaille, s.f., rock-work
rodomont, s.m., swaggerer
rodomontade, s.f., swaggering
roi, s.m., king
Rome, s.f., Rome
romain, -e, adj., Roman
rond, -e, adj., round
rondelet, adj., plump
rose, s.f., rose
rosier, s.m., rose-tree
roue, s.f., wheel
rouge, adj., red
rougeâtre, adj., reddish
rougeaud, -e, adj., ruddy, red-faced
rougir, v.a.n., to redden
rouler, v.a., to roll
roulade, s.f., trill
roulis, s.m., rolling (of ships)
route, s.f., road, route, way
roux, -sse, adj., sandy (of the hair)
ruade, s.f., kick
rude, adj., rough, rude
rudesse, s.f., roughness, rudeness
rue, s.f., street

ruelle, s.f., lane, bedside
ruer, v.n., to kick
rugir, v.n., to roar
rugissement, s.m., roaring
rumeur, s.f., rumour

S

sable, s.m., sand
sablier, s.m., hour-glass, sand-box
sac, s.m., sack, bag
sachet, s.m., little bag
sacrifier, v.a., to sacrifice
sage adj., wise
sagesse, s.f., wisdom
saison, s.f., season
salade, s.f., salad
saladier, s.m., salad-dish
salaud, adj., slovenly
sale, adj., dirty
saler, v.a., to salt
salir, v.a., to soil
saloir, s.m., salting-tub
salutaire, adj., salutary
sangle, s.f., strap, band, girth
sanglé, p.part. of sangler, to strap, to give blows
sans, prep., without
sans-dent, without teeth
sans-façon, loc.adv., unceremoniously
sans-gêne, s.m., free manners; adv., unceremoniously
satisfait, -e, adj., satisfied, pleased
sauteur, -se, s.m.f., leaper, jumper
sauvage, adj., wild
savant, -e, adj., learned
savoir, v.a., to know
savoir, s.m., knowledge
savonnage, s.m., washing with soap

savonner, v.a., to lather
scie, s.f., saw
science, s.f., science
scier, v.a., to saw
se, soi, pr.pers., (parag. 95, 96)
secours, s.m., succour, help, aid
Seigneur, s.m., Lord
séjour, s.m., stay
semer, v.a., to sow
semis, s.m., seed-plot
sens, s.m., sense, meaning
sentence, s.f., sentence
sentiment, s.m., sensation, feeling, sentiment
sentir, v.a., to feel
seoir, v.n., to be becoming
séparable, adj., separable
séparer, v.a., to separate
serrure, s.f., lock
serrurier, s.m., locksmith
servir, v.n., to serve, to be useful
si, conj., if, whether
si, adv., so
siècle, s.m., century, age, time, world
siége, s.m., seat
siéger, v.n., to preside
signal, s.m., signal
sincère, adj., sincere
sincérité, s.f., sincerity
singe, s.m., monkey
singerie, s.f., apishness, mimicry
situation, s.f., situation
sobre, adj., sober
sobriété, s.f., sobriety
social, -e, adj., social
société, s.f., society, company
sœur, s.f., sister
soigneux, -se, adj., careful
soin, s.m., care
soir, s.m., evening

soirée, s.f., evening, evening party
soixante, adj.ind., sixty
soixantaine, s.f., about sixty
sol, s.m., soil, ground
soldat, s.m., soldier
solde, s.f., pay
somme, s.m., nap, sleep
somme, s.f., sum
sommeil, s.m., sleep
son, sa, ses, adj.poss., his, her, its, one, one's
sortir, v.n., to go out
soulier, s.m., shoe
soumis, adj., obedient
sot, sotte, adj., foolish, silly
sottise, s.f., folly, foolery
souci, s.m., care, anxiety
soucier, (se), v.r., to care
souffrir, v.n., to suffer
souffrance, s.f., suffering
souhait, s.m., wish
souhaiter, v.a., to wish
soulèvement, s.m., heaving, rising, insurrection
soulier, s.m., shoe
souper, v.n., to sup
souper, s.m., supper
soupir, s.m., sigh
soupirail, s.m., air-hole
soupirer, v.n., to sigh
sourire, v.n., to smile
sous, prep., under
sous-axillaire, adj., subaxillary
sous-intendant, s.m., understewart
sous-jacent, -e, adj., subjacent
sous-maître, s.m., undermaster, usher
sous-marin, adj., submarine
sous-officier, s.m., non-commissioned officer
sous-préfet, s.m., subprefect

sous sol, s.m., basement
souvenir, s.m., remembrance
souvenir, (se), v.r., to remember
souvent, adv., often
stimulant, s.m., stimulant
stimuler, v.a., to stimulate
studieux, -se, adj., studious
style, s.m., style
succès, s.m., success
sucre, s.m., sugar
sucrier, s.m., sugar-basin
suffire, v.n., to suffice
suffisance, s.f., sufficiency
Suisse, s.m., Swiss
Suissesse, s.f., Swisswoman
suivre, v.a., to follow
sujet, s.m., subject
suppliant, adj. (pers.), suppliant, (things) beseeching
sur, prep., on, upon, over, above
sûr, -e, adj., sure, certain, safe
sûreté, s.f., safety
surface, s.f., surface
surmonter, v.a., to overcome, to surmount
surnager, v.n., to float (upon the surface), to swim
surpasser, v.a., to surpass
surprendre, v.a., to surprise
surseoir, v.n., to respite
surveiller, v.a., to watch
suspendre, v.a., to suspend
syllabe, s.f., syllable
symbole, s.m., symbol
syndic, s.m., syndic
syndicat, s.m., syndicate

T

Table, s.f., table
tablée, s.f., tablefull
tableau, s.m., picture, painting, table, board
tablette, s.f., tablet
tablier, s.m., apron
tache, s.f., spot, stain, blot
tacher, v.a., to spot
tâche, s.f., task
tâcher, v.n., to endeavour
tailler, v.a., to cut
tailleur, s.m., tailor
taillis, s.m., copse
tante, s.f., aunt
taper, v.a., to smack, to hit
tapis, s.m., carpet
tapissier, s.m., upholsterer
tapoter, v.a., to pat
tard, adv., late
tarte, s.f., tart
tartelette, s.f., tartlet
teindre, v.a., to dye
tel, telle, adj. and pr.ind., such
télégramme, s.m., telegram
témoignage, s.m., testimony
témoigner, v.a., to testify
tempérance, s.f., temperance
température, s.f., temperature
tempérer, v.a., to temper
tempête, s.f., tempest, storm
tendre, v.a., to stretch
tendre, adj., tender
tendresse, s.f., tenderness
tenir, v.a., to hold
terminaison, s.f., termination
terminer, v.a., to end
ternir, v.a., to tarnish, to stain

terrain, s.m., ground
terrasse, s.f., terrace
terre, s.f., land, earth
texte, s.m., text
thé, s.m., tea
thème, s.m., exercise
tige, s.f., stalk, stem
tigre, s.m., tiger
timide, adj., timid
timidité, s.f., timidity
tirer, v.a., to draw, to pull
tirage, s.m., drawing (of a lottery), pulling (printing)
tiroir, s.m., drawer
tombe, s.f., 1. tomb, tombstone; 2. tomb, grave
tombeau, s.m., 1. tomb (monument); 2. tombstone
tonne, s.f., tun
tonneau, s.m., cask
tonnelle, s.f., arbour
tonnerre, s.m., thunder
tordre, v.a., to wring, to twist
tort, s.m., wrong; avoir tort, to be wrong
tôt, adv., soon; tôt ou tard, sooner or later
touchant, -e, adj., affecting, touching
toucher, v.a., to touch
toucher, s.m., touch (the sense)
touffe, s.f., tuft
toujours, adv., always
Toulouse, s.p., Toulouse
Toulousain, s.m., native of Toulouse
tour, s.m., turn, trip, tour, trick
tour, s.f., tower
tourelle, s.f., turret
tourmenter, v.a., to torment
tout, adj. and pr.ind., every, all; loc., tous les jours, every day

tracer, *v.a.*, to trace, to draw out
trahir, *v.a.*, to betray
trahison, *s.f.*, treason
train, *s.m.*, train
traînée, *s.f.*, trail
traire, *v.a.*, to milk
traître, *s.m.*, traîtresse, *s.f.*, traitor, traitress
tranchant, *s.m.* edge
tranchée, *s.f.*, trench, cutting
trancher, *v.a.*, to cut
tranquille, *adj.*, tranquil
tranquillité, *s.f.*, tranquillity
travail, *s.m.*, work
travailler, *v.a.n.*, to work
travailleur, *s.m.*, labourer, workman, hard worker
travailleuse, *s.f.*, workwoman, painstaking person (woman, girl)
trentaine, *s.f.*, about thirty
trente, *adj.num.*, thirty
très, *adv.*, very, very much
triage, *s.m.*, sorting
tribun, *s.m.*, tribune
tribunat, *s.m.*, tribuneship
tribut, *s.m.*, tribute
tricher, *v.a.*, to cheat
tricheur, *s.m.*, trickster, cheat
trier, *v.a.*, to sort
triste, *adj.*, sad
tristesse, *s.f.*, sadness
trivial, *adj.*, trivial
trivialité, *s.f.*, triviality
tromper, *v.a.*, to deceive
se tromper, *v.r.*, to be mistaken, to make a mistake
trop, *adv.*, too, too much, too many, too far, too long
trou, *s.m.*, hole

trouble, *s.m.*, trouble, confusion
trouver, *v.a.*, to find, to think, to like
tuer, *v.a.*, to kill
tuile, *s.f.*, tile
turbulent, *adj.*, noisy

U

Ultra-libéral, *adj.*, ultra-liberal
ultra-mondain, *adj.*, ultra-mundane
ultra-royaliste, *adj.*, ultra-royalist
ultra-zodiacal, *adj.*, ultra-zodiacal
un, -e, *adj.*, and, *subs.*, one
un, -e, *art.ind.*, a or an
user, *v.a.*, to wear out
usure, *s.f.*, wear and tear, usury
utile, *adj.*, useful

V

Va, 3.*p. p.ind. of* aller (p. 112)
vache, *s.f.*, cow
vacher, *s.m.*, cow-keeper
vagabond, *s.m.*, vagabond
vagabondage, *s.m.*, vagrancy
vain, -e, *adj.*, vain; *loc.*, en vain, in vain, vainly
vaincre, *v.a.*, to conquer
vainqueur, *s.m.*, conqueror
vaisseau, *s.m.*, ship, vessel
valeur, *s.f.*, value, valour
valoir, *v.n.*, to be worth
vanter, *v.a.*, to praise
vantard, -e, *adj.*, boastful
vapeur, *s.f.*, vapour, steam
varié, *adj.*, varied
variété, *s.f.*, variety

vassal,
vaut,
to b
végéta
veille,
veiller
v.n.,
venda
venda
ther
vendre
vendre
venges
gear
venger
venge
venge
aver
venir,
venue,
verbe,
verdir,
gree
vérita
vérité,
vermei
lion,
vermei
verre,
verrou
vers, s
verset,
Scri
vert, a
vertu,
vertue
vestiai
veux,
voul
vexer,
viande
vice, s.
vice-ar
adm
vice-pr
vice-
vice-ro
vieux,
old
vieillot

vigne, s.f., vine
vigneron, s.m., vine-dresser
vilain, -e, adj., ugly, nasty, villanous
vin, s.m., wine
vingt, adj.num., twenty
vingtaine, s.f., about twenty
violent, -e, adj., violent
visite, s.f., visit
vite, adj., quick, swift
vite, adv., quickly, swiftly, fast
vitrail, s.m., stained glass-window
vivre, v.n., to live
vœu, s.m., vow, wish
voici, adv., here is, here are
voilà, adv., there is, there are

voiler, v.a., to veil
voilure, s.f., set of sails
voir, v.a.n., to see
voiture, s.f., carriage
volable, adj., 1. (persons) to be robbed; 2. (things) easily stolen
voler, v.a., to steal, to rob
voler, v.n., to fly
volée, s.f., flight, volley
volet, s.m., shutter
voleur, -euse, s.m.f., thief
volume, s.m., volume
voter, v.a.n., to vote
votre (pl. vos), adj.pos., your, thy
vôtre (le,la), vôtres (les), pron.pos., yours
vouloir, v.a., will, to be willing

vous, pron.pers., you, to you
voyage, s.m., travelling, journey, voyage
voyageur, s.m., traveller

Y

Y, adv., there, thither, at home, within
y, pron., (things) it, them, (pers.) him, her, them (with the preposition required by the verb)

Z

Zéro, s.m., nought, cypher
zone, s.f., zone

ENGLISH-FRENCH VOCABULARY.

A

A, *art.ind.*, un (*m.*), une (*f.*)
abolish, *v.t.*, abolir
abominable, *adj.*, abominable
above, *prep.*, au-dessus de, sur; above all, surtout
absolve, *v.t.*, absoudre
accept, *v.t.*, accepter
accusation, *s.*, accusation (*f.*)
act, *v.t.*, agir
admire, *v.t.*, admirer
advantage, *s.*, avantage (*m.*)
advice, *s.*, avis (*m.*)
affair, *s.*, affaire (*f.*)
afflicted, *s.* and *adj.*, affligé
again, *adv.*, de nouveau, encore
agreement, *s.*, convention (*f.*)
aim, *v.intr.* (at), tendre (à)
alarm, *v.t.*, alarmer
alarming, *adj.*, alarmant
Algeria, *s.*, Algérie (*f.*)
all, *adj.ind.*, tout, -e, tous (*m.pl.*)
already, *adv.*, déjà
alter, *v.t.*, changer
although, *conj.*, quoique
always, *adv.*, toujours

amiable, *adj.*, aimable
ancestor, *s.*, ancêtre (*m.*), aïeul (*pl.* aïeux)
and, *conj.*, et
another, *adj.ind.* un (e), autre
answer, *v.t.*, répondre
answer, *s.*, réponse (*f.*)
anxiety, *s.*, inquiétude (*f.*)
any, *adj.ind.*, tout, n'importe lequel
applaud, *v.t.*, applaudir
apply, *v.int.*, s'appliquer
apprehend, *v.t.*, pressentir
argument, *s.*, argument (*m.*)
arm, *v.t.*, armer
army, *s.*, armée (*f.*)
arrive, *v.int.*, arriver
as, *prep.*, (for), quant (à)
as, *adv.*, comme, aussi; as forward as they, aussi avancé qu'eux
assault, *v.t.*, assaillir
assess, *v.t.*, répartir, évaluer
attack, *v.t.*, attaquer
attention, *s.*, attention (*f.*)
attentive, *adj.*, attentif.
aunt, *s.*, tante (*f.*)
avenging, *adj.*, vengeur, -resse (*m.f.*)
avoid, *v.t.*, eviter

B

Bad, *adj.*, mauvais, méchant
bank-note, *s.*, billet de banque (*m.*)
battle, *s.*, bataille (*f.*)
be, *v.aux.*, être (p. 75)
beautiful, *adj.*, beau, bel (*m.*), belle (*f.*)
because, *conj.*, parce que
become, *v.int.*, devenir (*v.t.*), seoir (à)
bed, *s.*, lit (*m.*)
before, *prep.*, avant
behave, *v.int.*, se conduire
believe, *v.t.*, croire (p. 127)
bell, *s.*, cloche (*f.*)
belong, *v.int.*, appartenir
bend, *v.t.*, fléchir
benefactor, *s.*, bienfaiteur (*m.*)
benefactress, *s.*, bienfaitrice (*f.*)
benevolent, *adj.*, bienfaisant
best, *adj.sup.*, (the, my, le, mon, etc.), meilleur
betray, *v.t.*, trahir
better, *adj.comp.*, meilleur
better, *adv.*, mieux
bill, *s.*, lettre de change (*f.*)
bird, *s.*, oiseau (*m.*)
bite, *v.t.*, mordre

blow, s., coup (m.)
boast, v.int., s'enorgueillir, se vanter
boat, s., bateau (m.)
bonnet, s., chapeau (m.)
book, s., livre (m.)
boot, s., botte (f.)
born, adj.; né; to be born, naître
bottle, s., bouteille (f.)
bow, s., arc (m.)
branch, s., branche (f.)
bread, s., pain (m.)
break, v.t., casser, rompre
breakfast, v.int., déjeûner
bring, v.t., apporter; to bring to confusion, confondre; to bring back, rapporter
brother, s., frère (m.)
bullet, s., balle (f.)
burn, v.t., brûler
burst, v.int., éclater; burst into tears, fondre en larmes
but, conj., mais
button, s., bouton (m.)
buy, v.t., acheter
by, prep., par, de, en

C

Cake, s., gâteau (m.)
call, v.t., appeler
calumniate, v.t. calomnier
camp, s., camp (m.)
can, v.def., pouvoir
candlestick, s., chandelier (m.)
care, s., soin (m.)
cargo, s., cargaison (f.)
carriage, s., voiture (f.)
castle, s., château (m.)
cat, s., chat (m.)
catastrophe, s., catastrophe (f.)
cautious, adj., prudent
cellar, s., cave (f.)
ceremony, s., cérémonie (f.)

certainly, adv., certainement
chair, s., chaise (f.)
charming, adj., charmant
cherish, v.t., chérir
child, s., enfant (m.)
choice, s., choix (m.)
choose, v.t., choisir
church, s., église (f.)
circumstance, s., circonstance (f.)
citadel, s., citadelle (f.)
cloak, s., manteau (m.); cloak-room, vestiaire (m.)
close, v.t., fermer
cloth, s., drap (m.)
clothe, v.t., vêtir; one's self, se vêtir
coal, s., charbon (m.)
coat, s., habit (m.)
cold, s., rhume (m.); to catch cold, s'enrhumer
collar, s., col (m.)
collect, v.t., percevoir
collection, s., collection (f.)
colonel, s., colonel (m.)
colour, s., couleur (f.)
come, v.int., venir; to come down, descendre
comfortable, adj., commode
commerce, s., commerce (m.)
commission, s., commission (f.)
company, s., compagnie, société (f.)
compassionate, adj., compatissant
complain, v.int., se plaindre
conceited, adj., suffisant
conceive, v.t., concevoir
concert, s., concert (m.)
condemn, v.t., condamner
conduct, s., conduite (f.)
confess, v.t., avouer, confesser

confidence, s. confiance (f.)
confound, v.t., confondre
confusedly, adv., confusément
conquered, p.part., conquis
consecrate, v.t., bénir
consent, v.int., consentir
consent, s., consentement (m.)
consequence, s., conséquence (f.)
consider, v.t., considérer —as, regarder comme
consoler, s., consolateur (m.)
contempt, s., mépris (m.)
continual, adj., continuel, -le
correspond, v.int., correspondre
cost, v.int., coûter
country, s., pays (m.), campagne (f.); country-house, maison de campagne; in the country, à la campagne
countrywoman, s., paysanne (f.)
court, s., cour (f.)
cousin, s., cousin (m.)
cousin, s., cousine (f.)
cow, s., vache (f.)
criticise, v.t., critiquer
cross, v.t., traverser
crown, s., couronne (f.)
cruel, adj., cruel, -le
crystal, s., cristal (m.); Crystal Palace, Palais de Cristal
cup, s., tasse (f.)
curtain, s., rideau (m.)
custom, s., coutume (f.)

D

Danger, s., danger (m.);
dangerous, adj., dangereux, -se

day, s., jour (m.); journée (f.)
deal, s., quantité (f.); a great deal, beaucoup
dear, adj., cher, (adv.) cher
death, s., mort (f.)
deceive, v.t., tromper
defeat, v.t., défaire
defend, v.t., défendre
delicious, adj., délicieux
departure, s., départ (m.)
depth, s., profondeur (f.)
deserve, v.t., mériter
design, s., dessein (m.)
despair, s., désespoir (m.)
detail, s., détail (m.)
devote, v.t., consacrer
dictionary, s., dictionnaire (m.)
die, v.int., mourir
difficult, adj., difficile
difficulty, s., difficulté (f.)
diligent, adj., appliqué
dine, v.int., dîner
dinner, s., dîner (m.)
disappear, v.int., disparaître
discharge, v.t., accomplir
discouraged, adj.part., découragé
discreet, adj., discret
discuss, v.t., discuter
disgrace, v.t., déshonorer
disguise, v.t., déguiser
disobey, v.int., désobéir
disown, v.int., disconvenir de
disposition, s., disposition (f.)
distribute, v.t., répartir
distrustful, adj., méfiant
do, v.t., faire (p. 129)
door, s., porte (f.)
dozen, s.coll., douzaine (f.)
drawer, s., tiroir (m.)
drawing, s., dessin (m.)

dream, s., rêve (m.); idle dream, chimère (f.)
dress, s., robe (f.)
drink, v.t., boire
drive, v.t., conduire, mener, pousser; to drive to despair, réduire au désespoir
dumb, adj., muet
during, pr., pendant
dust, s., poussière (f.)
dust, v.t., épousseter; to dust a coat, battre un habit
duty, s., devoir (m.)

E

Each, adj.ind., chaque
each, pr.ind., chacun; each other, l'un l'autre
early, adv., de bonne heure; as early as, dès
eat, v.t., manger
effort, s., effort (m.)
either, adj. and pr., l'un ou l'autre, l'une ou l'autre
embroider, v.t., broder
end, s., but (m.), fin (f.)
enemy, s., ennemi (m.)
England, s.p., Angleterre (f.)
engrave, v.t., graver
engraving, s., gravure (f.)
enjoy, v.int., jouir de
enslave, v.t., asservir
entreat, v.t., supplier
envy, s., envie (f.)
equal, adj., égal
equivalent (to be) équivaloir
error, s., erreur (f.)
essential, adj., essentiel
establish, v.t., établir
estate, s., terre, (f.), propriété (f.)
event, s., événement (m.)

every, adj. ind., chaque, tout; tous les; everybody, tout le monde
everywhere, adv., partout
examine, v., (into) approfondir
excellent, adj., excellent
exercise, s., thème (m.)
expose, v.t., dévoiler
extremely, adv., extrêmement
eye, s., œil (m.), (pl. yeux); eye-glass, s., lorgnon (m.)

F

Face, s., face (f.), visage (m.), figure (f.)
fail, v.int., faillir
faint, v.int., (away) s'évanouir
fall, s., chute (f.)
fall, v.int., tomber; to fall due, échoir
false, adj., faux (m.), fausse (f.)
fan, s., éventail (m.)
far, adv., loin
farm, s., ferme (f.)
fatal, adj., fatal
father, s., père (m.)
fault, s., faute (f.)
favour, s., faveur (f.)
favourite, adj., favori (m.), -te (f.)
fear, s., crainte (f.)
fear, v.t., craindre
feed, v.t. (on), se repaître de
fell, v.t., abattre
field, s., champ (m.)
fill, v.t., remplir
find, v.t., trouver
fine, adj., beau, bel, belle
finish, v.t., finir
fire, s., feu (m.)
firm, adj., ferme

fish, s., poisson (m.)
flattering, adj., flatteur
fleet, s., flotte (f.)
flourish, v. int., fleurir
flower, s., fleur (f.);
　flower-bed, planche (f.)
follow, v.t., suivre
fond, adj., cher
food, s., nourriture (f.)
for, prep., pour, à
forbid, v.t., défendre
force, s., force (f.)
foresee, v.t., prévoir
forget, v.t., oublier
fork, s., fourchette (f.)
formerly, adv., autrefois
forward, adj., avancé
fox, s., renard (m.)
franc, s., franc (m.)
France, s., France (f.)
French, adj., français
frequent, v.t., fréquenter
Friday, s., vendredi (m.)
friend, s., ami (m.), amie (f.)
friendship, s., amitié (f.)
from, pr., de
fruit, s., fruit (m.)
full, adj., plein
future, s., avenir (m.)

G

Gain, v.t., gagner
garden, s., jardin (m.)
gardener, s., jardinier (m.)
general, s., général (m.)
gentle, adj., doux. -ce
gentleman, s., monsieur (pl. messieurs)
get (up), v. int., se lever
give, v.t., donner; to give up, abandonner
glass, s., verre (m.)
glove, s., gant (m.)
go, v.int., aller; go out, sortir
God, s., Dieu (m.)

good, adj., bon, bonne
goods, s., marchandises (fem. pl.)
goose, s., oie (f.)
government, s., gouvernement (m.)
grammar, s., grammaire (f.)
grandfather, s., grand-père, aïeul (m.)
grape, s., raisin (m.)
grass, s., herbe (f.)
grateful, adj., reconnaissant
great, adj., grand
greatness, s., grandeur (f.)
Greek, adj., grec, grecque
grief, s., chagrin (m.)
grind, v.t., moudre (a knife) émoudre
grow, v.int., croître
guilty, s. and adj., coupable
guinea, s., guinée (f.)
gun, s., fusil (m.)

H

Hand, s., main (f.)
hang, v.int., pendre (up) suspendre
happen, v.int., arriver
happiness, s., bonheur (m.)
happy, adj., heureux, -se
haste, s., hâte (f.), to make haste, se hâter
hasty, adj., emporté
hat, s., chapeau (m.)
hate, v.t., haïr
he, pr.pers., il; lui; celui
health, s., santé (f.)
hear, v.t., entendre
heart, s., cœur (m.)
heat, s., chaleur (f.)
heaven, s., ciel (m.)
heavy, adj., pesant, lourd

her, pr.pers., elle, la, lui, à elle; hers (pr.poss.) le sien, la sienne, les siens, les siennes; à elle (adj.) son, sa, ses
here, adv. ici
him, pr.p., le, lui, celui; himself, se, lui-même, lui
his, adj.poss., son, sa, ses
his, pr.poss., le sien, la sienne; les siens, les siennes; pr. pers. à lui, de lui
history, s., histoire (f.)
holiday, s., congé (m.)
honest, adj., honnête
honourably, adv., honorablement
hope, s., espérance (f.)
horse, s., cheval (m.)
house, s., maison (f.)
how, adv., comment; how much, combien
humane, adj., humain
hundred, adj. num., cent
hungry, adj., affamé; to be —, avoir faim
hurt, v.t., blesser
hypocrite, s., hypocrite (m.)

I

I, pr.pers., je, moi (m.f.)
ice, s., glace (f.)
idea, s., idée (f.)
if, conj., si
ill, adj., malade
importance, s., importance (f.)
immediately, adv., immédiatement
impossible, adj., impossible
in, pr., dans, en, à
inconsiderate, adj., indiscret
industrious, adj., laborieux

infirm, *adj.*, infirme
infirmity, *s.*, infirmité (*f.*)
infringe, *v.t.*, enfreindre
inhabit, *v.t.*, habiter
inkstand, *s.*, encrier (*m.*)
insult, *s.*, insulte (*f.*)
interest, *s.*, intérêt (*m.*)
intrenchment, *s.* retranchement (*m.*)
invade, *v.t.*, envahir
it, *pr. nom.*, il, elle; (*acc.*) le, la; (*dat.*) lui (*m.f.*); (*imp.*) il, ce

J

January, *s.*, janvier (*m.*)
jealous, *adj.*, jaloux, -se
jewel, *s.*, bijou (*m.*)
join, *v.t.*, joindre
journal, *s.*, journal (*m.*)
judge, *s.*, juge (*m.*)
justice, *s.*, justice (*f.*)

K

Keep, *v.t.*, garder, tenir, conserver
kill, *v.t.*, tuer
kind, *adj.*, bon, bonne
kindness, *s.*, bonté (*f.*)
king, *s.*, roi (*m.*)
knife, *s.*, couteau (*m.*)
know, *v.t.*, savoir, connaître

L

Ladder, *s.*, échelle (*f.*)
lady, *s.*, dame (*f.*); young lady, demoiselle (*f.*)
lamp, *s.*, lampe (*f.*)
landscape, *s.*, paysage (*m.*)
large, *adj.*, grand
last, *adj.*, dernier

late, *adj.*, en retard
lately, *adv.*, dernièrement
laugh, *v.int.*, rire;—at, se moquer de
law, *s.*, loi (*f.*)
learned, *adj.*, instruit, savant
lease, *s.*, bail (*m.*), (*pl.*) baux
least, *adj. s.*, moindre, plus petit
least, *adv.*, moins; at least; au moins, du moins
less, *adj. c.*, moindre, plus petit
less, *adv.*, moins
leg, *s.* (of mutton), gigot (*m.*)
legal, *adj.*, légal
leisure, *s.*, loisir (*m.*)
lemon, *s.*, citron (*m.*)
lesson, *s.*, leçon (*f.*)
letter, *s.*, lettre (*f.*)
liable, *adj.*, sujet
library, *s.*, bibliothèque (*f.*); circulating library, cabinet de lecture (*m.*)
lie, *v. int.*, gésir
like, *v. tr.*, aimer
like, *adj.*, pareil, semblable, tel; like master, like man, tel maître, tel valet.
little, *adj.*, petit, (*adv.*) peu
linen, *s.*, linge (*m.*)
live, *v. int.*, vivre; demeurer
long, *adj.*, long; all day long, toute la journée
lose, *v.t.*, perdre; to lose one's self, s'égarer
loss, *s.*, perte (*f.*)
love, *v.t.*, aimer
loyal, *adj.*, loyal
luck, *s.*, bonheur (*m.*)

M

Machine, *s.*, machine (*f.*)
magnificent, *adj.*, magnifique
make, *v.t.*, faire; to make happy, rendre heureux
man, *s.*, homme (*m.*)
many, *adj. ind.*, plusieurs, beaucoup (*de*); bien (*des*); many a time, mainte fois
marriage, *s.*, mariage (*m.*)
master, *s.*, maître (*m.*)
mayor, *s.*, maire (*m.*)
means, *s.*, moyen (*m.*)
meat, *s.*, viande (*f.*)
meet, *v. t.*, rencontrer; (*ref.*) se rencontrer
meeting, *s.*, rencontre (*f.*), séance (*f.*)
melt, *v.t.*, fondre
mend, *v. t.*, réformer
merchant, *s.*, marchand (*m.*)
merit, *s.*, mérite (*m.*)
merry, *adj.*, gai
mild, *adj.*, doux
milk, *v. t.*, traire
mind, *s.*, esprit; to make up one's mind, se décider
mine, *pr. poss.*, le mien, la mienne, les miens, les miennes, à moi
my, *adj. poss.*, mon, ma, mes
minister, *s.*, ministre (*m.*)
minute, *s.*, minute (*f.*)
misfortune, *s.*, malheur (*m.*)
mistake, *s.*, faute (*f.*); erreur (*f.*); to make a mistake, se tromper
moderate, *adj.*, modéré
money, *s.*, argent (*m.*)
month, *s.*, mois (*m.*)
moral, *adj.*, moral
more, *adv.*, plus
morning, *s.*, matin (*m.*)

morrow, s., demain; le lendemain; (adv.) to-morrow, demain
mother, s., mère (f.)
move, v. t., mouvoir, émouvoir
mouse, s., souris (f.)
much, adv., beaucoup, bien; too much, trop
murder, v.t., massacrer
museum, s., musée (m.)
music, s., musique (f.)
must, v.n.def., falloir
mutton, s., mouton (m.)

N

Nation, s., nation (f.)
nature, s., nature (f.)
near, prep., près de
necessary, adj., nécessaire; to be necessary, falloir
needle, s., aiguille (f.)
neglect, v.t., négliger
negotiate, v.t., négocier
neither, adj. and pr., ni l'un ni l'autre, ni l'une ni l'autre
neither, conj., ni
never, adv., ne .... jamais
new, adj., neuf, -ve, nouveau, nouvel, -le
news, s., nouvelle (f.)
no, adj., ne pas...de, nul, ne...aucun, pas un, ne ...pas or point
no, adv., non, ne...pas
none, pr. pers., nul, aucun, pas un, personne ne
nor, conj., ni
nosegay, s., bouquet (m.)
not, adv., ne...pas, ne... point, non, pas
note, s., billet (m.)

nothing, s.pr., rien; good-for-nothing, bon à rien
notice, v.t., remarquer
nut, s., noisette (f.)

O

Oar, s., rame (f.)
obedient, adj., obéissant
obey, v.int., obéir
oblige, v.t., obliger
observe, v.t., observer
obstinate, adj., obstiné
obstinately, adv., opiniâtrement
obtain, v.t., obtenir
of, pr., de
offence, s., offense (f.)
offend, v.t., offenser; to be offended, s'offenser
offensive, adj., offensant
offer, s., offre (f.)
office, s., bureau (m.)
officer, s., officier (m.)
often, adv., souvent
old, adj., vieux, vieil, vieille, ancien, ancienne; old man, vieillard, s.m.
on, pr., sur
one, adj. and s., un, (pr.) on, se, soi, en
open, v.t., ouvrir; open again, rouvrir; half-open, entr'ouvrir
opinion, s., opinion (f.)
orchard, s., verger (m.)
order, v.t., commander
original, adj., original
other, pr.ind., autre, pl. autres, d'autres, autrui
other, adj., autre
our, adj.poss., notre, nos
ours, pr.poss., le nôtre, la nôtre, les nôtres, à nous

ourselves, pr.pl., nous-mêmes, nous
out, pr., hors
over, pr., sur
owe, v.t., devoir; owe again, redevoir
owl, s., hibou (m.)
own, adj., propre

P

Pair, s., paire (f.)
palace, s., palais (m.)
paper, s., papier (m.)
pardon, v.t., pardonner (à)
parents, s., parents (m.pl.)
Paris, s.pr., Paris (m.)
parish, s., paroisse (f.)
parish, adj., paroissial, -e, communal; parish school, école communale
park, s., parc (m.)
party, s., parti (m.
pass, v.int., passer
past, prep., au delà de; it is past six, il est six heures passées; half-past two, deux heures et demie
path, s., chemin (m.)
patient, s., malade (m.f.)
pear, s., poire (f.)
pen, s., plume (f.)
penknife, s., canif (m.)
perceive, v.t., apercevoir (act.), s'apercevoir de (ref.)
perform, v.t., s'acquitter de
perish, v.int., périr
perseverance, s., persévérance (f.)
person, s., personne (f.)
pickle, v.t., confire
picture, s., tableau (m.)
piece, s., morceau (m.)

pistol, s., pistolet (m.)
pity, v.t., plaindre
place, s., place (f.)
plan, s., plan (m.)
play, v.int., jouer
play, s., comédie (f.)
please, v.int., plaire
pleased, adj., content
pleasure, s., plaisir (m.)
plot, s., complot (m.)
poem, s., poëme (m.)
poet, s., poëte (m.)
polish, v.t., polir
politeness, s., politesse (f.)
poor, adj., pauvre; the poor, les pauvres (m.)
pond, s., étang (m.)
pope, s., pape (m.); Pope Sixtus Quintus, le Pape Sixte-Quint
possession, s., possession (f.); to take possession, s'emparer de
postpone, v.t., différer
praise, v.t., louer
prefer, v.t., préférer
pretend, v.t., feindre
pretty, adj., joli
prevail, v.i., prévaloir
priest, s., prêtre (m.)
princess, s., princesse (f.)
principal, adj., principal
print, v.t., imprimer
printer, s., imprimeur (m.)
proposal, s., proposition (f.)
propose, v.t., proposer
protect, v.t., protéger
protest, s., protestant (m.)
provide, v.int., pourvoir (for...à)
provided, conj., pourvu que
prudent, adj., prudent
punish, v.t., punir
punishment, s., punition (f.)
pupil, s., élève (m.)
put, v.t., placer, mettre; put out, éteindre

Q

Quality, s., qualité (f.)
queen, s., reine (f.)
question, s., question (f.)
quiet, adj., tranquille
quire, s., main (f.)
quite, adv., tout-à-fait, tout, -e

R

Railway, s., chemin de fer (m.)
rain, v.imp., pleuvoir
read, v.t., lire, (past part., lu)
ready, adj., prêt
reason, s., raison (f.)
rebel, s., rebelle (m.)
recast, v.t., refondre
receive, v.t., recevoir
recompense, v.t., récompenser
red, adj., rouge; red (head of) hair, chevelure rousse
reflect, v.int., (on), réfléchir (à)
regularly, adv., régulièrement
reign, s., règne (m.)
rejoice, v.int., se réjouir (de)
relate, v.t., raconter
remain, v.int., rester
remember, v., se rappeler, se souvenir de
reputation, s., réputation (f.)
request, v.t., requérir
resell, v.t., revendre
reserve, v.t., réserver
resolve, v.t., se résoudre à
resound, v.i., retentir
retract, v.t., se rétracter
return, v.t., rendre
review, s., revue (f.)
reward, s., récompense (f.)

rich, adj., riche
ridiculous, adj., ridicule
right, adj., juste
ripe, adj., mûr
rise, v.int., (in price), enchérir
river, s., rivière (f.)
roast, v.t., rôtir
room, s., salle (f.), chambre (f.)
root, s., racine (f.)
rope, s., corde (f.)
royal, adj., royal
ruddy, adj., rouge
rule, s., règle (f.)
rumour, s., bruit (m.)
rush, v.int., se précipiter

S

Sail, v.i., mettre à la voile, appareiller, partir
sailor, s., marin (m.)
same, adj., même
sarcastic, adj., moqueur, -se
satisfy, v.t., satisfaire (irr.)
say, v.t., dire (p. 128)
scarf, s., écharpe (f.)
scatter, v.t., répandre
school, s., école (f.)
schoolmaster, s., maître d'école (m.)
scold, v.t., gronder
scribbler, s., écrivassier (m.)
seal, v.t., cacheter
see, v.t., voir (irr.)
seem, v.i., paraître (irr.)
sell, v.t., vendre
send, v.t., envoyer
sense, s., sentiment (m.)
servant, s., domestique (m.)
serve, v.t., servir (irr.)
several, adj. ind., plusieurs
severely, adv., sévèrement
sow, v.t. (on), coudre

ELEMENTARY-FRENCH GRAMMAR—ACCIDENCE. 203

't (f.), ac-	staircase, s., escalier (m.)	telegram, s., télégramme (m.)
elle	start, v.int., tressaillir (with...de)	tell, v.t., dire
ıdre	steady, adj., posé	temper, s., caractère (m.)
is (f.)	steal, v.t., voler — away (v.i.) s'esquiver	than, conj., que, de
elling (m.)	steeple, s., clocher (m.)	thanks, s., remerciment (m.)
eau (m.)	stocking, s., bas (m.)	that adj. dem., ce, cet, cette, ces
iise (f.)	street, s., rue (f.)	that, pr. dem., celui-là, celle-là, cela, ça, le
er (m.)	strengthen, v.t., affermir, fortifier	
ge (m.)	stretch, v.t., étendre	that, pr. rel., (nom.) qui ; (acc.) que, lequel, laquelle, lesquels, lesquelles
ntrer	strike, v.t., atteindre	
ner	studious, adj., studieux, -se	
let (m.)	stupid, adj., stupide	that, conj., que, afin que; in order that, afin que
sincère	subscribe, v.i., s'abonner	the, art., le, la, les
iter	succeed, v.i., réussir	their, adj. poss., leur, leurs
r (f.)	success, s., succès (m.)	
m, s'asseoir	such, adj., tel, telle	theirs, pr. poss., le leur, la leur, les leurs, à eux, à elles
ituation (f.)	suddenly, adv., soudainement	
n (m.)	suffer, v.t., souffrir	
ive (m. f.)	sully, v.t., ternir	themselves, pr. pers., se, eux-mêmes, elles-mêmes, mêmes
rmir (irr.)	sum, s., somme (f.)	
etit	supply, v.t., fournir	
arire	suppose, v.t., supposer	there, adv., là, y
aplanir	supreme, adj., suprême	they, pr. pers. (subj.) ils, elles; (when alone) eux, elles ; they who, ceux (m.), celles (f.) qui
i ; so...(as),	surprised, pr. and adj., surpris (at...de)	
utant, tant	suspect, v.t., soupçonner	
	suspend, v.t., suspendre	thick, adj., épais, épaisse
ciété (f.)	sweep, v.t., balayer	thine, pr. pers., le tien, la tienne, les tiens, les tiennes, à toi
doncir	sweet, adj., doux, douce	
ldat (m.)	sword, s., épée (f.)	
i, de la, des		
nelque	**T**	thing, s., chose (f.); everything, tout
elques-uns,		
nes, en	Table, s., table (f.)	think v.t.int., croire, penser
n.)	take, v.t., prendre ; take back, reprendre; (somebody in a carriage) reconduire	
j., chagrin		this, adj. dem., ce, cet (m.), cette (f.)
sound ad-		
is salutaire		thoroughly, adv., complètement
., spacieux,	talent, s., talent (m.)	thou, pr.p. 2 pers., tu, toi
Espagne (f.)	tax, s., impôt (m.)	thought, s., pensée (f.) ; to collect one's thoughts, se recueillir
parler	tea, s., thé (m.)	
scours (m.)	tea-pot, s., théière (f.)	
:penser	tear, v.t., déchirer	threaten, v.t., menacer
plendeur (f.)	tear, s., larme (f.)	three, adj. num. card., trois
dre (m.)	tedious, adj., ennuyeux, -se	
sort (m.)		
on (m.)		
ie (f.)		

through, *pr.*, à travers
thunder, *s.*, tonnerre (*m.*)
thunderstorm, *s.*, orage (*m.*)
thy, *adj.poss.*, ton, ta, tes
ticket, *s.*, billet (*m.*)
tiger, *s.*, tigre (*m.*)
time, *s.*, temps (*m.*)
timid, *adj.*, timide
to, *pr.*, à
together, *adv.*, ensemble
too, *adv.*, trop
torment, *v.t.*, tourmenter; torment one's self, se tourmenter
towards, *pr.*, euvers, vers
town, *s.*, ville (*f.*)
toy, *s.*, joujou (*m.*)
train, *s.*, train (*m.*)
translate, *v.t.*, traduire
treachery, *s.*, trahison (*f.*)
treatise, *s.*, traité (*m.*)
tree, *s.*, arbre (*m.*)
tribute, *s.*, tribut (*m.*)
trifling, *adj.*, léger
troop, *s.*, troupe (*f.*)
trunk, *s.*, malle (*f.*), tronc (*m.*)
trust, *v.t.*, se fier à
truth, *s.*, vérité (*f.*)
tune (in), *loc.*, juste
Turkish, *adj.*, turc, turque
two, *adj.num.*, deux

U

Undeceive, *v.t.*, détromper; undeceive one's self, se détromper
under, *pr.*, sous
undergo, *v.t.*, subir
understand, *v.t.*, comprendre

undertaking, *s.*, entreprise (*f.*)
unfeeling, *adj.*, insensible
unfurnish, *v.t.*, dégarnir
ungrateful, *adj.*, ingrat
unless, *conj.*, à moins que
unpolite, *adj.*, impoli
unravel, *v.t.*, débrouiller
unwell, *adj.*, indisposé, souffrant
use, *s.*, usage (*m.*)
useful, *adj.*, utile
uselessly, *adv.*, en vain, inutilement

V

Vegetable, *s.*, légume (*m.*)
very, *adv.*, très
village, *s.*, village (*m.*)
vinegar, *s.*, vinaigre (*m.*)
virtuous, *adj.*, vertueux, -se
visit, *v.t.*, visiter
voice, *s.*, voix (*f.*)

W

Wait, *v.*, attendre
walk, *v.int.*, marcher
walking, *s.*; marche (*f.*), promenade (*f.*); walking-stick, *s.*, canne
want, *s.*, besoin (*m.*)
warm (a bed), *v.t.*, bassiner
warn, *v.t.*, avertir
warrior, *s.*, guerrier (*m.*)
watch, *s.*, montre (*f.*)
watch, *v.*, surveiller
water, *s.*, eau (*f.*)
water, *v.t.*, arroser
way, *s.*, chemin (*m.*)
we, *pr.pers.*, nous
weak, *adj.*, faible
week, *s.*, semaine (*f.*)

wood, *s.*, bois (*m.*)
word, *s.*, parole (*f.*)
work, *s.*, ouvrage, travail ; work-box,*s.*,boîte (*f.*) à ouvrage
work, *v.t.*, travailler
worship, *v.t.*, adorer
worth (to be),valoir (*v.i.*)
wound, *v.t.*, blesser
wring, *v.t.*, tordre
write, *v.t.*, écrire

Y

Year, *s.*, an (*m.*), année (*f.*)
yesterday. *adv.*, hier
yet, *adv.*, encore
yield, *v.int.*, céder, se rendre (à)
you, *pr.pers.*, vous
young, *adj.*, jeune
your, *adj.poss.*, votre, vos
yours, *pr.poss.*, le vôtre, la vôtre, les vôtres, à vous
yourself, *pr.pers.*, vous-même, vous

Z

Zeal, *s.*, zèle (*m.*)

THE
PUBLIC SCHOOL ELEMENTARY FRENCH GRAMMAR

PART II.—SYNTAX

By AUGUSTE BRACHET

Adapted for the use of English Schools and Persons engaged in Elementary Teaching

BY

THE REV. P. H. E. BRETTE, B.D.
HEAD-MASTER OF THE FRENCH SCHOOL, CHRIST'S HOSPITAL,

AND

GUSTAVE MASSON, B.A.
ASSISTANT MASTER AND LIBRARIAN, HARROW SCHOOL,
EXAMINERS IN THE UNIVERSITY OF LONDON.

FIFTH EDITION.

𝔗𝔬𝔯𝔬𝔫𝔱𝔬:
JAMES CAMPBELL & SON.
1878.

[*All rights reserved.*]

PREFACE.

THE publication of the Syntax of our "ELEMENTARY FRENCH GRAMMAR" has been postponed much longer than we either wished or expected; we trust, however, that the result of this unavoidable delay will have been to render our work more worthy of the success already obtained by the "Accidence." Persons engaged in tuition know perfectly well how difficult it is to modify the explanation of Syntactic rules, originally addressed to French pupils, so as to meet the wants of English students; grammatical problems meet us as we go on, which we did not anticipate when we started; and thus, what was to have proved the occupation of a few weeks, has ended in being the labour of months.

The present volume, composed exactly on the plan of the previous one, is also followed by an alphabetical index, which, we trust, will be found useful for purposes of reference. In accordance with the wishes of many experienced masters, we have also added a complete French-English and English-French Vocabulary. Finally, a supplementary series of Exercises is in active preparation, and will be ready in the course of next August.

P. H. ERNEST BRETTE.
GUSTAVE MASSON.

LONDON, *February,* 1877.

TABLE OF CONTENTS.

BOOK III.—SYNTAX.

FIRST PART.

	PAGE
Syntax of Words	3

CHAPTER I.

	PAGE
Syntax of the Substantive	4
SECTION I.—Agreement of the Substantive.—Of Gender	4
SECTION II.—Of Number	8
I. Plural of Proper Nouns	9
II. Plural of Words taken from Foreign Languages	9
III. Plural of Compound Nouns	10
SECTION III.—Complement of the Substantive	12

CHAPTER II.

	PAGE
Syntax of the Article	15

CHAPTER III.

	PAGE
Syntax of the Adjective	19
SECTION I.—Agreement of the Adjective	19
SECTION II.—Of the Position of the Adjectives	21
SECTION III.—Complement of the Adjective	24
SECTION IV.—Degrees of Comparison	25

CHAPTER IV.

	PAGE
Syntax of Numeral, Possessive, and Indefinite Adjectives	28
SECTION I.—I. Numeral Adjectives	28
SECTION II.—II. Possessive Adjectives	30
SECTION III.—Indefinite Adjectives	32

CHAPTER V.

	PAGE
Syntax of the Pronouns	36
I. Personal Pronouns.—Conjunctive	36
Disjunctive	39
Reflective	39
Repetition of the Personal Pronouns	40
II. Possessive Pronouns	42
III. Demonstrative Pronouns	43
IV. Relative and Interrogative Pronouns	46
V. Indefinite Pronouns	50

CHAPTER VI.

Syntax of the Verb	55
I. Agreement of the Verb with one simple Subject	55
II. Agreement of the Verb with several Subjects	58
III. Complement of the Verb	61
IV. Use of the Auxiliary Verbs	64

CHAPTER VII.

Syntax of the Participles	67
SECTION I.—Agreement of the Present Participle	67
SECTION II.—Agreement of the Past Participle	70
1. General Principles	70
2. The Past Participle used with the Auxiliary Verb être ($=to\ be$)	70
3. The Past Participle used with the Auxiliary avoir ($=to\ have$)	71
4. Additional Remarks on the Agreement of the Participles	74
5. Summary	77

CHAPTER VIII.

Syntax of Adverbs	78

CHAPTER IX.

Syntax of Prepositions	84

CHAPTER X.

	PAGE
Syntax of Conjunctions	89

SECOND PART.

Syntax of Propositions	93
I. Definitions	93
II. Of the Subordinate Proposition	95
III. Use of the Indicative and of the Subjunctive in Conjunctive Propositions	96
IV. Use of the Tenses of the Subjunctive	100
V. Relative Propositions	103

APPENDIX.

Of Analysis	105
Index	111
French-English Vocabulary	115
English-French Vocabulary	122

BOOK III.

SYNTAX.

219. We have studied successively the ten kinds of words of which the French language is composed; it remains for us to show how these words can be brought together, in order to form sentences. That part of grammar which treats of the manner of connecting words so as to make sentences is called **syntax**.

Syntax comes from the Greek σύνταξις (=arrangement, construction).

220. We cannot express a thought by words, without making what is called a **proposition**. When we say: *Dieu est tout-puissant* (=God is almighty), *l'enfant aime ses parents* (=the child loves his parents), each of these phrases forms a *proposition*.

221. The *proposition* may be **simple**, as in *Dieu aime les hommes* (=God loves men), or **compound**, as in *Dieu, qui est clément, aime les hommes* (=God, who is merciful, loves men). This latter proposition is called *compound*, because, to the principal proposition (*Dieu aime les hommes*), a secondary proposition is added (*qui est clément*).

222. Syntax, then, is divided into two parts: the first teaches us how to combine two or more words in order to make of them a *simple* proposition; the second, how to combine two or more simple propositions, in order to make of them a *compound* proposition.

223. These two parts of syntax are called: the first, **syntax of words**, the second, **syntax of propositions.**

FIRST PART.

SYNTAX OF WORDS.

224. We have said that we cannot express a thought by words without making what is called a *proposition*.

Every proposition contains three terms: the *subject*, the *verb*, the *attribute*. When we say, for instance, *le juge est juste* (=the judge is just), we attribute to the person called *judge* the quality of *just*; we affirm that *the judge* possesses that quality. The word *just*, designating the quality which we **attribute** to the judge, is for that reason called **attribute**; the word *est* (=is), which serves to **affirm** that this quality of just *exists* in the judge, is called **verb**; finally, *the judge*, of whom we have affirmed that he possessed the quality pointed out by the attribute, is called **subject**.

Thus the *subject* of the proposition is that of which something is affirmed, the *verb* is the word which expresses this affirmation, and the *attribute* is the quality which we affirm to exist in the subject.

In every proposition, the verb and the attribute **agree** with the subject—that is to say, they take the number, the gender, and the person of the subject to which they refer. When we say *l'herbe est verte* (=the grass is green) *est* is the third person singular, and *verte* (=green) is the feminine of the same number, because the two words, *est* and *verte*, refer to the same object—*l'herbe* (=the grass)—which is in the feminine gender and singular number. If we compare the proposition to a little band of soldiers, we can say that the subject is the commander, and that the verb and attribute recognise his authority and wear his uniform. We ought then to begin syntax with the study of the rules, according to which different words *agree* together, when we wish to combine them in order to form a proposition.

When we say *l'herbe est verte* (= the grass is green), the word *grass* as yet only indicates a very vague idea; we know that *that which is green* is *the grass*, not *water* or *the earth*, but we do not know whether it is this or that grass which is green — if it is the grass of the garden, for instance, or that of the meadow. If, to particularise this general idea, we say *l'herbe du jardin est verte* (= the grass of the garden is green), the word *garden*, which comes in to *complete*, to explain the word *grass* to which it refers, is called, for this reason, its **complement**. To express an idea by the help of words joined together in a proposition, we must know how to render that idea clearer by adding to the proposition one or more **complements**, which explain or determine it.

225. The syntax of *words* has, then, the double object of determining for each of the ten parts of speech all the rules which concern the **agreement** and the **complement**.

CHAPTER I.
SYNTAX OF THE SUBSTANTIVE.

SECTION I.

AGREEMENT OF THE SUBSTANTIVE.

226. When two substantives following each other point out the same person or the same thing, the second agrees with the first in gender and in number. *Le roi chevalier* (= the king-knight), *la reine mère* (= the queen-mother), *les soldats laboureurs* (= the ploughmen soldiers), *Clotilde, reine illustre* (= Clotilda, an illustrious queen), *Turenne était un héros* (= Turenne was a hero).

OF GENDER.

227. The nouns **aide, critique, garde, manœuvre, statuaire,** are:—

A. Feminine when they denote **the action**:—

L'aide puissante de Dieu (= the powerful help of God)
La critique est bonne (= the criticism [review] is good)
La garde des frontières (= the watching over the frontiers)
La manœuvre d'un navire (= the working of a ship)
La statuaire des anciens (= the statuary of the ancients);

B. **Masculine** when they denote **the man who accomplishes those different actions** :—

    Un *critique* (= a critic)
    Un *garde-chasse* (= a gamekeeper)
    Un *aide-chirurgien* (= an assistant-surgeon)
    Un *manœuvre* (= a workman)
    Un *statuaire* (= a sculptor)

228. Aigle (= eagle), *properly* and *figuratively*, is *masculine* when it denotes the male bird or a man, as :—

    L'aigle est fier et courageux (= the eagle is proud and courageous)
    Cet homme est **un** *aigle* (= this man is a transcendent genius);

It is *feminine* when it means the female of the eagle, or a military standard, as :—

    Une *aigle attaqua un vautour* (= an eagle attacked a vulture)
    L'aigle romaine (= the Roman eagle).

229. Amour (= love), **délice** (= delight), and **orgue** (= organ), are *masculine* in the singular, and *feminine* in the plural :—

L'amour *filial* (= filial love)	*Les* **premières** *amours* (= first love)
Un *délice enivrant* (= an intoxicating pleasure, delight)	*De* **joyeuses** *délices* (= joyful delights)
Un bel *orgue* (= a fine organ)	*De* **belles** *orgues* (= fine organs).

230. Chose in the locution *quelque chose*, or *quelque chose de* is *masculine* :—

    J'ai appris quelque chose de fâcheux (= I have heard some sad news, *lit.*, something sad).

But in *quelque chose que je lui aie dite, je n'ai pu le convaincre* (= whatever I might tell him, I could not convince him), *quelque chose* means *quelle que soit la chose*, and is *feminine*.

231. Foudre is *feminine* when it means *lightning, thunderbolt* :—

    La *foudre sillonne les nues* (= the lightning flashes through the clouds);

but it is *masculine* when used *figuratively* :—

    Un *foudre de guerre* (= a doughty warrior)
    Un *foudre d'éloquence* (= a very eloquent orator).

232. Gent is *feminine* in the singular, and means *race, tribe, crowd* : —

>*La gent moutonnière* (= the ovine race)
>*La gent criarde* (= the noisy crowd).

In the plural (**gens**) it means *men, people*, and remains *feminine* if an adjective comes before it :—

>*Les bonnes gens* (= good folks) ;

but it becomes *masculine* if an adjective follows it :—

>*Les gens de ce pays sont bons* (= the people of that country are good).
>*Les vieilles gens sont soupçonneux* (= old people are suspicious).

The adjective **tout** is an exception, as it remains *masculine* whether it comes before or after the word *gens* :—

>*Tous les gens que j'ai vus* (= all the people I have seen)
>*Ces bonnes gens sont tous ennuyeux* (= these good folks are all tiresome).

Tout, however, becomes *feminine* when it precedes an adjective not having the same termination for both genders. Thus it is right to say : *tous les honnêtes gens* (= all honest people), because *honnête* is spelt alike for the masculine and feminine ; but we must say : *toutes les bonnes gens* (= all good people).

☞ **Gens de lettres** and other compounds are always *masculine*.

>*Gent* is feminine, and meant formerly *nation, people* :—
>
>"*O combien lors aura de veuves*
>*La gent qui porte le turban !*"—MALHERBE (1556-1628).

(= Oh how many widows will there be then among the people that wear turbans !) But it soon lost that meaning in the plural (which, however, is even now retained in *le droit des gens*, for *le droit des nations*, = the law of nations) for that of *men, individuals*, as : *les gens de ce pays* (= the men of that country), *les gens de mer* (= the sailors), etc. Just as the feminine word *personne* (see § 110), with the meaning of *man*, became masculine in such locutions as : *personne n'est bon dans ce pays* (= there is no good man in this country), *personne n'est venu* (= no one has come), the idea of *man* causing its proper gender to be forgotten ; in the same way, the new idea of *man, individual* caused the change of gender in the word *gens*. This conflict between the two genders has given rise to the double rule explained above.

233. Hymne, when meaning a hymn (of the church), is *feminine* :—

> *Les anciennes hymnes de l'église ont le mérite de la simplicité* (=the ancient hymns of the church have the merit of simplicity);

but it is *masculine* in all other cases :—

> *Chaque peuple a son hymne national* (=every nation has its national hymn).

234. Orge (=barley) is *feminine* :—

> *De belle orge* (=some fine barley);

but, according to the *Dictionnaire de l'Académie*, it is *masculine* in the expressions :—

> *Orge perlé* (=pearl barley),
> *Orge mondé* (=Scotch barley, husked barley).

235. The following substantives have different meanings according to their gender :—

	MASC.	FEM.
Crêpe	crape	pancake
livre	book	pound
manche	handle	sleeve
mémoire	memoir, bill, paper	memory
mode	mood	fashion
moule	mould	mussel
mousse	cabin-boy	moss
page	page (boy)	page (of a book)
pendule	pendulum	clock, timepiece
période	highest pitch	period
poêle	stove, pall	frying-pan
somme	nap, slumber	sum
souris	smile	mouse
tour	turn, trick, lathe	tower
vase	vase, vessel	slime
voile	veil	sail

QUESTIONS FOR EXAMINATION.

1. What is the rule for the agreement of substantives?
2. What have you to say on the gender of *aide, critique, garde, manœuvre*?
3. Give the rules concerning the gender of *aigle, amour, délice, orgue, foudre, chose*.
4. State fully the rules relating to the agreement of adjectives accompanying *gens*.
5. Give six nouns which are masculine in one sense and feminine in the other.

Exercise 40.

1. Les paratonnerres préservent les édifices de la foudre. 2. Cette critique est bonne. 3. Si vous cassez quelque chose, je le rabattrai sur vos gages. 4. Le moule est cassé. 5. Donnez-moi la poêle. 6. Tous les honnêtes gens le respectent, mais toutes les mauvaises gens le haïssent. 7. Les soldats chantèrent leur hymne national. 8. Certains gens de lettres sont venus me voir. 9. A Milan il y a deux grandes orgues. 10. On a placé un orgue de chaque côté du chœur. 11. Ce sont mes plus chères délices.

[1] salle (f.). [2] faisait, [3] garde, [4] pour, [5] chirurgien (m.), [6] trompeur, [7] cacher, [8] frapper, [9] foudre, [10] moine (m.).

1. All the eagles taken from the enemy were placed in the hall.[1] 2. It is a good help. 3. He kept[2] a good watch.[3] 4. All these people have been very kind to[4] me. 5. This surgeon[5] has two very good assistants. 6. This manœuvre was deceptive.[6] 7. If something remains he hides[7] it. 8. This tree was struck[8] by lightning.[9] 9. The monks[10] were singing a beautiful hymn. 10. All the good people were surprised.

SECTION II.

OF NUMBER.

236. Aïeul, ciel, œil, travail, see § 86.

237. Témoin (=witness) does not take the sign of the plural when it is placed at the beginning of a sentence, or in the locution *à témoin* :—

Témoin les blessures qu'il a reçues (=witness the wounds he has received)
Je vous prends tous à témoin (= I call you all to witness).

N.B.—*Prendre à témoin* means properly *prendre pour témoin;* the Old French said: *Élire un chevalier à roi* (=to elect a knight for king).

238. Some nouns are only used in the singular :—

le boire (= drinking)   *l'adolescence* (=youth)
le manger (= eating)   *la reconnaissance* (=gratitude)
la botanique (=botany)   *le silence* (=silence)

Others are used only in the plural :—

Alentours, m. (= neighbourhood, environs)
archives, f. (= archives)
catacombes, f. (= catacombs)
ciseaux,* m. (= scissors)

environs, m. (= neighbourhood, vicinity, environs)
mathématiques f. (= mathematics)
ténèbres, f. (= darkness, dark, night).

I. Plural of Proper Nouns.

239. In English proper nouns take the sign of the plural, but, in French, they do not, as :—

Les deux **Corneille** sont nés à Rouen (= the two Corneilles were born at Rouen)
Les **Corneille**, les **Molière**, les **Racine** ont illustré le siècle de Louis XIV (= men like Corneille, Molière, and Racine have rendered the age of Louis XIV illustrious);

EXCEPT (1) when they are common to great families or dynasties, as :—

Les deux **Gracques**, en flattant le peuple, commencèrent les divisions qui ne finirent qu'avec la République—(BOSSUET) (= The two Gracchi, by flattering the people, originated those quarrels which only ended with the Republic);

(2) when they are used as common nouns, as :—

Un Auguste aisément peut faire des **Virgiles** (i.e., des poètes comme Virgile) (= an emperor like Augustus can easily produce poets like Virgil);

(3) when the name of an author is used to designate his works, as :—

J'ai plusieurs **Virgiles** dans ma bibliothèque (= I have several copies of Virgil in my library).

240. Proper names of countries take the sign of the plural, as :—

Les deux **Guinées** (= Upper and Lower Guinea)
Les deux **Amériques** (= North and South America).

II. Plural of Words taken from Foreign Languages.

241. Words taken from foreign languages, and which have become French by frequent use, take *s* in the plural:

* *Ciseau* in the singular means chisel.

Un accessit (*proxime accessit* = honourable mention)	*des accessits*
un album (= album)	*des albums*
un examen (= examination)	*des examens*
un opéra (= opera)	*des opéras*
un pensum (= an imposition, task)	*des pensums*
un spécimen (= a specimen)	*des spécimens*, &c.

EXCEPT (1) names of prayers: *des ave, des credo*; (2) compound nouns: *des in-octavo, des ex-voto*; (3) terms of music borrowed from the Italian: *des allegro, des crescendo*.

Carbonaro, lazzarone, dilettante keep their Italian plural: *carbonari, lazzaroni, dilettanti*.

III. Plural of Compound Nouns.

242. Compound nouns written **in one word**, as *portemanteau* (= portmanteau, *lit.* that which *carries the cloak*), *contrevent* (= shutter, *lit.* that which protects *against* the *wind*), follow the rules for the formation of the plural of simple nouns: *des portemanteaux* (= portmanteaus), *des contrevents* (= shutters).

☞ **Gentilhomme** (= nobleman), **monsieur** (= Sir, Mr.), **madame** (= Madam, Mrs.), **mademoiselle** (= Miss), however, become *gentilshommes* **mes**sieurs, **mes**dames, **mes**demoiselles, in the plural.

243. When the compound nouns are written **in two words**, as *coffre-fort* (= strong-box, safe), *porte-drapeau* (= standard-bearer), the noun and adjective alone can take the sign of the plural; all the other words, whether verb, adverb, or preposition, remain invariable.

244. The rules for forming the plural of compound nouns are *six* in number.

When a compound noun is formed—

1. **Of two nouns,** *both nouns* take the sign of the plural:—

un chat-tigre (= a tiger-cat)	*des chats-tigres*
un chou-fleur (= a cauliflower)	*des choux-fleurs*.

2. **Of two nouns joined by a preposition,** *the first alone* takes the sign of the plural:—

un arc-en-ciel (= a rainbow)	*des arcs-en-ciel*
un chef-d'œuvre (= a masterpiece)	*des chefs-d'œuvre*.

When the preposition is understood, the same rule must be observed; thus *un hôtel-Dieu*, which stands for *un hôtel* **de** *Dieu* (= a house of God = a hospital) is in the plural *des hôtels-Dieu*;

> EXCEPT: *Un tête-à-tête* (= a private interview)
> *un coq-à-l'âne* (= a cock and bull story)
> *un pied-à-terre* (= temporary lodgings, a country box)

which remain the same: *des tête-à-tête*, &c.

3. Of a noun and an adjective, *both* take the sign of the plural:—

> *une basse-taille* (= a bass voice)   *des basses-tailles*
> *un coffre-fort* (= a safe)   *des coffres-forts*.

EXCEPT some expressions formed with Old French words such as: *terre-plein* (= platform, terre-plein), from the old adjective *plein*, *plain* (= flat, even); *chevau-léger* (= light horseman), properly *cheval léger*; *blanc-seing* (= signature on a blank paper), from the Old French *seing*, for *signature*. These nouns form their plural like the compounds written in one word — that is to say, that the last word alone takes the plural—*des terre-pleins, des chevau-légers, des blanc-seings*.

4. Of a noun and a verb, *the noun alone* takes the sign of the plural:—

> *un passe-port* (= a passport)   *des passe-ports*
> *un tire-bouchon* (= a corkscrew)   *des tire-bouchons*.

EXCEPT the compound nouns formed with the verb *garder*: *un garde-chasse* (= a game-keeper), *un garde-manger* (= a larder, meat-safe), in which *garde* takes *s* in the plural when it means a *keeper*: *un garde-chasse, des gardes-chasse*; but remains invariable when it designates an instrument or object: *un garde-manger, des garde-manger* (see § 227).

5. Of a noun and a preposition, or of a noun and an adverb, *the noun alone* takes the sign of the plural:—

> *un sous-officier* (= a non-commissioned officer)   *des sous-officiers*
> *un avant-coureur* (= a precursor, harbinger)   *des avant-coureurs*

6. Of invariable words (verb, preposition, adverb), *both words remain unchanged*:—

> *un ouï-dire* (= a hearsay)   *des ouï-dire*
> *un passe-partout* (= a master-key)   *des passe-partout*.

245. REMARKS.—In forming the plural of compound nouns we must first examine what is their exact meaning; thus we write *des serre-tête* (=head-bands) without *s* after *tête*, because the band is fastened round *one head* only, and *un couvre-pieds* (=a counterpane, quilt) because it covers *the feet;* again, *des abat-jour* (=shades), because it shades *the light;* but *un porte-clefs* (=a turnkey), because he carries *many keys*

Exercise 41.

1. Les deux Corneille sont nés à Rouen. 2. Les Boileau et les Gilbert furent les Juvénals de leur siècle. 3. J'ai deux Molières dans ma bibliothèque, ce sont des in-octavo. 4. Les porte-clefs arrivaient. 5. Je vous prends tous à témoin. 6. Il a remporté deux prix et trois accessits. 7 Permettez-moi de vous présenter mes beaux-frères. 8. Voici un casse-noisettes.

¹ essuie-mains (*m.*), ² tire-bottes (*m.*), ³ en haut, ⁴ renard (*m.*), ⁵ basse-cour (*f.*), ⁶ porte-plume (*m.*), ⁷ ivoire (*m.*), ⁸ Néron, ⁹ couvre-feu (*m.*).

1. These towels[1] are new. 2. Your boot-jack[2] is upstairs.[3] 3. The foxes[4] visited several poultry-yards.[5] 4. These penholders[6] are of ivory.[7] 5. The rainbows were beautiful. 6. The game-keepers were in the forest. 7. These kings were as many Neros.[8] 8. *Poets such as* (the *pl.*) Corneille and (the *pl.*) Milton are rare. 9. The sub-lieutenants were speaking with the vice-admirals. 10. I have lost my tooth-pick. 11. The curfew[9] was introduced into England by William the Conqueror. 12. These master-keys are well made.

SECTION III.

COMPLEMENT OF THE SUBSTANTIVE.

246. When one substantive is used as a complement to another, this use is generally marked by the prepositions **de** (=of) or **à** (=to): *un homme* **d'***honneur* (=a man of honour), *la maison* **de** *Paul* (=Paul's house), *un oiseau* **de** *proie* (=a bird of prey), *un fusil* **à** *aiguille* (=a needle-gun), *un chandelier* **à** *branches* (=a branch-candlestick), *un piano* **à** *queue* (=a grand piano), *un enfant* **aux** *cheveux noirs* (=a black-haired child).

In expressions like the above, which mark possession, **à** (=to) signifies **avec** (=with); *fusil à aiguille, piano à queue* are equivalent to *fusil* **avec** *aiguille, piano* **avec** *queue* (lit. a piano with a tail). Besides possession, **à** and **de** serve to mark the relation between cause and effect, that of a part to the whole, etc.

De is used when the idea of origin, composition, or possession is implied; à implies means or purpose, and is also used instead of with.

247. We find also **en, sans, autour,** etc. (=in, without, round, etc.) equally employed for this purpose: *un homme* **sans** *fortune* (=a man without fortune), *une épée* **en** *acier* (=a steel sword), *un voyage* **autour** *du monde* (=a voyage round the world).

248. The infinitives can also be used as complements to the substantive: *l'art d'écrire* (=the art of writing), *la façon de* **marcher** (=the way of walking), etc.

249. We must carefully distinguish between the case where the noun and its complement are united by the article **du** (=of the), and that where they are united by the preposition **de** (=of): *un palais de roi et le palais du roi* (=a kingly palace, and the palace of the king) do not by any means express the same idea; the former phrase is general, and qualifies a *palace* of *royal* appearance: *cette maison est un vrai palais de roi* (=that house is quite a royal palace); the latter phrase, on the contrary, is very special, and determines to whom the palace belongs: *cette maison est le palais du roi* (=that house is the king's palace).

250. When two nouns require after them the same preposition, they may have the same complement: *son ardeur et son application* **au** *travail* (=his ardour and his application to work), because *ardeur* and *application* both require after them the preposition *à*.

But we cannot say: *son dévouement et son obéissance pour son maître* (=his devotedness and his obedience to his master). Each word must take its appropriate complement. We shall say then: *son dévouement* **pour** *son maître et son obéissance* **envers** *lui.*

REMARK.—The use of a noun in the singular or the plural after a preposition depends entirely on the idea expressed. We must see whether the noun conveys or not an idea of plurality. Thus we must say: *marchand de* **lait** (=a milkman)=*qui vend du lait,* and *marchand de* **pommes** (=an apple-seller)=*qui vend des pommes; un fruit à* **noyau** (=a fruit with a stone in it—*i.e.,* apricots, peaches, cherries, etc.)=*qui a un noyau,* but *un fruit à* **pepins** (=a fruit with pips—*i.e.,* apples, pears, etc.)=*qui a des pepins.*

QUESTIONS FOR EXAMINATION.

1. Give the plural of *aïeul, œil.*
2. In what instances do nouns of persons take the sign of the plural?
3. Write out the plural of *pensum, ultimatum, dilettante, ave, te deum, post-scriptum.*
4. How do you form the plural of compound nouns composed of (1) two nouns, (2) an adjective and a noun, (3) a verb and a noun, (4) a preposition or adverb and a noun?
5. What is the best means to know whether any parts, and which, of a compound noun ought to be in the plural?
6. How is the use of the complement generally marked in French?
7. What are the ideas expressed by the two prepositions *à* and *de* respectively?
8. When do two nouns take the same complement?
9. When is a noun to be placed in the singular and when in the plural after a preposition?

Exercise 42.

1. Tout bon citoyen doit l'obéissance aux lois et à la constitution de son pays. 2. Les règles de l'honnêteté sont celles de la bienséance et des bonnes mœurs. 3. Le Pérou a de nombreuses mines d'or, d'argent et de diamants. 4. Le plaisir est souvent l'ennemi de la raison. 5. J'ai toujours des armes à feu chez moi. 6. Prenez un verre de vin. 7. La domestique a laissé tomber le pot au lait. 8. Où est la bouteille à vin? 9. Le raisin est un fruit à pepins et la pêche est un fruit à noyau.

¹ règle (*f.*), ² décence (*f.*), ³ manière (*f.*), ⁴ boîte (*f.*), ⁵ couverture (*f.*), ⁶ noyer (*m.*).

1. Has the servant broken the wine bottle? 2. Give a glass of beer to that brave soldier. 3. The rules[1] of decency[2] and good manners[3] condemn this action. 4. My sister has bought a grand piano. 5. Who is that lady with a blue bonnet? 6. I shall buy a pair of satin shoes. 7. Bring down the tea-caddy[4]; it is in my bedroom. 8. The peach is a stone-fruit, but the orange is a fruit with pips. 9. It is a book with a green cover[5]. 10. The cover of the book is green. 11. A walnut-wood[6] table. 12. A stone house.

CHAPTER II.

SYNTAX OF THE ARTICLE.

251. The article is used in French:—

1. Before nouns taken in their general as well as in their particular sense: **les** *livres sont les meilleurs amis de l'homme* (=books are man's best friends), **le** *livre que je lis* (=the book which I read).

2. Before nouns of measure, weight, number, etc.: *ce vin coûte six shillings* **la** *bouteille* (=this wine costs six shillings a bottle).

Instead of the article, the preposition *par* (=by) is placed before nouns expressing a subdivision of time, or the wages, salary, price of entrance paid, etc.: *il jouit d'un revenu de trois cent mille francs par an* (=he has an income of three hundred thousand francs a year).

3. Before nouns of kingdoms, countries, provinces, etc.: *l'Angleterre est un pays libre* (=England is a free country).

4. Before adjectives taken substantively: **le** *rouge est une couleur qui ne vous sied pas* (=red is a colour which does not become you).

5. Before titles followed by the name: **le** *docteur Nélaton* (=Doctor Nélaton).

252. Every noun which is either the subject, the attribute, or the object of a verb must have one of the two articles, *definite* or *indefinite*: **Le** *cheval mange* **du** *foin* (=the horse eats hay), **un** *ami est* **un** *trésor sans prix* (=a friend is a priceless treasure).

253. When the article refers to two substantives in the singular, it must be repeated before each of them: **le** *cousin et* **la** *nièce* (=the cousin and the niece), and not **les** *cousin et nièce*, except in the locution **les** *père et mère* (=the father and mother), which usage has consecrated.

SYNTAX OF THE ARTICLE.

254. When two adjectives united by *et* (=and) refer to the same substantive, and the substantive represents two distinct things, the article must be repeated before the second adjective: l'*histoire ancienne* **et la** *moderne* (=ancient and modern history), not l'*histoire ancienne* **et** *moderne;* but it would be correct to say **le** *brave* **et** *illustre Turenne*)=the brave and illustrious Turenne), because both adjectives qualify the same person (Cf. § 300).

255. No article is used in French:—

1. Before the ordinal numbers introduced in quotations: *livre premier* (=book the first).

2. Before the numbers expressing the succession of popes, kings, etc.: *Charles premier* (=Charles the First).

3. Before nouns expressing the title, profession, country, etc., of the person or thing represented by the preceding noun, the material of which a thing is made, and generally before a noun when it is used to complete the meaning of another: *une table de marbre* (=a marble table), *du vin d'Espagne* (=Spanish wine), *un homme d'esprit* (=a witty man), *mon père était libraire* (=my father was a bookseller).

4. Before substantives placed in apposition: *le roi fut reçu en triomphe, honneur qu'il méritait bien* (=the king was received in triumph, an honour he well deserved).

5. In the title of a book: *histoire de France* (=a history of France).

6. After the pronouns **quel, quelle, quels, quelles** (=which, what), used as exclamations: *quel magnifique coucher de soleil!* (=what a splendid sunset!)

7. After words of quantity, want, etc., except *la plupart* and *bien; votre thème a beaucoup de fautes* (=your exercise has many mistakes), *bien* **des** *années après la mort d'Alexandre* (=many years after Alexander's death).

8. In proverbs or in sentences of a general kind: *pauvreté n'est pas vice* (= poverty is no crime).

9. In enumerations, when we wish to give more rapidity to the phrase: *rois, peuples, ennemis, tout tremblait devant lui* (= kings, people, enemies, all trembled before him).

256. Before the adverbs **plus, moins,** and **mieux,** the articles *le, la, les* are employed when a comparison is meant: *la rose est* **la** *plus belle des fleurs* (= the rose is the finest of flowers), *les gazelles sont* **les** *plus agiles des quadrupèdes* (= gazelles are the nimblest of quadrupeds).

257. *Le,* however, remains invariable when we wish to express a quality carried to the highest degree, without making any comparison: *c'est en Asie que les montagnes sont* **le plus** *hautes* (= it is in Asia that the mountains are highest).

Le is further invariable before **plus, mieux, moins,** when these words are followed by another adverb, or employed by themselves: *c'est elle qui a répondu* **le plus** *adroitement* (= it is she who has answered the most skilfully), *c'est la rose que j'aime* **le mieux** (= it is the rose which I like the best).

258. The **indefinite** article **du, de l', de la, des** is used before all nouns taken in a partitive sense, except when an adjective precedes the noun, or when the sentence is negative (see § 48). Sometimes another preposition comes before *de*: *Charles est venu* **avec des** *amis* (= Charles came with some friends).

259. The article remains, however, (1) when the adjective follows the noun: **du** *pain excellent* (= excellent bread); (2) when the noun and adjective form a compound noun: *donnez-moi* **des** *petits-pois* (= give me some green peas); (3) when the negative question implies a positive meaning: *n'avez-vous pas* **des** *amis?* (= have you not any friends?)

260. With nouns expressing things which are not capable of enumeration we must not use *un* or *une*, but *du* or *de la*. Thus we cannot say: *donnez-moi* **un** *vin*, **une** *viande* (=give me a wine, a meat), as we say: *donnez-moi* **une** *cerise ou* **une** *pomme* (=give me a cherry *or* an apple); we must say: *donnez-moi* **du** *vin*, **de la** *viande* (=give me some wine, some meat).

Un must be used after *c'est*: *c'est* **un** *Français* (=he is a Frenchman), and **des** after *ce sont*: *ce sont* **des** *Anglais* (=they are Englishmen); but it is not expressed after *il est* (=he is): *il est Anglais* (=he is an Englishman).

QUESTIONS FOR EXAMINATION.

1. When is the definite article used in French?
2. Enumerate the various cases in which no article is used.
3. When is *le* invariable in connection with the adverbs *plus, moins, mieux*?
4. When is the article *du, de l', de la* *des* used?
5. What article is used with nouns expressing things which are not capable of enumeration?

Exercise 43.

1. La fortune est une divinité capricieuse. 2. Le printemps, l'été, l'automne et l'hiver sont les quatre saisons de l'année. 3. Le fromage coûte soixante-dix centimes la livre. 4. La charité est la première des vertus chrétiennes. 5. La Touraine est le jardin de la France. 6. Le bon et le mauvais sont mêlés ensemble dans toute la nature. 7. Donnez-moi du pain et du beurre. 8. Voici d'excellents fruits. 9. Le fer et l'acier sont des métaux utiles. 10. La politesse est souvent le fruit de l'usage, de l'expérience et de l'application. 11. Guillaume Trois monta sur le trône d'Angleterre à la suite d'une révolution. 12. Vous trouverez ce passage dans l'histoire de France d'Anquetil, chapitre cinq, livre trois. 13. Ampère était à la fois philosophe, chimiste et mathématicien. 14. Je reviens de Marseille, ville dont la fondation est attribuée à une colonie de Phocéens. 15. Quel malheur votre ami a éprouvé!

[1] n'importe qui, [2] boiteux, [3] valoir, [4] par, [5] Inde (*f.*), [6] crayon (*m.*), [7] en Espagne, [8] méchant, [9] esprit (*m.*), [10] bien, [11] s'étaient écoulées.

1. Good example is a language which anybody [1] can understand. 2. The horse which you have lent me is lame.[2] 3. Eggs are worth [3] a shilling a dozen. 4. I have passed through [4] Greece in coming from India.[5] 5. Blue is one of the primitive colours.

6. When you go out, buy me some pencils⁶ and colours. 7. I found in Spain⁷ wretched⁸ inns and detestable roads. 8. Italy produces oranges and olives. 9. Book the tenth, section the eighteenth. 10. What an accomplished man! 11. My friend is an officer. 12. I have read *Hernani*, a tragedy by Victor Hugo. 13. Charles II., king of England, had much wit⁹ but no prudence. 14. Many¹⁰ years had elapsed¹¹ since.

CHAPTER III.
SYNTAX OF THE ADJECTIVE.

SECTION I.
AGREEMENT OF THE ADJECTIVE.

261. The adjective agrees in gender and number with the noun which it qualifies: *Dieu est* **clément** (=God is merciful), *le ciel est* **bleu** (=the sky is blue), *les hommes sont* **mortels** (=men are mortal).

262. An adjective which relates to two or more nouns in the singular is put in the plural and agrees in gender with those nouns; thus: *la fouine et la belette sont également danger***euses** (=the polecat and the weasel are equally dangerous).

If the nouns are of different genders, the adjective generally takes the masculine, thus: *le roi et la reine sont génér***eux** (=the king and the queen are generous).

263. After two nouns separated by the conjunctions **ou** (=or), **ainsi que** (=as well as, like), **de même que** (=as, as well as), etc., the adjective agrees with the latter, provided it really qualifies that noun only: *les colonnes se construisent en bois* **ou** *en pierre très-dure* (=the columns are made of wood or of very hard stone).

264. When two or more substantives mark a gradation, or form a climax, and we wish to fix the attention particularly upon the last, we give to the adjective the gender and the number of this last substantive: *Condé montra à Rocroy un courage, un sang-froid, une audace étonnante* (= Condé showed at Rocroy courage, coolness, and wonderful audacity).

265. When an adjective is composed of two adjectives (or of an adjective and a participle), united by a hyphen, the two parts agree with the noun: *des poires aigres-douces* (= half-sweet, half-sour pears).

The only exception is the word **mort** (= dead), which never takes the sign of the feminine in compound adjectives: *une brebis mort-née* (= a still-born lamb).

266. But if the former of the two adjectives is employed adverbially, it does not vary, being then a real adverb: *l'herbe est très-**clair**-semée*—that is to say *très-**clairement** semée* (= the grass is very thinly sown), *ces personnages étaient **court**-vêtus*—that is to say, **courtement** *vêtus* (= those persons wore very short clothes). We say, likewise: *une fille **nouveau**-née* (= a new-born daughter).

267. Adjectives employed adverbially can never agree with the substantive, inasmuch as they are really adverbs—that is to say, words which from their nature are invariable: *elle chante* **faux** (= she sings out of tune), *cette fleur sent* **bon** (= this flower smells sweet), etc.

268. We have seen in § 232 that the substantive *gens* (= people) requires in the feminine the adjectives which precede it: *de **sottes** gens;* and masculine those which follow it: *des gens **sots*** (= stupid people).

For the details of this exception and the explanation of its origin, see § 232.

269. Demi, nu, feu, ci-joint, etc., see §§ 275-278.

270. Grand (= great, large, tall) remains invariable in certain locutions: *grand'mère* (= grandmother), *grand'route* (= high road).

In Old French *grand* and a few other adjectives had the same form for the masculine and the feminine. Later they became variable like *court, courte* (= short), but several expressions in which *grand* did not vary were retained.

271. Substantives, employed as adjectives to express certain colours, are invariable: *des étoffes* **noisette** (=nut-brown stuffs), *des robes* **olive** (=olive-coloured dresses).

Two adjectives combined for the purpose of expressing a colour remain invariable: *des cheveux* **châtain-clair** (=light brown hair), *des yeux* **bleu-foncé** (=dark blue eyes).

† In expressions such as *châtain-clair, bleu-foncé*, the former word is properly a substantive in the singular number (i.e., *des cheveux d'un châtain*), and the second word, *i.e.*, the adjective, agrees with that substantive.

Exercise 44.

1. La victoire que César gagna à Pharsale fut désastreuse pour le genre humain. 2. Mirabeau montrait dans tous ses discours un talent, une habileté étonnante. 3. Mon frère et ma sœur sont heureux. 4. Un style uni, simple et naturel est le seul recommandable. 5. Une personne sensible ne peut voir un vieillard ou une femme pauvres et souffrants sans être émue. 6. La grand'-route est bordée d'arbres. 7. Leurs vêtements sont gris-foncé.

¹ porter, ² nid *(m.)*, ³ construire, ⁴ robe *(f.)*, ⁵ posséder, ⁶ ardeur *(f.)*.

1. Charles and Emily are attentive. 2. He wore[1] black silk stockings. 3. These nests[2] are built[3] with an admirable art and skill. 4. Blue cotton stockings. 5. I do not see very distinctly. 6. Light blue dresses.[4] 7. These oranges have a good smell (translate: smell good). 8. Colbert had[5] profound judgment, indefatigable industry,[6] and a very extensive knowledge of foreign commerce. 9. Robespierre acquired in Paris an absolute power and authority.

SECTION II.

OF THE POSITION OF ADJECTIVES.

272. GENERAL RULE.—Adjectives are in French generally placed *after* the substantive to which they relate, as :—

un homme riche (=a rich man)
une pensée morale (=a moral thought)
une chambre obscure (=a dark room)
une table ronde (=a round table)
un climat chaud (=a warm climate)
un thème français (=a French exercise).

273. Although many adjectives may be placed either before or after the noun at pleasure, as *un homme habile*, or *un habile homme* (= a clever man), the best way to avoid mistakes in writing exercises is to put them *after* the substantive, except the following, which usually precede it:—

Beau (= fine)	*jeune* (= young)	*saint* (= holy)
bon (= good)	*joli* (= pretty)	*tel* (= such)
cher (= dear [denoting affection])	*mauvais* (= bad)	*tout* (= all)
	meilleur (= better)	*vieux* (= old)
digne (= worthy)	*moindre* (= less)	*vilain* (= ugly)
grand (= great)	*petit* (= little)	

N.B.—Past participles used as adjectives follow the noun: *un homme instruit* (= a learned man), *un livre reçu* (= a book which has been received).

274. Several adjectives take a different signification according as they are placed before or after the noun. The following are some of them:

une certaine nouvelle ([Lat. *quidam*] = certain news).
un mal certain ([Lat. *certum*] a positive evil).

mon cher frère (= my dear brother).
un livre cher (= an expensive book).

différentes / diverses } *choses* (= sundry things).
des objets { *différents / divers* } (= different, various objects).

un nouvel habit (= a fresh coat).
un habit nouveau (= a new-fashioned coat).

un pauvre poète (= an indifferent poet).
un poète pauvre (= a needy poet).

un plaisant conte (= an absurd tale).
un conte plaisant (= an amusing tale).

son propre habit (= his own coat).
un habit propre (= a clean coat).

son seul enfant (= his only child).
un enfant seul (= a child alone).

un vrai coquin (= an arrant [notorious] rogue).
une nouvelle vraie (= true intelligence).

un brave homme (= an honest man).
un homme brave (= a brave man).

un grand homme (= a man of genius).
un homme grand (= a tall man).

de méchants vers (= poor verses).
des vers méchants (= malicious, spiteful verses).

la dernière année (= the last year [of any period]).
l'année dernière (= last year).

275. The two adjectives, **nu** (=naked) and **demi** (=half), placed before the noun, are invariable, and are united to the substantive by a hyphen: *nu-pieds* (=bare-footed), *nu-tête* (=bare-headed), *une demi-livre* (=half-a-pound), *une demi-heure* (=half-an-hour); placed after the noun, they agree with it—the former in gender and number: *les pieds nus, la tête nue;* and the latter in gender *only: une livre et demie* (=a pound and a-half), *deux heures et demie* (=two hours and a-half).

REMARK.—When *demi* is used as a substantive, it is masculine when it means *a half* in arithmetic: *deux demis font un entier* (=two halves make a whole); but it is feminine when it applies to *hours: cette pendule sonne les demies* (=this clock strikes the half-hours).

276. The adjective **feu** (=late, deceased) is invariable when placed before the article: **feu** *la reine* (=the late queen); but when placed after it, it agrees with the noun in gender and in number: *la* **feue** *reine.*

277. Ci-joint, ci-inclus remain invariable :—

1. At the beginning of a sentence: **ci-joint** *la lettre de votre père* (=annexed is your father's letter), **ci-inclus** *les pièces du contrat* (=enclosed are the documents referring to the deed).

2. In the body of a sentence, when the following noun is used without an article or a determinative adjective: *vous trouverez* **ci-joint** *copie de sa lettre* (=you will find a copy of his letter annexed).

In every other case the agreement takes place: *les pièces* **ci-jointes** *sont précieuses* (=the annexed documents are valuable), *vous trouverez* **ci-jointe** *la copie du traité* (=you will find herewith the copy of the treaty).

278. Franc in the expression *franc de port* (= carriage, or postage paid), is invariable when it precedes the substantive: *vous recevrez,* **franc de port,** *la lettre que je vous envoie* (=you will receive the letter I send you, postage paid). Placed after the substantive, it agrees with it: *cette lettre est* **franche de port** (=this letter is prepaid).

Exercise 45.

1. Elle marchait nu-pieds. 2. La feue reine était très-estimée. 3. Dans une demi-heure je vous reverrai. 4. Cette caisse est franche de port. 5. Ce sont les propres termes dont il s'est servi. 6. C'est une vraie histoire que vous me contez là.

[1] montagnard (*m.*), [2] Écosse (*f.*), [3] dans, [4] revenir, [5] de devant, [6] règne (*m.*).

1. The Highlanders[1] of Scotland[2] have their legs bare in[3] all seasons. 2. I send you herewith the documents (which) you require. 3. I shall call again[4] in an hour and a-half. 4. Behind the house there was a large garden, but the front[5] garden was small. 5. It is an expensive hotel. 6. This war began in the last year of Henry's reign.[6] 7. I have bought a new book (*i.e.* lately published).

SECTION III.

COMPLEMENT OF THE ADJECTIVE.

279. Two adjectives qualifying the same noun must each have the same preposition as a complement. Thus we can say: *ce fils est* **utile** *et* **cher** *à sa mère* (=that son is useful and dear to his mother), because *être utile à quelqu'un* (=to be useful to some one), *être cher à quelqu'un* (=to be dear to some one) are grammatically correct; but we would not say: *ce fils est* **utile** *et* **chéri de** *sa mère*, because *être utile de quelqu'un* is wrong; in this case we must lengthen the proposition, and say: *ce fils est utile à sa mère et il* **en** *est chéri* (=that son is useful to his mother and he is beloved by her).

280. Some adjectives, having a determinate meaning, take no complement; thus **inviolable** in the following sentence: *les droits de la conscience sont* **inviolables** (=the rights of conscience are inviolable).

281. Adjectives, which signify plenty, scarcity, or want, take the preposition *de* before the word which they govern. Such are the following:—

absent (=absent)
affligé (=afflicted)
avide (=greedy)
capable (=capable)
comblé (=overwhelmed)
complice (=accessory, privy)
content (=content)
curieux (=curious)
désespéré (=disheartened)
désolé (=desolate, very sorry)
différent (=different)
digne (=worthy)
éloigné (=distant)
envieux (=envious)
esclave (=a slave to)
exempt (=exempt)
fatigué (=tired)
fier (=proud)
fou (=mad)
glorieux (=proud)
honteux (=ashamed)
impatient (=impatient)
incapable (=incapable)
indigne (=unworthy)
jaloux (=jealous)
las (=tired)
lassé (=tired)
mécontent (=dissatisfied)
plein (=full)
rassasié (=satisfied)
rempli (=filled)
soigneux (=careful)
sûr (=sure)
tributaire (=tributary)
victime (=a victim to)

282. Adjectives denoting aptness, fitness, inclination, ease, or any habit, take the preposition *à*; such are the following:—

accessible (=accessible)
accoutumé (=accustomed)
antérieur (=previous)
ardent (=ardent)
attentif (=attentive)
cher (=dear)
conforme (=conformable, agreeable)
contraire (=contrary)
enclin (=disposed, prone to)
exact (=punctual)
favorable (=favourable)
funeste (=baneful)
impénétrable (=impenetrable)
importun (=importunate)
invincible (=unconquerable)
invisible (=invisible)
nuisible (=injurious)
préférable (=preferable)
prompt (=prompt)
propice (=favourable)
propre (=good for)
redoutable (=redoubtable)
semblable (=similar)
sujet (=subject)
visible (=visible)

SECTION IV.

DEGREES OF COMPARISON.

283. We have seen, § 66, that the comparatives of superiority, inferiority, and equality are formed by means of the words **plus...que, moins...que, aussi ...que,** and **ne...si...que** in negative sentences.

284. When a numeral adjective or a substantive comes after the comparative, *que* is changed into **de**: *avez-vous plus* **de** *vingt francs dans votre bourse?* (= have you more than twenty francs in your purse?)

285. When a verb follows a comparative, **de** is placed after *que*, if the verb is in the infinitive, and **ne**, if it is in the indicative mood: *il est plus grand* **de** *vaincre ses passions* **que de** *conquérir des royaumes* (= it is greater to overcome one's passions than to conquer kingdoms); *vous vous flattez plus* **que** *vous* **ne** *le devriez* (= you flatter yourself more than you ought).

EXCEPT: 1. When the first infinitive is preceded by *à*, this preposition is repeated before the second: *il est plus disposé* **à** *vous plaindre* **qu'à** *vous punir* (= he is more disposed to pity than to punish you).

2. When the verb being in the indicative, a conjunction comes between *que* and the verb: *vous êtes plus enclin à travailler* **que** *quand vous étiez au collège* (= you are more inclined to work than when you were at college).

3. When the sentence expresses negation, interrogation, or doubt: *il n'est pas plus heureux* **qu'**il *l'était* (= he is not happier than he was).

286. When a comparative is repeated, no article should be used in French: **plus** *on lit*, **plus** *on aime à lire* (= the more one reads, the more one likes to read); **plus** *une chose est difficile*, **plus** *il y a de mérite à l'accomplir* (= the more difficult a thing is, the greater merit there is in accomplishing it).

NOTICE that *difficile* and *de mérite* are placed after the verb in French.

287. The article **le**, which precedes a superlative, agrees generally with the noun before an adjective, but not before an adverb (*see* §§ 256, 257): **les** *plus belles roses* (= the finest roses); *c'est elle qui agit* **le** *plus adroitement* (= it is she who acts with the greatest skill).

DEGREES OF COMPARISON. 27

208. The verb which follows a superlative with *que* is generally in the subjunctive mood: *Cet ouvrage est le meilleur que je* **connaisse** (= this work is the best I know).

QUESTIONS FOR EXAMINATION.

1. State the rule and exceptions for the agreement of one adjective with several substantives.
2. What is the rule for the agreement of compound adjectives?
3. How do adjectives agree with the substantive *gens*?
4. State the rule of agreement (1) for adjectives employed adverbially; (2) for substantives employed as adjectives.
5. Where are adjectives generally placed in French?
6. Write a list of the adjectives which precede the substantive.
7. Name a few adjectives which take a different meaning according as they are placed *before* or *after* the noun.
8. Explain the rule of agreement so far as it affects the adjectives *nu, demi, feu, franc.*
9. What are the ideas expressed by adjectives which govern their complement with (1) the preposition *de*; (2) the preposition *à*.
10. How is *than* expressed in comparative sentences?
11. State the rule for the comparative repeated.
12. How is the verb put in sentences with the superlative?
13. State the rules for the agreement of *le* in sentences where the superlative occurs.
14. When can two adjectives have the same complement?

Exercise 46.

1. Rien ne me plaît tant que les ouvrages de Raphaël. 2. La déesse Calypso était plus grande qu'Eucharis de toute la tête. 3. Rien n'est plus agréable à l'esprit que la lumière de la vérité. 4. Y a-t-il rien de plus injuste que de punir ce pauvre soldat? 5. L'armée avec laquelle Alexandre-le-Grand défit Darius ne s'élevait pas à plus de quarante mille hommes. 6. Moins vous étudierez, moins vous profiterez. 7. La ville de Troie fut autrefois la plus célèbre de l'Asie Mineure. 8. La probité est une des plus belles qualités qu'un homme puisse posséder. 9. Les hommes les plus savants font quelquefois les fautes les plus grossières.

[1] gagner, [2] dépense (*f.*), [3] faire, [4] goût (*m.*).

1. The public good is preferable to private interest. 2. Why are you dissatisfied with your condition? 3. He is not fit to discharge his duty. 4. I do not like people who are cruel to animals. 5. The Thames is not so rapid as the Rhine. 6. I am older than you by two years. 7. We flatter ourselves more than we should. 8. The more I examine this question, the more difficult I find it. 9. The less money he gets,[1] the less expense[2] he runs into.[3] 10. It is the best work which that author has written. 11. These three young ladies sing well, but Miss Martin is the best singer. 12. It is she who sings most tastefully (translate: with the most of taste [4]).

CHAPTER IV.

SYNTAX OF NUMERAL, POSSESSIVE, AND INDEFINITE ADJECTIVES.

SECTION I.

I. NUMERAL ADJECTIVES.

289. The names of cardinal numbers are invariable: **trois** *hommes*, **quatre** *femmes* (=three men, four women), except **un, vingt, cent** (=one, twenty, and one hundred).

290. Un (=one) makes **une** in the feminine: *deux coffrets et* **une** *boîte* (=two coffers and one box).

291. Vingt and **cent** do not vary as to gender, but they take **s** when they are preceded by a multiple: **quatre-vingts** *hommes* (=eighty men), **deux cents** *soldats* (=two hundred soldiers).

EXCEPT (1) when they are themselves followed by another number: *quatre*-**vingt**-**trois**, *deux* **cent trente** (=eighty-three, two hundred and thirty); (2) when they are used instead of the ordinal numbers: *page* **quatre-vingt** (=page eighty, *i.e.* eightieth), *l'an* **huit cent** (=the year eight hundred, *i.e.*, eight hundredth).

292. Mille (=thousand), invariable in gender and number, changes its form when it expresses the date of a year, or the date marked on coins; it is then written *mil* (but only in this case): *l'an* **mil** *huit cent soixante-seize* (=the year eighteen hundred and seventy-six). Note, further, that this spelling only applies to the years subsequent to the Christian era: *Ce fait arriva chez les Hébreux l'an du monde* **mille** *deux cent quarante* (=this happened among the Hebrews in the year of the world two thousand two hundred and forty).

The word *mil* is not, as is commonly supposed, an abbreviation of the French word *mille*, but comes from the Latin singular *mille*, whilst *mille* is derived from the Latin plural *millia*. The O.F. said: *mil hommes* (=one thousand men).

NUMERAL ADJECTIVES.   29

Mille (=mile) is a substantive, and, of course, takes the sign of the plural.

293. Ordinal adjectives agree in gender and in number with the noun which they determine : *les* **premières** *maisons, la* **seconde** *ville, la* **trentième** *année du règne de Louis XIV* (=the first houses, the second town, the thirtieth year of the reign of Louis XIV.).

294. We have seen (§ 80) that the ordinal adjectives indicate order and rank: *le* **dixième** *siècle, la* **vingtième** *année* (=the tenth century, the twentieth year) ; but the cardinal numbers are employed exceptionally to point out:—

1. The order of a sovereign in a dynasty: *Charles* **XII** (=Charles the Twelfth), not *Charles le* **douzième**; *Napoléon* **III** (=Napoleon the Third), not *Napoléon le* **troisième**.

2. The days of the month: *le* **deux** *avril, le* **trois** *juillet* (=the second of April, the third of July), not *le* **deuxième** *avril, le* **troisième** *juillet*. (Notice that the preposition *of* is not translated into French.)

3. In quoting paragraphs, pages, etc.: *livre* **dix** (=book ten); *page* **deux-cent** (page two hundred). *See* § 291.

The ordinal *premier* (=first), however, is alone exceptionally used: *Napoléon* **premier**, *le* **premier** *juillet* (=Napoleon the First, the first of July), and has never been supplanted by *un*.

295. Adjectives expressing the dimensions or the size of objects can be translated into French in several ways. Thus: *la nef de cette église a soixante pieds* **de long**, or **de longueur**: or *la nef de*, etc... **est longue de** *soixante pieds* (=the nave of this church is sixty feet long). The same rule applies to *haut...hauteur* (=high, height), and *large...largeur* (=wide, width); but *deep* must be expressed by *de profondeur*, not by *de profond*.

By or and, used when defining length and breadth, is translated by *sur*. Thus: *les murs de la citadelle*

ont trente-cinq pieds de hauteur **sur** *quinze d'épaisseur**
(=the walls of the citadel are thirty-five feet high and fifteen thick).

296. *More, less,* after a numeral, are expressed in French by **de plus, de moins** : *il a deux ans de plus que moi* (=he is two years older than I, *lit.* he has two years more than I).

Exercise 47.

1. La France est longue d'environ trois cents lieues. 2. Cette maison est haute de vingt mètres. 3. Cela est arrivé en mil huit cent deux. 4. Henri IV est un des meilleurs rois que la France ait eu. 5. C'est la cinquantième année de son règne. 6. Vous trouverez ce passage à la page quatre-vingt cinq. 7. Ce fossé a quatre pieds de large sur trois pieds de profondeur.

¹ retarder de, ² des Turcs, ³ États-Unis.

1. The room is 40 feet long, by 30 wide, and 15 high. 2. The crusades delayed the Turkish ² invasion by ¹ 300 years. 3. Napoleon the First was proclaimed emperor in 1804. 4. Eighty lords and more than 1200 knights perished at the battle of Crecy. 5. It was on the 4th July, 1776, that the independence of the United States ³ was proclaimed. 6. Have you read page 69? Yes; I am reading page 100. 7. Give him 10 francs more.

SECTION II.

II. POSSESSIVE ADJECTIVES.

297. Possessive adjectives, in French, agree in gender and number with the *object possessed*, and not with the *possessor* as in English :—

son âge (=his, her, or its age)   son frère (=his or her brother)
son mari (=her husband)   sa sœur (=his or her sister)
sa femme (=his wife)   sa mère (his or her mother)

298. The possessive adjectives are repeated in French before each substantive, and agree with it in gender and number :—

mon frère et ma sœur (=my brother and sister).

* *Un mur épais de quinze pieds,* or *de quinze pieds d'épaisseur* (=a wall fifteen feet deep), can be used, but not *un mur de quinze pieds d'épais.*

POSSESSIVE ADJECTIVES. 31

299. Where, in English, a possessive adjective refers to two or more nouns connected by a conjunction, it must be repeated in French: **sa** *sagesse et* **sa** *prudence* (= his wisdom and prudence).

300. When two adjectives of *dissimilar meaning* qualify the same noun, and the noun represents two distinct things, the possessive adjective is placed before each: **notre** *bonne et* **notre** *mauvaise fortune* (= our good and bad fortune).

But when the adjectives are of *similar meaning*, and the same things are signified by the noun, the possessive adjective is only placed before the first: **nos** *belles et fertiles plaines* (= our beautiful and fertile plains). (Cf. § 254.)

301. The name of the object possessed (when it belongs to several persons) is put in the singular, if the object is possessed in common: *le père et la mère attendaient* **leur** *voiture* (= the father and the mother were waiting for their carriage); it is put in the plural when there are as many objects possessed as there are possessors: *les ambassadeurs attendaient* **leurs** *voitures* (= the ambassadors were waiting for their carriages).

302. When the object possessed belongs to a person (and not to an inanimate being), *son, sa, ses* are used: *j'aime Henri, mais je connais* **ses** *défauts* (= I love Henry, but I know his faults).

When speaking of things **en** is generally used, followed by the definite article: *si je vous parle de ces fruits, c'est que j'***en** *connais* **la** *saveur* (= if I speak to you of those fruits, it is because I know the flavour of them).

303. The possessive adjectives *mon, ton, son,* etc. (= my, thy, his, etc.), are replaced by the article when they refer to something inseparable from the person, and when the sense of the phrase clearly indicates the possessor: *il s'est cassé le bras* (and not *son bras* [=he has broken his arm]); but we must say: *il a perdu sa fortune* (=he has lost his fortune).

Note that the expression *il s'est coupé la jambe* would mean: he has cut his leg off; whilst *il s'est coupé à la jambe* means: he has made an incision in his leg.

304. In French *votre* (in speaking of relations of the person addressed) is, out of politeness, often preceded by the words: *Monsieur, Madame, Mademoiselle* (=Mister, madam, miss); plural, *Messieurs, Mesdames, Mademoiselles*, which are not expressed in English:—

monsieur votre père (=your father)
mademoiselle votre sœur (=your sister)
messieurs vos frères (=your brothers).

305. Mon, ma, mes are used in speaking to relatives or friends: *venez, mon enfant* (=come, my child), *bonjour, ma tante* (=good morning, aunt). In the same way soldiers say to their officers: *mon capitaine* (=captain), *mon colonel* (=colonel), instead of: *monsieur le capitaine, monsieur le colonel*, expressions which would be used in society.

SECTION III.

INDEFINITE ADJECTIVES.

306. Indefinite adjectives do not call for any particular remarks as far as the Syntax is concerned, except in the case of the words *tout* (=all, every), *quelque* (=some), *chaque* (=each, every), *même* (=the same, even), and *maint* (=many, many a).

307. The adjective **tout** (=all, every) does not present any difficulty when it is used as an adjective, as it follows the ordinary rules bearing on that part of speech: **tout** *homme,* **toute** *femme* (=any, every man, any, every woman); *j'ai vu* **tous** *les hommes* (=I have seen all the men); *je ne puis vous accorder ceci, mais demandez-*

moi **toute** *autre chose et vous l'obtiendrez* [that is to say, **toute** *chose* **autre** *que celle que vous me demandez*] (= I cannot grant you this, but ask me for anything else, and you will obtain it [that is to say, anything else but what you have asked me for]).

In the same way, in **tout** *Paris*, **tout** *Londres* (=all Paris, all London), **tout** agrees with *people* understood: **tout** *le peuple de Paris* (=all the people of Paris), etc.

308. We have seen in §§ 266, 267 that adjectives can be used as adverbs: *parler* **haut**, *chanter* **faux**, *voir* **clair** (=to speak loud, to sing out of tune, to see clearly); in like manner *tout* (=all, every) can be employed adverbially, and it then means *tout-à-fait* (=altogether, quite): *je suis* **tout** *surpris* [*je suis tout-à-fait surpris*] (= I am quite surprised).

When used as an adverb *tout* is naturally invariable: *elle est* **tout** *heureuse du succès de son fils* (=she is quite happy in the success of her son); *ces mères sont* **tout** *heureuses des succès de leurs fils* [that is to say, *tout-à-fait heureuses*] (=those mothers are quite happy in the successes of their sons); *Londres est* **tout** *autre chose que Paris* [that is to say, *une chose tout-à-fait autre*] (=London is quite another thing from Paris).

But before *feminine* adjectives, or past participles, beginning with a consonant, such as *surprise* (=surprised), or an *h* aspirate, such as *honteuse* (=ashamed), the adverb *tout* is made to agree with the subject, like a simple adjective, for the purpose of softening the pronunciation: *elle est* **toute** *surprise* (=she is quite surprised), *elle est* **toute** *honteuse* (=she is quite ashamed).

In the same way, we can say: *ces gens sont* **tout** *yeux*, **tout** *oreilles* (=these people are all eyes and ears). **Tout** means also *quelque, si* [adverb] (=however): *la valeur,* **tout** *héroïque qu'elle est, ne suffit pas à faire des héros* (=valour, however heroic it may be, is not sufficient to make heroes).

Syntax.   D

309. Quelque (=some), used as an adjective, follows the ordinary rules of agreement with the noun to which it refers: **quelques** *hommes* (=some men), **quelques** *ennemis que vous ayez, vous triompherez* (=whatever enemies you may have, you will conquer).

But when it is used adverbially, *quelque* remains invariable, and signifies:

1. With substantives, *environ, à peu près* (=about, nearly): *j'ai rencontré* **quelque** *vingt personnes* (=I met about twenty people); *il vivait* **quelque** *cent ans après Jésus-Christ* (=he lived about one hundred years after Jesus Christ).

2. Joined to adjectives, it means the same as the adverb *si* : (**quelque** *puissants que soient vos ennemis* [that is to say, **si** *puissants que soient vos ennemis*] (=however powerful your enemies may be, *or* powerful as your enemies may be).

310. We must not confound **quelque** (used with its corresponding substantive) with another adjectival locution, **quel que**, which is never used except when separated from its substantive (and which is always followed by a verb in the subjunctive, to express doubt about the person or the thing spoken of): **quel** *que* **soit** *votre bonheur* (=whatever your happiness may be), **quelles** *qu'***aient** *été vos infortunes* (=whatever your misfortunes may have been).

Quelque, written in one word, must not, therefore, be mistaken for the expression *quel que* (formed from *quel*, *quelle*, and the conjunction *que*); this latter word is not at all, as some grammarians believe, the adjective *quelque* divided into two.

311. Même (=the same, self, very, even) varies when it is an adjective, and remains invariable when it is an adverb, that is to say, when it has the sense of *de plus, aussi, encore* (=besides, also, again, even). It is an adjective, for instance, in: *les* **mêmes** *hommes* (=the same men, the very men), *les dieux eux-***mêmes** *sont étonnés* (=the gods themselves are astonished). It is an adverb in: *le citoyen doit obéir aux lois,* **même** *injustes* (=the citizen ought to obey laws, even unjust ones).

INDEFINITE ADJECTIVES.

Même is an adverb when placed after several substantives: *les vieillards, les femmes, les enfants* **même** *furent égorgés* (=the old men, women, and even children were slaughtered).

312. Chaque (=each, every) being an *adjective*, must never be used except with its corresponding substantive, whilst **chacun, chacune,** being pronouns, are used without a substantive following them: **chaque** *pays a ses usages* (=every country has its customs), *ces villes ont* **chacune** *une citadelle* (=each of these towns has a citadel). We must not say, then: *ces fruits valent un franc* **chaque,** but *un franc* **chacun** (=these fruits are worth a franc each).

313. Maint (=many a) is used indiscriminately in the singular and in the plural: *j'ai lu dans* **maint** *auteur* (=I have read in many an author), *il m'a rendu* **maints** *services* (=he has rendered me many services).

QUESTIONS FOR EXAMINATION.

1. When do the numbers *vingt* and *cent* take the sign of the plural?
2. How is *mille* written in dates of the Christian era?
3. When does *taille* take the sign of the plural?
4. What is the rule for the agreement of ordinal numerals?
5. When are cardinal numbers used instead of the corresponding ordinal ones?
6. Explain the difference between the English and the French, so far as the agreement of possessive adjectives is concerned.
7. When are possessive adjectives repeated?
8. When is the possessive adjective replaced by the article?
9. State the rule and exceptions to the agreement of *tout*.
10. Explain thoroughly the syntax of *quelque*.
11. How does *même* (adjective) agree?
12. When is *même* used as an adverb?
13. Distinguish between *chaque* and *chacun*.
14. Explain the use of *maint*.

Exercise 48.

1. Mon frère a laissé tous ses livres dans sa chambre. 2. J'ai rencontré mademoiselle votre sœur au bal. 3. Nourri dans le sérail, j'en connais les détours. 4. Je me suis fait mal à la jambe. 5. Madame votre mère m'a paru toute surprise de me voir. 6. Ces livres sont tout couverts d'encre. 7. Vous ne pouvez manquer de lui trouver quelque mérite. 8. Quelque adroitement que vous vous y preniez, vous ne réussirez pas. 9. Quelles que soient ses protections, il obtiendra difficilement le poste qu'il souhaite. 10.

Quelques richesses qu'il ait, son avarice est insatiable. **11.** Ils se sont trompés eux-mêmes. **12.** Leurs vertus et même leurs noms étaient ignorés. **13.** On trouve mainte épine où l'on cherchait des roses.

¹ troublée, ² fouler, ³ laisser tomber.

1. How is your sister to-day? **2.** Your brothers have each a good place. **3.** This lady is quite confused¹ by your question. **4.** Whatever your motives may be, your conduct will be blamed. **5.** Whatever services you have done me, I have been thankful for them. **6.** I have sprained² my wrist. **7.** These peaches cost a shilling each. **8.** These are the same things I saw this morning. **9.** Even the wisest men are liable to make mistakes. **10.** Your sister has dropped³ her pocket-handkerchief. **11.** London is a very large city; I know well its parks and its principal monuments. **12.** Learned as they are, they could not discover these mistakes. **13.** I met one of your clerks at the Stock Exchange. **14.** This lady sings beautifully; every one admires her voice. **15.** Every age has its pleasures.

CHAPTER V.

SYNTAX OF THE PRONOUNS.

I. PERSONAL PRONOUNS.

Conjunctive.

314. We have seen (§ 89) that the personal pronouns are divided into *conjunctive*, *disjunctive*, and *reflective*, and that the conjunctive are called so on account of their position immediately *before* or *after* the verb.

315. These pronouns are placed *before* the verb:—

1. When used as subject in affirmative sentences: **je parle** (= I speak).

2. When used as direct or indirect object to a verb not in the imperative affirmative: *tu* **me** *remercies* (= thou thankest me), *il* **te** *l'a donné* (= he has given it to thee), *ne* **me le** *dites pas* (= do not tell it me), *l'avez-vous vu?* (= have you seen him); the indirect object coming first when two pronouns are used, except, however, when both are in the third person: *il* **le lui**

a donné (=he has given it to him); *ils le leur ont envoyé* =they have sent it to them).

316. They are placed *after* the verb:—

1. When subject of the verb:—

    (a) In interrogative sentences: *est-il heureux?* (=is he happy?)

    (b) In parenthesis: *non, a-t-il dit, ne le faisons pas* (=no, he said, let us not do it);

    (c) Sometimes after the expressions **à peine** (=scarcely, hardly), **aussi** (=and so, accordingly), **peut-être** (=perhaps): **peut-être** *ne viendra-t-il pas aujourd'hui* (=perhaps he will not come to-day);

    (d) In elliptical sentences when the subjunctive is used without a conjunction: **puissé-je** *de mes yeux y voir tomber la foudre* (=may I, with my own eyes, see it struck by lightning); **dût-il** *m'en coûter la vie* (=even if it were to cost me my life).

2. When object of the verb, in the imperative mood used affirmatively: *apportez-*le *moi demain* (=bring it me to-morrow). The pronoun dative is then changed from conjunctive to disjunctive, *i.e.*, *moi* is used instead of *me*, unless followed by *en, y* (see § 324): *vendez-***m'en** *la moitié* (=sell me half of it).

317. If the sentence is negative, *ne* is put directly after the subject, before the governed pronoun, as—

> *je* **ne** *vous donne pas* (=I do not give you)
> *tu* **ne** *me connais pas* (=you do not know me)
> *vous* **ne** *les avez pas vus* (=you have not seen them)

318. Nous, vous (=we, you), used for *je, tu* (=I, thou) govern the verb in the plural, but the past participel or adjective referring to them remains in the singular: **Nous** *sommes* **sûr**, *dit le roi, de votre fidélité* (=we are assured of your loyalty, said the king); **vous** *êtes* **enclin** *à la paresse* (=you are prone to idleness).

319. When the pronoun replaces two or more names of persons grammatically different, it is put in the first person, if there is one in the sentence; if not, it is put in the second person; thus: *vous, lui et moi*, **nous** *sommes fort âgés* (=you, he, and I are very old); *toi et lui*, **vous** *êtes malheureux* (=thou and he are unhappy). (See § 182.) This resuming pronoun is not required after **ni**: **ni** *vous* **ni** *moi ne l'avons vu* (=neither you nor I have seen it).

320. When the pronoun **le** represents a word which describes a state, such as *malade* (=ill), or a function, as *reine* (=queen), or a quality, as *mère* (=mother), it is invariable: *Madame, êtes-vous* **malade** ?—*je* **le** *suis* (=Madam, are you ill?—I am); *êtes-vous* **mère** ?—*je* **le** *suis* (=are you a mother?—I am); *êtes-vous* **reine** ?—*je* **le** *suis* (=are you a queen?—I am).

But when *le* represents a word which, instead of describing either a *state* or a *function*, stands for the *person* in that state, or exercising that function, or possessing that quality, it varies in gender and number: *êtes-vous* **la** *malade que l'on m'a recommandée?*—*Je* **la** *suis* (=are you the invalid who has been recommended to me?—I am); *êtes-vous* **la** *dame que nous cherchons ?*— *je* **la** *suis* (=are you the lady for whom we are looking ? —I am); *êtes-vous* **les** *soldats qui ont battu l'ennemi hier ?* —*oui, nous* **les** *sommes* (=are you the soldiers who beat the enemy yesterday ?—we are).

Le is invariable in the first case and variable in the second, because in the first instance it means *that, what you say*. This *le* is about the only trace of the Latin neuter which still exists in French. In the second instance it is used instead of the noun: *je la suis, i.e.* the lady [you look for].

321. Note that **le**, preceded by the negative **ne**, is used in French after a comparative, and is not expressed in English: *vous êtes plus avancé qu'il* **ne** *l'est* (=you are more advanced than he is).

322. When speaking of animals or things, the pronouns **en** and **y** are used instead of *de lui, d'elle, d'eux ; à lui, à elle, à eux,* etc. *: cet arbre est grandi, on*

PERSONAL PRONOUNS. 89

en ferait un mât (=that tree has grown, one could make a mast of it); *cette chaise est cassée, j'y ferai mettre un pied* (=this chair is broken, I shall have a leg put on to it).

En, y are also used with reference to persons, in order to avoid the repetition of a noun or pronoun: *quoique je parle beaucoup de vous, ma fille, j'y pense encore davantage* (=although I speak much of you, my daughter, I think of you still more).

Disjunctive.

323. We have seen (§§ 93—95) what is meant by *disjunctive* pronouns, and said that these pronouns are used as subject to give greater emphasis to the expression, or as object after the verb *être*, and after prepositions.

324. They are used also:—

1. After a comparative: *elle est meilleure que* **toi** (=she is better than thee).

2. After the imperative affirmative, to express the dative: *parlez-***moi** (=speak to me).

But the *conjunctive* pronoun is always used before *en, y: donnez-m'***en** (=give me some).

☞ Notice that **lui, leur** (=to him, to her, to them) are used both as *conjunctive* and *disjunctive* pronouns, *i. e. before* or *after* the verb (*see* §§ 315, 316).

325. When there are two imperatives in the same sentence, the *conjunctive* pronoun is sometimes used before the second imperative: *battez-***moi** *et* **me** *laissez rire* (=beat me and let me laugh); *apportez-***moi** *mes pantoufles et* **me** *donnez mon bonnet de nuit* (=bring me my slippers, and give me my night-cap).

Reflective.

326. Se (=one's self) is used for both genders and both numbers as direct or indirect object. It is always placed before the verb (*see* §§ 159 and 160): *il* **se** *fait une loi de lui écrire tous les mois* (=he makes it a duty to write to him every month).

327. Soi (= one's self) is used instead of *lui* (= him), *elle* (= her):—

1. After indefinite pronouns: *on* (= one), *chacun* (= every one), *personne* (= nobody), etc.: **on** *ne doit jamais parler de* **soi** (= one should never speak of one's self); **chacun** *vit pour* **soi** (= every one lives for himself).

2. After an impersonal verb, or an infinitive: **il faut** *penser à* **soi** (= one must think of one's self); **être** *toujours content de* **soi** *est une sottise* (= to be always satisfied with one's self is foolishness).

3. After a noun in the *singular* expressing *a thing*: *cette* **faute** *entraîne après* **soi** *bien des regrets* (= that fault entails [brings after it] many regrets). But if the noun is in the *plural*, **soi** cannot be used: **ces fautes** *entraînent après* **elles** *bien des regrets* (= these faults entail [bring after them] many regrets).

REMARK.—**Soi** is even used with a determinate subject, in order to avoid ambiguity: *l'avare qui a un fils prodigue n'amasse ni pour* **soi** *ni pour* **lui** (= the miser who has a prodigal son accumulates neither for himself nor for him).

Repetition of the Personal Pronouns.

328. Personal pronouns, used as subject, must be repeated in French:—

1. Before every verb, if these verbs are not in the same tense: *j'étudie et j'étudierai toujours* (= I study, and I will always study). But if the verbs are in the same tense, the repetition of the pronoun is optional: *je crains Dieu, et n'ai point d'autre crainte* (= I fear God, and have no other fear).

2. After a conjunction: *il est humble,* **parce qu'il est** *pauvre* (= he is humble, because he is poor).

329. Personal pronouns, used as object, must be repeated before each verb: *il* **vous** *estime et* **vous** *honore* (= he esteems and honours you). But when the verbs are in a compound tense, the pronoun need not be repeated, if the auxiliary is understood: *il les a flattés et loués* (=he has flattered and praised them).

330. When we wish to express ourselves with emphasis, the disjunctive pronouns are used as well as the conjunctive (*see* §§ 94, 95): *cela* **me** *frappa,* **moi** *et tous ceux qui l'entendirent* (=that struck me and all those who heard it); *il* **me** *l'a dit à* **moi-même** (=he said it to myself).

QUESTIONS FOR EXAMINATION.

1. When are the conjunctive personal pronouns placed before the verb?
2. When are they placed after the verb?
3. What pronoun is used after the imperative to express the dative?
4. What have you to remark on *nous* and *vous* used instead of *je, tu*?
5. When is *le* invariable? When does it vary?
6. Say what *en* and *y* are used for.
7. Remark on the use and place of the disjunctive personal pronouns.
8. Give the rules for the use of *se, soi.*
9. Say when the personal pronouns must be repeated, and in what cases they may be omitted.

Exercise 49.

1. Vous avez beaucoup de pommes, veuillez m'en donner. 2. Prêtez-moi votre grammaire; je vous la rendrai demain. 3. Chacun agit pour soi. 4. Ma tante est malade, et elle le sera longtemps. 5. Etes-vous la sœur de Monsieur Berthier? Oui, je la suis. 6. Ces enfants ont faim; donnez-leur à manger. 7. Je la vois et je lui parle tous les jours. 8. Il veut, il ne veut pas, il accorde, il refuse. 9. A peine étions-nous arrivés qu'il voulait déjà repartir. 10. Polissez votre ouvrage et le repolissez. 11. Il le lui fera savoir immédiatement. 12. Je veux le voir, le prier, le presser, l'importuner, le fléchir.

¹ rendre, ² partir, ³ gronder, ⁴ supplier, ⁵ sain et sauf.

1. If you have no pens I shall lend you some. 2. There is his grammar; why have you not returned[1] it to him? 3. Virtue is amiable of itself. 4. Are your sisters unwell? Yes, they are. 5. Are you my friend's mother? Yes, I am. 6. I assure you that I shall not do it. 7. He has deceived me, his best friend. 8. You and I shall leave[2] at the same time. 9. I will see her, herself. 10. He has scolded[3] and punished them. 11. We consulted, questioned, and entreated[4] him. 12. He will perhaps do it for me. 13. *I wish he may* (may he) return safely[5].

II. POSSESSIVE PRONOUNS.

331. The possessive pronouns **le mien, le tien**, etc. (=mine, thine, etc.), only refer to a noun already expressed: *j'achète* **votre** *maison et je vends* **la mienne** (=I buy your house, and I sell mine). These pronouns are never used as adjectives, except in a few old expressions: *un* **mien** *cousin* (=a cousin of his), *une* **sienne** *tante* (=an aunt of his). (*See* § 101.)

332. When used with the verb *être* (=to be), the possessive pronouns *mine, thine, his, hers, ours, yours,* and *theirs* are generally translated in French by **à moi, à toi, à lui, à elle, à nous, à vous, à eux,** or **à elles**: *ce chapeau est à moi* (=this hat is mine, *or* belongs to me).

333. *My own, thy own,* etc., are sometimes translated by **à moi**: *j'ai une maison* **à moi** (=I have a house of my own); and sometimes by the possessive adjectives **mon, ma, mes**, etc., followed by the adjective **propre** (=own): *je l'ai vu de* **mes propres** *yeux* (=I have seen it with my own eyes).

334. The possessive pronouns **le mien, le tien, le sien,** etc., when used absolutely, express *property* when they are in the singular: *j'ai demandé* **le mien**, *rien de plus* (=I asked for my own, nothing more); **le mien** *et* **le tien** *engendrent beaucoup de guerres et de procès* (=mine and thine give rise to many wars and lawsuits).

335. They express *relations, family, tribe, partisans,* when they are used in the plural: *on n'est jamais trahi que par* **les siens** (=one is never betrayed but by one's own people); *il est plein d'égards pour moi et pour* **les miens** (=he is full of attentions for me and mine).

In this case the possessive pronouns are real nouns, as they do not refer to any substantive previously expressed.

336. The English expressions: a friend of mine, a book of his, etc. are translated into French by *un de mes amis, un de ses livres,* etc.

DEMONSTRATIVE PRONOUNS.

QUESTIONS FOR EXAMINATION.

1. To what do the possessive pronouns refer?
2. How are possessive pronouns expressed when connected with the verb *to be*?
3. How are the expressions *my own, thy own* sometimes rendered in French?
4. When do the pronouns *le mien, le tien* express property? When do they express relations of family, tribe, or friendship?
5. When do the possessive pronouns become real nouns?
6. Translate into French: *he was going towards a house of his.*

Exercise 50.

1. Ces chapeaux sont à moi. 2. Vous avez perdu votre place, et j'ai conservé la mienne. 3. J'ai rencontré au musée un mien cousin. 4. Ce tableau est à moi; je l'ai acheté de mes propres deniers. 5. Ne m'accusez pas de convoitise; je ne demande que le mien. 6. Ce général fut lâchement abandonné des siens. 7. Il prit un des livres de son frère. 8. Cette maison n'est pas à lui, elle est à moi en propre; elle me vient des miens.

¹ se retirer, ² magnifique.

1. Whose is this umbrella? It is mine. 2. You have your pleasures; I have mine. 3. This old man is an uncle of mine. 4. I have retired¹ from business, and I have now a house of my own. 5. He has bought this splendid² picture with his own money. 6. That poor widow only claims what belongs to her. 7. I have been betrayed by my own family. 8. He had been using a pen of his brother's.

III. DEMONSTRATIVE PRONOUNS

337. We have seen (§ 99) that **ceci, celui-ci, celle-ci**, etc., are used when speaking of an object *close to us*, and **cela, celui-là**, etc., when we refer to an object *far from us*. We have now to add that **ceci** often refers to what *follows*: *n'oubliez pas* **ceci**: *aide-toi, le ciel t'aidera* (= do not forget *this*: help thyself, and Heaven will help thee), whilst **cela** applies to what comes *before* it: *l'orgueil est un grand défaut, retenez bien* **cela** (= pride is a great defect, remember *that* well). The same applies to **voici, voilà**.

In colloquial and rather familiar language, the contraction **ça** is used instead of cela: *ça m'est égal* (= I don't care). **Cela and ça**, referring to persons, are mostly used in contempt.

DEMONSTRATIVE PRONOUNS.

338. Celui, celle, ceux, celles cannot determine a simple adjective or participle; thus, instead of saying: *j'ai lu votre lettre et* **celle** *destinée à mon frère*, we must add the relative pronoun **qui** or **que** (see § 348) to the demonstrative, and say: *j'ai lu votre lettre et* **celle qui** *est destinée à mon frère* (=I have read your letter, and the one which is intended for my brother).

☞ **What**, meaning *that which*, must always be translated in that way, *i.e.*, by **ce qui** or **ce que**.

339. Ce is used with the third person singular or plural of *être, pouvoir, devoir:* **ce pourrait** *être lui* (=it might be he); **ce doit** *être touchant* (=it must be impressive).

340. When **ce** is used before those verbs, it refers either to persons or things, and the verb is always in the singular, unless the pronoun following the verb is in the third person plural: **ce** *n'est pas vrai* (=it is not true); *si jamais homme en a été capable,* **ce fut** *sans doute Alexandre* (=if ever a man could do it, it was doubtless Alexander); **ce sont** *eux* (=it is they).

341. Ce is used instead of *il, elle, eux, elles,* when the verb *être* is followed by an article, a possessive or a demonstrative adjective: **c'est un** *Français* (=he is a Frenchman); **c'est sa** *sœur* (=she is his sister); **ce** *sont vos amis* (=it is your friends); **ce** *n'étaient pas* **ces** *arbres qu'il voulait abattre* (=it was not these trees he wished to fell).

But we must say: **il** *est Français,* the noun (or rather adjective) being used without any article or adjective.

342. If the verb *être* is followed by an adjective, the English word *it* is expressed:—

1. By **ce**, when referring to what precedes: **c'est vrai** (=it is true).

2. By **il**, when *être* is used as an impersonal verb, and *it* refers to what follows: **il** *est vrai que c'est mon frère qu'il a vu* (=it is true that it is my brother he has seen).

DEMONSTRATIVE PRONOUNS.

343. Ce is used by redundance :—

1. When *être* is placed between two infinitives: *laisser un crime impuni, c'est s'en rendre complice* (= to leave a crime unpunished is to make one's self an accomplice of it).

2. When the second part of a sentence begins with the verb **être** followed by a substantive or an infinitive, the pronoun **ce** is repeated if it begins the sentence: ce *que j'aime,* c'est *la vérité* (= what I like is truth); ce *que je désire,* c'est *de vous voir réussir* (= what I wish is to see you succeed).

344. When either part of the sentence can be the predicate of the other, the pronoun **ce** may be used or not before the second: *boire, manger, dormir* **était**, or **c'était**, *leur seule occupation* (= drinking, eating, sleeping was their only occupation).

345. Que de, before an infinitive in the second part of the sentence, when **ce** begins the first part, gives great force to the expression : *c'est acheter cher un repentir* **que de** *se ruiner pour une fantaisie* (= it is buying repentance dear to ruin one's self for a mere fancy).

346. In interrogations, certain forms are to be avoided on account of their harsh sound ; such are: *furent-ce, doivent-ce;* another way must then be employed, such as *les Romains furent-ils...* (= were the Romans...). (See § 388).

QUESTIONS FOR EXAMINATION.

1. When are *celui-ci, celui-là, ceci, cela, voici, voilà* used ?
2. What does *ça* mean, and when is it used?
3. How do you translate : *the one which,* or *that which* ?
4. In what number is the verb put after *ce* ?
5. When is the English word *it* translated by *ce*, and when by *il* ?
6. State the cases when *ce* must be expressed in the second part of a sentence.
7. What is the effect produced by *ce... que de* before an infinitive ?

Exercise 51.

1. Vous êtes venu de bonne heure, c'est vrai. 2. Comment ça va-t-il chez vous ? 3. C'est nous qui avons payé le déjeûner. 4. Voyez-vous ces dames ? 5. Ce sont elles que j'ai eu l'honneur

d'accompagner au bal. 6. Ceci me convient mieux que cela. 7. Laplace et Newton furent deux célèbres mathématiciens; celui-là était Français, et celui-ci Anglais. 8. Je ne me soucie pas de ça. 9. C'est remporter la plus belle des victoires que de commander à ses passions. 10. Ce pourraient être vos motifs. 11. Il n'est pas sûr qu'il vienne aujourd'hui. 12. Je vous dis que c'est très-sûr.

¹ s'en prendre, ² ça, ³ devoir, ⁴ tout à fait.

1. It is a mistake to suppose that he is ill. 2. It is (to) you that I shall call to account.[1] 3. It is they who are making that noise. 4. I like this, but that seems to me very dangerous. 5. How are you this morning? 6. They[2] give themselves (de) such airs. 7. French and English are the two languages most generally spoken; the former in Europe, and the latter in the other parts of the world. 8. That is what you know, this is what you are going to learn. 9. They must[3] be the same gentlemen we saw yesterday. 10. He is a man you may trust. 11. It is quite[4] evident. 12. It is certain that in this circumstance he did not do his duty.

IV. RELATIVE AND INTERROGATIVE PRONOUNS.

347. Relative pronouns agree in gender, number, and person with their antecedent, even when they themselves do not change: *les maisons* **qui** *sont dans cette rue sont bien bâties* (= the houses which are in that street are well built). Although **qui** does not change, it agrees in gender, number, and person with *maisons*, and the verb *sont* which agrees with *qui*, is in the third person plural.

348. Qui in the nominative case, and **que** in the objective (*or* accusative), may be used for *persons* or *things*: *le livre* **qui** *est sur la table* (= the book which is on the table); *l'homme* **qui** *vient* (= the man who comes): *le livre* **que** *vous voyez* (= the book which you see); *l'homme* **que** *vous voyez* (= the man whom you see).

349. ☞ Great care must be taken to distinguish between **que** and **qui**, as, owing to the clear sense of those two words, inversions are very frequent in French :—

l'ours **qui** *tua la chasseur* (=the bear which killed the hunter);
l'ours **que** *tua le chasseur* (=the bear which was killed by the hunter, or which the hunter killed).

350. Qui can be used, without an antecedent, either as subject or as complement (or object). In that case, it applies to *persons only*, and is always *masculine*: **qui** *sert bien son pays n'a pas besoin d'aïeux* (=he who serves his country well has no need of ancestors); *à* **qui** *venge son père il n'est rien d'impossible* (=there is nothing impossible for the one who avenges his father); *choisis* **qui** *tu voudras* (=choose whom you like).

351. Qui, repeated, is used sometimes in the sense of *ceux-ci, ceux-là*: *chacun y est en action*, **qui** *à bâtir*, **qui** *à l'agriculture* (=every one there is busy, some in building, others in agriculture).

352. Qui, preceded by a preposition, applies to *persons* or *things personified*: *l'enfant* **à qui** (not **auquel**) *tout le monde cède est le plus malheureux* (=the child to whom everybody yields, is the most unhappy); *O rochers escarpés! c'est à vous que je me plains, car je n'ai que vous* **à qui** *je puisse me plaindre* (=O steep rocks! it is to you that I complain, for I have only you to complain to).

353. Quoi, as a relative pronoun, is used with a preposition, and is applied to *things only;* it generally refers to an antecedent having an indefinite meaning: *c'est* **à quoi** *l'on pensera* (=that is what we will think about); *la chose* **à quoi** (or **à laquelle**) *l'on pense le plus est souvent celle dont on parle le moins*(=the thing about which we think most, is often that of which we speak least).

354. De quoi forms an idiomatic expression which means *enough, the means, money*, &c.: *il y a* **de quoi** *se plaindre* (=there is reason to complain); *il n'a pas* **de quoi** *payer* (=he has not enough to pay); *il a* **de quoi** *vivre* (=he has enough to live upon).

355. Dont is used for both genders and numbers, and may apply to all nouns, as :—

le commis **dont** *vous parlez* (= the clerk of whom you speak)
les choses **dont** *vous parlez* (= the things of which you speak)
la nature **dont** *nous ignorons les secrets* (= Nature, whose secrets are unknown to us).

356. If the relative pronoun is separated from its antecedent by another substantive, *whose or of whom* is translated by **de qui**, and *of which* by **duquel, de laquelle, desquels, desquelles**, according to the gender and number of the antecedent: *c'est un ami à la générosité* **de qui** *je puis toujours faire appel* (= he is a friend to whose generosity I can always appeal); *c'est une entreprise à la réussite* **de laquelle** *je ne puis croire* (= it is an undertaking in the success of which I cannot believe).

357. When **dont** denotes the origin, lineage, descent, it applies to *persons only: la famille illustre* **dont** *il descend* (= the illustrious family from which he is descended). In every other case *from whom, from which* must be translated by **duquel, de laquelle**, etc.

With *nouns of things*, **d'où** is employed: *le pays* **d'où** *je viens* (= the country from which I come).

D'où is used also, instead of *dont*, to announce a conclusion: *c'est un fait* **d'où** *je conclus* (= it is a fact from which I conclude).

358. Où always refers to *inanimate objects* :—

le siècle **où** (or *dans lequel*) *nous vivons* (= the age in which we live)
les moyens par **où** (or *par lesquels*) *vous réussirez* (= the means by which you will succeed).

359. All the above pronouns being used for both numbers and genders, there is sometimes doubt as to which noun is their antecedent. This can be obviated by the use of **lequel**, which agrees with its antecedent in gender and number, as we have seen at § 104.

360. Lequel can be used for *persons* and *things* ; *l'homme* **de qui** (or **duquel**) *vous parlez* (= the man of whom you speak) ; *le cheval* **sur lequel** *il était monté* (= the horse on which he was mounted).

RELATIVE AND INTERROGATIVE PRONOUNS. 49

Duquel, de laquelle, etc., are used to translate *from whom, from which.*

361. Great care must be taken to place the relative pronoun in such a way that there can be no doubt as to what word is its real antecedent; thus: *il y a plusieurs pages dans ces manuscrits* **qui** *sont illisibles* is an incorrect sentence, because the relative pronoun **qui** seems to refer to *manuscrits*. The correct way is: *il y a dans ces manuscrits plusieurs pages* **qui** *sont illisibles* (= there are in these manuscripts several pages which are illegible).

362. Relative pronouns, which are often understood in English, must always be expressed in French:—

le livre **que** *vous voyez* (= the book you see)
la leçon **qu'il** *apprend* (= the lesson he learns).

363. The *relative pronouns* are also used as **interrogative pronouns.** They have not then quite the same meaning, and are subject to the following rules:—

Qui refers to *persons only*: **qui** *voulez-vous?* (= whom do you want?); **qui** *parle?* (= who speaks?)

Que refers to *things only*: **que** *voulez-vous?* (= what do you want?)

Quoi is used in exclamations, in a simple question, and after a preposition, instead of *que*: **quoi?** (= what?); **quoi** *de mieux!* (= what is there better?); *avec* **quoi?** (= with what?)

Lequel shows a preference, a choice made of some thing among a number: **lequel** *de ces tableaux voulez-vous?* (= which of those pictures will you have?)

Dont is never used as an interrogative pronoun.

364. To these must be added the **interrogative adjective** *quel* (= what, which). It varies in gender and number (see § 107), and is always followed by a noun: **quel** *homme* (= what a man)! **quelles** *maisons* (= what houses)!

☞ Notice that, in the singular, the English article *a* is not translated into French.

QUESTIONS FOR EXAMINATION.

1. To what substantives do *qui* and *que* apply?
2. What is the difference between *qui* and *que*?
3. How is *qui* used when it has no antecedent?
4. Explain the idiomatic force of *qui* repeated?
5. Explain the use of *quoi*.
6. Remark on *dont*. — Distinguish between *dont* and *d'où*.
7. To what class of substantives does *où* refer?
8. When are *lequel, laquelle*, &c., to be used?
9. Where are the relative pronouns to be placed?
10. What is the difference between *qui, que, quoi, lequel* used as interrogative pronouns?

Exercise 52.

1. Les malheurs que son administration déchaîna sur la France. 2. Toi qui sais ta leçon, viens la réciter. 3. Qui sert bien son pays n'a pas besoin d'aïeux. 4. Ils saisirent qui un fusil, qui un pistolet. 5. A qui est ce chapeau? 6. De qui parlez-vous? 7. Ce soldat dont le courage est connu recevra la médaille d'honneur. 8. C'est un soldat au courage de qui je me confie. 9. Le bonheur appartient à qui fait des heureux. 10. La famille dont je sors est une des plus illustres de l'Angleterre. 11. Qui habite la chaumière d'où vous sortez? 12. Par où irez-vous? 13. En quoi consiste la différence? 14. Que pensez-vous de cela?

[1] paletot (m.), [2] se plaindre de, [3] en bas, [4] se fier à, [5] dans toute l'Europe, [6] compter, [7] malheureux, [8] intéresser.

1. What has he told you? 2. Which of these two great-coats[1] is mine? 3. What do you complain of[2]? 4. The friend you love so much is downstairs.[3] 5. That is the aim to which he tends. 6. He is a writer on (to) whose good taste you can always rely,[4] and whose genius is known throughout the whole of Europe.[5] 7. With whom did you come? 8. I do not admit the principles from which you derive your system. 9. Death is an evil for which there is no remedy. 10. Where will you go after? 11. On what do you reckon[6]? 12. Which of these books do you like best? 13. What is more unfortunate[7] than his position? 14. I read a story in the book of that author which interests[8] me much.

V. INDEFINITE PRONOUNS.

365. The pronoun **on** expresses an idea of universality in a vague manner. It only refers to persons, and is only used as subject: **on** *mange pour vivre* (= one eats to live).

INDEFINITE PRONOUNS. 51

On is generally singular, but when it clearly designates a woman or several persons, it becomes either feminine or plural: *à votre âge, ma fille,* **on** *est bien curieuse* (=at your age, my daughter, one is very inquisitive); *ici* **on** *est égaux* (=here people are equal).

NOTE.—Instead of using the passive voice, the French put, whenever it is possible, the verb in the active, giving to it the pronoun *on* as a nominative: **on** *a reçu des lettres* (=letters have been received). (See § 149.)

366. L'on is frequently used instead of *on*, after the conjunctions *et* (=and), *si* (=if), *ou* (=or), and the adverb *où* (=where): **si l'on** *savait tout* (=if one knew all); *parlez,* **et l'on** *écoutera* (=speak, and we shall listen); *sachez* **où l'on** *va* (=know where we are going). Before the pronoun *le, la, les,* however, it is better to say *on* to avoid the repetition of the sound of *l*: *qu'il parle,* **et on** *l'écoutera* (=let him speak, and we shall listen to him); *si* **on le** *savait* (=if people knew it); *sachez où* **on la** *conduit* (=knew where she is led).

On, in the twelfth century *om,* and earlier *hom,* is simply the Latin word *homo,* and means properly "a man": **on** *lui amène son destrier* (=a man brings him his war-horse). Thus, *on* was originally a substantive; and this accounts for its being sometimes preceded by the article (**l'on**).

367. On is used to avoid naming the persons of whom we speak, and, in that case, it generally shows a certain amount of contempt, although not so much as *ça*: *vous, Narcisse, approchez, et vous, qu'***on*** se retire* (=as for you, Narcissus, draw near; and you [*i.e.* the other persons present], withdraw). (See § 337).

Vous takes sometimes the place of **on** in colloquial language: *si* **vous** *sortez après dix heures, on* **vous** *arrête et on* **vous** *mène en prison* (=if you go out after ten o'clock, you are arrested, and taken to prison); **vous** *savez bien quand* **vous** *y entrez, mais personne ne peut dire quand* **vous** *en sortirez* (=you know when you go in, but no one can tell when you will come out).

368. The pronoun **chacun** takes *son, sa, ses* after it :—

1. When it is the subject of the verb: **chacun** *doit parler à* **son** *tour* (=each one must speak in his turn).

2. When it is placed *after* the complement of the verb, or when there is no complement: *remettez ces livres-là* **chacun** *à* **sa** *place* (=put back these books, each in its place); *les animaux sont vêtus* **chacun** *selon* **ses** *besoins* (=the animals are clothed, each according to its wants).

369. Chacun takes *leur, leurs*, when it is placed *before* the direct complement: *les abeilles bâtissent* **chacune leur** *cellule* (=the bees construct each its cell); *les langues ont* **chacune leurs** *bizarreries* (=each language has its oddities); *les juges ont donné* **chacun leur** *opinion* (=each judge has given his opinion).

370. If **chacun** is preceded by a verb which cannot have a direct object, the use of *son, sa, ses*, or *leur, leurs* is optional: *ils sont venus,* **chacun** *avec* **ses,** or **leurs** *gens* (=they came each with his servants).

371. The locution **l'un l'autre** (=one another, each other) expresses reciprocity, and takes both genders and both numbers; thus: *ils s'aimaient* **les uns les autres** (=they loved one another); *elles se nuisent* **les unes aux autres** (=they injure one another).

The locution **l'un et l'autre** (=both) does not express reciprocity, but merely the idea of two or more persons, two or more things; placed before a noun it is an adjective, and agrees in gender with the noun: *j'ai parcouru* **l'une et l'autre** *régions* (=I have gone over both regions).

372. Autrui (=others, other people) is always used as a substantive, and does not take the plural: *ne parlez jamais mal d'***autrui** (=never speak ill of other people).

373. The indeterminate pronouns *whosoever, whoever* are usually expressed:—

1. By **quiconque**, when they mean *all those who:* **quiconque** *touchera à mon livre sera puni* (=whoever touches my book shall be punished).

2. By **qui que ce soit qui,** or **que** (followed by the verb in the subjunctive mood), when they mean *whatever the person may be who,* or *whom:* **qui que ce soit qui** *vienne, dites-lui que je rentrerai dans une demi-*

heure (=whosoever may come, tell him that I shall be back in half-an-hour).

374. Quoi que ce soit (=whatever) is used in like manner for things: *quoi que ce soit que vous disiez, on vous croira* (=whatever you may say, you will be believed).

375. Rien means properly *quelque chose* (=something), and it has still that meaning in interrogative sentences: *y a-t-il rien de plus beau?* (=is there anything more beautiful?).

376. Used with a negative, it means *nothing*: *je ne fais* **rien** (=I do nothing).

377. Rien is used in the sense of *nothing*, and *without a negative*:—

(1) After a comparative: *il a moins que* **rien** (=he has less than nothing);

(2) After a preposition: *il fait cela avec* **rien** (=he does that with [almost] nothing);

(3) in answers: *que faites-vous?* **rien** (=what are you doing? nothing); *que voyez-vous?* **rien** (=what do you see? nothing).

378. Rien and **tout** are placed *after the verb* in simple tenses, and *between the auxiliary and the participle* in compound tenses: *il ne voit* **rien** *et vous voyez* **tout** (=he sees nothing, and you see everything); *il n'a* **rien** *vu mais vous avez* **tout** *vu* (=he has seen nothing, but you have seen all). With an infinitive, they generally come first: *vous ne devez* **rien** *faire* (=you must do nothing); *il faut* **tout** *dire* (=you must say all).

379. Personne, meaning *anybody*, does not take **ne**:—

(1) in interrogative sentences: *y a-t-il* **personne** *de mieux renseigné?* (=is there any one better informed?).

(2) In sentences expressing doubt: *je doute qu'il vienne* **personne** (=I doubt whether anybody will come);

(3) In answers: *qui est là?* **personne** (=who is there? no one);

(4) After a comparative: *il le fera mieux que* **personne** (=he will do it better than any one).

380. Personne, with a negative sense, is masculine, unless it clearly refers to a woman: **personne** *n'est entièrement* **bon** (=no one is entirely good); **personne** *n'est plus* **jolie** (=no one [lady] is prettier). When **personne** is used as a noun, *i.e.*, when preceded by an article or an adjective (demonstrative or possessive), it is feminine: *une* **personne** *de qualité* (=a man [or woman] of title).

For the other pronouns, **tout**, etc., see *Indefinite Adjectives* (§ 306, § 314).

QUESTIONS FOR EXAMINATION.

1. Explain the various idiomatic uses of *on*.
2. When does the pronoun *chacun* take *son, sa, ses* after it?—When does it take *leur?*
3. Distinguish between *l'un l'autre* and *l'un et l'autre*.
4. When is *autrui* used?
5. How are the pronouns *whoever, whosoever, whatever* translated?
6. What is the real meaning of *rien?*
7. When are *rien* and *personne* followed by *ne?*—when are they not?
8. Where are *rien* and *tout* placed?
9. When is *personne* masculine?—when is it feminine?

Exercise 53.

1. On dit qu'il y a eu un violent incendie à Londres. 2. On est égaux quand on s'aime. 3. Les dix tribus de l'Attique avaient chacune leur président. 4. Ces messieurs ont voté chacun selon ses opinions. 5. Par soi-même on peut juger d'autrui. 6. Quiconque aura fini son devoir à midi pourra aller jouer. 7. Je n'en parlerai à qui que ce soit. 8. Prêtez-moi un ouvrage quelconque. 9. Ne vous maltraitez pas l'un l'autre. 10. Ils sont toujours à se moquer l'un de l'autre. 11. Je n'aime ni l'un ni l'autre. 12. Quand vous êtes là, vous n'avez plus que quelques pas à faire pour arriver à la gare. 13. On ne peut rien faire de mieux. 14. Personne ne l'a vu.

¹ apporter, ² s'occuper, ³ place (*f.*), ⁴ envers, ⁵ à la maison.

1. News have been brought[1] from Paris. 2. They say that the king is dead. 3. Every one must take care[2] of himself. 4. These two gentlemen have each a good situation.[3] 5. Of whom—

soever you speak, avoid calumny. 6. Whosoever is not ashamed of his faults deserves to be punished. 7. You are guilty of great injustice towards [4] each other. 8. Both suspect him, but neither will say why. 9. Mention this fact to nobody. 10. You should never speak evil of others. 11. We wish to see everything. 12. There is nothing to see. 13. There is nobody at home.[5] 14. This person is very good. 15. What is in that box? nothing.

CHAPTER VI.

SYNTAX OF THE VERB.

I. AGREEMENT OF THE VERB WITH ONE SIMPLE SUBJECT.

381. Every verb agrees with its subject in number and person: *les hommes* **sont** *mortels* (= men are mortal); *nous* **avons** *le livre* (= we have the book); *le courage* **est** *une vertu* (= courage is a virtue).

382. When the subject is a collective noun, that is to say, a noun which denotes an assemblage, a collection of objects of the same kind, the verb is put in the singular, if the *collective noun* is taken as the subject: *une* **nuée** *de sauterelles* **obscurcit** *l'air* (= a swarm of locusts obscured the air).

It is put in the plural, if the *complement* of the collective noun is taken as the subject: *une nuée de* **barbares** **désolèrent** *le pays* (= a swarm of barbarians desolated the country).

Practice will teach when to put the plural and when the singular. The invariable rules, which grammarians pretend to establish on this point, are more than doubtful. It is, in reality, with the most important word, that the verb agrees.

383. After **la plupart** (= most part), **le plus grand nombre** (= the greatest number), **une foule de** (= a crowd of), **une infinité de** (= a multitude of), etc., the verb always agrees with the *complement* of these collective locutions, either expressed or understood: *la plupart des* **gens** *ne* **font** *réflexion sur rien*

(= most people think of nothing); *la plupart* **écrivent** *ce nom de cette manière* (= most people write this name thus).

334. After the adverbs of quantity, **beaucoup** (= much), **peu** (= little), **moins** (= less), **assez** (= enough), **trop** (= too much), etc., followed by a plural, the verb never agrees with the adverb, but always with the noun: *beaucoup de* **personnes ignorent** *la gravité de cette affaire* (= many people are ignorant of the gravity of that affair); *peu de* **gens supportent** *la contradiction* (= few people bear contradiction).

335. Plus d'un requires the verb in the *singular*, although it calls forth an idea of *plurality*: **plus d'un** *brave* **mord** *la poussière* (= more than one brave man bites the dust).

But when *reciprocity* is implied, the verb is put in the *plural*: **plus d'un** *avocat qui* **s'insultent** *au palais se* **serrent** *la main en sortant* (= many barristers, who insult each other in court, shake hands when they go out).

336. The verb **être** (= to be), preceded by **ce** (**c'est**, **c'était**, etc.), remains in the singular:—

(a) When it is followed by one or more nouns, the first of which is singular: **c'est** *la pluie et le brouillard qui attristent l'Angleterre* (= it is the rain and the fog which make England gloomy); **ce sera** *le même théâtre et les mêmes décorations* (= it will be the same theatre and the same scenery).

(b) If the pronoun **ce** recalls the idea of a singular substantive expressed before: *pour lui le bonheur,* **c'est** *de grandes richesses* (= as for him, he thinks that happiness consists in being very rich).

(c) When **être** is followed by a pronoun of the *first or second* person: **c'est nous** *qui sommes les vrais coupables* (= it is we who are the real culprits); **c'est vous** *qui auriez dû le faire* (= it is you who should have done it).

AGREEMENT OF THE VERB WITH ONE SIMPLE SUBJECT. 57

(d) When the noun coming after **être** is preceded by *de*: **c'est** *de vos parents que nous parlons* (=it is of your relations we speak).

387. But the verb **être** is put in the plural:—

(a) When the first noun is in the plural: **ce sont** *les mêmes décorations, le même théâtre* (=it is the same scenery, the same theatre); **ce sont** *les arbres, le chemin, la maison que j'ai vus autrefois* (=it is the trees, the road, the house, I saw formerly); **ce sont** *les rois qui sont les chefs des nations* (=it is the kings who are the chiefs of the peoples).

(b) When the pronoun *ce* recalls the idea of a plural noun expressed before: *il y a dix espèces de mots*: **ce sont** *l'article, le nom*, etc. (=there are ten kinds of words: they are the article, the noun, etc.).

(c) When **être** is followed by pronouns of the third person plural: **ce sont eux** *qui m'ont accusé* (=it is they who have accused me).

388. The verb **être**, however, although followed by a pronoun of the third person plural, is put in the singular: (a) in order to avoid expressions disagreeable to the ear, such as *sont-ce, seront-ce, furent-ce*. Thus, we must say: **sera-ce** *vos amis qui vous tireront d'affaire?* (=will it be your friends who will get you out of difficulty?).* (b) In the locution *si ce n'est* (=unless it be, if it is [or was] not): **si ce n'est eux**, *quels hommes eussent osé l'entreprendre?* (=what men, besides them, would have dared to undertake it?).

389. Impersonal verbs (or verbs employed as such) remain invariable, even when they are followed by a plural noun: **il tomba** *des milliers de projectiles sur le champ de bataille* (=thousand of projectiles fell on the battle-field); **il vint** *plusieurs personnes* (=several persons came).

* *Est-ce que* may also be used in this case. See § 179.

See § 162 for the particular nature of the word *il*. Impersonal verbs may be used figuratively in the the third person plural: *les traits* **pleuvent** (= darts are showered); *les canons* **tonnent** (= the cannons roar).

Exercise 54.

1. Ces enfants sont très-aimables. 2. Une foule de soldats se précipitèrent dans l'enceinte de l'assemblée. 3. La plupart pensent que la guerre sera bientôt déclarée. 4. Une multitude de sauterelles dévorèrent la récolte. 5. Beaucoup de maisons ont été détruites par l'incendie. 6. A Paris, au collége de France, un très-grand nombre de jeunes gens suivent gratuitement les cours des meilleurs professeurs. 7. Plus d'un philosophe s'y est trompé. 8. Peu de gens savent cette nouvelle, et je vous engage à ne pas l'ébruiter. 9. Ce furent les Phéniciens qui inventèrent l'écriture. 10. C'est des anciens habitants de cette région que je vous parle. 11. Il est venu plus de deux mille personnes à la cérémonie.

[1] enclin, [2] sortir, [3] impasse (*f.*), [4] assistance (*f.*), [5] échapper à.

1. These men are not so rich as we thought. 2. He and I are inclined[1] to do it. 3. Many *people* think this news is false. 4. A crowd of children came out[2] of the court.[3] 5. Half the passengers were so ill that they could not give any help.[4] 6. Few persons put into practice the saying: Time is money. 7. It is the barkings of the dogs that I hear. 8. What are the chief towns of France? They are: Paris, Lyons, Marseilles, Bordeaux, Lille, Toulouse, Nantes, Rouen. 9. It is of them (*f. pl.*) they speak. 10. Was it the Phenicians or the Egyptians who invented writing? 11. The multitude of errors which escaped[5] his attention have been corrected since.

II. AGREEMENT OF THE VERB WITH SEVERAL SUBJECTS.

390. A verb which has two or more subjects in the same person of the singular is put in the same person of the plural: *le chien et le chat* **recherchent** *le voisinage de l'homme* (= the dog and the cat seek the vicinity of men).

But if the subjects are of different persons, the verb follows the same rule as the pronoun (*see* § 319), that is to say, it is put in the first person plural if there is one in the sentence: *vous, lui et moi, nous* **sommes** *heureux*

AGREEMENT OF THE VERB WITH SEVERAL SUBJECTS. 59

(=you, he and I are happy); and if there is not a first person, it takes the second: *vous et lui, vous êtes coupables* (=you and he are guilty).

391. The verb is put in the singular after several subjects:—

1. When the subjects form either an enumeration or a kind of climax: *un regard, une parole, un serrement de main* **suffit** *pour relever le courage du malheureux* (=a look, a word, a grasp of the hand is enough to raise the courage of the unhappy man).

2. When the enumeration is summed up by a word, such as *chacun, tout, rien*, etc.: *un souffle, une ombre, un rien*, **tout** *lui* **donnait** *la fièvre* (=a breath, a shadow, a trifle, everything gave him a fever).

392. When the subjects are connected together by **comme** (=as), **ainsi que** (=as well as), **de même que** (=as well as), **autant que** (=as much as), **plus que** (=more than), **moins que** (=less than), **aussi bien que** (=as well as), the verb agrees with the first only: *la vérité,* **comme** *la lumière,* **est** *inaltérable* (=truth, as well as light, is unalterable); *l'or* **autant que** *les honneurs* **séduit** *l'homme* (=gold seduces man as much as honours). In this last example, the verb of the secondary proposition is understood: *l'or* **séduit** *l'homme autant que les honneurs le* **séduisent.**

393. After **l'un et l'autre** (=both) the verb takes the plural: **l'un et l'autre sont** *morts* (=both are dead); **l'un et l'autre** *guerrier* **sont** *de haute taille* (=both warriors are of tall stature);

But **l'un ou l'autre** (=one or the other), **ni l'un ni l'autre** (=neither one nor the other) require the verb in the singular: **l'un ou l'autre a** *raison, mais lequel des deux?* (=either one or the other is right, but which of the two?); **ni l'un ni l'autre** *ne remportera la victoire* (=neither one nor the other will gain the victory).

394. The conjunctions **ou** and **ni** (=or *and* nor) also lead to some violations of the rules on the agreement of verbs. Ni and ou sometimes take the verb in the plural: **ni** *l'or* **ni** *la grandeur ne nous* **rendent** *heureux* (=neither gold nor greatness make us happy); *le courage* **ou** *le bonheur* **ont** *pu faire des héros* (=courage or happiness have been able to make heroes); and sometimes they take the verb in the singular: **ni** *Jean* **ni** *Pierre n'***a** *voulu travailler* (=neither John nor Peter would work); *la peur,* **ou** *la misère lui* **a** *fait commettre une lâcheté* (=fear or misery made him commit a cowardly act).

Habit will teach how to distinguish between these shades of difference. As a general rule, when **ou, ni** are *distributive*, the verb is in the *singular*; when they are *collective*, the verb is put in the *plural*.

395. When the verb has for its subject the relative pronoun **qui** (=who), it agrees in number and person with that pronoun which agrees itself with its antecedent: *c'est* **moi qui** *vous le dis, qui* **suis** *votre tuteur* (=it is I who tell you this, I who am your guardian).

Exercise 55.

1. Les convenances, son intérêt, l'honneur l'exige. 2. Prières, menaces, coups, rien ne peut le corriger. 3. Camille ainsi que Maxime est très-paresseux. 4. La vérité comme la conscience est inaltérable. 5. C'est vous qui avez jeté des pierres dans mon jardin. 6. L'un et l'autre sont parfaitement oubliés. 7. Mon cousin ou son frère aura sa place. 8. Votre sœur ou ma tante viendront ce soir. 9. Le prince avec ses compagnons se cacha dans une caverne. 10. J'espère que ni vous ni lui ne parlerez. 11. Ni l'un ni l'autre n'étaient musiciens. 12. 'Un seul mot, un soupir, un coup d'œil nous trahit.

[1] Sarrasins, [2] Damiette, [3] réussir à.

1. He and I, we shall go into the country. 2. Fear or want cause all his movements. 3. Our peril or safety is not a thing which interests you. 4. The elephant, like the castor, likes

society. 5. It is a satire, not a useful book, that he has written. 6. Neither of them will come. 7. Neither you nor I are wrong. 8. It was Themistocles and Miltiades who vanquished the Persians. 9. I am Louis, king of France, who repulsed the Saracens[1] at Damietta.[2] 10. Entreaties, threats, harsh measures, nothing succeeded in[3] making him speak. 11. His courage, his perseverance, his endurance astonishes me.

III. COMPLEMENT OF THE VERB.

396. Two or more verbs can have a common complement, but only when these verbs do not require complements of a different nature: *l'enfant doit* **chérir** *et* **respecter** *ses parents* (=the child ought to love and respect his parents); in this sentence, *parents* may serve as a complement to both verbs *chérir* and *respecter*, because we say *chérir quelqu'un, respecter quelqu'un* (=to love a person, to respect a person); but with a verb governing an indirect complement like *obéir* (=to obey), for instance, we could not use *parents* as a common complement; we could not say, for example: *l'enfant doit* **obéir** *et* **respecter** *ses parents* (=the child ought to obey and respect his parents); it is then necessary to express both complements: *l'enfant doit respecter* **ses parents** *et* **leur** *obéir*.

397. When a verb has two or more complements, these complements ought to be of the same nature; we might say correctly: *il* **aime à** *chanter et à dessiner* (=he likes to sing and to draw), or *il aime* **le** *chant et* **le** *dessin* (=he likes singing and drawing), but we cannot say: *il aime* **le** *chant et* **à** *dessiner* (=he likes singing and to draw).

398. A verb cannot have two indirect complements, when the latter is a mere repetition of the former; thus, we must not say: *c'est* **à vous à qui** *je parle, c'est* **de vous dont** *il s'agit*, but *c'est* **à vous que** *je parle* (=it is to you I am speaking), *c'est* **vous dont** *il s'agit* (=it is you who are in question); or *c'est* **vous à qui** *je parle, c'est* **de vous qu'il** *s'agit*.

The same remark applies to the adverb *où*; we must not say: *c'est ici où il demeure, c'est là où je vais*, but *c'est ici qu'il demeure* (= it is here that he lives), *c'est là que je vais* (= it is there that I am going).

399. Some verbs are both transitive and intransitive; such are: *aider* (= to help), *présider* (= to preside), *satisfaire* (= to satisfy), *suppléer* (= to supply or fill up). *Aider quelqu'un* and *aider à quelqu'un* both mean to help a person; *présider une séance* (= to take the chair at a meeting), *présider à une solemnité* (= to have the management of a solemnity); *satisfaire* takes *à* before a noun of thing: *j'ai satisfait à mes engagements* (= I have met my liabilities), but *j'ai satisfait mon maître* (= I have satisfied my master); *suppléer quelqu'un* (= to supply a person's place), *suppléer quelque chose* (= to supply a deficiency in some article which is not complete), *suppléer à quelque chose* (= to make up for one thing by another).

400. The passive verbs govern their complement with the preposition **de** or **par**; **de** must be used when the action expressed results from an operation of the soul: *il est redouté de tout le monde* (= he is dreaded by everybody); **par** should be used if the action expressed is *bodily* or *mental*: *il a été tué par un soldat* (= he has been killed by a soldier); *il a été instruit par son frère aîné* (= he has been taught by his eldest brother).

401. Par, however, is sometimes used to avoid the repetition of **de**: *la proposition a été approuvée d'une commune voix par tous les membres présents* (= the proposal was accepted unanimously by all the members present).

402. NOTICE that any preposition used in English in the sense of *in order to* is generally expressed in French by the preposition **pour**: *il est venu pour faire votre portrait* (= he came to make your portrait). Sometimes the preposition is not expressed: *allez le voir* (= go and see him), *venez me chercher* (= come and fetch me).

403. The following verbs take no preposition before their direct object:—

aimer mieux	(=to like better)	défendre * †	(=to forbid)
apercevoir	(=to perceive)	demander * †	(=to ask for)
approuver	(=to approve)	désirer	(=to desire)
assurer *	(=to assure)	payer *	(=to pay for)
attendre†	(=to wait, to expect)	prier	(=to beg of)
chercher‡	(=to look for, to seek)	regarder	(=to look on)
compter	(=to count, to reckon)	vouloir	(=to be willing, to wish).
craindre†	(=to fear)		

404. The following verbs, which take no preposition in English, must be followed by **à** in French:—

attenter à	(=to attempt)	pardonner à*	(=to pardon)
convenir à	(=to suit)	permettre à†	(=to allow)
défendre à†	(=to forbid)	plaire à	(=to please)
dire à†	(=to tell, to say)	promettre à†	(=to promise)
se fier à	(=to trust)	répondre à	(=to answer)
obéir à	(=to obey)	succéder à	(=to succeed).

405. The following verbs are followed by **de** in French:—

abuser de	(=to abuse)
approcher de	(=to approach)
avoir garde de	(=to take care not to, to mind lest)
changer de	(=to change)
convenir de	(=to agree to)
douter de	(=to doubt)
jouir de	(=to enjoy)
manquer de	(=to want)
se moquer de	(=to laugh at)
se servir de	(=to use)
se souvenir de	(=to remember)
user de	(=to use).

Exercise 56.

1. Elle le regrette et s'en repent. 2. Il obéit à son général et le respecte beaucoup. 3. Est-ce à moi que vous parlez ? 4. C'est sur le mont Sinaï que Dieu donna sa loi à Moïse. 5. C'est à lui

---

* *Assurer une chose à quelqu'un* (=to assure some one of a thing)
  défendre „ „ (=to forbid some one to do a thing)
  demander „ „ (=to ask some one for a thing)
  payer „ „ (=to pay some one for a thing)
  pardonner „ „ (=to pardon some one for a thing).

† *Attendre, craindre, défendre, demander, dire, permettre, promettre* take the preposition **de** before an infinitive.

‡ *Chercher* requires the preposition **à** before an infinitive.

que j'écris. 6. M. Bourdet a présidé à la distribution des prix. 7. J'ai satisfait tout le monde. 8. Il touchait au port quand il a fait naufrage. 9. Nous avons loué une salle pour recevoir nos amis ce soir-là. 10. Il a été blessé de votre manière de parler. 11. Son père a été grièvement blessé par la chute d'une poutre.

[1] aller à cheval, [2] aimer, [3] coup de pistolet, [4] malle (*f.*)

1. Charles went out to look for his brother. 2. He assured my father that the letter had been sent. 3. This house does not suit your uncle. 4. You ought not to trust him. 5. Can you agree about the price? 6. He asked his father for the newspaper. 7. I don't think he ever assured any one of a thing of which he was not certain. 8. The letter was written by James. 9. He rode [1] to and returned from Kingston in two hours and a-half. 10. He is very fond of [2] [to] walking and riding. 11. The gamekeeper was wounded by a pistol-shot [3] by the gardener. 12. I had this trunk [4] made to go to America.

IV. USE OF THE AUXILIARY VERBS.

406. We have seen (§ 153) that some neuter verbs take **avoir** and others **être** in their compound tenses. The former is used to mark the *action*: *il* **a passé** *en Australie au mois de mai* (=he went to Australia in the month of May). The auxiliary **être** expresses a *state*; *il* **est passé** *en Australie depuis vingt ans* (=he has been in Australia these twenty years); we here express the state of his being a resident in Australia.

407. When these verbs can be used in an *active* sense they naturally take the verb *avoir*: *il* **a** *monté l'escalier* (=he has gone upstairs); *nous* **avons** *descendu nos livres* (=we have taken down our books); *il a passé la rivière* (=he has crossed the river).

408. A few neuter verbs change their auxiliary according to the difference of meaning; thus *convenir*, used instead of *plaire* (=to please), takes *avoir*: *cet homme ne m'a pas convenu* (=that man has not pleased me); in the sense of *to make an agreement* it takes *être*: *nous* **sommes** *convenus d'agir ainsi* (=we have agreed to act thus).

The verbs *demeurer* (=to remain), *expirer* (=to expire), *rester* (=to stay), the sense of which is susceptible of variation, follow the same rule.

409. The following verbs only take the auxiliary **avoir**:—

courir	(=to run)	*périr*	(=to perish)
dormir	(=to sleep)	*succomber*	(=to succumb)
languir	(=to languish)	*vivre*	(=to live)
marcher	(=to walk)	*survivre*	(=to outlive)
paraître	(=to appear)	*triompher*	(=to triumph)

410. Twelve neuter verbs, of which a list is given in § 153, take the auxiliary **être** only.

411. The English make frequent use of auxiliaries. and such words as *do, did, shall, will,* etc., (1) in answers, (2) to question the truth of a statement, (3) to express surprise: (a) *Has Mr. Smith arrived? Yes, he has;* (b) *Is it Spanish he is reading? Yes, it is;* (c) *Will your brother come to-day? No, he will not;* (d) *He has bought a country house. Has he?*

The French language is less elliptical, and requires the sentence to be complete. The above sentences would be translated thus: (a) *Mr. Smith est-il arrivé? Oui,* **il est arrivé**; (b) *Est-ce de l'espagnol qu'il lit? Oui,* **c'en est**; (c) *Votre frère viendra-t-il aujourd'hui? Non,* **il ne viendra pas**; (d) *Il a acheté une maison de campagne.* **Vraiment!** or **en vérité**, or any other exclamation suited to the occasion.

NOTICE, therefore, that the auxiliary is not used alone, but that the principal verb and a noun or pronoun must be expressed; and that in exclamative sentences some suitable exclamation must be used in the shape of an adverb, a verb, or an interjection. (*See* § 139, and the rules on the position of pronouns.)

QUESTIONS FOR EXAMINATION.

1. State the rule for the agreement of the verb with its subject.
2. How is the rule affected when the subject is a collective noun?
3. In what number is the verb put after *la plupart?—le plus grand nombre,* etc.
4. What number does the verb take after *beaucoup* followed by a noun in the plural?—after *plus d'un?*
5. When does the verb *être*, preceded by *ce*, take the singular?—When does it take the plural?

6. State the exception to the rule.
7. When *impersonal* verbs are followed by a plural noun, what number do they take?
8. When is the verb, following several subjects, put in the singular?
9. In what number should the verb be written after two subjects connected by *ni?*—by *ou?*
10. When is the verb put in the singular after *ou* and *ni?*
11. In what number is the verb written after *l'un et l'autre?*
12. State the rule which affects the verb having as its subject the pronoun *qui.*
13. Can a verb have two complements?
14. Correct the fault in the expression *c'est à vous à qui je parle.*
15. What auxiliary do neuter verbs take when they express (*a*) *action,* (*b*) *state?*
16. Give a few neuter verbs conjugated (*a*) with *être,* (*b*) with *avoir,* (*c*) with either.
17. Explain how certain verbs alter their meaning, according to the auxiliary verb with which they are conjugated.

Exercise 57.

1. Est-ce à moi que vous parlez? Oui, c'est à vous. 2. J'ai passé quatre mois à Paris. 3. Mon frère est passé en Russie depuis plusieurs années. 4. Avez-vous descendu ma boîte à ouvrage? Oui, je l'ai descendue. 5. Cette maison lui a convenu. 6. Nous sommes convenus d'aller ensemble. 7. Elle a survécu à toute sa famille. 8. Il est tombé du haut de la maison. 9. Que sont devenus vos cousins? 10. Ils sont parvenus aux postes qu'ils cherchaient à obtenir. 11. Est-ce un roman que vous lisez? Oui, c'en est un. 12. Jacques est arrivé hier d'Afrique. Vraiment! déjà!

¹ revenir, ² *to bring upstairs* = monter, ³ descendre, ⁴ de.

1. You will write to your uncle, will you? Yes, I will. 2. Your brother has not yet returned¹ from America. 3. We agreed to meet at the station at twelve o'clock. 4. James and Henry have brought the table and the chairs upstairs.² 5. These books have not yet been taken down.³ 6. The lease has expired yesterday. 7. He stayed three years in that town. 8. Charles triumphed over⁴ all his enemies. 9. Is that your carriage? Yes, it is. 10. Is it an Italian book you are reading? Yes, it is. 11. Do you give these boys translations to do? No, I do not. 12. Should you like to stay there? Yes, indeed, I should. 13. The lease is expired since yesterday.

CHAPTER VII.

SYNTAX OF THE PARTICIPLES.

SECTION I.

AGREEMENT OF THE PRESENT PARTICIPLE.

412. The present participle is always invariable: *cette personne* **obligeant** *tous les malheureux est vraiment charitable* (= that person being kind to all the unfortunate is really charitable) ; *l'orage, nous* **effrayant** *tous, redoubla* (= the storm, frightening us all, redoubled in violence).

413. Taken as an adjective, the present participle is called a *verbal adjective*, and, like all other adjectives, follows the rules of agreement. The verbal adjective expresses a *state*: *l'obscurité est* **effrayante** (= the darkness is alarming) ; while the present participle expresses an *action*: *l'orage, en* **effrayant** *les animaux, dispersa tout le troupeau* (= the storm, in frightening the animals, dispersed the whole flock); we must, therefore, whilst examining a sentence, ascertain whether a *state* or an *action* is expressed.

414. There is *action*, and, consequently, no agreement:—

1. When the participle *has a direct complement*: *on n'entend plus les marteaux* **frappant** *l'enclume* (= the hammers are no longer heard striking the anvil);

2. When the participle is *preceded* by the preposition **en**: *la mer s'avance* **en** *mugissant* (= the sea advances, roaring);

3. When the participle is *followed* by an adverb: *une fille* **obéissant** *bien* (= a girl obeying faithfully), *des esprits* **agissant toujours** (= minds always busy).

415. *State* is expressed, and, therefore, agreement takes place :—

1. When the verbal adjective *is accompanied by the verb* **être**: *cette fleur* **est charmante** (= this flower is charming);

2. When the verbal adjective is *preceded by an adverb*: *une fille* **bien obéissante** (= a very obedient girl).

When the form in -*ant* is followed by an indirect or circumstantial complement, the sense alone can show whether there should be agreement or not. Thus we shall write: *voyez-vous ces débris* **flottant** *vers la côte?* (= do you see those fragments drifting towards the shore?); but *Calypso vit des cordages* **flottants** *sur la côte* (= Calypso saw on the shore floating cables). In the former example, *flottant* is invariable, because it is a participle and implies action; in the latter, *flottants* agrees with the noun, because it is an adjective, and shows the state of the cables which had long been left to the mercy of the waves.

☞ The present participle, so often used in English, must be translated into French by the indicative: *je la vois* **qui parle** *avec votre sœur* (= I see her speaking with your sister).

416. We have seen (§ 44) that the French language makes up fresh nouns with the help of the present participle: from *croyant, tranchant, débitant* the present participles of *croire* (= to believe), *trancher* (= to cut), *débiter* (= to retail), it forms *un croyant* (= a believer), *le tranchant* (= the edge [of a knife]), *un débitant* (= a retailer). All these words naturally follow the general rule for the formation of the plural of substantives: *des croyants, des tranchants, des débitants.*

We must not confound the present participles, such as *négligeant* (= neglecting), *adhérant* (= adhering), *différant* (= differing), *extravaguant* (= saying or doing odd things), with the adjectives *négligent* (= negligent), *adhérent* (= adherent), *différent* (= different), *extravagant* (= extravagant). The former are regularly derived from the French verbs *négliger, adhérer, différer, extravaguer*; the latter are real adjectives taken directly from the Latin. These adjectives cannot therefore, in any case, be called the verbal adjectives of *négliger, adhérer*, etc.

AGREEMENT OF THE PRESENT PARTICIPLE. 69

The following comparative list of present participles and verbal adjectives or nouns will be found useful:—

PRESENT PARTICIPLES.		ADJECTIVES.	
Adhérant	(=adhering)	Adhérent	(=adherent)
affluant	(=abounding)	affluent	(=confluent)
différant	(=differing)	différent	(=different)
excellant	(=excelling)	excellent	(=excellent)
expédiant	(=dispatching)	expédient	(=expedient)
extravaguant	(=rambling)	extravagant	(=extravagant)
fabriquant	(=manufacturing)	fabricant	(=manufacturer)
fatiguant	(=fatiguing)	fatigant	(=tiresome)
intriguant	(=plotting)	intrigant	(=intriguing)
négligeant	(=neglecting)	négligent	(=negligent)
précédant	(=preceding)	précédent	(=previous)
présidant	(=presiding)	président	(=president)
résidant	(=residing)	résident	(=resident)
violant	(=violating)	violent	(=violent)

QUESTIONS FOR EXAMINATION.

1. What is a *participle*?
2. How is the participle connected with the adjective?—with the verb?
3. How many kinds of participles are there?
4. Define a *verbal adjective*.
5. What is the difference between a verbal adjective and a present participle?
6. When is an *action* expressed?
7. When is a *state* expressed?
8. What rule does the present participle follow when used as a substantive?
9. Remark on the spelling of certain verbal adjectives or nouns.

Exercise 58.

1. Votre sœur est une charmante personne. 2. Les soldats d'Alexandre oubliant leur patrie ne songeaient qu'au butin. 3. Une dame obligeant ses amis. 4. Une preuve convainquante. 5. Les ennemis surprenant nos troupes n'eurent pas de peine à les vaincre. 6. Les émigrants sont partis de France sous Louis XVI. 7. Les fabricants ont décidé d'élever leurs prix. 8. En expédiant demain, les marchandises arriveront lundi. 9. Cet homme est des plus négligents.

[1] bêler, [2] convaincre, [3] amener, [4] s'efforcer, [5] attendrir, [6] passant, [7] soieries (*f.*), [8] gâter.

1. This delicious music, charming my senses, produces the desired effect. 2. My sister is more obliging than yours. 3. The effects of electricity are surprising. 4. We hear the bleating[1] sheep. 5. Your arguments, convincing[2] the judges, brought about[3] the prisoner's acquittal. 6. Beggars always endeavour[4] to work on the feelings of[5] the passers-by.[6] 7. It is in making silk

goods⁷ that the Lyons manufacturers become rich. 8. This is an excellent remedy. 9. The gummed paper adhering to the drawing had entirely spoiled⁸ it. 10. He has written to his adherents.

SECTION II.
AGREEMENT OF THE PAST PARTICIPLE.
1. General Principles.

217. When the past participle is joined to the substantive without the help of an auxiliary verb it is treated as an adjective—that is to say, it always agrees with the noun to which it refers in gender and number: *des mérites* **récompensés** (=merits rewarded), *des bonheurs* **passés** (=happiness past), *des lettres* **reçues** (=letters received).

218. When the past participle is preceded by the auxiliary verb **être** (=to be), it always agrees with the subject in gender and number: **il** *est venu* (=he is come), **elle** *est venue* (=she is come), **elles** *sont venues* (=they are come).

219. When the past participle is preceded by the auxiliary verb **avoir** (=to have), and is not accompanied by any complement, it is always invariable: **il** *a chanté* (=he has sung), **elle** *a chanté* (=she has sung), **ils** *ont chanté* or **elles** *ont chanté* (=they have sung).

2. The Past Participle used with the auxiliary verb être (=to be).

420. We have said that the past participle joined to the auxiliary verb **être** (=to be) always agrees with the subject: **la** *ville est ouverte* (=the town is open), **le** *port est fermé* (=the port is shut), **ces** *fleurs sont épanouies* (=these flowers are full-blown).

421. Consequently, **passive verbs**, being all conjugated with the auxiliary verb **être**, always have their past participle agreeing with the subject: **le** *roi est aimé* (=the king is loved), **la** *reine est aimée* (=the queen is loved), **les** *princes sont aimés* (=the princes are loved).

422. A few **neuter verbs** are conjugated with **être** (see § 153) and follow the same rule, such as *aller* (=to go), *venir* (=to come), *partir* (=to set out), *arriver* (=to arrive); conformably with the rule given in § 418, their past participle always agrees with the subject: **il est venu, elle** *est* **venue, ils** *sont* **venus, elles** *sont* **venues** (=he, she, they are come).

423. In the case of **impersonal verbs** conjugated with être, the participle agrees with the subject *il* (§ 420), and this pronoun being always invariable, it follows that the past participle never changes in verbs of this kind: **il** *est survenu un orage* (=a storm came on), **il** *est arrivé des malheurs* (=misfortunes happened).

For **reflexive verbs** see §§ 431-435.

424. We have seen (§ 205) that the French language creates new prepositions with the help of certain past participles, such as *excepté* (=except), *attendu* (=considering), *passé* (=past), etc., for instance, *excepté sa mère* (=except his mother), *attendu l'heure* (=considering the hour), *passé l'époque* (=the epoch being past), etc. In these cases the words *excepté, attendu*, etc., are always placed *before* the noun; but the same words are participles and agree with the noun when they are put *after* it: *sa mère except*ée, *l'heure attend*ue, *l'époque pass*ée.

3. The Past Participle used with the auxiliary avoir (=to have).

425. While the past participle with **être** depends upon the subject and agrees with it, the past participle united to **avoir** is always independent of the subject, and only agrees with the complement: **j'ai** *vu le roi*, **ils** *ont vu le roi* (=I have seen the king, they have seen the king), **le** *roi que j'ai* **vu, les** *rois que j'ai* **vus** (=the king whom I have seen, the kings whom I have seen).

426. The past participle with **avoir** varies when it is preceded by its direct complement, and it then agrees with that complement: les *chevaux que j'ai* **vus** (=the horses that I have seen); les *fleurs que j'ai coupées* (=the flowers that I have cut);

But it always remains invariable when the complement which precedes it is indirect: **de** *tous ces malheurs j'ai maintes fois* **gémi** (=I have oftentimes sighed over all these misfortunes); or when the direct complement follows the participle instead of preceding it: *j'ai* **vu la** *rose, j'ai* **vu des** *roses* (=I have seen the rose, I have seen some roses).

427. Neuter verbs, never having a direct complement, the past participle of these verbs, conjugated with **avoir,** is always invariable: *cette mauvaise action nous a* **nui** (=that bad action has proved injurious to us); *les mères ont* **gémi** *de tous ces malheurs* (=the mothers have groaned over all those misfortunes).

428. We have seen (§ 399) that a few verbs are employed sometimes as active, sometimes as neuter verbs. In the former case they follow the rule of the past participle conjugated with *avoir: cet homme nous a fidèlement* **servis** (=this man has served us faithfully, *i.e., a servi nous*).

But when they are employed as neuter verbs, they have no direct complement, and their participle remains invariable: *ces livres nous ont beaucoup* **servi** (=these books have been of much use to us, *i.e., ont servi à nous*).

429. Remarks.

1. The participles **coûté, valu** are invariable when employed in their proper sense—that is to say, when they express the idea of price, of value: *je regrette les dix mille francs que cette maison m'a* **coûté,** *parce qu'elle ne les a jamais* **valu** (=I regret the ten thousand francs which that house has cost me, because it was never worth so much).

These participles vary when employed in a figurative sense— that is to say, with the meaning of *to cause, to procure*: *n'oubliez jamais les peines que vous avez* **coûtées** *à votre mère* (=never forget the pangs you have cost your mother); *voilà les chagrins que vous a* **valus** *votre paresse* (=such are the sorrows which your idleness has brought upon you).

2. The past participle of the verbs **vivre** (=to live), **dormir** (=to sleep), régner (=to reign), is always invariable: *les jours qu'on a vécu dans l'oisireté sont perdus* (=the days spent in idleness are lost); *les heures qu'elle a dormi l'ont reposée* (=the hours she has slept have rested her); just as if the sentences had stood: *pendant lesquels on a vécu..., pendant lesquelles elle a reposé...*

430. Impersonal verbs, conjugated with *avoir,* having no direct complement, their past participle is always necessarily invariable: *il a neigé* (=it has snowed), *il a plu* (=it has rained). By analogy, this invariableness has been extended to the participle of active verbs employed as impersonal verbs: *les grandes chaleurs qu'il a fait* (=the great heat there has been), although these verbs have a direct complement, exactly like active verbs properly so called.

431. Reflexive verbs, as we have seen in § 156, can either be *verbs reflexive by nature* (*s'écrouler*=to fall down), or *active verbs* (*laver*=to wash), or *neuter verbs* (*nuire*=to injure), employed reflexively (*se laver*=to wash one's self, *se nuire*=to injure one's self). According to these three cases, the rule for the syntax of the past participle differs.

432. In the case of **verbs reflexive by nature,** like *s'écrouler* (=to fall down), *s'évanouir* (=to faint), *se cabrer* (=to rear), etc., the past participle is always variable, and agrees with the pronoun *se*, which represents the subject: *la jument s'est* **cabrée** (=the mare has reared); *la malade s'est* **évanouie** (=the invalid lady has fainted); *la maison s'est* **écroulée** (=the house has fallen down).

☞ In these verbs the auxiliary *être* is used instead of *avoir;* that is to say: *la jument a cabré* **elle,** *la malade a évanoui* **elle. Se** is then a direct object, and, as it precedes the participle, there must be agreement. (*See* § 426.)

REMARKS.—1. The verb *s'arroger*(=to arrogate to one's self) is the only verb *reflexive by nature* which does not take the preceding pronoun as its direct complement. We must accordingly write: *elles se sont* **arrogé** *certains droits qu'elles n'avaient pas* (=they have arrogated to themselves certain rights to which they had no claim). *Se* here stands for *à soi*, and is the indirect complement. But we shall write: *elles n'avaient pas les droits qu'elles se sont* **arrogés** (= they had not the rights which they have arrogated to themselves), because *arrogés* agrees with *que*, standing for *droits*, direct complement, and preceding the verb.

2. Under the category of verbs *reflexive by nature* certain verbs are placed, such as *apercevoir* (= to perceive), *attaquer* (= to attack), *attendre* (= to wait), *douter* (= to doubt), *plaindre* (= to pity), *prévaloir* (= to prevail), *saisir* (= to seize), *taire* (= to keep secret), etc., the meaning of which changes when they become reflexive: *elles se sont* **prévalues** *de leur jeunesse* (= they have taken advantage of their weakness); *elles se sont* **tues** (= they have remained silent).

433. For the reason given in § 432, the past participle of **active verbs** *employed as reflexive* always agree: *je me suis* **lavée** (= I washed myself); *ils se sont* **lavés** (= they have washed themselves), that is to say: *ils ont lavé eux*; and the past participle of **neuter verbs** *used as reflexive* is always invariable, because these verbs cannot have a direct complément: *elles se sont* **nui**, i.e., *elles ont nui* **à elles** (= they have injured themselves); *bien des rois se sont* **succédé** *sur le trône* (= many kings have occupied the throne in succession); *elles se sont* **ri** *de nos menaces* (= they have scorned our threats); *ils se sont* **plu** *à mal faire* (= they have delighted in doing evil).

434. When the direct complement follows, the past participle of the reflexive verb naturally remains invariable: *elle s'est* **brûlé** *le doigt* (= she has burnt her finger); *se* is here an indirect complement (*elle a brûlé le doigt* **à elle**). We must not confound this case with the former one, where we have seen that the past participle agrees, as in *elle s'est* **brûlée** *au doigt*—that is to say, *elle a brûlé* **elle** *au doigt*—*se* here being a direct complement.

4. Additional Remarks on the Agreement of the Participles.

435. When followed by an infinitive, the past participle agrees with the preceding noun or pronoun, provided that noun or pronoun is its direct complement:

ces femmes chantent bien; je les ai **entendues** *chanter* (=those women sing well; I have heard them sing). Here, *entendues* agrees with the pronoun *les*, standing for *femmes*: *j'ai entendu qui?* (=I have heard whom?) *ces femmes chanter* (=those women singing).

But the past participle remains invariable when it has the infinitive for its direct complement: *ces romances sont bien connues; je les ai* **entendu** *chanter à Paris* (=those ballads are well known; I have heard them sung in Paris). In this case, the past participle remains unchanged, as it is followed by its direct complement (*see* § 426), the infinitive *chanter*, which, moreover, is naturally invariable:* *j'ai entendu quoi?* (=I have heard what?) *chanter ces ballades* (=those ballads sung in Paris).

NOTE that when the past participle agrees, the infinitive is expressed in English by the present participle, and when the past participle does not agree, the infinitive is translated by the English past participle.

The past participle **fait**, followed by an infinitive, is always invariable: *les maisons qu'il a fait construire* (=the houses which he has had built). The participles **dû, pu, voulu** are invariable when we can supply a verb after them; *je lui ai rendu tous les services que j'ai pu et que j'ai* **dû** ([*lui rendre* is understood] =I have rendered him all the services which I could, and which it was my duty to render him); *je lui ai lu tous les livres qu'il a* **voulu** ([*que je lui lusse* is understood] =I have read to him all the books he wished that I should read [to him]). But we must say: *j'ai payé les sommes que j'ai* **dues** (=I have paid the sums I owed); because the past participle *dues* agrees with its direct object *que*, standing for the substantive feminine plural *sommes*.

436. When **le**, signifying *cela* (=this, that), precedes the past participle, this latter word is always invariable: *sa tranquillité n'est pas aussi assurée qu'il l'aurait* **désiré**, (=his tranquility is not so secure as he would have wished), i.e., *il aurait désiré cela, à savoir, que sa tranquillité fût définitivement assurée* (=he would have

---

* Remember that the infinitive is always in the masculine gender, when used as a substantive: *le boire et le manger* (=eating and drinking).

wished that, namely, that his tranquility would have been quite secure).

We have seen (§ 320) that *le* (in the sense of *cela*) is a vestige of the Latin neuter, and that for this reason the invariableness of the participle is easily explained.

437. The past participle placed between **que**, relative, and **que**, conjunction, is invariable: *les livres* **que** *j'avais* **présumé que** *vous liriez* (= the books which I thought you would read); here the relative *que* is the direct complement, not of the past participle, but of the following proposition. Locutions of this kind should be avoided.

438. The past participle preceded by **en** is invariable: *tout le monde m'a offert des services, mais personne ne m'en a rendu* (= everyone has offered me services, but no one has rendered me any).

But the agreement takes place when the pronoun **en** is preceded by an adverb of quantity: *plus il a eu de livres,* **plus** *il* **en** *a lus* (= the more books he has had, the more he has read, *i.e. plus de livres il a lus*).

However, there is no agreement if the adverb follows the pronoun **en** instead of preceding it: *j'***en** *ai* **beaucoup** *vu* (= I have seen many of them); *j'***en** *ai* **tant** *visité* (= I have visited so many of them).

439. The past participle preceded by the locution **le peu** varies according to the meaning of that locution.

When **le peu** signifies *a small quantity*, the participle agrees with the noun: **le peu** *de nourriture qu'il a* **prise** *l'a sauvé* (= the little nourishment he has taken has saved him, *i.e.* the amount of nourishment, however small, has sufficed to save him).

When **le peu** means *insufficiency, want, lack*, the participle is invariable: *c'est* **le peu** *de nourriture qu'il a* **pris** *qui a causé sa mort* (= it is the insufficient amount of food he has taken which has caused his death).

5. Summary.

440. To sum up, the past participle, joined to the auxiliary **être** (=to be), agrees with the subject;

Joined to the auxiliary **avoir** (=to have), it agrees with the direct complement if the complement precedes it, and remains invariable if the direct complement follows it, or if there is no complement at all.

441. We have seen successively the application of this general rule to the past participles of *active* verbs (§ 419), *passive* (§ 421), *neuter* with *être* (§ 422), *impersonal* with *être* (§ 423), *neuter* with *avoir* (§ 427), *impersonal* with *avoir* (§ 430), *reflexive by nature* (§ 432), *reflexive by accident*, either *neuter* (§ 433) or *active* (§ 433); finally, to participles followed by an *infinitive* (§ 435), or accompanied by certain locutions (§§ 436—439).

QUESTIONS FOR EXAMINATION.

1. State the rule of the past participle used as an adjective.
2. Explain the rules applicable to the past participle used with (*a*) *avoir*, (*b*) *être*.
3. What is the rule for the past participle of (*a*) *passive* verbs, (*b*) *neuter* verbs, (*c*) *impersonal* verbs?
4. Remark on *attendu, passé, supposé*.
5. When does the past participle accompanied by *avoir* agree?
6. When does it remain unchanged?
7. State the rule for the *neuter* past participle accompanied by *avoir*.
8. State the rule which affects *coûté, valu, vécu, dormi*, etc.
9. What is the rule for the past participle of *impersonal* verbs conjugated with *avoir*?
10. How do verbs *reflexive by nature* agree?
11. Remark on *s'arroger, s'apercevoir, s'attaquer*.
12. State the rule which affects (1) *active* verbs used *reflexively*; (2) *neuter* verbs used in the same manner.
13. Explain the rule for the past participle followed by an infinitive.
14. What is the rule for *dû, pu, voulu*?
15. What happens when the participle is (1) placed between two *que*'s, (2) preceded by *en*, (3) preceded by *le*?
16. When does the participle agree with *le peu*? When does it agree with the complement of *le peu*?

Exercise 59.

1. Que de remparts détruits! Que de villes forcées! 2. Il a quatre maisons, y compris sa maison de campagne. 3. Vous trouverez mes trois lettres ci-incluses. 4. Dieu nous a distingués des autres animaux, surtout par le don de la parole. 5. Didon a fondé sur la côte d'Afrique la superbe ville de Carthage. 6. Les jours qu'il a conversé avec ses enfants. 7. Bossuet a créé une

langue que lui seul a parlée. 8. Elles s'en sont allées sans me voir. 9. Saturne eut trois fils qui se sont partagé le domaine de l'univers. 10. La disette qu'il y a eu pendant l'hiver. 11. Il s'est trouvé dix personnes chez moi. 12. Je l'ai rendue horrible à ses yeux inhumains. 13. Ils se sont percé le corps. 14. Elles se sont tranquillisées peu à peu.

1. The books which I have bought are well bound. 2. His fortune was greater than I had believed it. 3. You have made her laugh. 4. How many hares did you kill? I killed four (of them). 5. We must deduct from life the hours we have slept. 6. He has helped us with his purse. 7. I have helped her to come downstairs. 8. The soldiers whom the general condemned were put to death yesterday. 9. I know the tune to which you allude; I heard it sung last week. 10. We have met, but have not spoken to one another. 11. Great misfortunes have happened to your father. 12. The troops have marched across a barren country. 13. They seemed astonished. 14. She has broken both her arms.

CHAPTER VIII.
SYNTAX OF ADVERBS.

442. We may give, as a general rule, that the adverb is placed *after the verb* in the simple tenses: *il réussira* **probablement** *dans cette entreprise* (= he will probably succeed in this undertaking); and *between the auxiliary and the verb* in the compound tenses: *il l'a* **entièrement** *oublié* (= he has entirely forgotten it).

Bien, mal, fort, beaucoup, peu always follow this rule.

443. NOTE that the adverb is never placed in French, as in English, between the conjunctive pronoun subject and the verb: *vous venez* **toujours** *en retard* (= you *always* come late).

444. Adverbs of *time* or *place* are sometimes put at the commencement, and sometimes at the end of the sentence: *il est venu me voir* **hier** *avec son frère*, or **hier** *il est venu me voir avec son frère* (= yesterday he came to see me with his brother).

SYNTAX OF ADVERBS. 79

445. The *negative* consists of two parts, one of which is always **ne**, when the two words are to be expressed; the other varies according to the meaning. The principal adverbs of negation are:—

ne...pas	(=not)
ne...point	(=not at all)
ne...rien	(=nothing)
ne...jamais	(=never)
ne...plus	(=ne...more)
ne...que	(=only)

446. If **pas** or **point** is followed by a noun in the partitive sense, this noun is simply preceded by **de**:—

Affirm.: *j'ai du pain* (=I have some bread)
Negat.: *je n'ai pas de pain* (=I have no bread)

447. Ne is always placed *before*, and **pas, point**, etc. *after the verb* in the simple tenses, and *between the auxiliary and the verb* in the compound tenses: *je* **ne** *vois* **pas** (=I do not see); *je* **n'ai pas** *mangé* (=I have not eaten).

448. With the *present* infinitive the two parts of the negative are not separated, as:—

ne pas *se venger* (=not to revenge one's self)
ne plus *écrire* (=to write no more).

449. If the verb is in the perfect of the infinitive, it is optional to separate them or not, as:—

Not to have slept { **ne pas** *avoir dormi*
{ **n'***avoir* **pas** *dormi*.

450. When used without a verb, the negatives stand without **ne**, as:—

pas *à la fois* (=not at once)   **pas** *moi* (=not I)
pas *beaucoup* (=not much)   **pas** *trop* (=not too much)
pas *tant* (=not so much)   **pas** *aujourd'hui* (=not to day).

451. Non plus (=neither) requires the full negation **ne...pas** before it, as:—

je **ne** *le veux* **pas non plus** (=neither will I have it).

452. If the words **nor...either** are only connected with a noun or pronoun without a verb, the noun or the pronoun is preceded in French by **ni**, as :—

ni *Charles* **non plus** (= nor Charles either).

453. Observe the expression **ne...que** meaning *only*, as :—

je n'ai **que** *deux sœurs* (= I have only two sisters).

454. Ne is used before the second verb :—

1. After words expressing apprehension or fear, such as the verbs **appréhender** (= to apprehend), **avoir peur** (= to dread), **prendre garde** (= to take care), **empêcher** (= to prevent), etc. : *empêchez qu'on* **ne** *lui parle* (= prevent any one from speaking to him) ; *prends garde qu'il* **ne** *sorte* (= take care lest he should go out) ;

2. After the verb **craindre** (= to fear), and the conjunctive locutions **de crainte que, de peur que** (= for fear lest...), etc., when the thing expressed by the second proposition is *not* desired (see § 510) : *taisez-vous, de peur qu'on* **ne** *vous entende* (= hold your tongue, lest any one should hear you) ;

3. After a comparative of *inferiority* or *superiority*, and the words **autre, autrement** : *il est plus savant que vous* **ne** *pensez* (= he is more learned than you think) ; *il est moins riche qu'on* **ne** *croit* (= he is less rich than people imagine) ; *il pense autrement qu'il* **ne** *parle* (= he thinks differently from what he says) ;

4. When both propositions are negative : *le singe n'est pas plus de notre espèce que nous* **ne** *sommes de la sienne* (= the monkey no more belongs to our species than we belong to his, *i.e.*, we do not belong to his).

5. After **il s'en faut** accompanied by a negative or the negative expressions **peu, presque, rien** : *il ne s'en faut pas de beaucoup que la somme* **n'y** *soit* (= it wants little to make up the necessary sum) ; *peu s'en faut que je* **n'**interrompe *mon discours* (= a little more would make me interrupt my speech) ;

SYNTAX OF ADVERBS. 81

6. After **à moins que**: *il partira demain à moins que vous n'alliez le voir ce soir* (=he will leave to-morrow unless you go and see him this evening).

455. Ne is suppressed before the second verb:—

1. After a verb accompanied by a negative: *je ne crains pas qu'il vienne* (=I do not dread his coming);

2. After **défendre** (=to prohibit): *il défendit qu'aucun étranger entrât dans la ville* (=he prohibited all strangers from entering the town);

3. After the locutions **avant que** (=before), **sans que** (=without): *j'irai le voir avant qu'il parte* (=I shall go and see him before his departure); *je ne puis parler sans qu'il m'interrompe* (=I cannot speak without his interrupting me).

Ne may be inserted after **empêcher** (=to hinder), **douter** (=to doubt), **nier** (=to deny), **disconvenir** (=to disagree), **contester** (=to contest), used negatively: *on ne peut douter que les pôles ne soient couverts de glace* (=we cannot doubt but that the poles are covered with ice).

456. Pas and **point** may be suppressed:

1. After the verbs **pouvoir, cesser, oser**, and the conjunction **si**, especially in the locutions: *si ce n'est* or *si ce n'était* (=were it not, unless, except); *il ne cesse de parler* (=he does not leave off speaking); *je n'ose l'aborder* (=I dare not approach him); *je ne puis me taire* (=I cannot remain silent); *mon frère me ressemble, si ce n'est qu'il est plus petit* (=my brother resembles me, only he is shorter); *si ce n'était la crainte de vous déplaire* (=were it not for the fear of displeasing you);

2. After **il y a, depuis que**, in the compound tenses: *il y a un an que je ne l'ai vu* (=it is a year since I saw him).

3. When **autre...que** is used: *je n'ai d'autre but que de vous être utile* (=I have no other object than to be useful to you);

Syntax   G

If *autre* is understood, **pas** or **point** must be suppressed: *il n'a de volonté que la mienne* (=he has no other will but mine).

4. After **prendre garde** (=to avoid): *prenez garde qu'on ne vous trompe* (=take care that they do not deceive you).

457. Pas and **point** must be suppressed:—

1. After **savoir** used instead of *pouvoir*: *je ne saurais vous montrer le chemin* (=I cannot show you the way).

2. After **que** meaning *pourquoi* (=why): *que n'êtes vous arrivé plus tôt?* (=why did you not come sooner)?

3. When two negatives are joined by **ni**: *je ne parle ni n'écris* (=I neither speak nor write).

458. Point is more emphatic than **pas**: *je ne l'aime* **pas** (=I do not like him, her, or it); *je ne l'aime* **point** (=I do not like him, her, or it at all).

459. Plus tôt, plutôt. Plus tôt, in two words, means *avant* (=sooner), and is the opposite of **plus tard** (=later): *il est arrivé* **plus tôt** *que vous* (=he arrived sooner than you).

Plutôt, in one word, expresses an idea of choice, preference: **plutôt** *la mort que le déshonneur!* (=death rather than dishonour!).

460. Auparavant, davantage. Both these adverbs, being taken absolutely, must never be followed by either *de* or *que*. *Il a* **davantage** *de livres* **que** *moi* is wrong; we should say: *il a* **plus** *de livres* **que** *moi* (=he has more books than I). **Auparavant** *qu'il vienne* is also wrong; we should say: **avant** *qu'il vienne* (=before he comes).

461. Si, aussi, tant, autant.—Aussi and **autant** are used *exclusively* in partitive, whilst **tant** and **si** are *generally* used in negative sentences: *j'ai* **autant** *de livres que vous* (=I have as many books as you); *il est* **aussi** *savant que son ami* (=he is as learned as his friend); *je n'ai pas* **tant** *d'argent que vous* (=I have not so much money as you); *il n'est pas*

si *riche que son frère* (=he is not so rich as his brother). **Aussi** and **autant**, however, are sometimes used in negative sentences.

462. Mal parler, parler mal. Care should be taken to distinguish between these two expressions; **mal parler** means *to slander, to make use of offensive or insulting language;* **parler mal** means *to speak ungrammatically.*

463. Oui, si. Oui is used in answer to an affirmative question: *avez-vous de la monnaie?* **oui**, *monsieur* (=have you any change? yes, sir); **si** is employed when the question is put negatively: *n'avez-vous pas perdu votre bourse?* **si**, *madame* (=have you not lost your purse? yes, madam).

464. Aussi, non plus. These two adverbs, taken in the sense of *likewise, equally,* are used, the former in affirmative, the latter in negative sentences: *j'irai le voir, et moi* **aussi** (=I shall go and see him; so shall I); *je n'ai pas lu ce livre; ni moi* **non plus** (=I have not read that book; no more have I).

465. De suite, tout de suite. De suite means *successively, without interruption:* il ne *travaille pas deux heures* **de suite** (=he does not work two hours successively); **tout de suite** means *immediately:* je viens **tout de suite** (=I am coming immediately).

466. Partant, pourtant. Partant means *therefore, accordingly: peu courtisan,* **partant** *homme de foi* (=little of a courtier, therefore a man to be trusted); **pourtant** means *nevertheless: c'est un grand général, et* **pourtant** *il a été battu* (=he is a great general, nevertheless, he has been defeated).

QUESTIONS FOR EXAMINATION.

1. What is the place of the adverb?
2. What is the distinctive sign of negation in French?
3. When is *ne* used?
4. When is *ne* suppressed?
5. After what verbs are *pas* and *point* left out?
6. What is the difference between *pas* and *point?*
7. Distinguish between *plutôt* and *plus tôt—si, aussi* and *tant, autant—mal parler* and *parler mal—oui* and *si—aussi* and *non plus—de suite* and *tout de suite—partant* and *pourtant.*

Exercise 60.

1. On se repent rarement de parler peu, mais souvent de parler trop. 2. Ce qui se fait avec plaisir est ordinairement bien fait. 3. Il a plu aujourd'hui. 4. Autrefois on commençait plus tôt ses études, et on les terminait beaucoup plus tard. 5. Nous périrons jusqu'au dernier plutôt que de nous rendre. 6. Quelque méchants que soient les hommes, ils n'oseraient paraître ennemis de la vertu. 7. On se voit d'un autre œil qu'on ne voit son prochain. 8. Vous ne sauriez nier qu'un homme apprend beaucoup de choses en voyageant. 9. Plus on aime une personne, moins on doit la flatter. 10. Plus d'amour, partant plus de joie. 11. Cromwell couchait rarement deux nuits de suite dans la même chambre. 12. Faites votre devoir tout de suite.

1. There are persons who write better than they speak, and others who speak better than they write. 2. He does nothing but play from morning till night. 3. I do not blame him the less for it. 4. My clerk is more punctual than he was. 5. My little girl can scarcely write, and she reads with difficulty. 6. Have you ever been to Paris? 7. He disappeared suddenly. 8. I lost £10,000 at one single stroke. 9. However clever you may be, you should not despise the advice of your friends. 10. Your brother expresses himself incorrectly. 11 Never speak evil of any one. 12. It is now two years since I met with that accident. 13. I tremble lest you should be seen. 14. His wants are small, and therefore he is happy.

CHAPTER IX.
SYNTAX OF PREPOSITIONS.

467. Prepositions are always placed in French *before* the words to which they relate, and never *after*, as is sometimes the case in English, as:—

de *quoi se plaint-il?* (= what does he complain of?)

Durant is the only exception, as we can say: *sa vie* **durant** (= during his life). (See § 205.)

468. The preposition **à** is used for *to,** *at,* or *in,*

* NOTICE that the preposition *to,* when it is used in English as the sign of the infinitive, is not translated into French: *manger trop nuit* (= *to* eat too much is hurtful).

before proper names of places, such as towns, villages, etc., and the preposition **en** is used for *to* or *in* before names of countries and provinces, as:—

mon père est **à** *Paris* (=my father is at or in Paris)
nous allons **en** *Ecosse* (=we are going to Scotland).

If, however, the name of the country requires the article, the preposition **à** is used; as: *il est* **au** *Brésil* (=he is in Brazil).

NOTICE the difference between the expressions **à terre** and **par terre**: **à terre** is used when a thing raised above the ground falls; and **par terre** when the accident happens to a thing or person standing on the ground.

469. En is used with nouns taken in a vague and indeterminate sense, and is not generally followed by the article. **Dans**, on the contrary, is used with nouns taken in a more determinate sense, and requires the article; as: *je demeure* **en** *Angleterre*, **dans** *le comté de Middlesex* (=I live in England, in the county of Middlesex). **En** is used before a pronoun; as: *mon espoir est* **en** *vous* (=my hope is in you).

NOTICE the difference of meaning between **en** and **à** in the following phrases: *le général est* **à** *la campagne* (=the general is in the country); *le général est* **en** *campagne* (=the general has taken the field); *mon maître est* **à** *la ville* (=my master is in town, [by opposition to the country]); *je dîne* **en** *ville* (=I dine out).

470. *In* is translated by **en** when we speak of the time it takes to do a thing: *on va de Londres à Paris* **en** *dix heures* (=it takes ten hours to go from London to Paris).

In is translated by **dans** when we point out the time at which a thing is to be begun: *j'irai à Rome* **dans** *six mois* (=I shall go to Rome six months hence).

471. Avant means *before*, with reference to time or order; **devant** is used for *before*, with reference to place: *ne vous tenez pas* **devant** *moi* (=don't stand before me); **avant** *la fin du mois* (=before the end of the month).

472. Parmi (=among) is used when the person or thing alluded to is in the midst of others: *je l'ai trouvé* **parmi** *mes livres* (=I have found it amongst my books). **Entre** should be used (*a*) when only two persons or things are mentioned; and (*b*) when the persons or things alluded to are not connected together: *je suis* **entre** *mes amis* (=I am between my [two] friends); *la jalousie* **entre** *poëtes est chose assez commune* (=jealousy amongst poets is common enough).

473. Vers (=towards) is used with reference to nouns which indicate *place* or *time:* **vers** *la porte* (=towards the door), **vers** *le quatorzième siècle* (=towards the fourteenth century). **Envers** means *with regard to*, and is used after words implying *behaviour: charitable* **envers** *les pauvres* (=charitable to the poor).

474. Care must be taken not to confound the prepositions **sur** (=upon), and **sous** (=under) with the corresponding adverbs **dessus** (=above) and **dessous** (=underneath).

475. Dessus and **dessous** are used as prepositions when both are used together: *j'ai cherché* **dessus** *et* **dessous** *le lit* (=I have looked on and under the bed).

476. Pour is the word generally used to express *for: faites cela* **pour** *moi* (=do this for me). **Malgré, nonobstant** mean *for* in the sense of *notwithstanding:* **malgré** *tout cela, il n'a pas réussi* (=for all that, he did not succeed).

477. Pendant, durant refer to *time: il a été en Turquie* **pendant** *un mois* (=he has been in Turkey for a month).

478. Depuis corresponds to *since: je n'ai pas vu votre ami* **depuis** *six mois* (=I have not seen your friend for [or since] six months)

SYNTAX OF PREPOSITIONS.

479. Vis-à-vis (=opposite) is construed with **de**: *je me plaçai* **vis-à-vis de** *lui* (= I placed myself opposite to him).

In the colloquial style custom sanctions the following phrases: **vis-à-vis** *notre maison*, (=opposite our house) **vis-à-vis** *le palais* (=opposite the palace).

On *vis-à-vis*, see § 206

480. The prepositive locution **vis-à-vis** is never used figuratively. We must say *ingrat* **envers son** *bienfaiteur*, and not **vis-à-vis de** *son bienfaiteur* (=ungrateful towards his benefactors).

481. Au travers is always followed by the preposition **de**, whilst **à travers** never takes it: *il se fit jour* **au travers des** *ennemis* (=he fought his way through the enemies); *il marchait* **à travers** *les épines* (=he was walking through the thorns).

482. Voici announces what we are about to say; **voilà** recalls what has been said: **voici** *ce que je vous apporte: une histoire, une grammaire, un atlas* (=here is what I bring you: a history, a grammar, an atlas); *la prudence et la sagesse,* **voilà** *ce que Salomon demanda à Dieu* (=prudence and wisdom, that is what Solomon asked of God).

483. All prepositions in French require the following verb in the infinitive (present *or* perfect), except **en**, which takes the present participle.

484. The prepositions **à, de**, and **en** are always repeated before every complement: *il dut la vie* **à** *la clémence et* **à** *la magnanimité du vainqueur* (=he owed his life to the clemency and the magnanimity of the conqueror).

The other prepositions should also be repeated, unless the various complements are synonyms: **dans** *la paix et* **dans** *la guerre* (=in peace and in war); **dans** *le désordre et l'intempérance* (=in disorder and intemperance).

285. De and **à.** In the following sentences the idea of duty is implied:—

c'est à vous de me suivre (=it is your duty to follow me).
c'est à moi d'obéir (=it is my duty to obey).

The idea expressed in the following phrases is that of turn, rotation:—

est-ce à lui à jouer ? (=is it his turn to play ?)
c'est à elle à parler (=it is her turn to speak).

486. The use of the preposition **de** often alters entirely the meaning of certain phrases:—

il ne fait que parler (=he does nothing but speak).
il ne fait que **de** parler (=he has only just spoken).

De is also used in some particular sentences:—

1. After *quelque chose, rien, quoi, quelqu'un, personne, pas, point,* etc.: *je* **n'ai rien** *vu* **d'**étonnant (=I have not seen anything astonishing).

2. Before a past participle preceded by a noun of number (in this case the use of *de* is optional): *il y a eu vingt-cinq hommes tués* or **de** *tués* (=there have been twenty-five men killed).

487. Chez (=at the house of) can be preceded by **de**: *je sors* **de chez** *vous* (=I come from your house).

☞ **Chez moi, chez soi,** etc., can also be used as substantives: *j'ai* **un chez moi** (=I have a home).

QUESTIONS FOR EXAMINATION.

1. State the rule and exception for the placing of prepositions.
2. Explain the difference between *à, en,* and *dans*.
3. When is *devant* used ? What relation does *avant* express ?
4. Distinguish between *entre* and *parmi*.
5. What are the adverbs corresponding to the prepositions *sur* and *sous* ?
6. State the difference between *vis-à-vis* and *envers, à travers* and *au travers, voici* and *voilà* ?
7. What prepositions must always be repeated ? When should all prepositions be repeated ?
8. Show, by examples, in how many ways the English preposition *for* can be translated into French.
9. Remark on certain idiomatic uses of *de* and *à*.

Exercise 61.

1. Il y a une inscription curieuse sur cette médaille. 2. Ils se sont battus pendant deux jours. 3. Il se place toujours devant moi à table. 4. Le bateau à vapeur de Boulogne est arrivé avant

celui de Calais. 5. Les troupes du roi de Prusse sont en campagne. 6. Madame dinera-t-elle en ville aujourd'hui ? 7. Le trajet de Paris à Bordeaux se fait en quelques heures. 8. Le général partira dans trois jours. 9. J'ai cinquante volumes à vendre, et il y en a de bien reliés. 10. A qui dois-je m'adresser ? 11. La charité ne fait rien sans réflexion ni sans ordre. 12. L'orage a éclaté vers cinq heures. 13. Nous arriverons jeudi prochain. 14. Voici des fleurs que j'ai cueillies pour vous. 15. La droiture du cœur, la vérité, l'innocence, l'empire sur les passions : voilà la véritable grandeur. 16. En essayant de ramasser les livres qui étaient tombés à terre, je suis tombé par terre.

1. Alexander took the field at the head of an army of forty thousand men. 2. Be dutiful to your parents. 3. I never dine out more than once a week. 4. He will arrive on Tuesday, a week before my brother. 5. The elm was planted in front of the house. 6. I shall remain in London for a month. 7. Has the servant looked for my bracelet upon and under the table? Yes, she has. 8. All the plums have fallen down. 9. On arriving at Dover, we went to the hotel. 10. I have not read Homer for several years. 11. You are to play first. 12. It is your business to countersign the minister's letter. 13. There were three new operas performed last season. 14. I walk every day from ten to twelve. 15. It is not far from my house to the river. 16. What do you complain of?

CHAPTER X.
SYNTAX OF CONJUNCTIONS.

488. Among the simple conjunctions **quoique** (=though *or* although), with its synonyms **bien que, encore que,** is the only one which governs the subjunctive mood :—

> *Quoique* (or *bien que*, or *encore que*) *je sois malade* (=though I am ill). *See* § 494.

489. A moins que (=unless), **de crainte que** or **de peur que** (=for fear that), require **ne** before the following verb in the subjunctive mood :—

> *Il n'ira pas,* **à moins que** *vous ne lui demandiez* (=he will not go unless you ask him);
> *Allez-vous-en bien vite,* **de peur** *qu'il ne soit trop tard* (=go away quickly, lest it should be too late).

SYNTAX OF CONJUNCTIONS.

490. À moins que (=unless), followed by a verb in the infinitive mood, requires the preposition **de** without the negative; as: *je ne pourrais pas lui parler plus fortement à moins que* **de** *le quereller* (=I could not speak to him in stronger terms unless I scolded him). The *que* may be omitted: *à moins de le quereller.*

491. When a conjunction governs *several* verbs, it is placed before the first verb only, and *que* is used before the other verbs:—

<blockquote>
Comme il est appliqué et qu'il prend de la peine (=as he is diligent and takes pains).
</blockquote>

492. The conjunction **ni** serves to unite:—

1. Two negative propositions: *il ne boit* **ni** *ne mange* (=he neither eats nor drinks);

2. Two propositions depending on a negative proposition: *je ne crois pas qu'il vienne,* **ni** *même qu'il pense à venir* (=I do not believe that he will come, or that he even thinks of coming).

Ni is also used instead of **pas**: *il n'est* **ni** *bon* **ni** *mauvais* (=he is neither good nor bad).

493. Quand is a conjunction, and expresses the same idea as *quoique* (=although), and *lorsque* (=when): *je viendrai* **quand** *même il pleuvrait* (=I shall come even if it were to rain); *je partirai* **quand** *j'aurai fini* (=I shall go when I have done).

Quant followed by **à** is a prepositive locution, meaning the same thing as *pour, à l'égard de* (=as for…): **quant à** *moi, je n'en ferai rien* (=as for me, I shall do nothing of the kind).

494. The conjunction **que** is often employed:—

1. Instead of the conjunctive locutions *afin que* (=in order that), *sans que* (=without), *depuis que* (=since), etc.: *venez* **que** *je vous le montre* (=come, in order that I may show it to you); *je ne puis parler* **qu'il** *ne m'interrompe* (=I cannot speak without his interrupting me).

SYNTAX OF CONJUNCTIONS. 91

2. In order to avoid the repetition of the conjunctions *comme, quand*, and *si*: *comme il était tard et* **qu'on** *craignait la chute du jour, on battit la retraite* (=as it was late, and they were afraid of the dusk coming on, they sounded a retreat); *quand on est jeune et* **qu'**on *se porte bien, on doit travailler* (=when one is young, and in good health, one must work); *si vous y allez et* **qu'il** *vous* **rende** *mon livre, envoyez-le-moi* (=if you go, and if he gives you back my book, send it me).

When **que** is used instead of **si**, it requires the subjunctive, but the conjunction *si* is always followed by the indicative, not by the subjunctive, as in English: **si j'allais** *vous voir* (=if I were going to see you); **s'il venait,** *le recevriez-vous?* (=if he should come, would you receive him?).

<small>*Que,* at the beginning of a sentence, and before the third person of the subjunctive present, points out that the words *let him, let them, I wish, they should*, etc., are understood before it: *qu'il nous avertisse lorsqu'il sera prêt* (=let him give us notice when he is ready).</small>

495. Care must be taken not to confound **parce que** and **par ce que**. **Parce que**, in two words, is a conjunctive locution, which is the same as the phrase *par la raison que* (=for the reason that): *je me tais* **parce que** *je crains* (=I am silent, because [for the reason that] I am afraid).

Par ce que, in three words, is a locution identical with *par la chose que, d'après la chose que* (=from *or* by the thing which): *je suis instruit* **par ce que** *mon père m'a dit* (=I am informed in consequence of what my father has told me, *i.e., par cela que mon père m'a dit*).

496. Quoique should not be confounded with **quoi que**. **Quoique**, in one word, is a conjunction corresponding to *bien que* (=although): **quoique** *paresseux, il réussit assez bien* (=although he is idle, he succeeds tolerably well).

Quoi que, in two words, means *quelle que soit la chose que* (=whatever the thing may be): **quoi que**

vous disiez, il fait la sourde oreille (= whatever you may say, he turns a deaf ear). See § 374.

For the government of conjunctive locutions *see* § 508 and following sections.

QUESTIONS FOR EXAMINATION.

1. Which French conjunctions require the subjunctive?
2. After what conjunctions is *ne* used with the verb in the subjunctive?
3. Explain the rule for *à moins que*.
4. Enumerate the various idiomatic uses of the conjunction *que*.
5. How is *ni* used?
6. Distinguish between *quand* and *quant—parce que* and *par ce que—quoique* and *quoi que*.

Exercise 62.

1. Dieu existe, car ce qui pense en moi, je ne le dois point à moi-même. 2. Venez, que je vous dise un fait qui vous intéressera. 3. Il y a un siècle que je ne vous ai vu. 4. Que ne me disiez-vous que vous avez besoin d'argent? 5. Qu'il le veuille ou non, il prendra sa médecine. 6. Si vous rencontrez un sage, et que vous deveniez son ami, estimez-vous heureux. 7. Il ne sait ni le Latin ni le Grec. 8. Je vois, par ce que vous me dites, que j'étais mal informé. 9. Je crois que j'étais mal informé, parce que vous me le dites. 10. Quoi que vous écriviez, évitez la bassesse. 11. Le mérite est souvent négligé parce qu'il est trop modeste. 12. De crainte qu'ils n'entrassent dans le port, il ordonna à ses guerriers de les poursuivre.

[1] il est inutile que je, [2] d'après, [3] à la fois, [4] tandis que, [5] d'une manière profitable.

1. That poor man neither speaks nor hears. 2. Since you do not like the play, it is no use my[1] sending you a ticket. 3. When I am in Paris, and have plenty of spare time, I attend the lectures at the Sorbonne. 4. What is the matter with you that you do not eat? 5. Whatever you may do, you will always succeed. 6. Although he knew I was out, he called upon me. 7. As for that rascal, he shall be sent to prison forthwith. 8. From [2] what I have just heard, I think we shall soon have war. 9. The king was loved, because he was both [3] firm and just. 10. You lose your time, whereas [4] you ought to spend it profitably.[5]

SECOND PART.

SYNTAX OF PROPOSITIONS.

I. Definitions.

497. The first part of the Syntax has taught us to join together two or more *words* in order to form a **simple proposition**; the second part will teach us to unite two or more *simple propositions* in order to make a **compound proposition**.

There are only three ways of uniting simple propositions in order to form a compound proposition:—

1. Either simple propositions remain independent of one another, and we merely place them side by side: *je suis venu, j'ai vu, j'ai vaincu* (=I came, I saw, I conquered);

2. Or we join them together by a conjunction: *Dieu est juste et sa bonté est infinie* (=God is just, and His goodness is infinite);

3. Or if we take simple propositions, the one depends upon the other, is subject to it, is its *subordinate*, and we then obtain a compound proposition composed of two simple propositions, the one *principal*, the other *dependent*. Thus, *l'homme* **sait que** *l'âme est immortelle* (=man knows that the soul is immortal) is a proposition composed of two simple propositions: *l'homme sait* and *l'âme est immortelle*; but the second *depends* upon the first, which is called the *principal* proposition.

We have seen (§ 224) that every proposition has three terms: the *subject*, the *verb*, the *attribute*.

498. Generally speaking there are in a sentence as many propositions as there are verbs: *quand il* **arriva**, *son fils* **se jeta** *dans ses bras, en* **pleurant** (=when he arrived, his son fell into his arms, weeping); there are in this sentence three verbs, and, therefore, three propositions.

499. But in certain sentences containing only one verb in the subjunctive: *que Dieu vous assiste* (=may God help you); or in the imperative: *allez!* (=go!); or, lastly, in an interrogative form: *qui a dit cela?* (=who has said that?), there is always an indicative understood: **je désire** *que Dieu vous assiste* (=I wish that God may help you); **je veux** *que vous alliez* (=I insist on your going); **je demande** *qui a dit cela* (=I ask who has said that); because in such cases the mind really discovers two propositions.

These sentences are called *elliptical*, because there is in them an *ellipsis* or suppression of words.

500. The same thing occurs when, in order to impart greater rapidity to the speech, we suppress one of the verbs of the compound proposition: *je l'aime* **comme** *mon frère*, i.e., **comme j'aime** *mon frère* (=I love him as my brother); or even both verbs: thus, *au feu!* (=fire!) really means **allons** *au feu!* (=let us go to the fire!), i.e., *il* **est** *nécessaire que nous* **allions** *au feu* (=it is necessary that we should go to the fire). In this sentence, although no verb is expressed, there are, nevertheless, two propositions.

We have said (§ 497) that propositions are either *principal* or *subordinate*.

501. The verb of the principal proposition is always in the indicative mood,* because the indicative is the *affirming* mood, and every principal proposition conveys some affirmation: *je doute que vous veniez* (=I doubt your coming); *je doute*, being in the indicative, is the principal proposition.

Every verb in another mood than the indicative belongs to a *dependent* or *subordinate* proposition. In

---

* *Je ne sache* is the only instance of a verb in the subjunctive appearing in the principal proposition: *des enfants étourdis deviennent des hommes vulgaires;* **je ne sache point** *d'observation plus générale et plus certaine que celle-là* (=heedless children become vulgar men; I do not know any observation more general and more certain than that).

the following sentence: *je doute que vous veniez,*—**que vous veniez**, being in the subjunctive mood, constitutes the *dependent* proposition.

II. Of the Subordinate Proposition.

502. The *subordinate* or *dependent* proposition is formed, either:—

1. By the help of a **participle**: *je lis* **en marchant** (= I read whilst walking); *l'homme*, **poussé par la faim**, *devient criminel* (= man, driven by hunger, becomes criminal).

2. By the help of an **infinitive**: *j'aime* **à travailler** (= I like to work).

3. By the aid of a **conjunction**: *je sais* **que** *Dieu est bon* (= I know that God is good).

4. By the help of a **relative pronoun**: *aimez Dieu*, **qui** *vous protège* (= love God, who protects you).

503. We thus divide dependent or subordinate propositions into *four* classes, calling them respectively, **participial** *propositions*, **infinitive** *propositions*, **conjuntive** *propositions*, and **relative** *propositions*. Let us now review them briefly:—

504. The name of **participial** is given to every dependent proposition of which the verb is in the participle, either present: *je lis en* **marchant** (= I read whilst walking), or past: *l'homme*, **poussé** *par la faim, devient criminel* (= man, driven by hunger, becomes criminal). *En marchant, poussé par la faim* are participial propositions.

505. When the participial proposition refers to the subject, and when the subject precedes it: *l'enfant*, **ayant mangé des mets empoisonnés**, *mourut sur-le-champ* (= the child, having eaten some poisoned food, died at once), the subject must not be repeated before the verb. It would, therefore, be wrong to say: *l'enfant, ayant mangé des mets empoisonnés*, **il** *mourut sur-le-champ*.

506. Every dependent proposition, of which the verb is in the infinitive, is called an **infinitive proposition**: *il aspire* **à régner** (=he aspires to reign); *il aime* **à travailler** (=he likes to work).

507. Every dependent proposition, united to the principal one by a conjunction, is called a **conjunctive proposition**: *j'espère* **que** *vous viendrez* (=I hope you will come). *Que vous viendrez* is a conjunctive proposition.

For **relative** *propositions*, see § 519.

QUESTIONS FOR EXAMINATION.

1. How many terms does a proposition contain?
2. Define a *dependent* proposition.
3. How many propositions are there in a sentence?
4. In what mood is the verb of the principal proposition to be put?
5. How many kinds of subordinate propositions are there? How are they distinguished from one another?
6. Define a *participial* proposition.
7. What is an *infinitive* proposition? A *conjunctive* one?

Exercise 63.

Translate the following sentences into English, and underline the conjunctive propositions:—

1. Nul ne sait s'il vivra demain; et tous nous faisons des projets, comme si nous devions vivre toujours. 2. Les Romains soumettaient les villages voisins pendant qu'Alexandre conquérait l'Asie. 3. Arrangez votre vie de telle sorte que les envieux n'y reprennent rien. 4. Je doute que les vertus soient plus grandes depuis que les richesses ont augmenté.

III. Use of the Indicative and of the Subjunctive in Conjunctive Propositions.

508. The *seventeen* following conjunctive locutions must always have the **indicative** after them:—

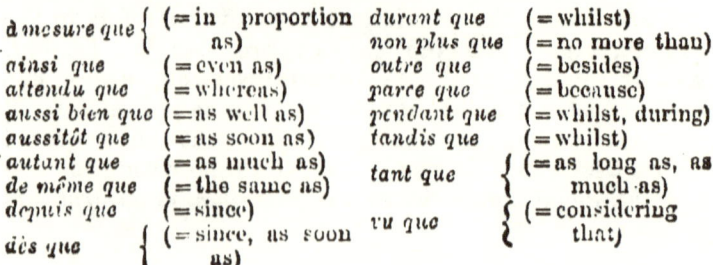

à mesure que	(=in proportion as)	durant que	(=whilst)
ainsi que	(=even as)	non plus que	(=no more than)
attendu que	(=whereas)	outre que	(=besides)
aussi bien que	(=as well as)	parce que	(=because)
aussitôt que	(=as soon as)	pendant que	(=whilst, during)
autant que	(=as much as)	tandis que	(=whilst)
de même que	(=the same as)	tant que	(=as long as, as much as)
depuis que	(=since)	vu que	(=considering that)
dès que	(=since, as soon as)		

SYNTAX OF PROPOSITIONS.

509. The *six* conjunctive locutions :—

de manière que	(= so that)	*si ce n'est que*	(= were it not)
de sorte que, en	(= in such a man-	*sinon que*	(= except that)
sorte que	ner that)	*tellement que*	(= so much that)

are sometimes followed by the **indicative**, and sometimes by the **subjunctive** :—

1. They are followed by the indicative when the sentence expresses a fact *positive, certain, absolute* : *cet enfant s'est conduit de telle sorte que tous ses parents* **ont été** *contents* (= that child conducted himself in such a manner, that all his relations were pleased with him).

2. They are followed by the subjunctive when the sentence expresses a fact in the *future, and which may not take place at all* : *faites en sorte qu'il* **vienne** (= act so that he may come) ; *conduisez-vous de telle sorte que tout le monde* **soit** *content de vous* (= conduct yourself in such a manner that everyone may be pleased with you).

510. The *seventeen* following conjunctive locutions always require the **subjunctive** after them :—

afin que	(= in order that)	*non que*	(= not but that)
à moins que	(= unless)	*pour que*	(= in order that)
avant que	(= before)	*pourvu que*	(= provided that)
en cas que	(= in case that)	*sans que*	(= without that)
bien que	(= although)	*pour peu que*	(= for ever so little that)
de peur que, de crainte que	(= for fear lest)	*soit que*	(= whether that)
jusqu'à ce que	(= until)	*supposé que*	(= supposing that)
loin que	(= far from)	*quoique*	(= although)

J'irai le voir **avant qu'il parte** (= I shall go and see him before he starts) ;

la terre ne s'épuise jamais, **pourvu qu'on sache** *la cultiver* (= the earth is never exhausted, provided one knows how to cultivate it) ;

je lirai **jusqu'à ce que** *vous* **veniez** (= I shall read till you come).

511. When the sentence includes two dependent propositions beginning with *si* (= if) : *ma tristesse serait grande,* **si** *Charles venait en France, et s'il passait par Paris sans me voir* (= my sorrow would be great if Charles came to France, and if he passed through Paris without seeing me), the second **si** may be replaced by **que**; but in this case the verb preceded by *que* is put in the **subjunctive**; *ma tristesse serait grande* **si** *Charles* **venait** *en France et* **qu'il passât** *par Paris sans me voir*.

512. The **subjunctive** is used:

1. After verbs which express *doubt, desire, fear, surprise, supposition, will*: *je* **doute** *qu'il* **sache** *sa leçon* (=I doubt whether he knows his lesson); *je* **crains** *qu'il ne* **parte** (=I fear lest he should go); *je* **désire** *qu'il* **vienne** (=I wish he may come); *je* **suis surpris** *que vous* **soyez** *arrivé* (=I am surprised at your having arrived); *je* **suppose** *qu'il* **lise** *ce livre* (=I suppose that he will read this book); *je* **veux** *qu'il* **sorte** (=I insist upon his going out).

2. After verbs used *interrogatively* or accompanied by a *negative*: *croyez-vous qu'il* **parte**? (=do you think he will start?); *pensez vous qu'il* **vienne**? (=do you suppose he will come?); *je ne présume pas qu'il soit* **arrivé** (=I do not presume he has arrived).

3. After the *impersonal verbs*: *il faut* (=it is necessary), *il importe* (=it is of consequence), *il convient* (=it is proper), *il est possible* (=it is possible), and, generally speaking, after all those which express *will, supposition*, or *doubt*: *il faut qu'il* **vienne** (=he must come); *il importe qu'il* **soit** *ici* (=it is of consequence that he should be here); *il convient qu'il* **sorte** (=it is proper that he should go out); *il est possible qu'il* **dorme** (=it is possible that he is asleep), etc.

513. But the **indicative** is used:—

1. Even after verbs expressing *supposition* or *will*, when the thing in question is considered as very probable: *je suppose qu'il* **lit** *le livre que vous lui avez prêté* (=I suppose that he is reading the book you have lent him); *je prétends qu'il* **est** *là* (=I maintain that he is there).

SYNTAX OF PROPOSITIONS.

2. In the case of a verb conjugated *interrogatively*, or accompanied by a *negative*, when the thing alluded to is considered as certain or extremely probable. Thus, we shall say: *croyez-vous que l'âme* **est** *immortelle?* (=do you believe that the soul is immortal?), because we consider the immortality of the soul as a *certain* fact; *vous ne dites pas que Paul* **est** *mon ami* (=you do not say that Paul is my friend), because, by these words, I *affirm* that Paul is my friend.

3. After *impersonal verbs* such as: *il est clair* (=it is clear), which express *certainty or probability*: *il est certain que la terre* **se meut** *dans l'espace* (=it is certain that the earth moves in space); *il est clair que deux et deux* **font** *quatre* (=it is clear that two and two make four); *il est probable que* **le ciel** *s'éclaircira* (=the sky will probably clear up).

But as a negative destroys certainty or probability, the same verbs conjugated negatively require the subjunctive after them: *n'est-il pas probable que le ciel* **s'éclaircisse**? (=is it not likely that the sky will clear up)?

514. To sum up, if the idea expressed in the subordinate proposition is looked upon as certain and positive, the verb of that proposition is put in the **indicative**. If the idea expressed is considered as doubtful or simply probable, the verb is put in the **subjunctive**.

QUESTIONS FOR EXAMINATION.

1. Which are the *conjunctive* propositions which require the *indicative* after them?
2. Enumerate those which require sometimes the *indicative*, sometimes the *subjunctive*, and state when?
3. Which are those which always take the *subjunctive*?
4. When does *que* require the subjunctive?
5. In what mood is the verb of the subordinate proposition put (a) after verbs expressing *doubt, desire*, etc.?—(b) after verbs employed *interrogatively* or *negatively*?—(c) after the verbs *il faut, il convient,* etc.?
6. When is the *indicative* used (a) after verbs expressing *supposition* and *will*?—(b) after verbs employed *interrogatively* or *negatively*?
7. When do *impersonal* verbs require (a) the indicative?—(b) the subjunctive?

Exercise 64.

Translate the following sentences, and put in the proper moods the verbs in italics :—

1. Que de gens se font du tort parce qu'ils *vouloir* parler avant d'avoir appris à écouter. 2. Autant que je le *pouvoir*, j'évite la rencontre des bavards et des importuns. 3. La femelle du rossignol couve ses œufs pendant que le mâle *chanter* sur la branche voisine. 4. Vous marchez de manière que ces enfants ne *pouvoir* vous suivre. 5. Faites en sorte que tout le monde *être* content de vous. 6. Cet enfant a travaillé de telle sorte que tout le monde *être* content de lui. 7. Pour peu qu'on *connaître* le défaut dominant d'un homme, on est assuré de lui plaire. 8. Quoique l'Espagne soit au midi et que la température y *être* plus élevée qu'en France, il y gèle quelquefois. 9. S'il arrive quelque chose, faites en sorte que j'en *être* informé immédiatement. 10. Il importe que les enfants *aller* de bonne heure à l'école. 11. Ignorez-vous que l'hiver *être* l'époque où le soleil est le plus rapproché de nous?

IV. Use of the Tenses of the Subjunctive.

515. Having examined the cases in which the verb of the dependent proposition ought to be used in the subjunctive, we have now to point out in which tense of the subjunctive mood this verb ought to be put:—

516. The use of the tenses of the subjunctive depends entirely on the idea we wish to express; the only rule to be observed, therefore, is the following one : <u>see in what tense of the **indicative** or the **conditional** you would put the second verb, if the sentence required one of these two moods, and use the corresponding tense of the subjunctive.</u>

REMARKS.—1. The *present* subjunctive corresponds to the indicative *present* and *future*.

2. The *imperfect* subjunctive corresponds to the *imperfect* of the indicative, and the *present* conditional.

3. The *perfect* subjunctive corresponds to the *past definite*, the *past indefinite*, and the *future anterior*.

4. The *pluperfect* subjunctive corresponds to the *pluperfect* indicative and the *past conditional*.

SYNTAX OF PROPOSITIONS. 101

517. In the choice of the tenses of the subjunctive, the verb of the subordinate proposition always depends upon the verb of the principal proposition, and is subject to the two following rules:—

1. If the verb of the principal proposition is in the **present** or the **future** of the **indicative**: *je défends, je défendrai* (= I defend, I will defend); the verb of the dependent proposition is put:—

   (*a*) In the **present** of the **subjunctive**, when the action has still to be performed: *je défends qu'il* **vienne** (= I forbid him to come), *je défendrai qu'il* **vienne** (= I will forbid him to come);

   (*b*) In the **perfect subjunctive**, when the action is already performed: *je doute que* **vous ayez pu** *le faire* (= I doubt whether you have been able to do it), *je douterai toujours que* **vous ayez pu** *le faire* (= I shall always doubt...).

2. If the verb of the principal proposition is in one of the **past or the conditional** tenses: *je voulais, je voulus, j'avais voulu, je voudrais* (= I was wishing, I wished, I had wished, I should wish), the verb of the dependent proposition is put:—

   (*a*) In the **imperfect** of the **subjunctive**, provided the action has still to be performed: *je voulais qu'il* **vînt** (= I wished that he might come), *je voudrais qu'il* **vînt** (= I should wish...), *j'ai voulu qu'il* **vînt** (= I have wished...);

   (*b*) In the **pluperfect** of the **subjunctive**, when the action has already been performed: *je ne savais pas que vous* **eussiez** *déjà* **étudié** *ce livre si complétement* (= I did not know that you had already studied that book so thoroughly); *je n'aurais pas voulu qu'il* **eût fait** *cette déclaration* (= I should not have wished him to make that declaration).

518. These rules only admit of two exceptions:—

1. When the sentence expresses the idea of any condition (the principal verb being in the *present* or in the *future* of the **indicative**), the verb of the dependent proposition is placed in the *imperfect* or in the *pluperfect* of the **subjunctive**: *je ne* **croirai** *jamais qu'il* **eût osé** *le faire,* **si** *on le lui avait défendu* (=I will never believe that he would have dared to do it, if he had been forbidden to do so).

2. When the sentence expresses a permanent fact, which reproduces itself or which has existed for a long time, the dependent verb (whatever may be the tense of the principal one) is always put in the *present* of the **subjunctive**: *Dieu a voulu que l'homme* **éprouve** (and not **éprouvât**) *sa puissance* (=it has been God's will that man should feel His power).

QUESTIONS FOR EXAMINATION.

1. State the general rule for the use of the tenses of the *subjunctive*.
2. To what tenses of the indicative do the *present, imperfect, perfect,* pluperfect subjunctive respectively correspond?
3. What are the principal rules?
4. State the exceptions.

Exercise 65.

Translate the following sentences into English, and put the verbs in italics in the proper tense:—

1. Ne dites jamais: "je veux que cela *être*;" dites plutôt: "je voudrais que cela *être*." 2. Le petit Saint-Bernard était le passage le plus facile qu'Annibal *pouvoir* trouver pour pénétrer en Italie. 3. Vous ne saviez pas que Louis XI *avoir encouragé* les lettres et les arts. 4. Il a fallu, pour me faire revenir de mes premières idées, qu'un nouveau jour se *faire* dans mon esprit. 5. Les oiseaux de rivage étant destinés à vivre dans la vase, la nature leur a donné de longues jambes pour qu'ils *pouvoir* s'y promener. 6. Il faut que celui qui parle se *mettre* à la portée de ceux qui l'écoutent. 7. Les Romains ne pouvaient voir sans indignation que les Carthaginois *oser* les attaquer. 8. Il faut qu'un homme *être* bien lâche pour persécuter la vertu opprimée. 9. On raconte que Henri IV voulait que chaque paysan *mettre* la poule au pot tous les dimanches. 10. Un philosophe ancien disait que le soleil *être* grand comme le Péloponèse.

V. Relative Propositions.

519. Every dependent proposition, united to the principal one by a relative pronoun, is called a **relative proposition**: *craignons Dieu* - **qui nous protége** (=let us fear God - who protects us); *j'aime l'enfant*- **qui est courageux** (=I love the child - who is courageous). *Qui nous protége, qui est courageux* are *relative propositions*.

520. After a relative in sentences which express *will, desire, doubt, negation,* the verb of the dependent proposition is put in the **subjunctive**: *je veux un serviteur* **qui m'obéisse** (=I wish for a servant who will obey me); *je ne connais personne* **qui soit** *vraiment heureux* (=I don't know anybody who is really happy).

REMARK.—This rule applies to the case of the adverb **où**: *allez dans une retraite* **où** *vous soyez heureux* (=go into a retreat where you may be happy).

521. The dependent verb is likewise put in the subjunctive when the relative is preceded by the word **seul** (=only, one), or by a **superlative**: *votre frère est le* **seul-qui soit** *habile* (=your brother is the only one who is clever); *il est aussi l'homme* **le plus adroit- que je connaisse** (=he is also the most skilful man I know).

522. The only exception to these two rules is when the verb of the dependent proposition includes an absolute affirmation: *j'ai rencontré un ouvrier* **qui m'a tiré** *d'embarras* (=I met a workman who extricated me from my difficulties); *achetez tous les meilleurs vins* **que** *vous* **trouverez**, *et expédiez - les - moi* (=buy all the best wines you find, and send them to me) (*see* § 513).

QUESTIONS FOR EXAMINATION.

1. What is meant by *a relative proposition*?
2. In what mood is the verb of the relative proposition put after (*a*) verbs expressing doubt?—
   (*b*) the word *seul*?—(*c*) the *superlative*?
3. What is the exception to that rule?
4. State the rule for *où*.

Exercise 66.

After having translated the following piece into English, the pupils should

1. Mark out:—
   - (a) the principal propositions;
   - (b) the subordinate propositions;
   - (c) the participial, the infinitive, the conjunctive, and the relative propositions;

2. Write in the proper tenses the verbs printed in italics.

LE MADRIGAL DE LOUIS XIV.

Il faut que je vous *écrire* une petite historiette, qui est très-vraie et qui vous divertira. Le roi se mêle depuis peu de faire des vers; MM. de Saint-Aignan et Dangeau lui apprennent comment il faut qu'il s'y *prendre*. Il fit l'autre jour un petit madrigal que lui-même ne trouva pas trop joli. Un matin il dit au maréchal de Grammont: " Monsieur le maréchal, je voudrais que vous *lire* ce petit madrigal, et que vous me *dire* si vous en *avoir* jamais vu un si impertinent: parce qu'on sait que depuis peu j'aime les vers, il n'est pas de jour que je n'en *recevoir* de toutes les façons." Le maréchal, après avoir lu, dit au roi: " Sire, Votre Majesté juge divinement bien de toutes choses: il est vrai que voilà le plus sot et le plus ridicule madrigal que j'*avoir* jamais vu." Le roi se mit à rire, et lui dit: " N'est-il pas vrai que celui qui l'*avoir* fait *être* bien fat? — Sire, il n'y a pas moyen de lui donner un autre nom. — Eh bien! dit le roi, je suis ravi que vous m'en *avoir* parlé si bonnement; c'est moi qui l'ai fait. — Ah! sire, quelle trahison! que Votre Majesté me le *rendre*; je l'ai lu trop brusquement. — Non, monsieur le maréchal; les premiers sentiments sont toujours les plus naturels." Le roi a fort ri de cette folie, et tout le monde trouve que voilà la plus cruelle petite chose que l'on *pouvoir* faire à un vieux courtisan. Pour moi, qui aime toujours à faire des réflexions, je voudrais que le roi en *faire* là-dessus et qu'il *juger* par là combien il s'en faut qu'il *connaître* jamais la vérité.—

Mme. DE SÉVIGNÉ.

APPENDIX.

OF ANALYSIS.

1. There are three kinds of analysis: 1. the *grammatical analysis*; 2. the *logical analysis*; 3. the *etymological analysis*.

2. The *grammatical analysis* treats of the nature and form of words, and determines the part they perform in the sentence.

Example:

L'écureuil est un joli petit animal qui n'est qu'à demi sauvage, et qui, par sa gentillesse, par sa docilité, par l'innocence même de ses mœurs, mériterait d'être épargné : il n'est ni carnassier ni nuisible, quoiqu'il saisisse quelquefois des oiseaux.

l' (for *la*), def. art., masc. sing., referring to *écureuil*.
écureuil, common subs., masc. sing., subject of *est*.
est, verb subs., 4th conj., ind. pres., 3rd pers. sing.
un, indef. art., masc. sing., referring to *animal*.
joli, qualif. adj., masc. sing., qualifying *animal*.
petit, qualif. adj., masc. sing., qualifying *animal*.
animal, common noun, masc. sing., complement of *écureuil*.
qui, relative pron., masc. sing., having as its antecedent *animal*, subject of *est*.
n' (for *ne*)...*que*, adverbial locution.
est, verb substantive, 4th conj., ind. pres., 3rd pers. sing.
à demi, adverbial locution.
sauvage, qualif. adj., masc. sing., qualifying *qui*.
et, conjunction.

qui, relative pron., masc. sing., having as its antecedent *animal*, subject of *mériterait*.
par, preposition.
sa, possess. adj., fem. sing., determining *docilité*.
docilité, common noun, fem. sing., indirect complement of *mériterait*.
par, preposition.
sa, possess. adj., fem. sing., determining *gentillesse*.
gentillesse, common noun, fem. sing., indirect complement of *mériterait*.
par, preposition.
l' (for *la*), def. art., sing. fem., referring to *innocence*.
innocence, common noun, fem. sing., indirect complement of *mériterait*.
même, indef. adjec., fem. sing., referring to *innocence*.
de, preposition.
ses, possess. adj., fem. plural, determining *mœurs*.
mœurs, common noun, fem. plural, complement of *innocence*.
mériterait, active verb, 1st conj., cond. pres., 3rd pers. sing.
de, preposition.
être épargné, passive verb, 1st conj., infin. pres.
il, pers. pron., 3rd pers. sing. masc., subject of *est*.
n' (for *ne*), adverb of negation.
est, verb substantive, 4th conj., ind. pres., 3rd pers. sing.
ni, conjunction.
carnassier, qualif. adj., masc. sing., qualifying *il*.
ni, conjunction.
nuisible, qualif. adj., masc. sing., qualifying *il*.
quoique, conjunction.
il, pers. pron., 3rd pers. sing. masc., subject of *saisisse*.
saisisse, verb active, 2nd conj., pres. subj., 3rd pers. sing.
quelquefois, adverb of time.
des, indef. art., plur. masc., agreeing with *oiseaux*.
oiseaux, common noun, masc. plur., direct complement of *saisisse*.

2. The *logical analysis* shows the relation in which propositions, and also words belonging to the same proposition, stand to one another.

We subjoin an example of logical analysis, in which the subordinate propositions have been placed after the principal propositions to which they respectively belong:—

Le lézard gris *aime* à *recevoir* la chaleur du soleil; *ayant* besoin d'une température douce, il *cherche* les abris; et lorsqu'une lumière pure *éclaire* vivement un gazon en pente ou une muraille, on le *voit s'étendre* sur ce mur, ou sur l'herbe nouvelle, avec un plaisir qui se *devine* aisément.

In the above sentence, there are eight propositions, viz., three principal ones:—

1. *le lézard gris aime.*
2. *il cherche les abris.*
3. *on le voit.*

And five dependent propositions:—

1. *à recevoir la chaleur du soleil.*
2. *ayant besoin d'une température douce.*
3. *lorsqu'une lumière pure éclaire vivement un gazon en pente ou une muraille.*
4. *s'étendre sur ce mur, ou sur l'herbe nouvelle, avec un plaisir.*
5. *qui se devine aisément.*

1. *Le lézard gris aime*, principal proposition. Subject: *le lézard gris;* simple, because there is only one; complex, because its complement is *gris;* verb: *est*, attribute: *aimant*, simple and complex, because its complement is the infinitive proposition *à recevoir la chaleur*, etc.

A recevoir la chaleur du soleil, dependent *infinitive* proposition. Subject: *lézard gris*, simple and complex; verb: *être;* attribute: *recevant*, simple and complex, because its complement is *la chaleur du soleil*.

2. *Il cherche les abris*, principal proposition. Subject: *il* (placed instead of *lézard*), simple and incomplex, because it has no complement; verb: *est;* attribute: *cherchant*, simple and complex, having as a complement *les abris*.

Ayant besoin d'une température douce, dependent *participial* proposition. The subject is *le lézard gris* (understood), simple and complex; verb: *est;* attribute: *ayant*, simple and complex, because it has for its complement *besoin d'une température douce*.

3. *On le voit*, principal proposition. Subject: *on*, simple and incomplex; verb: *est;* attribute: *voyant*, simple and complex, having for its complement *le* (put instead of *lui*).

Lorsqu'une lumière pure éclaire vivement un gazon en pente ou une muraille, dependent *conjunctive* proposition. Subject: *une lumière pure*, simple and complex; verb: *est;* attribute: *éclairant*, simple and complex, having as its complement *un gazon en pente*, etc.

S'étendre sur ce mur, ou sur l'herbe nouvelle, avec un plaisir, dependent *infinitive* proposition. Subject: *lézard gris* (replaced by *le*), simple and complex; verb: *être;* attribute: *étendant*, simple and complex, having as its direct complement *se*, and as its indirect complement *sur ce mur ou sur*, etc.

Qui se devine aisément, *relative* dependent proposition. Subject: *qui* (=*un plaisir*), simple and incomplex; verb: *est;* attribute: *devinant*, simple and complex, because it has for its complements *se* and *aisément*.

---

3. The *etymological* analysis studies the formation of words, and shows how the derived words are formed from the primitive ones.

Example:

Sur le penchant de quelque agréable coteau bien ombragé, je voudrais une petite maisonnette rustique, toute blanche, avec des contrevents verts.

Sur, simple preposition, used as a prefix, before adjectives and verbs.
le, simple article.
penchant, common noun derived from the verb *pencher*, through the *participle present*.
de, simple preposition.
quelque, adjective composed of *quel* and of the conjunction *que*.
agréable, adjective derived from the verb *agréer* with the suffix *able*.
coteau, common noun derived from *côte* with the suffix *eau*.
bien, adverb employed as prefix before adjectives and verbs.
ombragé, adjective derived from the verb *ombrager* through the past participle.
je, pronoun.
souhaiterais, verb in the cond. pres. derived from the infin. pres. with the imperf. of the verb *avoir*.
une, feminine article derived from *un* with the *e* mute, sign of the feminine.
maisonnette, common diminutive noun, formed from *maison*, with the suffix *ette*.
rustique, adjective, primitive word.
toute, feminine adjective formed from *tout* with the *e* mute, sign of the feminine.
blanche, feminine adjective formed from *blanc*, by the changing of *c* into *che*.
avec, simple preposition.
des, article formed from *de les*.
contrerents, common noun, derived from *rent* with the prefix *contre*, and *s*, sign of the plural.
verts, adjective, primitive word, to which *s*, sign of the plural, is added.

The pupils might now be required to give *vivâ voce*.—

1. A few adjectives or verbs formed with the help of the prefix *sur*, such as *surabondant, surnaturel, surpasser, surmonter, surmener*, etc.

2. Adjectives or verbs formed with the help of the prefix *bien*, such as *bienséant*, *bienveillant*, *bienfaire*.

By taking, also, the *primitive* words in the above exercise, they might be asked to form the derived ones; thus: from *rus*, root of *rustique*, we have *rustre*, *rustaud*, *rusticité*. Again, from *vert* (formerly *verd*), we have *verdâtre*, *verdelet*, *verdeur*, *verdir*, *verdure*, *verdoyer*, etc.

INDEX.

The numbers refer to the paragraphs in the grammar.

à and en, 468; repeated, 484.
à and de, 485.
adjective, agreement, 261–271; after nouns separated by *ou*, *ainsi que*, etc., 263; after a gradation, 264; after a verb having for its subject *nous*, *vous* used instead of *je*, *tu*, 318; compound adjective, 265; adjective used adverbially, 266, 267; adjective used with *gens*, 232; adjectives of colour, 271; position of the adjective, 279–282; degrees of comparison in adjectives, 283–288; how formed, 66; when followed by *de*, 234; by *que de*, 285; comparative repeated, 286; mood of the verb after a superlative, 288. *Numeral* adjectives. cardinal, 289–292; used instead of the ordinal, 294; ordinal, 293; adjective of dimensions, age, 295, 296. *Possessive*, 297–305; repeated, 298–300; replaced by *en* and the article, 302; replaced by the article, 303; before names of relations, 304, 305. *Indefinite*, 306–313. *Interrogative*, 364.
adverb, adjectives used as adverbs, 266, 267; syntax of adverbs, 442–465; their place, 442–444.
aide, 227.
aïeul, 236, see 36.
aigle, 227.
amour, 227.

analysis, in appendix.
article, *definite*, when used, 251, 252; repeated, 253, 254; when not used, 255; before *plus*, *mieux*, *moins*, 256, 257; *indefinite* and *partitive*, 258, 259; article used instead of the possessive adjective, 302, 303.
attribute, 224.
auparavant, 460.
aussi, 461, 464.
autant, 461.
autrui, 372.
auxiliary verbs, 406–411.
avant, devant, 471.
avoir, as auxiliary, 406–409.

ça, 337, 367.
ce, followed by a verb in the sing. or plur., 339, 340; instead of *il*, *elle*, etc., 341, 342; used by redundance, 343, 344; followed by *que de* in the second part of the sentence, 345; used in interrogations, 346, 388; number of the verb *être* after *ce*, 386, 387; before *ce*, 388.
cent, 291.
chacun, followed by *son*, *sa*, *ses*, 368–370; by *leur*, *leurs*. 369–370.
chaque, 312.
chez, 487.
chose, 227.
ciel, 236, see 38.
ci-inclus, 277.
ci-joint, 277.

comparative, 283; followed by *de, que* or *que de*, 284, 295; repeated, 286.
comparison, degrees of, *see* adjective and comparative.
complement, 225; of substantive, 246-250; of adjective, 279-282; of verbs, 396-405.
conjunction, 488-496; require the subjunctive mood, 488.
coûté, its agreement, 429.
de crainte que, followed by *ne* or *de*, 489, 490.
crêpe, 235.
critique, 227.

dans and **en**, 469, 470.
davantage, 460.
de, instead of *du*, etc., after *pas point*, 446; repeated, 484; *de* and *à*, 485, 486.
délice, 229.
demi, 275.
depuis, 478.
dessous, sous, 474, 475.
dessus, sur, 474, 475.
de suite, tout de suite, 465.
devant, avant, 471.
do, did, how translated, 411.
dont, 355; *dont, duquel, d'où*, 357.
dormi, its agreement, 429.
dû, its agreement, 435.

en (pronoun), instead of *son, sa, ses*, etc., 302; used for persons and things, 322.
en (preposition) and **à**, 468; *en* and *dans*, 469, 470; repeated, 481; what tense it governs, 483.
entre, parmi, 472.
envers, vers, 473.
envers, vis-à-vis, 480.
être, as auxiliary, 406-410.

fait, its agreement, 430, 435.
feu, 276.
for, how to translate it, 476, 477, 478.

foudre, 227.
franc de port, 278.

garde, 227.
gender of nouns, 227-235.
gent, gens, 232.
gentilhomme, its plural, 242.
grand, 270.

hymne, 233.

il, replaced by *ce*, 341, 342.
impersonal verbs, their past participle, 423, 430.
indicative, after conjunctions, 488; after conjunctive locutions, 508, 509, 513, 514.
in order to, translated by *pour*, 402.

le (pronoun), 320, 321.
lequel and **qui**, 360, 363.
livre, 235.
l'un l'autre, 371.
l'un et l'autre, 371.

madame, its plural, 242.
mademoiselle, its plural, 242.
maint, 313.
mal parler, parler mal, 462.
manche, 235.
manœuvre, 227.
même, 311.
mémoire, 235.
mille, 292.
mine, a friend of, 336.
modo, 235.
à moins que, followed by *ne* or *de*, 489, 490.
monsieur, its plural, 242.
moule, 235.
mousse, 235.

ne, its place, 447-449; used before the second verb, 454; suppressed, 450, 455.
neuter verbs, their past participle, 422, 427-429.
ni, 492.
non plus, 464.

INDEX. 113

noun, *see* substantive.
nu, 275.

œil, 236, *see* 36.
on, its gender and number, 365; preceded by the article, 366; used to avoid naming a person, 367.
orge, 234.
orgue, 229.
où, 358; *d'où* and *dont*, 357.
oui and si, 463.
own, 333.

page, 235.
par and de after a passive verb, 400, 401.
parce que, par ce que, 495.
parler mal, mal parler, 462.
parmi, entre, 472.
partant, pourtant, 466.
participle, after a verb having for its subject *nous*, *vous*, used for *je*, *tu*, 318; present participle, 412; distinguished from the adjective, 413-416; past participle, general rules, 417-419, 440; past participle used with *être*, 420-423; with *avoir*, 425-430; past participle of reflexive verbs, 431-435; past participle followed by an infinitive, 435; preceded by *le*, 436; placed between two *que*'s, 437; preceded by *en*, 438; preceded by *le peu*, 439.
pas, used without *ne*, 450; suppressed, 457; suppressed or expressed, 456.
passive verbs, their past participle, 421; prepositions they govern, 400.
pendant, durant, 477.
pendule, 235.
période, 235.
personne, 379, 380.
de peur que, followed by *ne* or *de*, 489, 490.
plus tôt, plutôt, 459.
poêle, 235.

point, stronger than *pas*, 458.
pour, 402.
preposition, meaning *in order to* translated by *pour*, 402; syntax, 467-487; place of the preposition, 467; what tense prepositions govern, 483; prepositions repeated, 484.
pronouns, personal, conjunctive, 314-322; placed before the verb, 315; after the verb, 316; *le* when it agrees, 320; *le* after a negation, 321; *en*, *y*, 322; disjunctive, 323-325; reflective, 326, 327; personal pronouns repeated, 328-330; *possessive*, 321-336; absolutely in the singular, 334; in the plural, 335; demonstrative, 337-346; relative, 347-360; always expressed in French, 362, and as near the antecedent as possible, 361; interrogative, 363, 364; indefinite, 365-380.
proposition, 220; simple, 221, 497; compound, 221, 497; number of propositions in a sentence, 498-501; subordinate, 502-507; relative, 519-522.
pu, its agreement, 435.

quand, quant, 493.
que and qui, 348, 349, 363; *que de* after a comparative, 285; after *ce*, 345; *que* used instead of another conjunction, 491-494.
quel, 364.
quelque, 399.
qui and que, 348, 349, 363; qui relative, without antecedent expressed, 350; repeated, 351; preceded by a preposition, 352; *de qui* and *duquel*, etc., 356; qui and lequel, 360, 363; qui interrogative, 363.

Syntax

quiconque, 373.
qui que ce soit, 373.
quoi, relative pronoun, 353; *de quoi*, 354; interrogative pronoun, 363.
quoique and **quoi que**, 496.
quoi que ce soit, 374.

reflexive verbs, their past participle, 431–435.
rien, 375–378.

shall, will, how translated, 411.
si, 461, 463.
somme, 235.
souris, 235.
sous, dessous, 474, 475.
statuaire, 227.
subject, 224; verb after one subject, 381–389; after several, 390–395.
subjunctive, after a superlative, 288; after a conjunction, 488; after conjunctive locutions, 509, 510; after *que* used for *si*, 511; after verbs of doubt, etc., 512, 514, 520, 522; after *le seul*, 521; use of tenses of the subjunctive, 515–518.
substantive, its agreement, 226; gender of substantives, 227–235; number of substantive, 236–238; substantive used only in the singular, 238; in the plural, 238; plural of proper nouns, 239–240; of nouns of foreign origin, 241; of compound nouns, 242–245; complement of the substantive, 246–250.
de suite, tout de suite, 455.
superlative, *see* adjective.
sur, dessus, 474, 475.

tant, 461.
témoin, 237.
tenses of the subjunctive, use of, 515–518.

à terre, par terre, 468.
tour, 235.
tout (adj.) 307, (adv.) 308, (pronoun) its place, 378.
travail, 236, *see* 36.
à travers, au travers, 491.

un, 290.

valu, its agreement, 429.
vase, 235.
vécu, its agreement, 429.
verb, 224; agreement with one simple subject, 381; after a collective, 382, 383; after an adverb of quantity, 384, 385; *être* after *ce*, 386, 387; before *ce*, 388; impersonal, 389; agreement with several subjects, 390–395; complement, 396–405; preposition governed by passive verbs, 400; verbs followed by no preposition, 402; by *à*, 404; by *de*, 405; verbs which take *avoir* or *être*, and when, 406–410; past participle of passive verbs 421; of neuter verbs, 422; of impersonal verbs, 423; of reflexive verbs, 431–435.
vers, envers, 472.
vingt, 291.
vis-à-vis, 479, 480.
voici, voilà, 337, 482.
voile, 235.
voulu, its agreement, 435.
vous, used instead of *tu*, 318; used instead of *on*, 367.

what, how to translate it, 338.
whatever, how to translate it, 374.
whoever, whosoever, how translated, 373.
will, shall, how translated, 411.

y, used for persons and things, 322.

FRENCH-ENGLISH VOCABULARY.

A

ier, v.a., to for-
.m., honorable
ner, v.a., to ac-
y
v.a., to grant
.a., to accuse
v.a., (achetant, j'achète, j'ache-
hèterai), to buy
., steel
ation, s.f., ad-
ation
r.a., to address;
ier, v.r., to ap-
nt, adv., clever-
.p. Africa
to act
adj., agreeable,
t
(plur., aïeux),
r
aïeul
adj., lovely
a., to love, to
. (allant, allé, j'allai, j'irai),
friend
m., love
lj., old, ancient

Anglais, adj., English
Angleterre, s. prop., England
animal, s.m., animal
année, s.f., year
appartenir, v. n. (appartenant, appartenu, j'appartiens, j'appartins, j'appartiendrai), to belong
appartient, see appartenir
apprendre, v.a. (apprenant, appris, j'apprends, j'appris), to learn
appris, see apprendre
arbre, s.m., tree
argent, s.m., silver
arme, s.f., arm
armée, s.f., army
arranger, v.a., to arrange, to order
arriver, v.n., to arrive
Asie, s. prop., Asia
assemblée, s.f., assembly
assurer, v.a., to assure
attaquer, v.a., to attack
Attique, s.p., Attica
attribuer, v.a., to attribute
augmenter, v.a., to increase
aujourd'hui, adv., to-day
autant, adv., as much, as many
automne, s.m., autumn
autrefois, adv., formerly

autrui, adj., others
avant, prep., before, previous to
avarice, s.f., avarice

B

bal, s.m., ball (to dance at)
bassesse, s.f., meanness
bateau, s.m., boat
battre, v.a., to beat, to strike; se battre, v.r., to fight
bavard, s.m., talker, chatterbox
beaucoup, adv., much, many
beau-frère, s.m., brother-in-law
Bernard (Saint), s. prop., St. Bernard
besoin, s.m., want
beurre, s.m., butter
bibliothèque, s.f., library
bienséance, s.f., good manners, propriety
bientôt, adv., soon
blanc, adj., white
blesser v.a., to wound
boîte, s.f., box; boîte à ouvrage, workbox
bon, adj., bonne, good
bonheur, s.m., happiness
bonnement, adv., simply
bordé, adj., lined, hemmed, trimmed
bouteille, s.f., bottle

branche, s.f., branch
brusquement, adverb, quickly
butin, s.m., booty

C

ça, pron., that
se cacher, v.r., to hide one's self
caisse, s.f., case, box
campagne, s.f., country; en campagne, campaining, in the field
capricieux, adj., capricious, whimsical
carnassier, adj., flesh eating
Carthage, s.p., Carthage
casser, v.a., to break
casse - noisettes, s.m., nut-cracker
caverne, s.f., cave
cela, pron. dem., that
célèbre, adj., celebrated
cent, adj. num., hundred
centime, s.m., centime
cérémonie, s.f., ceremony
César, s. prop., Cæsar
chacun, pron., each
chambre, s.f., room
chanter, v.a., to sing
chapeau, s.m., hat
chapitre, s.m., chapter
chaque, adj., each
charité, s f., charity
charmant, adj., lively
chaumière, s.f., cottage, little thatched house
chercher, v.a., to try
chez, prep., at the house of; chez moi, at my house
chimiste, s.m., chemist
chœur, s.m., choir
chose, s.f., thing
chrétien, adj., christian
chûte, s.f., fall
cinq, adj. num., five
cinquante, adj. num., fifty

cinquantième, adj. num., fiftieth
citoyen, s.m., citizen
cœur, s.m., heart
colonie, s.f., colony
commander, v.a., to command
comme, prep., like, as
commencer, v.a., to begin
comment, adv., how
compagnon, s.m., companion
comprendre, v.a. (comprenant, compris, je comprends, je compris), to understand, to include
compris, see comprendre
connaître, v.a. (connaissant, connu, je connais, je connus), to know
se confier, v.r., to trust one's self
connu, see connaître
conquérir, v.a. (conquérant, conquis, je conquiers, je conquis), to conquer
conscience, s.f., conscience
conserver, v.a., to keep, to preserve
consister, v.a., to consist
constitution, s.f., constitution
content, adj., satisfied
conter, v.a., to relate, to tell
contrevent, s.m., shutter
convainquant, adj., convincing
convenance, s.f., propriety
convenir, v.n. (convenant, convenu, je conviens, je convins, je conviendrai), to suit, to agree
convenu, see convenir
converser, v.n., to converse, to talk

corps, s.m., body
corriger, v.a., to correct
côte, s.f., coast
côté, s.m., side
côteau, s.m., hill, hillock
coucher, v.a. and n., to lie down, to sleep
coup, s.m., knock, blow
coup d'œil, s.m., glance
courage, s.m., courage
cours, s.m., course of lectures
courtisan, s.m., courtier
cousin, s.m., cousin
coûter, v.a., to cost
couver, v.a, to hatch, to sit (for hatching)
couvert, adj., covered
de crainte que, conj., for fear that
créer, v.a., to create, to establish
critique, s.m., critic
critique, s.f., criticism
cruel, adj., cruel
cueillir, v.a. (cueillant cueilli, je cueille, j cueillis, je cueillerai) to gather
curieux, adj., curious strange

D

dame, s.f., lady
dans, prep., in, into
déchaîner, v.a., to loose, to bring on
décider, v.a., to decide
déclarer, v.a., to declare
déesse s.f., goddess
défaire, v a. (défaisan défait, je défais, j défis), to defeat, to und
défaut, s.m., fault, defect
défit, see défaire
déjà, adv., already
déjeûner, s.m., breakfast
délice, s.m. or f., delight
demain, adv., to-morrow

demander, *v.a.*, to ask, to demand
demi, *adj.*, half
depuis, *prep.*, since
dernier, *adj.*, last
désastreux, *adj.*, disastrous
descendre, *v.a.*, to descend
destiner, *v.a.*, to destine
détour, *s.m.*, turn, ways
détruire, *v.a.* (détruisant, détruit, je détruis, je détruisis), to destroy
deux, *adj.num.*, two
devant, *prep.*, before, in front of
devenir, *v.a.* and *n.* (devenant, devenu, je deviens, je devins), to become
devenu, *see* devenir
devoir, *s.m.*, exercise, duty
devoir, *v.a.* (devant, dû, je dois, je dus, je devrai), to owe
dévorer, *v.a.*, to devour, to eat up
diamant, *s.m.*, diamond
Dieu, *s.m.*, God
différence, *s.f.*, difference
difficilement, *adv.*, with difficulty
dimanche, *s.m.*, Sunday
dîner, *v.n.*, to dine
dire, *v.a.* (disant, dit, je dis, je dis), to say, to tell
discours, *s.m.*, discourse, speech
disette, *s.f.*, scarcity, dearth
distinguer, *v.a.*, to distinguish
distribution *s.f.*, distribution
dit, *see* dire
divertir, *v.a.*, to divert
divinité, *s.f.*, deity, god, goddess

dix, *adj.num.*, ten
docilité, *s.f.*, docility
doit, *see* devoir
domaine, *s.m.*, dominion
domestique, *s.m.* or *f.*, servant
dominant, *adj.*, chief, ruling
don, *s.m.*, gift, present
dont, *pron.*, of which
douter, *v.n.*, to doubt
droiture, *s.f.*, straightforwardness, uprightness

E

ébruiter, *v.a.*, to spread about
éclater, *v.n.*, to burst
école, *s.f.*, school
écouter, *v.a.*, to listen
écriviez, *see* écrire
écrire, *v.a.* (écrivant, écrit, j'écris, j'écrivis), to write
écriture, *s.f.*, writing
écureuil, *s.m.*, squirrel
édifice, *s.m.*, building
égal, *adj.* equal
eh bien ! *int.*, well !
élever, *v.a.*, to raise, l'armée s'élevait, the army numbered
émigrant, *s.m.*, emigrant
empire, *s.m.*, empire, command
ému, *adj.*, moved
en, *pron.*, of it, of that, of him, of her, of them
en, *prep.*, in, into
enceinte, *s.f.*, enclosure
encourager, *v.a.*, to encourage
encre, *s.f.*, ink
enfant, *s.m.*, child
engager, *v.a.*, to advise, to engage
ennemi, *s.m.*, enemy
ensemble, *adv.*, together

envieux, *s.m.*, envious people
environ, *adv.*, about
épine, *s.f.*, thorn
épargner, *v.a.*, to spare, to save
époque, *s.f.*, epoch, time
éprouver, *v.a.*, to prove, to experience
Espagne, *s. prop.*, Spain
espérer, *v.a.*, to hope
esprit, *s.m.*, wit, mind
essayer, *v.a.*, to try
estimer, *v.a.*, to esteem
été, *s.m.*, summer
étonnant, *adj.*, astonishing, surprising
étude, *s.f.*, study
étudier, *v.a.*, to study
éviter, *v.a.*, to avoid
exiger, *v.a.*, to exact
exister, *v.n.*, to exist
expédier, *v.a.*, to send

F

fabricant, *s.m.*, maker
facile, *adj.*, easy
façon, *s.f.*, fashion, manner, kind
faim, *s.f.*, hunger
fait, *s.m.*, fact
faire, *v.a.* (faisant, fait, je fais, je fis, je ferai), to do, to make
falloir, *v.n.unip.* (fallu, il faut, il fallut, il faudra), to be necessary
fallu, *see* falloir
famille, *s.f.*, family
fat, *adj.*, foppish
faute, *s.f.*, mistake
femelle, *s.f.*, female
femme, *s.f.*, woman
fer, *s.m.*, iron
fera, *see* faire
feu, *s.m.*, fire
feu, *adj.*, deceased
finir, *v.a.*, to finish
flatter, *v.a.*, to flatter

fléchir, v.a., to make to yield
fois, s.f., time; à la fois, at the same time
folie, s.f., folly
fondation, s.f., foundation
fonder, v.a, to build, to erect
font, see faire
forcer, v.a., to break open
fortune, s.f., fortune
fossé, s.m., ditch
foudre, s.f., thunderbolt
foule, s.f., multitude, crowd
franc, adj., frank, free, open
français, adj., French
frère, s.m., brother
fromage, s.m., cheese
fruit, s.m., fruit
fusil, s.m., gun

G

gage, s.m., wages, pledge
gagner, v.a., to win
gare, s.f., station, terminus
geler, v.a., to freeze
général, s.m., general
genre, s.m., gender, kind; genre humain, mankind
gens, s.m. or f., people; gens de lettres, s.m.pl., men of letters
gentillesse, s.f., gentleness
grammaire, s.f., grammar
grand, adj., tall, great, large
grandeur, s.f., greatness
grand'route, s.f., high road
gratuitement, adv., gratuitously
grec, s.m., Greek
grièvement, adv., seriously

gris-foncé, adj., dark grey
grossier, adj., coarse, great
guerre, s.f., war
guerrier, s.m., warrior
Guillaume, s.prop., William

H

habileté, s.f., cleverness
habitant, s.m., inhabitant
habiter, v.a., to live, to dwell
haïr, v.a., to hate
haut, adj., high
Henri, s.prop., Henry
heure, s.f., hour; de bonne heure, early
heureux, adj., happy
hier, adv., yesterday
histoire, s.f., history, story
historiette, s.f., little story
hiver, s.m., winter
homme, s.m., man
honnête, adj., honest
honnêteté, s.f., honesty
honneur, s.m., honour
horrible, adj., horrible
huit, adj.num., eight
humain, adj., humane, human
hymne, s.m. or f., hymn

I

ignorer, v.a., to ignore
illustre, adj., illustrious
il y a, there is, there are
immédiatement, adv., immediately, at once
impertinent, adj., impertinent
importer, v.unip., to be important
importun, s.m., importunate person, troublesome person
importuner, v.a., to importune, to trouble
inaltérable, adj., unchangeable

incendie, s.m., fire
inclure, v.a., to include
indignation, s.f., indignation
inhumain, adj., inhuman
informer, v.a., to inform
injuste, adj., unjust
innocence, s.f., innocence
insatiable, adj., unsatiable, unquenchable
inscription, s.f., inscription
intéresser, v.a., to interest
intérêt, s.m., interest
inventer, v.a., to invent
irez, see aller
Italie, s.p., Italy

J

jamais, adv., never
jambe, s.f., leg
jardin, s.m., garden
jeter, v.a., to throw
jeudi, s.m., Thursday
jeune, adj., young
joie, s.f., joy
joli, adj., pretty
jouer, v.a. and n., to play
jour, s.m., day, light
juger, v.a., to judge

L

lâche, adj., coward
lâchement, adj., cowardly
laisser, v.a., to let, to leave
lait, s.m., milk
large, adj., wide
latin, s.m., Latin
leçon, s.f., lesson
lettre, s.f., letter
leur, adj., their
lieue, s.f., league
lire, v.a. (lisant, lu, je lis, je lus), to read
lisez, see read
livre, s.f., pound (sterling), pound (weight)
livre, s.m., book
loi, s.f., law
Londres, s.p., London

long, *adj.*, long
longtemps, *adv.*, a long time
louer, *v.a.*, to let, to hire, to praise
lui, *pron.*, him, to him, to her, to it
lumière, *s.f.*, light
lundi, *s.m.*, Monday

M

mademoiselle, *s.f.*, miss
madrigal, *s.m.*, madrigal
maint, *adj.*, many
mais, *conj.*, but
maison, *s.f.*, house
maisonnette, *s.f.*, little house
majesté, *s.f.*, majesty
mal, *adv.*, ill
mal, *s.m.*, evil, hurt, injury, harm, pain
malade, *adj.*, ill
mâle, *s.m.*, male
malheur, *s.m.*, misfortune
maltraiter, *v.a.*, to ill treat
manger, *v.a.*, to eat
manière, *s.f.*, manner; de manière que, so that
manquer, *v.a.*, to fail
marchandise, *s.f.*, goods, merchandise
marcher, *v.n.*, to walk
maréchal, *s.m.*, marshal
Marseille, *s.prop.*, Marseilles
mathématicien, *s.m.*, mathematician
matin, *s.m.*, morning
mauvais, *adj.*, bad
méchant, *adj.*, naughty, evil
médaille, *s.f.*, medal
médecine, *s.f.*, medicine
meilleur, *adj.*, better, best
mêler, *v.a.*, to mix
menace, *s.f.*, threat
mère, *s.f.*, mother
mérite, *s.m.*, merit
messieurs, *see* monsieur

métal, *s.m.*, metal
mètre, *s.m.*, metre
midi, *s.m.*, south
midi, *adv.*, noon
mien, *pron.*, mine
mieux, *adv.*, better
mil, *see* mille
mille, *adj.num.*, thousand
mine, *s.f.*, mine
mineur, *adj.*, minor, lesser, under age
modeste, *adj.*, modest
mœurs, *s.f. pl.*, manners
moi, *pron.*, me
moins, *adv.*, less
mois, *s.m.*, month
monde, *s.m.*, world; tout le monde, every one, everybody
monsieur, *s.m.*, gentleman, sir, Mr.
mont, *s.m.*, mount, mountain
monter, *v.a.* and *n.*, to ascend
montrer, *v.a.*, to show
se moquer, *v.r.*, to joke
motif, *s.m.*, motive
moule, *s.m.*, mould, shape
moule, *s.f.*, mussel
moyen, *s.m.*, means
musée, *s.m.*, museum
musicien, *s.m.*, musician
naître, *v.* (naissant, né, je nais, je naquis, je naîtrai), to be born

N

nature, *s.f.*, nature
naturel, *adj.*, natural
naufrage, *s.m.*, shipwreck
naufrage, *s.m.*, wreck; faire naufrage, to be wrecked
né, *see* naître
négligent, *adj.*, negligent
nier, *v.a.*, to deny
nom, *s.m.*, name, noun
nombre, *s.m.*, number

nombreux, *adj.*, numerous
nourri, *see* nourrir
nourrir, *v.a.*, to feed, nourish
nouvelle, *s.f.*, news
noyau, *s.m.*, stone
nu-pieds, *adj.*, barefooted
nuisible, *adj.*, hurtful
nul, *adj.*, no one

O

obéir, *v.n.*, to obey
obéissance, *s.f.*, obedience
obliger, *v.a.*, to oblige
obtenir, *v.* (obtenant, obtenu, j'obtiens, j'obtins, j'obtiendrai), to obtain
œuf, *s.m.*, egg
œil, *s.m.* (pl., yeux), eye
oiseau, *s.m.*, bird
ombrager, *v.a.*, to shade
opinion, *s.f.*, opinion
opprimer, *v.a.*, to oppress
or, *s.m.*, gold
orage, *s.m.*, storm
ordonner, *v.a.*, to order
ordre, *s.m.*, order
orgue, *s.m.* or *f.*, organ
oser, *v.a.*, to dare
ou, *conj.*, or
où, *adv.*, where
oublier, *v.a.*, to forget
oui, *adv.*, yes
ouvrage, *s.m.*, work

P

page, *s.f.*, page
pain, *s.m.*, bread
paraître, *v.n.* (paraissant, paru, je parais, je parus), to appear
parler, *v.n.*, to speak
paratonnerre, *s.m.*, lightning rod
parce que, *conj.*, because
paresseux, *adj.*, idle

parfaitement, *adj.*, perfectly
parole, *s.f.*, word, language
partager, *v.a.*, to divide
partant, *adv.*, therefore
partir, *v.n.* (partant, parti, je pars, je partis), to go, to depart, to leave
paru, *see* paraître
parvenir, *v.n.*(parvenant, parvenu, je parviens, je parvins, je parviendrai), to attain
parvenu, *see* parvenir
pas, *s.m.*, step
passage, *s.m.*, passage
passer, *v.a.*, to live, to pass
passion, *s.f.*, passion
patrie, *s.f.*, country
pauvre, *adj.*, poor
payer, *v.a.*, to pay
pays, *s.m.*, country
paysan, *s.m.*, peasant
pêche, *s.f.*, peach, fishing
peine, *s.f.*, trouble, difficulty; à peine, hardly
Péloponnèse, *s.p.m.*, Peloponnesus
penchant, *s.m.*, slope
pendant, *prep.*, for, during
pénétrer, *v.a.*, to enter
penser, *v.a.*, to think, to believe
pepin, *s.m.*, pip (break
percer, *v.a.*, to pierce, to
perdre, *v.a.*, to lose
perdu, *see* perdre
périr, *v.n.*, to perish
permettre, *v.a.* (permettant, permis, je permets, je permis, je permettrai), to permit, to allow
Pérou, *s.pr.*, Peru
persécuter, *v.a.*, to persecute

personne, *s.f.*, person
petit, *adj.*, little
peu, *adv.*, little
peut, *see* pouvoir
Pharsale, *s.prop.*, Pharsalia
philosophe, *s.m.*, philosopher
phocéen, *s.pr.*, Phocean
pied, *s.m.*, foot
pierre, *s.f.*, stone
pistolet, *s.m.*, pistol
place, *s.f.*, place, situation
placer, *v.a.*, to place
plaire, *v n.* (plaisant, plu, je plais, je plus), to please
plaisir, *s.m.*, pleasure
plait, *see*, plaire
pleuvoir, *v.imp.* (pleuvant, plu, il pleut, il plut, il pleuvra), to rain
plu, *see* pleuvoir and plaire
la plupart, *adv.*, most
plus, *adv.*, more
plusieurs, *adj.*, many
plutôt...que, *loc. conj.*, rather...than
poêle, *s.m.*, stove
poêle, *s.f.*, frying-pan
polir, *v.a.*, to polish
politesse, *s.f.*, politeness
pomme, *s.f.*, apple
port, *s.m.*, carriage, port
porte-clefs, *s.m.*, turnkey
portée, *s.f.*, reach
poste, *s.f.*, post (for letters
poste, *s.m.*, place, office
pot, *s.m.*, jug; pot au lait, milk-jug
poule, *s.f.*, hen
poursuivre, *v.a.* (poursuivant, poursuivi, je poursuis, je poursuivis), to pursue
poutre, *s.f.*, beam

pouvoir, *v.a.* (pouvant, pu, je peux, je puis, je pourrai), to be able
se précipiter, *v.r.*, to rush
prendre, *v.a.* (prenant, pris, je prends, je pris), to take
prends, *see* prendre
premier, *adj.num.*, first
prenez, *see* prendre
présenter, *v.a.*, to present, to introduce
préserver, *v.a.*, to keep, to preserve
président, *n.m.*, president
présider, *v.a.* and *n.*, to preside
presser, *v.a.*, to press
prêter, *v.a.*, to lend
preuve, *s.f.*, proof
prier, *v.a.*, to pray, to beg
prière, *s.f.*, prayer
prince, *s.m.*, prince
printemps, *s.m.*, spring
prix, *s.m.*, prize
probité, *s.f.*, honesty
prochain, *adj.*, next
professeur, *s.m.*, teacher, professor
profiter, *v.a.*, to profit
profondeur, *s.f.*, depth
projet, *s.m.*, project
se promener, *v.r.*, to walk
propre, *adj.*, proper, own clean
protection, *s.f.*, protection
Prusse, *s.prop.*, Prussia
puisse, *see* pouvoir
punir, *v.a.*, to punish

Q

qualité, *s.f.*, quality
quand, *conj.*, when
quarante, *adj.num.*, forty
quatre, *adj.num.*, four
que, *adv.*, how; que de, how much, how many

que, *conj.*, that; ne... que, only
quel, *adj.*, what, which
quelque, *adj.*, some
quelque, *adv.*, however
quelquefois, *adv.*, sometimes
quiconque, *adj.*, whoever

R

rabattre, *v.a.*, to beat down (a price), to take off (money)
raconter, *v.a.*, to relate
raisin, *s.m.*, grapes, raisin
raison, *s.f.*, reason
ramasser, *v.a.*, to pick up
rapprocher, *v.a.*, to bring near
rarement, *adv.*, rarely, unfrequently
ravi, *adj.*, delighted
recevoir, *v.a.*, to receive
recevra, *see* recevoir
réciter, *v.a.*, to recite
récolte, *s.f.*, harvest
recommandable, *adj.*, commendable
réflexion, *s.f.*, reflexion
refuser, *v.a.*, to refuse
région, *s.f.*, region
règle, *s.f.*, rule
regretter, *v.a.*, to regret
reine, *s.f.*, queen
relier, *v.a.*, to bind (a book)
règne, *s.m.*, reign
rempart, *s.m.*, rampart, bulwark
remporter, *v.a.*, to carry away, to win, to obtain, to gain
rencontre, *s.f.*, meeting
rencontrer, *v.a.*, to meet
rendre, *v.a.*, to make, to render, to give back
rendu, *see* rendre
repartir, *v.n.*, to set out again (*see* partir)

se repentir, *v.r.*, to repent
repolir, *v.a.*, to polish again
respecter, *v.a.*, to respect
revenir, *v.n.* (revenant, revenu, je reviens, je revins, je reviendrai), to come back, to return, to reconsider, to retract
reverrai, *see* revoir
revoir, *v.a.* (revoyant, revu, je revois, je revis, je reverrai), to see again
réussir, *v.a.* and *n.*, to succeed
richesse, *s.f.*, wealth, riches
ridicule, *adj.*, ridiculous
rien, *adv.*, nothing
rire, *v.n.*, to laugh
rivage, *s.m.*, coast
roi, *s.m.*, king
roman, *s.m.*, novel
Romain, *s.m.*, Roman
rose, *s.f.*, rose
rossignol, *s.m.*, nightingale
Russie, *s.p.*, Russia
rustique, *adj.*, rustic

S

sage, *s.m.*, sage, wise man
Saint-Bernard, *s.p.*, St. Bernard
sais, *see* savoir
saisir, *v.a.*, to take hold of
saison, *s.f.*, season
salle, *s.f.*, hall, room
sans, *prep.*, without
satisfaire, *v.a.* (satisfaisant, satisfait, je satisfais, je satisfis, je satisferai), to satisfy
savant, *adj.*, learned
savoir, *v.a.* (sachant, su, je sais, je sus, je saurai, que je sache, que je sasse) to know

sauterelle, *s.f.*, grasshopper
sauvage, *adj.*, savage, wild
selon, *prep.*, according to
sensible, *adj.*, sensitive, kind hearted
sentiment, *s.m.*, sentiment
sérail, *s.m.*, seraglio
sert, *see* servir
servir, *v.* (servant, servi, je sers, je servis), to use
seul, *adj.*, only, only one, alone
si, *conj.*, if
siècle, *s.m.*, century
sire, *s.m.*, sire
sœur, *s.f.*, sister
soi-même, *adj.*, himself, herself, itself
soi, *pron.*, one's self
soir, *s.m.*, evening
soixante, *adj.num.*, sixty
soldat, *s.m.*, soldier
soleil, *s.m.*, sun
songer, *v.a.*, to think, to believe
sors, *see* sortir
en sorte que, *conj.*, so that
sortir, *v.a.* and *n.* (je sors, je sortis, sortant, sorti) to go out, to come out
sot, *adj.*, stupid
se soucier, *v.r.*, to care
souffrant, *adj.*, suffering
souhaiter, *v.a.*, to wish
soumettre, *v.a.* (soumettant, soumis, je soumets, je soumis), to submit
soupir, *s.m.*, sigh
souvent, *adv.*, often
style, *s.m.*, style
suite, *s.f.*, sequence, following; à la suite de, after
suivre, *v.a.* (suivant, suivi, je suis, je suivis), to follow

superbe, *adj.*, superb, splendid
sur. *prep.*, on
cûr, *adj.*, certain
surprenant, *see* surprendre
surprendre, *v.a.* (surprenant, surpris, je surprends, je surpris) overtake, surprise
surpris, *adj.*, surprised
surtout, *adv.*, especially, above all
survécu, *see* survivre
survivre, *v.n.* (survivant, survécu, je survis, je survécus), to outlive

T

tableau, *s.m.*, picture
talent, *s.m.*, talent
tant, *adv.*, so much
tante, *s.f.*, aunt
tard, *adv.*, late
témoin, *s.m.*, witness
température, *s.f.*, temperature
terme, *s.m.*, term, word
terminer, *v.a.*, to terminate, to finish
terre, *s.f.*, earth, land, ground
tête, *s.f.*, head
tomber, *v.n.*, to fall
tort, *s.m.*, wrong
toucher, *v.a.*, to touch, to be close to
toujours, *adv.*, always
Touraine, *s.m.*, Touraine (the country in the neighbourhood of Tours)

tous, *see* tout
tout, *adj.* (toute, tous, toutes), all
tout le monde, *pron.*, every body
tout de suite, *loc.adv.*, directly
trahir, *v.a.*, to betray
trahison, *s.f.*, treason
trajet, *s.m.*, journey, distance
tranquilliser, *v.a.*, to quiet
travailler, *v.n.*, to work
très, *adv.*, very
tribu, *s.f.*, tribe
trois, *adj.num.*, three
tromper, *v.a.*, to deceive
se tromper, *v.r.*, to mistake, to deceive one's self
trône, *s.m.*, throne
trop, *adv.*, too, too much
troupe, *s.f.*, troop
trouver, *v.a.*, to find

U

un, *adj.num.*, one
uni, *adj.*, smooth
univers, *s.m.*, universe
usage, *s.m.*, custom
utile, *adj.*, useful

V

vaincre, *v.a.*, to conquer
vapeur, *s.f.*, vapour, steam
vase, *s.f.*, mud
vendre, *v.a.*, to sell
venir, *v.n.* (venant, venu, je viens, je vins, je viendrai), to come

venu, *see* venir
véritable, *adj.*,
vérité, *s.f.*, tru
verre, *s.m.*, gla
vers, *s.m.*, vers
vers, *prep.*, about
vert, *adj.*, greer
vertu, *s.f.*, virt
vêtement, *s.m.*,
veuillez, *from* please
veux, *see* voulo
victoire, *s.f.*, vi
vieillard, *s.m.*,
viens, *see* venir
village, *s.m.*, vi
ville, *s.f.*, town
vin, *s.m.*, wine
vingt, *adj.num.*
violent, *adj.*, vi
vivre, *v.n.*, to li
voici, *adv.*, here are
voir, *v.a.* (voya vois, je vis, to see
voisin, *adj.*, neig
volume, *s.m.*, v
voter, *v.a.*, to v
vouloir, *v.a.*, t wish
voyager, *v.n.*, t
vrai, *adj.*, tru
downright
vraiment, *adv* indeed
vu, *see* voir

Y

y, *adv.*, there
y, *pron.*, to it

ENGLISH-FRENCH VOCABULARY.

A

About, *prep.*, pour, à propos de
accident, *s.*, accident (*m.*)
accomplished, *adj.*, accompli
acquittal, *s.*, acquittement (*m.*)
action, *s.*, action, acte
adhering, *adj.*, adhérant
admit, *v.*, admettre *irr.*
admire, *v.*, admirer
advice, *s.*, avis (*m.*), conseil (*m.*)
after, *prep.*, après
age, *s.*, âge (*m.*)
agree, *v.*, s'accorder, tomber d'accord
aim, *s.*, but (*m.*)
air, *s.*, air (*m.*)
all, *adj.*, tout
allude, *v.*, faire allusion
although, *conj.*, quoique
America, *s.*, Amérique (*f.*)
amiable, *adj.*, aimable
animal, *s.*, animal (*m.*)
anybody, *pron.*, qui que ce soit, n'importe qui
author, *s.*, auteur (*m.*)
argument, *s.*, argument (*m.*)
arm, *s.*, bras (*m.*)
army, *s.*, armée (*f.*)
as *conj.*, comme, que
as ... as, aussi ... que
as, *conj.*, comme; as much, as many, autant de
ashamed, *adj.*, honteux
assistant, *s.*, aide
assure, *v.*, assurer
astonish, *v.*, étonner
at home, *adj.*, à la maison, chez moi, chez toi, chez lui, etc.
attend, *v.*, suivre
attention, *s.*, attention (*f.*)
avoid, *v.*, éviter

B

bare, *adj.*, nu
barking, *s.*, aboiement (*m.*)
battle, *s.*, bataille (*f.*)
beautiful, *adj.*, beau, bel
become, *v.*, devenir *irr.*
bed-room, *s.*, chambre à coucher
beer, *s.*, bière (*f.*)
beggar, *s.*, mendiant (*m.*)
begin, *v.*, commencer
behind, *prep.* and *adv.*, derrière
believe, *v.*, croire, *irr.*
belong, *v.*, appartenir, *irr.*, être à
betray, *v.*, trahir
bind, *v.*, lier, relier
blame, *v.*, blâmer [(*m.*)
bleating, *s.*, bêlement
blue, *adj.*, bleu
bonnet, *s.*, bonnet (*m.*), chapeau (*m.*)

book, *s.*, livre
boot-jack, *s.*, t
both, *pron.*, l'u tre; both, o fois
bottle, *s.*, bout
box, *s.*, boîte
boy, *s.*, garçon fant (*m.*)
bracelet, *s.*, bra
break, *v.*, casse
bring, *v.*, appor down, descen about, amen
brother, *s.*, frè
business, *s.*, af (trade) affair
but, *prep.*, mai
buy, *v.*, acheter
by, *prep.*, par,

C

caddy, *s.*, bo caddy, boîte
call, *v.*, appeler passer chez passer à; ca revenir, *ir.*
call to acco prendre à
calumny, *s.*, cal
can, *v.*, pouvoir
carriage, *s.*, voi
castor, *s.*, casto
certain, *adj*, c
chair, *s.*, chais
Charles, *s.*, Ch

charm, v., charmer
chief, adj., principal
child, s., enfant (m.)
circumstance, s., circonstance (f.)
city, s., ville (f.), cité (f.)
claim, v., demander
clerk, s., commis (m.)
colour, s., couleur (f.)
come, v., venir, irr.;
come out, sortir. irr.
complain, v., se plaindre
condemn, v., condamner
condition, s., condition (f.)
confused, adj., troublé
conqueror, s., conquérant (m.)
consult, v., consulter
convince, v., convaincre, irr.
correct, v., corriger
cost, v., coûter
countersign, v., contresigner
country, s., campagne (f.)
courage, s., courage (f.)
court, s., cour, impasse (f.)
cover, s., couverture, (f.) couvercle (m.)
croud, s., foule (f.)
Crecy, s., Crécy
crusade, s., croisade (f.)
curfew, s., couvre-feu (m.)

D

Damietta, s., Damiette
dangerous, adj., dangereux
dead, adj., mort
death, s., mort (f.)
deceive, v., tromper
decency, s., décence (f.)
deceptive, adj., trompeur
deduct, v., déduire, irr.
delay, v., retarder
delicious, adj., délicieux
derive, v., dériver, tirer

deserve, v., mériter
desire, v., désirer
despise, v., mépriser
detestable, adj., détestable
difficult, adj., difficile
difficulty, s., difficulté (f.)
dine, v., dîner
disappear, v., disparaître, irr.
discharge, v., décharger, s'acquitter de
discover, v., découvrir,
dissatisfied, adj., mécontent
do, v., faire; to do a service, rendre service
document, s., document (m.)
dog, s., chien
Dover, s., Douvres
downstairs, adv., en bas
dozen, s., douzaine (f.)
drawing, s., dessin (m.)
drop, v., laisser tomber
duty, s., devoir
dutiful, adj., respectueux

E

each, pron., chacun
each other, l'un l'autre
eagle, s., aigle
endeavour, v., s'efforcer
endurance, s., patience (f.)
effect, s., effet (m.)
egg, s., œuf (m.)
Egyptian, s., Egyptien
eighteen, adj., dix-huit
eighteenth, adj., dix-huitième
eighty, adj., quatre-vingts
elapse, v., s'écouler
electricity, s., électricité (f.)
elephant, s., éléphant (m.)
elm, s., orme (m.)
emperor, s., empereur (m.)
enemy, s., ennemi (m.)

England, s., Angleterre (f.)
English, adj. and s., Anglais
entirely, adv., entièrement
entreat, v., supplier
entreaty, s., supplication (f.)
error, s., erreur (f.)
escape, v., échapper à
even, adv., même
ever, adv., jamais, toujours
every one, pron., chacun
everything, tout
evident, adj., évident
evil, s., mal (m.)
Europe, s., Europe (f.)
examine, v., examiner
example, s., exemple (m.)
expense, s., dépense (f.)
expensive, adj., cher
expire, v., expirer
express, v., exprimer, parler

F

fact, s., fait (m.)
fall, v., tomber
false, adj., faux
family, s., famille (f.)
far, adv., loin
father, s., père (m.)
fault, s., faute
fear, s., crainte (f.)
feeling, s., sentiment (m.)
few, adv., peu
fifteen, adj., quinze
find, v., trouver
firm, adj., ferme
first, adj., premier
fit, adj., capable, convenable, to be fit for or to, être capable de
flatter, v., flatter, se flatter
fond, adj., fou; to be fond of, aimer à
forest, s., forêt (f.)

ENGLISH-FRENCH VOCABULARY. 125

forthwith, *adv.*, tout de suite, immédiatement
forty, *adj.*, quarante
foot, *s.*, pied (*m.*)
four, *adj.*, quatre
fox, *s.*, renard (*m.*)
franc, *s.*, franc (*m.*)
French, *adj.* and *s.*, Français
friend, *s.*, ami (*m.*)
from, *prep.*, de
front, *s.*, devant (*m.*)
front, *adj.*, de devant
fruit, *s.*, fruit (*m.*)

G

game-keeper, *s.*, garde-chasse (*m.*)
garden, *s.*, jardin (*m.*)
gardener, *s.*, jardinier (*m.*)
general, *s.*, général (*m.*)
genius, *s.*, génie (*m.*)
gentleman, *s.*, monsieur; _gentlemen, messieurs
get, *v.*, gagner, obtenir
girl, *s.*, fille (*f.*)
give, *v.*, donner
glass, *s.*, verre (*m.*)
go, *v.*, aller (*irr.*); go out, sortir (*irr.*)
good, *s.*, bien (*m.*)
goods, *s.*, marchandises (*f.*)
grammar, *s.*, grammaire (*f.*)
grand, *adj.*, grand; grand piano, piano à queue
great, *adj.*, grand
great-coat, *s.*, paletot (*m.*)
green, *adj.*, vert
guilty, *adj.*, coupable
gummed, *adj.*, gommé

H

half, *s.*, moitié, demi; half, *adj.*, demi
hall, *s.*, salle
happen, *v.*, arriver
hare, *s.*, lièvre (*m.*)
harsh, *adj.*, dur, sévère

have, *v.*, avoir (*irr.*); to have just, venir de
head, *s.*, tête (*f.*)
hear, *v.*, entendre
help, *v.*, aider
help, *s.*, aide (*f.*), assistance (*f.*)
Henry, *s.*, Henri
herewith, *adj.*, ci-inclus
hide, *v.*, cacher
high, *adj.*, haut
highlander, *s.*, montagnard (*m.*)
Homer, *s.*, Homère
horse, *s.*, cheval (*m.*)
hotel, *s.*, hôtel (*m.*)
hour, *s.*, heure (*f.*)
house, *s.*, maison (*f.*)
how, *adv.*, comment
hundred, *adj.*, cent
hymn, *s.*, hymne

I

if, *conj.*, si
ill, *adj.*, malade
in, *prep.*, dans, en, à
inclined, *adj.*, enclin, disposé
incorrectly, *adv.*, ne...correctement
indeed, *adv.*, vraiment
independence, *s.*, indépendance (*f.*)
India, *s.*, Inde (*f.*), les Indes
injustice, *s.*, injustice (*f.*)
inn, *s.*, auberge (*f.*)
interest, *s.*, intérêt (*m.*)
into, *prep.*, dans
introduce, *v.*, introduire
invasion, *s.*, invasion (*f.*)
invent, *v.*, inventer
it, *pron.*, le, la
Italian, *adj.*, italien
Italy, *s.*, Italie (*f.*)
ivory, *s.*, ivoire (*m.*)

J

James, *s.*, Jacques
judge, *s.*, juge (*m.*)

July, *s.*, juillet (*m.*)
just, *adj.*, juste

K

keep, *v.*, garder, conserver, préserver
kill, *v.*, tuer
kind, *adj.*, bon
king, *s.*, roi
Kingston, *s.*, Kingston
knight, *s.*, chevalier (*m.*)
know, *v.*, savoir (*irr.*), connaître (*irr.*)

L

lady, *s.*, dame (*f.*), young lady (*f.*), demoiselle (*f.*)
lame, *adj.*, boiteux
language, *s.*, langue (*f.*), langage (*m.*)
large, *adj.*, large, grand
last, *adj.*, dernier
laugh, *v.*, rire
learn, *v.*, apprendre (*irr.*)
learned, *adj.*, instruit, savant
lease, *s.*, bail (*m.*)
leave, *v.*, laisser, abandonner
lecture, *s.*, cours (*m.*), conférence (*f.*)
leg, *s.*, jambe (*f.*)
lend, *v.*, prêter
less, *adv.*, moins de
lest, *conj.*, de peur que
letter, *s.*, lettre (*f.*)
liable, *adj.*, sujet, exposé
lieutenant, *s.*, lieutenant (*m.*)
life, *s.*, vie (*f.*)
lightning, *s.*, foudre (*f.*), éclair (*m.*)
like, *v.*, aimer
look, *v.*, regarder; look for, chercher
London, *s.*, Londres
long, *adj.*, long
lord, *s.*, lord (*m.*), seigneur (*m.*)

lose, v., perdre
love, v., aimer
Lyons, s., Lyon

M

make, v., faire (*irr*.)
man, s., homme (*m*.)
manœuvre, s., manœuvre
manner, s., manière (*f*.)
manufacturer, s., fabricant (*m*.)
many, *adv*., beaucoup de
Marseilles s., Marseille
master-key, s., passe-partout (*m*.)
matter, s., matière (*f*.);
What is the matter with you? qu'avez-vous?
me, *pron*., moi, me
measure, s., mesure (*f*.)
meet, v., rencontrer
mention, v., mentionner
Milton, s. *prop*., Milton
mine, *pron*., à moi
minister, s., ministre (*m*.)
misfortune, s., infortune (*f*.), malheur (*m*.)
miss, mademoiselle (*f*.)
mistake, s., erreur (*f*.), faute (*f*.)
money, s., argent (*m*.)
monk, s., moine
month, s., mois (*m*.)
monument, s., monument (*m*.)
morning, s., matin (*m*.)
mother, s., mère
movement, s., mouvement (*m*.)
multitude, s., foule (*f*.)
music, s., musique (*f*.)
must, v., devoir

N

Napoleon, s., Napoléon
neither, *conj*., ni l'un, ni l'autre
Nero, s. *prop*., Néron
never, *adv*., jamais

news, s., nouvelle (*f*.)
night, s., nuit (*f*.)
nine, *adj*., neuf
no, *adj*., aucun, ne...pas de
nobody, *pron*., personne
noise, s., bruit (*m*.)
nothing, *pron*., rien
now, *adv*., maintenant
new, *adj*., nouveau, nouvel, neuf
newspaper, s., journal (*m*.)

O

oblige, v., obliger
o'clock, *adv*., heure (*f*.)
of, *prep*., de
officer, s., officier
old, *adj*., vieux, vieil
on, *prep*., sur
once, *adv*., une fois
olive, s., olive (*f*.)
only, *adv*., seulement, ne...que
opera, s., opéra (*m*.)
orange, s., orange (*f*.)
other, *pron*., autre
ought, v., devoir
ourselves, *pron*., nous-mêmes
out, *prep*., hors; dine out, dîner en ville
own, *adj*., propre, à moi, à toi, etc.

P

page, s., page (*f*.), page (*m*.)
pair, s., paire (*f*.)
paper, s., papier (*m*.)
park, s., parc (*m*.)
part, s., part (*f*.), partie (*f*.)
pass, v., passer
passenger, s., passager (*m*.)
passer-by, s., passant (*m*.)
peach, s., pêche (*f*.)
pencil, s., crayon (*m*.)
pen, s., plume (*f*.)
penholder, s., porte-plume
people, *s. pl*., gens

perform, v., jouer
perhaps, *adv*., peut être
peril, s., péril (*m*.)
perish, v., périr
perseverance, s., persévérance (*f*.)
Persian, s., Perse
person, s., personne (*f*.)
Phenician, s., Phénicien
pip, s., pepin (*m*.)
pistol, s., pistolet (*m*.); pistol-shot, coup de pistolet
place, v., placer, poser
plant, v., planter
play, v., jouer
play, s., jeu (*m*.), comédie (*f*.)
pleasure, s., plaisir (*m*.)
plenty, *adv*., beaucoup
plum, s., prune (*f*.)
pocket-handkerchief, s., mouchoir (*m*.)
poor, *adj*., pauvre
position, s., position (*f*.)
poultry-yard, s., basse-cour (*f*.)
practice, s., pratique (*f*.)
preferable, *adj*., préférable
price, s., prix (*m*.)
primitive, *adj*., primitif
principal, *adj*., principal
principle, s., principe (*m*.)
prison, s., prison (*f*.)
prisoner, s., prisonnier (*m*.)
private, *adj*., privé
proclaim, v., proclamer
produce, v., produire, *irr*.
profitably, *adv*., d'une manière profitable
prudence, s., prudence (*f*.)
public, *adj*., public
punctual, *adj*., ponctuel, exact
punish, v., punir
purse, s., bourse (*f*.)
put, v., mettre, *irr*.

ENGLISH-FRENCH VOCABULARY. 127

Q

[q]uestion, v., questionner
[q]uite, adv., tout à fait

R

[r]ainbow, s., arc-en-ciel (m.)
[r]apid, adj., rapide
[r]are, adj., rare
[r]ascal, s., coquin (m.)
[r]ead, v., lire, irr.
[r]eckon, v., compter
[r]eign, s., règne (m.)
[R]hine, s., Rhin (m.)
[r]ely on, v., se fier à
[r]emain, v., rester
[r]emedy, s., remède (m.)
[r]epulse, v., repousser
[r]equire, v., demander, avoir besoin de
[r]etire, v., retirer, se retirer
[r]eturn, v., retourner, revenir, rendre
[r]ich, adj., riche
[r]ide, v., aller à cheval
[r]oad, s., chemin (m), route (f.)
[r]oom, s., chambre (f.)
[r]ule, s., règle (f.)
[r]un, v., courir, irr.

S

[s]afely, adv., en sûreté, sain et sauf
[s]ame, adj., même
[S]aracen, s., sarrasin
[s]atin, s., satin (m.)
[s]atire, s., satire (f.)
[s]ay, v., dire, irr.
[s]aying, s., maxime (f.)
[s]carcely, adv., à peine
[s]cold, v., gronder
[S]cotland, s., Ecosse (f.)
[s]eason, s., saison (f.)
[s]ection, s., section (f.)
[s]ee, v., voir. irr.
[s]eem, v., sembler
[s]end, v.; envoyer

sense, s., sens (m.)
servant, s., domestique (m. and f.)
service, s., service (m.)
several, adj., plusieurs
seventy, adj., soixante-dix
shall, v., devoir (not to be mistaken for shall which indicates the future)
sheep, s., mouton (m.)
shilling, s., shilling (m.)
shoe, s., soulier (m.)
should, see shall
silk, s., soie (f.); silk goods, soiries
since, prep. and adv., depuis
since, conj., puisque
sing, v., chanter
singer, s., chanteur
sister, s., sœur (f.)
situation, s., situation, place
six, adj., six
small, adj., petit, modéré
society, s., société (f.)
soldier, s., soldat (m.)
some, adj., du, des, quelque
something, s., quelque chose
so much, adv., tant
soon, adv., bientôt
Spain, s., Espagne (f.)
spare, adj., de reste
speak, v., parler; speak evil, mal parler (used only in the pres. inf. and comp. tenses)
spend, v., dépenser; spend time, passer le temps
spoil, v., gâter
sprain, v., fouler
station, v., station (f.)
stay, v., rester
stock exchange, s., bourse (f.)
stone, s., pierre (f.)

stone-fruit, s., fruit à noyau
story, s., histoire (f.)
strike, v., frapper
sub-lieutenant, s., sous-lieutenant (m.)
succeed, v., réussir
such, adj., tel
suddenly, adv., tout à coup
suit, v., convenir, irr.
suppose, v., supposer
surgeon, s., chirurgien
surprised, adj., surpris
suspect, v., soupçonner
system, s., système (m.)

T

table, s., table (f.)
take, v., prendre, irr.; take care of, s'occuper de; take down, descendre; take the field, entrer en campagne
taste, s., goût (m.)
tastefully, adv., avec goût
tea, s., thé (m.)
tell, v., dire, irr.
ten, adj., dix
tend, v., tendre
tenth, adj., dixième
Thames, s., Tamise (f.)
than, conj., que
thankful, adj., reconnaissant
that, adj., ce, cet
that, pron-, cela, celui-là
that, conj., que
their, adj., leur
them, pron., eux; for them, pour eux, en
Themistocles, s., Thémistocle
therefore, adv., donc, par conséquent, c'est pourquoi, aussi
thing, s., chose (f.)
think, v., penser, croire, irr.
thirty, adj., trente

this, *adj.*, ce, cet
this, *pron.*, ceci, celui-ci
thousand, *adj.*, mille, mil
threat, *s.*, menace (*f.*)
three, *adj.*, trois
through, *prep.*, à travers
throughout, *prep.*, dans, à travers de
ticket, *s.*, billet (*m.*)
till, *conj.*, jusqu'à
time, *s.*, temps (*m.*); at the same time, en même temps
to, *prep.*, à, pour, envers
to-day, *adv.*, aujourd'hui
tooth-pick, *s.*, cure-dents
towards, *prep.*, vers, envers
towel, *s.*, essuie-mains (*m.*), serviette (*f.*)
town, *s.*, ville (*f.*)
tragedy, *s.*, tragédie (*f.*)
translation, *s.*, traduction (*f.*)
tree, *s.*, arbre (*m.*)
tremble, *v.*, trembler
triumph, *v.*, triompher
trunk, *s.*, malle (*f.*)
trust, *v.*, avoir confiance en
Tuesday, *s.*, mardi (*m.*)
tune, *s.*, air (*m.*)
Turkish, *adj.*, turc, des Turcs
twelve, *adj.*, douze
two, *adj.num.*, deux

U

umbrella, *s.*, parapluie
uncle, *s.*, oncle (*m.*) (*m.*)
understand, *v.*, comprendre, *irr.*

unfortunate, *adj.*, malheureux
United-States, *s.*, Etats-Unis
unwell, *adj.*, indisposé
upstairs, *adv.*, en haut
use, *s.*, usage (*m.*); it is no use, il est inutile
use, *v.*, se servir de, *irr.*, employer
useful, *adj.*, utile

V

vanquish, *v.*, vaincre, *irr.*
very, *adv.*, très
vice-admiral, *s.*, vice-amiral
virtue, *s.*, vertu (*f.*)
visit, *v.*, visiter, faire visite
voice, *s.*, voix (*f.*)

W

walk, *v-*, marcher, faire une promenade à pied, aller à pied
walnut, *s.*, noix (*f.*)
walnut-wood, *s.*, noyer (*m.*)
want, *s.*, besoin (*m.*) désir
war, *s.*, guerre (*f.*)
watch, *s.*, garde, montre (*m.*)
week, *s.*, semaine (*f.*)
well, *adv.*, bien
what, *adj.*, quel
what, *pron.*, ce qui, ce que
whatever, *adv.*, quelque
when, *conj.*, quand
whereas, *conj.*, tandis que
which, *pron.*, qui, que, lequel

who, *pron.*, **qui**
whole, *s.*, tout (*adj.*)
whose, *pron.*, à qui
whosoever, *pron.*, quiconque
why, *adv.*, pourquoi
wide, *adj.*, large
will, *v.*, vouloir, *irr.* (not to be mistaken for **will** which indicates the future)
William, *s.*, Guillaume
widow, *s.*, veuve (*f.*)
wine, *s.*, vin (*m.*)
wise, *adj.*, **sage**
wish, *v.*, vouloir, *irr.*
wit, *s.*, esprit (*m.*)
with, *prep.*, avec
work, *s.*, ouvrage, travail
work, *v.*, travailler
world, *s.*, monde (*m.*)
worth, *s.*, **valeur**; to be worth, valoir, *irr.*
would, *see* will
wound, *s.*, blesser
wretched, *adj.*, méchant, mauvais
wrist, *s*, **poignet**
write, *v.*, **écrire**, *irr.*
writer, *s.*, écrivain (*m.*)
writing, *s.*, écriture (*f.*)
wrong, *adj.*, mauvais; to be wrong, avoir tort

Y

year, *s.*, **an** (*m.*); année (*f.*)
yes, *adv.*, oui
yesterday, *adv.*, hier
yours, *pron.*, le vôtre